PLANET OF GOLD

White Powder of Gold and the Christian Forgery

by

Andreas A Paris

Eloquent Books
An imprint of AEG Publishing Group
845 Third Avenue, 6th Floor – 6016
New York, NY 10022
www.eloquentbooks.com

ISBN: 978-1-60693-455-5

Printed in the United States of America

Book Design: Dedicated Business Solutions, Inc.

Eloquent Books
New York, New York

Dedicated to my family with love

Blessed be the poor in mind
who have not the ability
to question God's actions

Table of Contents

Genealogy of the Anunnaki

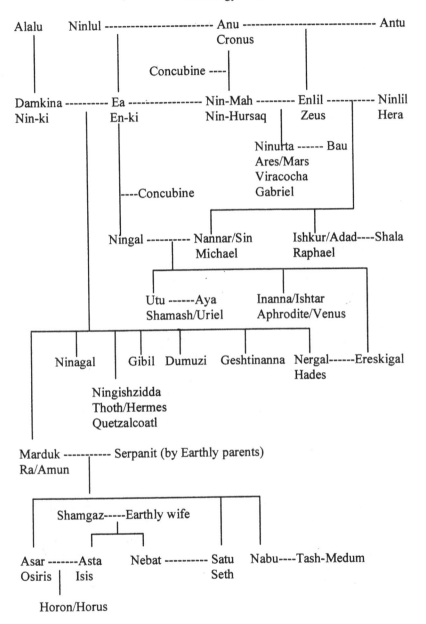

PREFACE

Enlil was the chief deity of the Sumerian pantheon. He was also the one who initiated the Sumerian civilization. His name means "Master of the Air," "Master of the Command."

According to Sumerian and Babylonian clay tablets, stone cylinders and other 'documents', Enlil came to Earth in charge of an alien expedition from the planet 'Nibiru'. Their planet was in great need of **gold powder**, and by chance or not, they found a **planet of gold**. Their mission was to take home as much gold as they could. They called themselves 'Anunnaki', meaning those who came from heaven to Earth. They created the human race to use as gold miners and servants. They also called themselves 'gods'. The purpose was to exercise dominion over humanity. Enlil was the Commander of the gods on Earth, assisted by family members, and other 'gods'.

We have no reason to disbelieve the Sumerians. In fact, the Anunnaki puzzle is fitting precisely in our history map, enabling us to understand our own history.

Enlil was neither god nor some mythological being, according to the Sumerians. They knew, he was a human being, although very powerful and very cruel. He did not allow anything to disturb the flow of gold to his home planet. His advanced weapons of 'brilliance', (the thunders of Zeus in the Greek Mythology) and other chemical and biological weapons (causing plagues and famines), were also very real to both Sumerians and other people. He instigated the deluge as a means to depopulate Earth. Some other gods, called the Igigi (the Titans in Greek Mythology), supported by humans and their king Nimrod, and leaded by another god by the name Marduk, revolted against him. They challenged him by building a Tower at the same location as the city of Babylon made its appearance, more than a thousand years later. Enlil ordered an aerial attack to destroy the Tower. That was the second time alien advanced weapons, like missiles, were used against humans. He also punished the participating humans by 'confusing their tongues'. He declared Marduk as his adversary and the Titans as betrayers, because they revealed the secrets about the gold powder to the humans.

The god Yahweh of the Hebrews presented himself as 'the only god' and forced them to recognize and obey him.

Was Yahweh interested in gold too? As we shall see, he was. He said to Moses (Exodus 20:22) 'Tell the children of Israel that you have seen that I have spoken to you from the heaven'! That was a prerequisite for establishing himself as God. That would allow him to present a corrupted history and establish religions. The religions could, in turn, neutralize human development and control the future of humanity. The tools have been, fear, punishments, threats and artful manipulations. Yahweh's treachery of the human race has been taken over by Christianity.

Some of the corrupted stories of our history are: The creation of Man, the incident of the Tower of Babylon, the Babylonian captivity, the destruction of Sodom and Gomorrah, the assertion that the Pharaohs of Egypt and the kings of Babylon were evils, the Exodus of the Israelites out of Egypt. Since these stories are included in the Christian Bible, then this book has been mediating a corrupted human history for over two thousand years. The early human history, as presented by the OT, intentionally and systematically corrupted, appears to be a forgery, a conspiracy against the human race and its future.

Yahweh has been identified by us and many other writers as the Sumerian god Enlil. He is also known in many other cultures by different names. He was even called 'Ilu-Kur-Gal' by the Sumerians and 'El-Shadai' by the Hebrew patriarch Abraham, which, in both tongues, means 'God of the Great Mountain'. This epithet has its origins in the fact that Enlil's temple/adobe was a big ziggurat called the 'E-Kur', meaning 'House like a mountain'. We wouldn't care about Enlil, had he been a mythological character. We wouldn't care about Yahweh either, had it been a matter of faith. We believe, however, that, as Yahweh, he is directing our future in the same manner as Enlil directed our past. Although he left, he never gave up the idea that to the Royal House of Nibiru, the so-called 'Kingdom of Heavens', is the owner of the 'planet of gold'. He probably left but he promised to come back.

The path of development of the Western civilization has mainly been determined by Christian values as defined by Yahweh. The picture established by Yahweh and repeated by the Church fathers, is that religion is a matter of faith, up to everyone to believe or not. It sounds good but the taste is rather bitter. More than 95% of our ancestors, at the time of Emperor Constantine, were forced to convert to Christianity. Besides, Christianity is much more than a religion. He established a global institution spreading disinformation since then. As God, he was certain that we would follow his instructions. Actually, it means that he has been directing human development since then, through Judaism, Christianity, and Islam.

In order to make the above accusations credible, we will present evidence that Yahweh is responsible for the corruption of our history, the neutralization of human advancement through destroying knowledge, and by directing humanity into a path of mental bondage.

Only a small portion of ancient 'documents', unearthed under the last 150 years, has reached the public. The rest of them are still waiting to be interpreted in the valves of different museums.

We shall present evidence connecting the members of the alien expedition, not only with gold, but also with most of the major events in human history. The Gold Mission of Enlil/Yahweh was the instigator of such events like the creation of man, the deluge, the Tower of Babili, probably the poisoning of Alexander the great, Christianity, Emperor Constantine, visions and holograms, and much more.

In order to understand our own history, we have to take into account the history of the Anunnaki. This is the history of the gods on Earth, the common history of gods and men. This is also the history of a man who managed to establish himself as God. The purpose was to keep human civilization at a level not permitting advanced resistance at the time of his comeback.

At this point I would like to make a statement. My standpoint concerning 'God' is quite simple. It may exist some force or some kind of being out there in the universe, we could call 'God'. Either it does or not, it's not possible to prove the one or the other. If indeed such a force does exist, we like to imagine that it is benevolent, just, powerful, all knowing, omnipotent and, perhaps most important, peaceful. This 'God' has nothing in common with the god of the OT.

Any opposition against Yahweh, the powerful Church fathers, or Christianity in general, was punished with the death penalty until recently. There are two important reasons why only a few writers have opposed the doctrines of Christianity in modern times. Religiosity is considered to be a matter of faith, not very popular to argue about. The other reason is the occurrence of all the incredible doctrines Christianity forced on people. The doctrines about Paradise, Hell, Trinity, remission of sins through payment of money and the like, have been hiding the real reason behind the creation of Christianity, which was to be a control instrument in the hands of the Brotherhood of the Gold. Yet, it is not easy to understand the silence of intellectual and prominent persons who disagree with the Christian Bible.

The merged identity of Enlil and Yahweh into Enlil-Yahweh is the start point of this book. We shall, however, take the opportunity, whenever it appears, to note the connection between the two. We shall also scan those Sumerian tablets, as well as the OT to find out why this Enlil of the Sumerians became Yahweh of the Hebrews, and much later even the God of the Christians and the Moslems. Consequently, Marduk, the adversary of Enlil, became the adversary of Yahweh/God in Judaism and Christianity. The doctrine, 'it's sinful to question God's identity', or actions, will not discourage us.

Most Christians have no intention, whatsoever, in studying other aspects of the stories included in the bible. On the other hand, most of them have never read the whole bible. Many of them have never read a single page of this book. Their frequent visit in the church is kind of social obligation. Others, like the believers in the letter of the bible, are seeking vindication for almost any crime through studying the violent actions of God, described in this holy book.

Science needs evidence in order to accept God. This is why Christianity has been persecuting scientists and philosophers. We have been manipulated since childhood, by parents, Sunday schools, schools, priests and by the society we are living in, that God exists. We have been manipulated to accept Yahweh as God. We have been accustomed to expressions we do not really believe in, like the 'Kingdom of Heavens', 'Paradise and Hell', 'God is always right' and the like. Things nobody can possibly know anything about. We have also been manipulated to justify his evil actions we are unable to understand, by saying 'mysterious are the ways of God'. He said, we are all sinful, so he offers remission of sins. In exchange, we offer him forgiveness for his many crimes against humanity. It sounds like a fair agreement among people with bad conscience! Beside the payment of money, remission of sins can also be achieved by offering gold! Christians of the Orthodox Church use to pay for covering the features of the icons with gold or silver. They believe it would easily open the gates to the Kingdom of heavens!

Under the time of Emperor Constantine and thereafter, Christianity was forced on people through imperial decrees. Philosophers and educated people were convinced that Christianity was a conspiracy against science, a conspiracy that would bring darkness and neutralize human development. Unfortunately, they were right. Patriarchs and Popes became rulers, more powerful than emperors. Yahweh has been exercising dominion over humanity through holy men, holy emperors, holy books, holy inquisitions, holy crusades, and of course, through fear and punishment.

Under the times of darkness, no other written records were allowed, except for the books about Yahweh. No other god and no other religion, beside Judaism, were allowed. Some 1500 years are forever lost. That is the cost humanity had to pay for shifting allegiance from other gods to Yahweh! Not to mention the cost in human lives. Today, the power of the doctrines of Yahweh is decreasing, not able to stop scientific achievements any more. The fear, however, is still here, fear for punishment as well as hope for reward.

At the time when emperor Theodosius outlawed other faiths and declared Christianity as the exclusive state religion of the Roman Empire (380 CE), no other option was given to 95% of the citizens of the empire than to accept! The first generation born 'Christians' could not protest either. It was a matter of life and death. Generation after generation kept silent. We are one of the first generations that have that option. Nevertheless we are keeping silent too. Why? Because the reality has been changed. As Christians we want our religion to be strong and able to stand against Islam. Without Islam and without the fear for punishment, we would have more options. We have to admit that the alien founders of those religions have been very clever. From being a matter of faith it's now a matter of competition and a matter of pride. We have forgotten that we are the descendants of people who have been forced to accept Christianity. We are not mentally free to cast a scrutinizing look at our 'holy' books!

We are living in mental bondage, like our ancestors spent their lives in physical slavery. We have been manipulated by Christianity to 'fear God'. We agree to that. Although we do not have to fear a benevolent, almighty and just God, we should fear the powerful God of the Old Testament, as we shall see.

Laughing at the Anunnaki and fearing one of them, the god of the OT, is an unexplainable paradox!

Chapter 1

HISTORY AND MYTHOLOGY

History preserved through Mythology

Our past, history and Mythology, has been documented in oral traditions and in 'written records' of different kinds all over the world. We can study something that happened long ago, but to treat it as history, it has to be documented in more than one source, otherwise it is classified as mythology. Therefore we have a lot of 'mythological' stories around the world, and very little history from the older times.

The Old Testament of the Christian bible is history, we have been told, the words of God. No supporting evidence is needed, as religion is a matter of faith. Without the old 'documents' unearthed under the last 100–150 years, the OT could, by definition, be classified as mythology too.

There is some kind of magical line beyond the year 1500 BCE. If we are interested in the history of humanity beyond that time, then the normal procedure is to consult the references in different mythologies. Mythical stories have been passed down from generation to generation, and we find them (same or similar) in many cultures around the world. We believe that Mythology is not entirely created out of the imagination of our ancestors. Some myths are actually reflecting real historical events. Graham Hancock says:

> Could it be that the myths themselves are historical records?
> Could it be that these cunning and immortal stories, composed
> by anonymous geniuses, were the medium used to record such
> information and pass it on in the time before history began? [1]

1

Archaeological discoveries of the last hundred and fifty years have turned our comprehension of history beyond the magical 1500 BCE, upside down. Sumerian, Egyptian, Babylonian, Akkadian and Greek 'documents', have been unearthed by several expeditions. These cylinder seals, clay tablets, art items, cuneiform texts, mechanical and electrical items, and other 'documents', written by both humans and 'gods', have recorded humanity's early history, from the creation of man, to about 2000 BCE. Most of these discoveries have been stored in different museums in decades, until it became possible to interpret them. Some pioneers, like N.S. Kramer, Torskild Jacobsen, and others, discovered that many bible stories have their parallels in those older documents. Which of them is most credible? Unfortunately, the much older stories are still regarded as myths, and the involved 'gods' are explained as mythological figures associated with nature. For most people they still are. The stories of the OT are still regarded as the 'words of God', witnessing of the enormous power hidden in religiosity.

In resent times, some writers have had the courage to state that the stories described in the OT have been copied from those older documents. One of them, Zecharia Sitchin takes these tales about the Anunnaki 'gods' seriously, stating that they were not 'gods' but human beings from the planet Nibiru, as the Sumerians, Babylonians and Egyptians stated.

The bible believers, even scientists, reject this theory although, because of different reasons. It is generally accepted that the creation of man, described by the Sumerian and Babylonian 'documents', is indeed the original text used in the bible. The obvious difference is that the bible story is intentionally and unintentionally corrupted, as we shall see.

We can understand why the bible believers feel very near God, and we hope that they also can be able to understand that they are indeed far away from the truth. The stories of, and about those 'gods' are closely connected with human history. When N. S. Kramer says that, 'history begins at Sumer', he refers, as we understand, to human history. We also know by now that the Sumerian civilization was the creation of those gods. If history began at Sumer, then it is the common history of gods and men. We have not the right to dismiss them, either we are part of their history, or they are part of our history.

By following those 'gods' through the ages, like Theseus followed the thread given to him by Ariadne to help him find his way

out of the labyrinth in Knossos, we shall see that the thread is leading us to our own times through the **gold powder**, and through the
struggles among the 'gods'.

Enlil and Marduk have been haunted by the struggle about which
of them would rule the Earth. Since, both gods and humans were involved in that struggle, their actions have also been directing most of
our history since then. The influence of Christianity, also a result of
the struggle among the gods, has formed our civilization in the West.
During the journey, we intent to present some facts given to us by
those 'gods', but also uncover the reasons behind their actions; like
the creation of man, the deluge, the wars among the gods, executed
by themselves as well by the humans, the creation of kingdoms and
empires, the passing of some knowledge to the humans, the hiding
of some knowledge, and other significant events. Throughout the
journey, in every single action taken by them, there is always an
invisible factor influencing them, which, in turn, influenced the actions of our ancestors. The invisible cause was and still is the **gold**,
which was the very reason they came here for. We believed that gold
dust could bring health and longevity. We believe that it is a matter
of time until it would be confirmed by science. Enlil, however, classified that knowledge as top secret, and the gods were forbidden to
reveal the secret to the humans.

Most of our knowledge of today is based on ancient knowledge.
After fifteen hundred years of darkness in Europe, Greek, Egyptian,
and Babylonian ancient knowledge, what had been remained of it,
found its way to Europe under the renaissance, thanks to Arab traders.

Ptolemy Philadelphus (309–246 BCE) commissioned the Egyptian priest Manetho to compile the history of Egypt from all available sources. The Seleukid king Antiochus Soter (reigned 281–261)
commissioned the Babylonian priest and astronomer Berossus to do
the same concerning the history of Babylonia. Most of our knowledge about Sumer, Egypt, Babylon, and their gods, comes from
those two writers.

After these, as well as other influences, Europe began to wake up
from the deep sleep caused by a more than millennia long absence
of education and freethinking. Most people could not read at all, and
for the few who could, there were only religious texts available.

In 1650 CE the Irish Protestant Archbishop, James Ussher announced in his Annales Veteris Testamenti that, by calculating the

age of each patriarch named in the bible, the first man, Adam was created in 4004 BCE. Although Ussher's calculations contradicted old Sumerian and Babylonian records, the church forbade any kind of opposition against Ussher. Laurence Gardner says:

> In 1654 the Vatican Council had decreed that anyone daring to contradict the 4004 BCE date was a heretic—an attitude that was not relaxed until Pope Pius XII addressed the 1952 Papal Academy of Science in Rome.[2]

Herodotus of Halicarnassus (5th century BCE) wrote that the world was tens of thousands of years old. That was of course, unacceptable to the Christian Church, as well as to Christian scientists and theologians. The time about 4000 BCE is very important all right, but not because the world was created then, but because it was the beginning of the first human civilization on Earth after the deluge. Initiated and administrated by the alien gods.

The great number of scientific and archaeological discoveries of the last hundred and fifty years, highlights mankind's limited knowledge about its own history. We present just a few of the archaeological discoveries in modern times.

- The city of Nineveh, Mesopotamia, (Iraq), was excavated 1842 and in 1852 the library under the palace of Ashurbanipal.
- The city of Nimrud, also known as Kalhu or Calah, in Iraq unearthed 1845.
- The library of Ashur-bani-pal in Nineveh, the greatest library of the time, was unearthed between 1848 and 1876.
- The ancient city of Mycenae, metropolis of the Mycenaean civilization in Hellas was unearthed in 1876.
- The city of Troy, the capital of the mythical Greek colony in Asia Minor, was excavated 1870–90 by Heinrich Schliemann, 1893–94 by Wilhelm Doerfelf, and 1932–38 by Carl Blegen.
- The palace of Knossos in Crete, Hellas, unearthed 1900-1936, by Arthur Evans.
- The Karnak cachette in Thebes, Egypt, discovered in 1904 by Georges Legrain.
- The city of Ur in Mesopotamia, Iraq, unearthed in 1920–1930 by Leonard Woolley.
- Manchu Picchu in Peru discovered 1911, by Hiram Bingham.

- The Nag Hammadi scriptures, in Egypt, unearthed 1945, translated and accessible to public first in 1977.
- The Dead Sea scrolls in Qumran, Israel discovered 1947.
- Discoveries at Harappa, (Indus Valley) dating back to 3300 BCE excavated as late as 1995–1998.

Note that the information that directed the steps of archaeologists, professionals, and amateurs, to many of the above places was not history but mythology. Acharya S says:

Rather than being an entertaining but useless "fairytale," as myths are erroneously considered to be, the mythos is designed to pass along from generation to generation information vital to life on Earth, so that the humans do not have to learn it repeatedly but can progress. Without the knowledge, or gnosis, of the celestial mythos, humankind would still be in caves.[3]

Nobody knows how many clay tablets, scrolls, cylinders, and other types of 'documents' are still underground. We must also keep in mind that quite a lot of already unearthed material is still waiting to be interpreted in different museums. Many historical 'documents' exist only at one location, completely unavailable to the public, and even to most writers. Not until 1920 and thereafter, Sumerian and other texts have been deciphered, and not until the marching of the Internet have some of them been available to the public.

Not until now, the last fifty years or so has it been possible to compare the original scriptures with the "copies" included in the bible. In case of disagreement between the older Sumerian, Babylonian, Egyptian texts, and the OT, the original source would, naturally, be worthy of more recognition. However this is not always the case. According to Lawrence Gardner, in his book "Genesis of the Grail Kings," the Memorandum and Articles of Association of the Egypt Exploration Fund, first established in Britain 1891 to expedite archaeological digs in Egypt states:

. . . the Fund's objective is to facilitate surveys and excavations for the purpose of elucidating or illustrating the Bible narrative.[4]

Religiosity has always been haunting our minds. The current procedure is that if something contradicts the bible, then it is classified as 'myth', or the work of devil. Take Troy for example, the story of the war between the Hellenic states and the Hellenic colony of Troy, as told by Homer in "Iliad." The site is now unearthed and the Trojan War is regarded as history. According to Homer, several gods participated too, on both sides. Ares and Aphrodite on the Trojan side, Athena and Hera on the opposite side, just to name a few. This however is still regarded as myth. The reason is that any information about 'gods' is against the doctrine of the 'only God' of the bible. But if the war and the protagonists were real, why would Homer invent the participation of some gods? Did he chose the names by random? And why are these flying gods of the Trojans, or the flying Horus of the Egyptians, or the flying Athena of the Athenians regarded as mythological beings, whereas the flying messengers (angels) of the bible are regarded as real? Besides, the angels were gods too!

The early Christian Julius Africanus of Edessa (200-245 CE), observed that:

> . . . as well as having godly status, the Elohim were defined in some non-canonical works as 'foreign rulers' and 'judges'.[5]

'Elohim' is the plural form of 'Eloh', meaning 'gods'. It is just one among several words and names that the corruption failed to adjust. 'Non canonical works' are all kinds of religious documents not included in the Christian Bible.

According to Greek Mythology, Hades is the god of the underworld ruling over the dead. Hades is not very sympathetic since he can expose the 'inhabitants' of the place for every kind of torture and punishment.

This is a very realistic description of the underground gold mines in Southern Africa. Nergal, also known as Hades, was the administrator of the underground mines and the god of the underworld.

The concept of the 'underworld' derives partially from the fact that the mines were beneath the surface and because they were located in the Abzu, probably a Nibiruan word from which the word 'abyss' derives. Both names, Nergal and Hades, have been connected with death, punishment and Hell. In fact, Christianity adopted the concept of Hell as a place where the sinful are destined to 'live miserably' after death.

Nergal, being a member of the alien Brotherhood of the Gold, was a very result-oriented executive. He could travel around in Africa, Asia and Europe, selecting men to use as labor in the mines. Being selected by Nergal was equivalent to be considered as dead. The mineworkers were transported to the underground mines, where they worked as long as they lived. They were provided with food and water to keep them alive, although they probably had been manipulated to believe they were dead. Those people lived the rest of their lives in the mines. They were 'living dead'. When they no longer were able to work, they were just buried under the excavated soil. They never came up again. The 'underworld' was a place of no return. Surely, it was a terrible fate for those ancestors of ours. It was literally a place of Hell, not for the souls but for living people. It was a place where the slaves provided the Nibiruans with gold.

Do we have any evidence, beside mythology, that Nergal/Hades used to take (by force) workers to use in the mines? Indeed we have. In 1887 some 350 clay tablets were found in Egypt at El Amarna, the capital city of Pharaoh Amenhotep IV. Those tablets, today in European Museums, were written under the time of Amenhotep III and his son, Amenhotep IV who later changed his name to Akhenaten (Servant of Aten).

The Amarna tablets were 'written' in the diplomatic language of the time, Akkadian, reflecting a correspondence between Egyptian and other leaders. One of those 'letters', with the ID 'EA35', is from the king of Cyprus (Alashiya) to the Egyptian Pharaoh. Here is what he says:

Speak to the King of Egypt, my brother. Thus says the King of Alashiya [9], your brother:

All goes well with me. With my houses, my wife, my sons, my chief men, my horses, my chariots, and in my lands, it is well. And with my brother may it be well. . . .

My brother, behold, my messenger I have sent with your messenger to you to Egypt. Now I have sent 500 talents [1] of copper to you; I have sent it to you as a gift [2]—for my brother. Do not let my brother be concerned that the amount of copper is too little, **for in my land the hand of Nergal** [3], **my lord, has killed all the men of my land, and so there is not a** (single) **copper-worker** [emphasis added].[6]

Note that only men were 'killed' by the hand of Nergal. They were, of course, not 'killed' but taken away and considered as dead. Had it been some kind of disease, or plague, then Nergal/Hades/Death would have taken women and children as well. As we shall see, the gods created the humans to be used as labor in the gold mines. They were slaves under the powerful Brotherhood of the Gold. However not all the gods treated them as slaves. Some of them considered them as equals and friends. Unfortunately, even that would cause human suffering, as we shall see. Another god who used to send young men and women to Hades was Nannar/Sin, a son of Enlil who later became St Michael in the bible, the collector of souls!

The right to believe in God (or not) is a fundamental right free to exercise. But if our free will is directed only by faith based on fear, and not by facts and faith based on free will, then we become victims to everyone who is clever enough to use some advanced manipulative technique to keep us under control. We shall show that this is precisely what happened. We have been manipulated, cheated, persecuted, and forced to surrender. Unfortunately, even people suspecting that this is the case, are keeping silent because of fear.

We have to learn from our past in order to be able to make the right decisions for the future. If Enlil/Yahweh is our enemy, as his actions are witnessing, and the one who said he would come back, then, we have to be prepared to meet him. He would not come back to 'bless us', that is for sure. He would come back for more gold. He is a very powerful man who has the means to break down our civilization, throwing us back thousands of years, so he could use us again as labor.

The most unpleasant discovery of my research is the connection between the god of the OT and the gold of Earth. 'KI' (Earth) has also been a planet exclusively governed by Enlil/Yahweh—the prince from the Royal House of Nibiru. Ki represents 'the Planet of Gold', and the human race represents the slaves-gold-miners who dug the gold for them. The question is if Christianity, established by him, is a gift to humanity, or a control instrument? Even so, it is better to find some scary answers, than no answers at all.

[1] Graham Hancock, Fingerprints of the Gods, p. 187
[2] Laurence Gardner, Genesis of the Grail Kings p. 16
[3] Acharya S, The Christ Conspiracy, p. 150
[4] Laurence Gardner, Genesis of the Grail Kings, p. 76
[5] Ibid., p. 30
[6] The Amarna Letters from: www.reshafim.org.il/ad/egypt/alasiya.htm

Chapter 2

ALIEN AUTHORS AND THEIR LANGUAGE

Mediating History and Fear

The Book of Enki

Two of the most known gods who were among the first to come to
Earth, left behind 'words' as a heritage to the human race.

'The Lost Book of Enki', by Zecharia Sitchin, is compiled from
old Sumerian tablets two millennia after the time of Jesus. It is a com-
pound of fourteen stone tablets interpreted and presented together.
The tablets are supposed to have been 'written' down in Egypt sometime around the year 2000 BCE, just after the destruction of Sodom and
Gomorra. Soon after that, Enki's son, Marduk replaced Enlil as the
chief of the gods on Earth. Enki is supposed to dictate 'his memoirs'
to a scribe, in order to preserve the history of gods and men, equally
the history of the human race. The purpose was to pass down that
unknown part of our history to future generations.

Endubsar, (Master scribe) the scribe, who engraved the words of
Enki on those stone tablets, says in page 13:

> And the voice [of Enki] said: These are the tablets upon which
> you shall inscribe my words . . .

> Do not deviate from my words and utterances!

It is possible that similar stories to those 'the book of Enki' is compiled from, was preserved as papyrus in the great library of Alexan-

dria. The books of the library, some 500–700 thousands, are forever lost, destroyed by both Christians and Moslems. Surprisingly, the translation into Greek of the first five books of the Hebrew Bible, survived!

Enki tells Endubsar 'the History of Earth', from the arrival of the Anunnaki until ca 2000 BCE. Most of the stories told by Enki, like the creation of man, the Deluge, the Tower of Babylon and the confusion of the tongues, are the original stories of the copies we find in the OT.

Enki is completely unknown among ordinary people. We don't know that he was the creator and protector of the human race. We don't know that it was he who helped the human race to survive the Deluge. His identity has been stolen by Enlil. In the Bible he is referred to as the evil serpent. To us, he is some unimportant lesser god associated with the waters.

The Book of Enlil/Yahweh

'The Book of the OT', written at the time of the Babylonian Captivity (536–539 BCE is compiled from older Hebrew Scriptures, the last one by St Jerome about 400 CE. Those scriptures were written under the Babylonian Captivity (536–539 BCE). The OT is supposed to mediate the words of Enlil/Yahweh to the Hebrews. He didn't actually mediate history, but violently forced them to accept whatever he had to say. Later the Christians were forced to do the same. They too subjected to his will. As we shall see, Enlil/Yahweh was the great enemy, almost exterminating the human race, destroyed cities and civilizations and created mental bondage through religious doctrines. This man has been elevated to the creator and protector of the human race. He became our God.

The Conflict

Enlil and Enki were probably among the last to leave Earth too. The first we note about them is that Yahweh was not willing to reveal his real identity, probably because it would be easier to be accepted as God that way. Enki, on the other hand, 'signed' his book with his own name.

These two books are often in conflict with each other. The freedom to believe in the one or the other is not given to us. The 'Holy Book' stands above everything, as Enlil-Yahweh stands above all the other gods! Those who refused to believe have been exterminated, or forced to surrender by imperial decrees, and fear for punishment. The antagonism between the two brothers, Enki and Enlil and their different opinions directed both the history of the gods on Earth and the history of humanity. Not many people in the whole world have heard of the Book of Enki, while every Christian owns a copy of the book of Enlil (the Bible).

A book is the expression of passion and the ability to clothe the passion in suitable words. Yahweh is, however, skillfully hiding his passion and his revulsion against the human race. He is pretending to be the protector of humanity. Nowhere in that book do we find anything supporting such a quality. The most obvious passion through the whole book is Yahweh's outstanding devotion to establish himself as God. As it is stated even in the New Testament, those who do not believe in him 'should be stoned to death'.

Enki delivers history as experienced by him. It is obvious that he cared about us, but he could only observe with much trepidation the destructive actions of the powerful Enlilite brotherhood, not always being able to supply some assistance. The passion is, in both cases, expressed in all honesty. But while Enki deplores and deprecates most of the major events in human history, Enlil justifies every evil action as the work of God, always being right! While Enki is delivering history, Enlil is meditating fear, threatening with punishment!

The Language of the gods
The original language spoken by the humans could not have been any other than the god's own language. It was the common language of all humans until God decided to allot different languages to different groups. The reason, as stated in the OT, was to prevent them from communicating with one another! While this book is claiming that God had the right to do that, and did right by doing so, we find this action as a crime against humanity.

The only group, probably allowed to retain the original language, was the Sumerians. As a result of the disappearance of this people, their language disappeared too. The overabundance of new languages has caused a lot of confusion through the eons. That was, on the other hand, the very purpose of Enlil/Yahweh. Sumerian names were not used outside Mesopotamia any more. Different people assigned different names to the same god. For example, Enlil in Sumerian (the language of the gods) became Adon to the Phoenicians, El to the Hebrews and Canaanites, and Zeus to the Greeks. Historical events have been lost because the different names could not be associated to the same personality.

In order to understand this book, it is necessary to give some information available concerning the language of the gods. Sometimes, it is also helpful to understand the connection between a name and its signification in the Bible.

Alien tongue	Meaning
Ab	Shepherd
Ab-a-el	Shepherd of the watered Meadows
Ab-ra-ham	Bright Shepherd father
Ab-zu	The wise shepherd
An	Heaven
Anu-nna-ki	Those who came from heaven to Earth
Dub	Scribe
En	Master
En-dub-sar	Prince master scribe
En-Ki	Master of Earth
En-Lil	Master of the Air, Commander (Yahweh)
E-ri-du	Home far away
Ham	Father, Kinsman
Ib	Son
Igigi	Watchers, observers (came down from Mars)
Il/Ilu	God
Ilu-kur-gal	God of the great mountain
Ish	Physicist, Chemist
Ka-in	Farmer
Ki	Earth
Kish	Throne (city)
Kur/Hur	Mountain, Head
Ish-Kur	Head Physicist, healer (Raphael)
Lil	Air, Command
Na	Bearer
Nnar	Power
Na-nnar	Bearer of heavenly power (Michael)
Nin	Lord/Lady
Urta	He of strength
Nin-urta	Lord of strength (Gabriel)
Shar /Sar	Prince, also the time needed for Nibiru to complete a full orbit around the Sun

Shara/Sara	Princess
Ra	Bright
Utu	The Shining (Uriel)

The Connection

Despite every action to avoid revealing their names, the connection of some of them with names given to them in the Hebrew language is obvious. The names in Hebrew appear to be a direct interpretation of the alien names, without doubt provided by Yahweh's messengers. Yahweh is supposed to have changed the name of Ibruum to Abraham and the name of Sarai to Sara.

Abel	Shepherd of God
Anakim	Same as Anunnaki (plural)
An-na	The heavenly
Ab-Ra-Ham	Father of a multitude
El	God
Elohim	Gods
El-Shadai	God of the great mountain
Gabriel	Strength of God
Kain	Farmer
Nephilim	Those who came down (from Mars), the Igigi
Michael	He who is like god
Raphael	Healer of God
Sara	Princess, half sister and wife of Abraham
Uriel	Light/Fire of God
YHWH	(I am) the Commander, (cause to happen)

Chapter 3

GENESIS OF THE HUMAN RACE

The creation of God or the result of science

Two of the most important events, described in the OT, are about slavery and captivity, the slavery of Jews in Egypt, and the Babylonian captivity. Both Egypt and Babylon happened to be the domains of Marduk, Enlil's greatest antagonist.

Most scholars agree by now that the Jews wrote down most of the stories of the OT under the Babylonian captivity, from older Babylonian and Sumerian records. However, they had some hard time with the many names of the gods. In the Babylonian stories the protagonists were several deities like Enlil, and the whole multitude of his family, as well as Enki, the Wise Serpent, Marduk, Ninmah and Ningishzidda.

This contradicted the beliefs of the scribes and the doctrine of the 'only one God'. Their God had to be deprived of his family members. Enki on the other hand had such a crucial roll in those happenings that it was impossible to ignore him, so he became 'The Lord' too, as Enlil. In other cases, the god Enki became the 'evil serpent', like Marduk. The 'gods' had been translated into 'Lord' too, but in some cases they made, by mistake, the right translation into 'Elohim', meaning 'gods'.

In The Lost Book of Enki by Z. Sitchin, we read that the very first day Enki and his companions became uncomforted when they saw the sun setting down. Alalu informed them that this was normal on Earth. It was the ending of the day and the beginning of the

15

night. They found the day and night 'beyond imagination short'. Therefore, they worked hard for several days to accomplish their temporary encampment, which later became the city of Eridu. After six days the camp was finished and Enki said:

> Let this day be a day of rest; the seventh day hereafter a day of resting always be!

> Let this place henceforth by the name Eridu be called, Home in the Faraway the meaning thereof will be![1]

'Enki' was translated into 'God' since the proposition of resting at the seventh day was of good character. Genesis 2:3 says:

> And God blessed the seventh day, and sanctified it because that in it He had rested from all his work which God created and made.

Since we don't believe that the all-knowing God, the all powerful, the Creator of all could be tired, we believe those words are the words of Enki. The day of rest proposed by Enki to his crew became the day of worship of Enlil/Yahweh. In many societies it is 'ungodly' and unsocial to work on Sunday, even forbidden by law, as in the islands of Tonga. The constitution of Tonga is the work of Shirley Baker, an English (and Christian) missionary.

The task to create a "Lulu," (primitive worker) began in "The House of Life," in the Abzu (South Africa). The first Homo sapiens male was born by Ninmah through insemination.

> Like dark red blood was his color, like the clay of the Abzu was its hue. They looked at his male hood: Odd was its shape, by a skin was its forepart surrounded, . . . Let the Earthlings from us Anunnaki by this foreskin be distinguished! So was Enki saying.

*   *   *

> Adamu I shall call him! Ninmah was saying. One Who Like Earth's Clay Is, that will be his name![2]

A boy they called Adamu, 'One Whose color was like the clay of Earth'. Uneducated scribes have corrupted the above expression into 'the creation out of clay 'and' from ashes to ashes. 'Skin from its forepart was hanging'. Enki says 'let the Earthlings from us Anunnaki by this foreskin be distinguished'. Enlil, on the other hand, ordered the Jews to circumcise their boys. He avoided explaining the reason for such an unnecessary operation.

Then a girl called Ti-Amat (Mother of Life) was born by Ninki. The two were so perfected that Enki decided that they should not work in the mines. Note that 'Enki' is still 'God' in the bible while the names of Ninmah and Ninki are completely erased in Genesis 1:26-27.

> And God said, Let us make man in our image, after our likeness. So God created man in his own image, in the image of God created he him: male and female created he them.

The statement 'do-not-make-any-images-of-me' is therefore not easy to understand. If he created humans in his own image, then we know that he was of a similar appearance, even if the 'creator' actually was not one, but three, Enki, Ninmah, and Ningishzidda.

The three of them brought Adamu and Ti-Amat to Eridu, the city of Enki in Sumer, and all the gods came to see the wonder, the first Homo sapiens. The event was so important that Marduk, Enki's son, came down from Mars to see the first Earthlings. It is worthy to note that Marduk's journey is witnessing of some advanced, space technology where neither energy power nor time was a problem to them. "An adobe in the enclosure for them, they built, to roam therein they could." The enclosure was in the land of the "E-din" that later became "Eden" in the bible. The two Earthlings however were not capable of procreating. Let us see what Ningishzidda did.

> Let us the essence of Adamu and Ti-Amat afresh examine! Ningishzidda was saying. Their ME's bit by bit to be studied, what is wrong to ascertain! In Shurubak, in the House of Healing, the essences of Adamu and Ti-Amat were contemplated, With the Life essence of Anunnaki males and females they were compared. Like two entwined serpents Ningishzidda the essence separated, Arranged like twenty-two branches on a Tree of Life were the essences, Their bits were compatible, the images and likenesses they properly determined. Twenty-two they were in number, the ability to procreate they did not include! Another two bits of the essence in the Anunnaki present

Ningishzidda to the others showed. One male, one female: without them there was no procreating! They locked the doors behind them, the three with the two earthlings alone remaining. Upon the four others Ningishzidda a deep sleep caused to descend, the four he made unfeeling.

From the rib of Enki the life essence he extracted, Into the rib of Adamu the life essence he inserted: From the rib of Ninmah the life essence he extracted, Into the rib of Ti-amat the life essence he inserted. Where the incisions were made, the flesh thereon he closed up. Then the four of them by Ningishzidda were awakened. It is done! He proudly declared.

To their Tree of Life two branches have been added, With procreating powers their life essences are now entwined!

* * *

In the heat of the day Enlil in the orchard was scrolling, the shade he was enjoying. Without expectation Adamu and Ti-amat he encountered, the aprons on their loins he noticed.

What is the meaning of this? Enlil wondered: Enki for explaining he summoned. The matter of procreation Enki to Enlil explained:

* * *

Great was Enlil's anger, furious his words were: . . . Now the last bits of our life essence to these creatures you have given, To be like us in procreation knowing, perchance our life cycles on them to bestow!

* * *

My Master Enlil! Ningishzidda was saying. Knowing of procreation they were given, The branch of Long Living, to their essence tree was not!

Ninmah then spoke up, to her brother Enlil she was saying: What was the choice, my brother? To end it all in failure, Nibiru in doom to face its fate, Or to try and try and try, and by procreation let Earthlings the toil undertake? Then let them be where they are needed! Enlil with anger said. To the Abzu, away from the Edin, let them be expelled![3]

Then the corrupted version in Genesis 2:21-22:

And the LORD God caused a deep sleep to fall upon Adam, and he slept: and he took one of his ribs, and closed up the flesh thereof: And the rib, which the LORD God had taken from man, Made he a woman, and brought her unto the man.

Was the above corruption 'made a woman from the rib' unintentional caused by ignorance? It is hard to believe. We have three persons involved, including God, according to Genesis, while there were five persons in the original story. All the gods, except one, must be excluded, as there was only one God according to the beliefs of the scribes. Not only the corruption is obvious, but also God's actions are contradicting each other'. Why bother to 'create' a woman, perform a high skilled operation in order to give them the ability to procreate and then be angry because they made used of that ability? What was the purpose of the creation of the woman? Unless, of course, the different actions were performed by several 'gods'. Besides, why does God need a special room, complete with surgical and other medical equipment while he only had to utter some words in order to create the universe?

The purpose of the surgical operation was to give them the ability to procreate. Ningishzidda appears to be, not only a great surgeon but also a scientist who knew what was lacking the two Earthlings and how to remedy it.

Ninmah's explanation is also interesting here. She admits that the surgery was needed so that the Earthlings would be able to produce more Earthlings-mine-workers without whom, the Gold Mission would end in failure! Should we be grateful or should we say:

Our fathers in the heavens, thank you for giving us our daily work as mine workers so we can dig the gold for you! Amen!

The ability of procreating is documented in Genesis 1:24:

Therefore shall a man leave his father and his mother, and shall cleave unto his wife: and they shall be one flesh.

It must have been very hard for the scribes of the OT to corrupt the truth and at the same time describe the real events. It is possible that the story was partly corrupted unintentionally. The part dealing with the creation of the woman from the ribs of Adam could be the result of ignorance. We cannot expect that the scribes of Genesis could understand the meaning of that surgical operation. The replacement of Ningishzidda by 'God', however, was certainly intentional, and the surgery was the reason for expelling them from the Edin.

Now this is the story of Adamu and Ti-Amat. The story described in Genesis chapter 1, 2 and 3, the first two Homo sapiens. These are however not the parents of Cain and Abel. They are only partially the Adam and Eve of the Genesis. The parents of Cain and Abel were two other young people, called Adapa, and Titi. In fact there are two stories in Genesis too, concerning the creation of human-kind. We find the first one in Genesis 1:27 when God created male and female and the second one in Genesis 2:22 when the LORD God created the woman out of the rib of Adam. This is in agreement with 'the Lost Book of Enki' where we find two parts of the creation story, the creation of a boy and a girl and later the operation that made it possible for the two first Earthlings to procreate.

Adamu and Ti-amat were "expelled" from the Edin (the land of Sumer), after Enlil's order, and brought back to Abzu, (in South Africa or somewhere in Africa), where they multiplied and lived in some kind of freedom, we assume. We hear no more about them.

Later on, Enki mated with two earthly women who born Adapa and Titi. They were demigods and they lived much longer than we do. This was however a secret between Enki and his vizier. Enki was probably afraid that Enlil could have them killed if he knew the truth.

If the Tree of Life in Genesis is actually a real tree, or a symbolic one, like the DNA tree, is not the significant here. The significant is that all of them, the Lord God, Enki, Ninmah, and Ningishzidda denied humans the essence of "Long Living." That essence existed according to Gen. 3:22:

And the LORD God said, Behold, the man is become as one of us, to know good and evil: and now, lest he put forth his hand, and take also of the tree of life, and eat, and live for ever.

Even according to Enlil, the longevity was quite reachable.

> To be like us in procreating knowing, perchance our life cycles
> on them to bestow![4]

Neither the Lord God, nor the Master Enlil allows humankind a
"Long Life." The three protagonists, Enki, Ningishzidda and Ninmah, might wish to give us the essence or not, or just they did not
have the authority to do that. We never know. On the other hand,
why should they have given long life to humans created to be used
as slaves?

It is possible that there was indeed a real tree, the tree of life. We
know also that they brought both plants and animals from Nibiru.
By watering that particular tree with an admixture of water and gold
dust, the tree could produce fruits that were more 'effective' than the
consuming of gold dust, as being 'reworked' by the tree. The fruits
were indeed some of the 'essences' of longevity; otherwise he would
not need to guard the tree. The 'House of Life', the laboratory where
the 'admixture' of the DNA was worked out, could not be the tree,
as it was not situated in the Edin, but in the Abzu. The tree of life
was, after Adamu and Ti-amat were expelled from Edin, guarded by
some kind of automatic guard machine, as Genesis 3:24 states.

> So he drove out the man; and he placed at the east of the gar-
> den of Eden Cherubims, and a flaming sword which turned
> every way, to keep the way of the tree of life.

How the Cherubims looked like, there is no knowledge about. The
Jewish historian, Flavius Josephus (1st century CE), stated that: in
his day no one knew what a cherub looked like.

There are a lot more striking similarities between the book of
Genesis and the Lost Book of Enki. Sometimes they are correctly
copied sometimes not, and yet sometimes totally corrupted. What
we have learned from them, however, is that it is possible to extend
human life, perhaps much longer than we can imagine.

More out of logic is the fact that Eve's action, eating from the
tree of knowledge is regarded as sin, the original sin according to
the church. What theologians and church fathers really have missed
here is that without that "eating" (without the "adding" to our DNA

and the mating), none of us would exist today. Out of logic is also
the fact that the original patriarchs in the service of Enlil/Yahweh
loaded that 'sin' on the woman alone. In fact it is easier to understand Enlil's' standpoint than that of the church. At least he was
sincere in that he only wanted dumb workers, not procreating intelligent beings, who would come to create a lot of problems for him,
and perhaps some day, consume the gold powder and be able to live
as long as he.

And God said to them that they would die by eating of the tree
of knowledge, or of the tree of life. Apparently they ate of the tree
of knowledge and lived much longer than we do. How can the Lord
be right while he is lying? Here we have the two of them, Enlil and
Enki merged into the same epithets, 'God' and 'Lord'. It is not difficult to guess which of them 'dictated' the OT!

The surgical operation in "the House of Life," (or the eating of
fruits in the garden of Eden), so closely connected with humankind's
very existence, has been turned against humankind as something
evil. It is witnessing of the enormous power of religious doctrines,
the manipulative abilities of Master Yahweh and the architects behind Christianity. The creation of Man is, as we have seen, the result
of a high-tech level of genetic engineering; it is the result of science.
The result of love making between a man and a woman is definitely
not the result of some sinful action. Enlil/Yahweh had several children of his own, even with different women.

The corruption of the creation story, from older historical records,
was partly intentional and partly the result of ignorance, miss understanding and miss interpretations due to the confusion of the tongue
by Yahweh. The fact that it was Enlil/Yahweh who sent the Jews into
the Babylonian captivity, as we shall see, witnesses of an action according to plan. Although some corruption was inevitable, as the Jews
could not accept the involvement of other gods than their own, it is
possible that some of the interpretations were indeed the work of some
'angels'. The corruption itself is one of the greatest frauds ever. The
reason was to keep humanity ignorant of what actually happened.

---

[1]Zecharia Sitchin, The Lost Book of Enki, p. 77
[2]Ibid., p.139, 140
[3]Ibid., p.147–148
[4]Ibid., p. 149

Chapter 4

THE REVOLT OF THE TITANS

Betrayers of the secrets of the gods Heroes of Mankind

Enlil took over the command of the Gold Mission on Earth from his brother Enki. This was decided by casting lots. For how long his assignment would last, or who was supposed to replace him some day, of that there are no records. Alalu, the deposed king who fled to earth, discovered gold and informed the Nibiruans about, says:

> Return to Nibiru I was promised, in fairness the throne to regain! Then to earth came Ea; the one by compromise the next to reign Nibiru he was designated. Then came Enlil, the succession from Anu to himself claiming. Then Anu came, by lots he tricked Ea; Enki, the Lord of Earth, he was proclaimed, Of Earth, not Nibiru, to be the master. Then to Enlil command was granted, Enki to the distant Abzu was delegated.[1]

Alalu claims that both he and Enki were tricked by Anu. This was probably true. Enki was supposed to succeed Anu since he was the firstborn son of his. Later the rules of succession were changed, and Enlil, the son from another bloodline, became the successor. That was the beginning of the struggle between the half brothers. Enki had also been deprived the right to rule Earth. Most of the children of Enki didn't care, except for Marduk. He not only cared, but did everything he could to replace Enlil on Earth.

The casting of lots 'decided' that Anu was to return and rule Nibiru, Enlil was given the most important post on Earth, as the High Commander of the Gold Mission, (Master of the command) and Enki was reduced to something as unimportant as the chief of a gold mine in Southern Africa (Abzu). The reason Enlil was 'chosen' to lead such a vital operation on another planet, was certainly his enormous devotion to the mission. He proved through the times that there was absolutely nothing as important as that. Not even life. Since Alalu was deposed by Anu because he was unsuccessful in 'repairing the atmosphere of Nibiru', Enlil knew too well how essential the task was.

Since they knew (or so they said) that their planet was in desperate need of gold, once they found it, they were determined to take home as much as possible. Besides, Anu managed to leave behind both sons that had the pretension to succeed him. In addition, he sent Alalu, the former king who also demanded to get back his kingdom, to exile on Mars.

From being a matter of succession, the struggle became a matter of bilateral relations that could affect the future of the expedition. Anu returned to Nibiru feeling safe on the throne. By appointing Enlil as the High Commander on Earth, he was certain that Enlil was to stay here for a very long time. He also knew that Enki was deprived of his rights twice, and the brothers would be busy in counteracting each other. Anu, the wise heavenly father was obviously wise, but perhaps not so nice to his children.

Another important fact that strengthened the enmity between the two clans was their different opinions about the human race. The humans had been created to be miners and servants. The Enlilites treated the humans as some kind of lower race compared to them, and they wished them to stay under the original slave-status. Marduk, on the other hand, and some others from the Enki House, considered the 'new race', the Homo sapiens, as their equals and wished to release more knowledge, power and freedom to them.

The ministry of Enlil was sturdy. The decisions were taken by a Council dominated by him and his family. The executives of every important section of the gold operations were of the Enlil family. Except for the administration of the mines in the Abzu, entrusted to Enki. Enlil certainly wished him as far away from Ki-Engi (Sumer) as possible. In time, Enki was to be replaced by his son, Nergal, who became more Enlilite than the Enlilites themselves, through his marriage with Ereskigal, a grand daughter of both Enlil and Enki. All other posts of importance were in Ki-Engi.

Ninurta was the chief administrator of the metallurgical installations in Badtibira. Ishkur was the commander of the Landing place in Baalbek. Nannar was the governor of Ur, and the whole land of Sumer. The whole machinery of the Gold Mission was administrated and served by the Enlilite brotherhood. The brotherhood operated much like a secret brotherhood. Only the members of the highest decrees could be entrusted some vital decisions.

The only possible opposition was to come, occasionally, from Enki. But Enki alone could not make his voice heard. Besides, he had some other interests too. He spent most of his time in scientific observations and the development of the new Earthlings. The Earthlings, and their development, were under observation by Enlil too, although, because of different reasons. From being a livestock of workers, they soon multiplied, and became a power not to be ignored. Enlil used to complain that the Earthlings made too much noise disturbing his sleep. In order to understand this lamentation we have to consider that the gods didn't sleep as long as the humans, one night, but several weeks, corresponding to one night on their home planet.

According to the 'Lost Book of Enki', at about this time, just before the Deluge, the conditions on Mars probably disturbed by the nearing of Nibiru. Sandstorms were stronger and occurred more often than before. Nibiru was 'absorbing' the planet's atmosphere. The future of the Chariots Landing place on Mars was uncertain.

Enlil decided to build a landing place for the chariots on Earth. Who would be the commander? Enki suggested Marduk who had a long experience from the landing place on Mars, as the most suitable for the task. Enlil answered that the task was for his son, Ninurta. As always, when Enlil was unwilling to take responsibility, he turned to his father for help. Despite the long distance separating Earth and Nibiru, the Anunnaki were always able to communicate with their home planet through 'beaming words'. Anu selected Utu, a grandson of Enlil for the task. The appointing of the new Landing place to a member of a new generation would mark the coming of a new age.

Marduk felt as being passed over and humiliated, but there was nothing he could do. It was now a matter of time when the Watchers (Igigi/Titans) as the Anunnaki on Mars were called, would be forced to leave Mars because of the unbearable conditions there. He visited Earth to ask for permission to marry an Earthly woman, Serpanit, a daughter of Earthlings serving on Mars. Those humans were highly educated, and could perform the jobs assigned to them, at least as well as the Igigi. They probably knew most of the secrets of the Anunnaki too. Only the fact that Marduk needed permission to marry an Earthling, explains much of the relationship between the Anunnaki and the Earthlings. In the eyes of the Anunnaki, Marduk's wish was unheard. All of them had occasionally relations with Earthly women, but to marry one? The Earthlings could serve them, they could be of equal skills, but, yet, they were treated as a lower race. Marduk's own words concerning the situation:

> What my father once had said, I with my own eyes witnessed:
> Step by step on this planet a primitive being, one like us to be,
> we have created, In our image and in our likeness Civilized
> Earthling is, except for the long life, he is we! A daughter of
> Enkime my fancy caught, her to espouse I wish![2]

As Marduk says, the only difference between the two species was the longevity of the Anunnaki. He was, however, one among very few, to see the Earthlings as equals in everything else. His father Enki and his mother Ninki approved Marduk's wish. The juridical authority of the High Commander was stretched to cover even matters like this one. When Marduk asked for permission to marry Serpanit, Enlil said:

> It was one thing for the father with Earthlings intercourse
> have, It is another matter for the son an Earthling to espouse,
> lordship on her to bestow! [3]

What master Enlil was saying, was 'go to bed with them, but do not marry them'. By marrying Marduk, Serpanit would become Nin-Serpanit, a 'lady'. Something Enlil considered as 'not worthy her'. In Enlil's opinion, the Earthlings were created to be slaves, and they ought to stay that way. They should not be allowed to rise to 'lords', or 'ladies'.

Enlil says nothing here about Marduk was to 'defile' himself by marrying an earthly woman. The bible however, states that those Igigi, by marrying earthly women, had defiled themselves, and that the children from such a union were 'giants'. Enlil appealed to Anu, 'by beamed words', in order to prohibit the marriage. Anu allowed this to happen, but Marduk, by doing so, would lose his princely title (Shar). Besides, his wife was not welcome to Nibiru. The ladies of the Nibiruan aristocracy would not be forced to associate themselves with the offspring of a slave race.

Anu's decision might not have been as liberal as it appears to be. He was not only wise but also shrewd, and he might have known that the decision would cause additional problems, which perhaps, might have been his intention. The most problem that his children had to face, the longer they should stay on Earth.

What Enlil feared most of everything, was that Marduk and his earthly family would stay on Earth. It was, in fact, the only option Marduk had, since he had been deprived of his princely title. A man, a lord from Nibiru, who knew the secret of the gold dust, would certainly reveal the secret to his family members. What would happen if the earthlings suddenly begun to use gold powder for themselves? The future of the whole Gold Mission would be in danger. Enlil decided that Marduk and his wife were not welcome to stay in the Edin (Sumer). They were expelled like Adamu and Ti-Amat. The first Anunnaki who saw the humans on Earth as his equals (beside Enki) was humiliated both on Nibiru, and on Earth.

By this act, Enlil and Anu were creating a rebellion that was to side with the humans even more. Marduk's decision to marry an earthly woman and the consequent humiliation of him was one of the most fateful events in the history of the Anunnaki, greatly affecting the history of humanity too. The consequences are still existed to this day. As we shall see, all the future actions of the Enlilites, from this time on, as well the actions of Marduk were directed by the relationship between them. A relationship that now was on tracks that soon or later would lead to collision. The behavior of the humans, who chose or being forced to side by the one or the other side, was affected too. The whole humanity would also be divided. Marduk's allies, most of the humans, became the enemies of Enlil.

Some scholars state that the instigator of the enmity between the two lords was Marduk by marrying the woman he loved. This event, however, as well as consequent events, revealed the type of their character. Enlil revealed his racial feelings about the human race, while Marduk was to be the protector of humanity. Either way, the humans were destined to suffer.

Marduk chose to lose his princely title, and married Serpanit. The decision might have been easy but the consequences were certainly of a very bitter taste. He was no longer a prince and the possibility to replace Enlil as the chief of the gods on Earth had also shrunk. The extremely vital gold mission could not be entrusted to a god with interests in the future of humanity.

On the occasion of Marduk's marriage, two hundred of the Igigi-watchers on Mars came 'down' to Earth to celebrate Marduk's wedding. Or so they said. Their purpose was to marry earthly women too. They demanded to be permitted to marry Earthling women, like Marduk. When their demand was not granted by Enlil, all two hundred of them married Earthly women at the site of Baalbek, (Lebanon), all at the same time. Probably most of the women were taken by force. The action was illegal since it had not been approved by the authorities i.e. Enlil. The name of their leader was Shamgaz. We assume that most of them were well educated for the job at the landing place. They were called 'heroes' as all the other Anunnaki who left Nibiru for the mission of the gold, far away from home. Most of them were probably technicians, but even scientists and other people of high skills.

They have been called Nephilim in the bible, which means 'those who descended' (from Mars). They and their offspring are also known by other names, like Anakim, watchers, angels, fallen angels, the sons of God and even Giants in the bible and some apocryphal books. 'Angel' is the same as messenger. 'Watcher' was the original Sumerian name. 'Fallen angels' can be explained by the fact that 'they came down to earth', but, since they married earthly women without the permission of Enlil, they considered as 'morally fallen'. The 'sons of God' applies to all Anunnaki on Earth. Anakim is a corruption of the word Anunnaki. Since they were considered as outlaws, they were forced to defend themselves, and their families, against eventual attacks from the Enlilites.

They settled down in Baalbek (Lebanon), which was some kind of military establishment, fortified the place, and demanded that Enlil should approve their marriage. Although the crime seems to have been rather harmless, it was very serious indeed. Now there were two hundred earthly women that eventually would begin to consume gold powder together with their children.

Marduk, not permitted to live in Eridu, his father's city in Sumer, moved to Egypt. Some of the Igigi with their families moved to Egypt too, invited by Marduk to settle down there. Marduk's action was a friendly action to his Igigi friends but equally hostile to the Enlilites, because he offered refuge to those 'outlaws'. It seems that Enlil was unable to sustain his status as the ruler because of the rebellious Igigi/Titans. His reputation as 'Master of the Command' was damaged.

The Titans were too many and too powerful. Enlil accused Marduk as the instigator and responsible for their actions. He proclaimed himself as the victim of a conspiracy. He proclaimed Marduk as his evil adversary. He proclaimed the Watchers too as evils, 'the fallen angels'. His low self-confidence was a hinder for solving the problem.

The expression 'fallen angels' is completely ridiculous, implying some religious association. Besides, it all depends on which side one stands. In the 'Second Treatise by the Great Seth', one of the scrolls found in Egypt, collectively named 'The Nag Hammadi Library', Jesus is supposed to speak in his own words. He called the Watchers, 'those of the race that came down'. The Igigi, being religious or not, longing after women and family life, their marriage cannot be associated with any religion. Their actions were of social, political and military character. This is another example of how the scribes of the OT forwarded their own, uneducated, opinion instead of history.

Enlil feared that Marduk and the Titans would not only plan to replace him, but perhaps send the gods home in order to put an end to the Gold Mission. It was a logical assumption indeed. But he declared everyone who tried to prevent him from carrying on the gold operations as his enemy. After he became Yahweh in the OT, his enemies were 'blazed' with attributes like 'wicked' or 'evil' and the enemies of God! He was already making plans about how to exterminate Marduk, the Igigi, and their offspring.

The book of Enoch is one of the so-called 'apocrypha', hidden or secret books. There were many different opinions in the early Christian times, as to which books would be compiled together in order to assemble the bible. The book of Enoch was excluded. However this book is part of the Ethiopian bible. It was also part of the Talmud (the Jewish bible) until the year 90 CE, when the Sanherdin (the Jewish High Council) declared it as 'apocryphal'. In Enoch I 6:1–6 we read:

And it came to pass when the children of men had multiplied that in those days were born unto them beautiful and comely

daughters. And the angels, the children of the heaven, saw
and lusted after them, and said to one another: 'Come, let us
choose us wives from among the children of men and beget us
children'. And Semjaza [Shamgaz], who was their leader, said
unto them: 'I fear ye will not indeed agree to do this deed, and
I alone shall have to pay the penalty of great sin'. And they all
answered him and said: 'Let us all swear an oath, and all bind
ourselves by mutual impressions not to abandon this plan but
to do this thing'. . . . And they were in all two hundred.

And in chapter 7:1:

And all the others together with them took unto themselves
wives, and each chose for himself one, and they began to go in
unto them and to defile themselves with them, and they taught
them charms and enchantments, and the cutting of roots, and
made them acquired with plants. And they became pregnant,
and they bare great giants, whose height was three thousand
ells: . . .

We find similar information in 'The lost book of Enki', by Zecharia
Sitchin. Except that they were not 'giants', and, of course, they were
not defiling themselves. From the above we understand that the Igigi
were willing to share their skills with their families. Probably was a
good life on Earth more important than the gold mission. In the bible
as well as in the book of Enoch, the Igigi offspring are monsters of
some 16 feet high (over 5 meters!), who used to kill people and drink
their blood. Nowhere, whatsoever, there is any record to support this
description. It must have been the sole imagination of the scribe of
the book of Enoch. We understand that Enlil considered them as 'defiling themselves', as he was a man of racial opinions. Accordingly,
the scribe of the book of Enoch was also acting for the accounts of
his master. The story of the Igigi is also recorded in Greek Mythology where the Titans revolted again Zeus. Here we have yet another
example of a historical event recorded as mythical.

Although the word 'Titan' was first used in the Greek Mythology, neither the meaning nor the origins of the word is known. As
we believe that the origins of the word is to be found in the tongue
of the gods, our contribution is that 'Tit-an' could mean 'Those of
heavenly life'.

'Made them acquire with plants' is also of great significance. As we shall see, the Anakim (Watchers and their descendants) cultivated wheat of which they could bake bread containing gold dust. The 'giants' are mentioned in the bible too, Genesis 6:4. This is yet another evidence connecting Enlil with Yahweh.

> There were giants on the earth in those days; and also after that, when the sons of God came in unto the daughters of men, and they bare children to them, the same became mighty men which were of old, men of renown.

Except for the word 'giants' the description here is similar to that in the 'Lost Book of Enki'. The expression 'in those days and after that too' means 'in the days before the deluge, and after the deluge too'. The expression 'the same became mighty men which were of old, men of renown' comes from earlier versions stating: **'They were the Mighty Ones of Eternity, the People of the Shem'**. This is more in accordance with the Lost Book of Enki. 'Shem' means both name and rocket, as we shall see. Enki says:

> To the Landing place in the Cedar Mountains the Igigi with the females went, Into a stronghold the place they made, to the leaders a challenge they issued: Enough of deprivation and not having offspring! The adaptive daughters to marry we wish. Your blessing to this you must give, else by fire all on Earth destroy we will! Alarmed the leaders were, of Marduk, the Igigi commander, charge to take they demanded. If in the matter I a solution must seek, with the Igigi my heart in agreement is!

* * *

> One evil deed by another has been followed, fornication from Enki and Marduk the Igigi have adopted,

* * *

> With much disgust was Enlil speaking..

* * *

> Children there to them were born, Children of the Rocketships they were called.

Marduk and Serpanit his spouse also had children, Asar and
Satu were the first two sons called.[4]

Naturally Marduk sided with the Titans and that was an additional
reason for Enlil to declare him responsible for their revolt. Note that
the Igigi demanded that Marduk should replace Enlil as the chief of
the gods on Earth. The story that began with a wedding ended up as
a revolt against the Commander Enlil.

The Children of the Rocket ships', became 'Anakim' in the bible,
meaning 'those who came down from the heavens', a corruption of
the word 'Anunnaki'. The bible stating that they were giants, sons of
the giant Anak, cannot be taken seriously as there is no supporting
evidence for that at all. 'Anak' means 'Anunnaki made', 'Anakim'
is the plural form of Anak, meaning 'the descendants of Anunnaki'.
The great anger of the commander Enlil is easy to understand. The
Igigi were probably in the possession of some weapons since they
threatened to put the whole Earth on fire. The whole Gold Mission
was threatened. And for the time being, there was nothing Enlil
could do. Except for proclaiming them as evil, and later manipulate
people to believe that.

It is also easy to understand his point that 'and they began to go
in unto them', was equal to 'defile themselves'. A union between
Anunnaki and humans was in the benefit of the human race, according to his understanding. The winners were the offspring of
such a union. 'Better' than ordinary humans, which could explain
the word 'giants'. We can also understand the bible scribes stating
that this was an evil thing to do, since the Igigi didn't side with
Enlil, the god of the OT, but with his adversary and their fellow
humans.

The word 'giants' (from Greek gigantes) can be used to describe
someone physically big, but also big in mind and skills. The Igigi
and their children were indeed 'giants' compared with ordinary humans, due to their education and skills. A similar meaning can be
applied to the word 'Titan'. Adapa, and Titi were the offspring of
a similar union between Enki and two Earthly women. But there is
no record that they, or their children, Abel, Cain and Seth were 'giants'. Not even in the bible. Asar (Osiris), and Satu (Seth), the sons
of Marduk and the Earthly Serpanit were not giants either, but perfectly normal people. The sons and daughters of the Igigi and their

Earthly wives couldn't have been different in that matter. Laurence Gardner says about the Nephilim:

> . . . Josephus did not say that the Nephilim were giants. In fact, he did not mention the nephilim at all; he mentioned only the 'angels of God' whose sons (by earthly women) performed acts of physical strength reminiscent of the Titans: 'those whom the Grecians call giants'. The Genesis text relates that these offspring were 'mighty men' and 'men of renown' - but such descriptions (irrespective of any perceived physical stature) referred to extraordinary ability, just as Nimrod was himself called 'a mighty one in the earth'.[5]

How much knowledge should the Earthlings be allowed to gain? Enlil was angry when the first Earthlings were given the knowledge (ability) of procreating. Now he was angry because the Igigi revealed knowledge to their wives and children as stated in Enoch I chapter 8:

> And Azazel, [one of the leaders], taught men to make swords, and knives, and shields, and breastplates, and made known to them the metals of the earth and the art of working them, and bracelets, and ornaments, and the use of antimony, and the beautifying of the eyelids, and all kinds of costly stones, and all coloring tinctures. And there arose much godlessness, and they committed fornication, and they were led astay, and became corrupt in all their ways. Semjaza taught enchantments, and root-cuttings, Armaros the resolving of enchantments, Baraqijal astrology, Kokabel the constellations, Ezeqeel the knowledge of the clouds, Araqiel the signs of the earth, Shamsiel the signs of the sun, and Sariel the course of the moon. And as men perished, they cried, and their cry went up to heaven.

Here the writer is trying to tell us something important, deliberately or not. No human being, no matter how indoctrinated and manipulated by Enlil and his 'angels', can deny the benefit of this knowledge. The Igigi provided every kind of knowledge contributing to human development. Only a manipulated agent of Enlil/Yahweh could describe them as 'godless and corrupted in all their ways'. Since 'by godless' they meant nothing else that the Igigi and their families were not supporters of Enlil/Yahweh, the god of the scribes, then the Igigi and their offspring ought to be proud of that. They were against the god whose only purpose on Earth was to obtain gold for Nibiru, and to achieve that he was keeping mankind as slaves. He could not accept that some of his comrades treated the humans as equals.

We know that Enlil wanted mankind to get just the knowledge needed for serving him and the other gods. In fact, the Book I of Enoch states that it was Azazel who sinned most, by learning the earthlings 'of the metals of the earth and the art of working them'.

The gold is one of 'the metals of the earth'. Did Azazel revealed the secrets of the 'gold dust'? Did he reveal the secret why the Anunnaki wanted our gold? He probably did according to Enoch I 9:6.

> ... Thou seest what Azazel hath done, who hath taught all unrighteousness on earth and revealed the eternal secrets which were (preserved) in heaven, which men were striving to learn ...

According to this, the humans must have had some idea about gold dust since 'they were striving to learn'. For every human using gold dust for himself, it would be less gold left for the commander Enlil to send to Nibiru. Not to think about future consumption. 'The eternal secrets which were (preserved) in heaven', means that the Brotherhood of the Gold had decided to classify anything concerning gold dust as top secret, and keep it away from mankind's knowledge. It was a part of their mission equally important, as the Gold Mission itself, at least, for some of them, including the High Commander, himself. But we cannot understand why a single human could think of Enlil as being right, and the Titans/Igigi and the earthlings, as being wrong. Here we have additional evidence that the agents of Enlil, who probably were forced to side with the enemies of mankind, wrote many of the scriptures of the OT. These stories are the version promoted by Enlil. The other version has been lost and it is only known as 'hidden knowledge'.

Enlil could not stop the Igigi from providing mankind with 'forbidden knowledge'. Not yet. But he was making plans against Marduk and the Earthlings. Plans to be materialized in the future, no matter how long time it would take.

In his heart [Enlil] things against Marduk and his Earthlings was plotting.

* * *

How Marduk of Earthlings his strength increases, Ninurta carefully observed.[6]

Marduk and the Igigi became the enemies of Enlil. 'Being enemy of Enlil/Jehovah', has been corrupted into 'being enemy of God'. The truth appears to be quite the opposite. Enlil was already giving orders how to punish the Titans and their children, as stated in Enoch I 10:8–11 and 12:4–6.

> . . . And the whole earth has been corrupted through the works that were taught by Azazel: to him ascribe all sin. And to Gabriel said the Lord: 'Proceed against the bastards and the reprobates, and against the children of fornication: and destroy [the children of fornication] and the children of the Watchers from amongst men [and cause them to go forth]: send them one against the other that they may destroy each other in battle: for length of days shall they not have. And no request they (i.e. their fathers) make of thee shall be granted unto their fathers on their behalf; for they hope to live an eternal life, and that each one of them will live five hundred yeas . . .

> . . . declare to the Watchers of the heaven who have left the high heaven, the holy eternal place, and have defiled themselves with women, and have done as the children of earth do, and have taken unto themselves wives: 'Ye have wrought great destruction on the earth: And ye shall have no peace nor forgiveness of sin: and inasmuch as they delight themselves in their children, The murder of their beloved ones shall they see, and over the destruction of their children shall they lament, and shall make supplication unto eternity, but mercy and peace shall ye not attain.

No end of God's vengeance! Is it possible that God can be full of such hatred, vengeance, anger and violence? Is God bloodthirsty? We do not believe so, but Enlil/Yahweh proved to be. Here we have additional evidence that the children of the Igigi knew about the gold powder. 'They hope to live an eternal life and that each one of them would live five hundred years'. We understand 'eternal life' as 'healthy life' otherwise the statement is in conflict with 'five hundred years'.

Note that the Lord says that the Watchers would see 'the murder of their beloved ones' and not 'the death of their beloved ones'. He had already decided to murder them. He was able to kill for the sake of the gold dust. Once again, we need to emphasize the unexplainable agreement between Enlil/Yahweh and the scribes of the OT and other religious books. We understand that he was protecting his own interests, the interests of the Gold Mission. What interests were the scribes protecting?

To defeat Marduk and the Igigi, and 'make them vanished from off the face of the Earth', was now a matter of high priority for the Brotherhood of the Gold. The future of the Gold Mission was depended on that. Since they couldn't destroy the Igigi themselves, they needed some support from the humans. Not humans in general, but humans who would obey every word of them, and execute every command given to them. Humans not allowed thinking by themselves, only obeying and acting according to orders. Since such humans were not to be found anywhere, Enlil had to create them, i.e. he had to educate them, manipulate them, make them fear him and obey him. He had to 'program' them for the task. As we shall see, most of his actions were according to plan. Time was never a problem.

The Brotherhood of the Gold needed a plan describing how to destroy Marduk, how to destroy the Igigi and their offspring and how to force the humans to obey them in order to maintain dominion over the human race.

Whoever threatened the Gold Mission of Yahweh, god or human, was risking his life. Everybody was expendable as long as there were enough humans left to send to the gold mines in the 'underworld', and some to be exposed to systematic indoctrination.

[1]Zecharia Sitchin, The Lost Book of Enki p.96
[2]Ibid., p. 197
[3]Ibid., p. 198
[4]Ibid., p. 201
[5]Laurence Gardner, Genesis of the Grail Kings p. 52
[6]Zecharia Sitchin, The Lost Book of Enki p. 202, 20

Chapter 5

THE DELUGE

The vengeance of God

The time of the Deluge varies greatly from about 6,000 to 13,000 BCE, depending on the source. There have also been some natural calamities of local character, which some scholars count as the global flood described in the bible.

The Babylonian historian, Berossus, (ca 278–290 BCE) reported in his 'Babyloniaca':

According to Mesopotamian records, 432,000 years elapsed between the crowning of the first earthly king and the deluge.

The first king on Earth, according to the Sumerian king list, was Alorus, who reigned 162,000 years. Enki supports the information given by Berossus:

In the one hundred and twentieth Shar was the Deluge awaited, In the tenth Shar in the life of Ziusudra was the Deluge forthcoming, In the station of the constellation of the Lion was the avalanche looming.[1]

The constellation of the Lion was visible in the skies from about 10,970 to 8810 BCE. One hundred and twenty Shar is 432,000 years, if we accept the Sumerian information that one Shar is equivalent to

3,600 years. Note that Ziusudra/Noah was ca 36,000 years old at that
time and he had not yet been 'blessed' by Enlil with long life! Here
we can clearly see how Anunnaki-genes and the consuming of gold
dust could affect their lifetime and even the lifetime of the demigods. Both Ziusudra, and Adapa, were the sons of Enki by earthly
women. Ziusudra had lived for more that 36,000 years, Adapa died
at the age of ca 55,000 years.

> In the midst of the ninety-third Shar was he [Adapa] born, by
> the end of the one hundred and eighth he died. A long life for
> an Earthling he had; the life cycle of Enki he did not have.[2]

A long life for an Earthling (half-Earthling), indeed! Yet, not as long
as the life cycle of Enki. Think about it. It is hard to accept for people like us living some 75 years! Yet, we have no reason to dismiss
the information just because it sounds 'unbelievable'. Serious scientists have made more unbelievable statements that the one above.
They have concluded many ideas as impossible until the day those
ideas became practically materialized. It is worthy to note that for
just about a hundred years ago, our scientists declared aircrafts as
impossible to use for transportation. Steamships could never cross
the Atlantic Ocean with passengers or cargo, because all the space
available was needed for fuel (coal). 'Impossible' is certainly everything that could be possible 'tomorrow'.
    Ziusudra was then born sometime in the one hundred and tenth
shar, and Adapa died in the one hundred and eighth shar, which
means that Adapa died some 7,000 years before Ziusudra's birth, or
some 43,000 years (12 shar), before the deluge. By accepting this
information, it enables us to understand the actions of the gods and
their plans, often spanning over hundreds or thousands of years.
    The Sumerians regarded the Deluge as a historical event. It could
also be dated, because they had lists of kings who reigned before
the Deluge. After the Deluge, the Anunnaki established kingship on
Earth once more. Most people have difficult to accept the lengths assigned to the reigns of the antediluvian kings, since these reigns are
so incredibly long. From the Sumerian king list, we note between
others: Alorus ruled for 162,000 years, En-tarah-ana 420 years, Emmerkar 420 years, Lugal-Banda 1,200 years, just to mention a few of
them. These lengths being right or not, we have to consider the dif-

ference between the life lengths of the Anunnaki and our life cycle. Even the difference between the half-Anunnaki, the demigods, and our own life lengths is considerable.

According to Enki, Adapa (Adam) lived about 55,000 years whereas the bible states 930 years, which sounds to us like more credible. 'Sounds to us', is not necessarily the same as true. In fact, most figures mentioned in old records, including the bible, sounds incredible. We do not believe the Anunnaki have been here either. Laurence Gardner says:

> . . . fed with extracts from Anunnaki Star Fire to increase their perception, awareness and intuition, so that they became masters of knowingness, almost like gods themselves. At the same time their stamina levels and immune systems were dramatically strengthened so that the anti-ageing properties of the regularly ingested Anunnaki melatonin and serotonin facilitated extraordinary lifespans. All records of the era confirm that this was the case-and in this regard there is no reason to be over-sceptical about the great ages of the patriarchs given in the book of Genesis.[3]

The Deluge in Different Cultures

The story of the Deluge is widely spread all over the Earth. We find such stories in Alaska, India, Mesoamerica, in the Norse mythology, in Hellas, and many other places.

According to the Greek historian Hesiodos (eight century BCE), there have been four ages or races of man on Earth, the Golden race, the Silver race, the Bronze race and the Heroic race. The Iron race is the present one. The golden race were men who lived like gods. It all started with gods and their gold operations!

According to the Greek Mythology Prometheus, who had presented humanity the gift of fire, and had been punished by Zeus, warned his son Deucalion to make a wooden box, and in it save himself and his wife Pyrrha. The bronze race, with strength like giants, was the living race at the time of the deluge, which Zeus destroyed by an overwhelming flood.

In India we find a similar story. There the hero, called, Manu, had been warned by a fish, (the manifestation of the god Vishnu), about the coming Deluge. He sent him a large ship and advised him to go on board after loading it with two of every living species, and the seeds of every living plant.

The Deluge as told by Enki

According to 'The Lost Book of Enki' by Zecharia Sitchin, the hero of the deluge was his son, Ziusudra, by an earthly mother.

> In the one hundred and tenth Shar was Ziusudra born, In Shurubak he grew up and espoused Emzara, and she bore him three sons, In his days the sufferings on Earth intensified; plagues and starvations the Earth afflicted.

> * * *

> Aches, dizziness, chills, fevers the Earthlings overwhelmed. Let us the Earthlings curing teach, how themselves to remedy to learn! So did Ninmah say. This by decree I forbid! Enlil to her pleas retorted.[4]

Enlil tried every possible way to decrease the human race. By using chemical and biological weapons, the brotherhood of the gold could cause famines and plagues at every location of their choice. Serious protests by other gods, like Ninmah and Enki, were without result. They were not even allowed to handle some help. As if that was not enough with all the sufferings of the people, a new opportunity arose, adding a new dimension to his evil plans. A great flood, that nothing could stop, was expected.

Enlil, the High Commander of the Anunnaki and chief of the council of the gods, (controlled by him) decided not to reveal the coming calamity to the humans, as he wished them to perish. Enki revealed the secret to his son Ziusudra, and instructed him to build a boat, (some kind of submarine) and there save himself together with his family and friends who helped him.

The approaching Nibiru was expected to pass nearer Mars, and Earth, than any time before. Mars was losing most of its atmosphere. On Earth an enormous flood would start from the South, destroying everything on its way. It was an opportunity from heavens, right in Enlil's hand. And he was determined to make use of it. The target was the whole humanity. He made every single one of the gods to take an oath that they would not reveal the information to the humans. But Enki found a way to warn Ziusudra without 'breaking' the oath. He made sure that life on Earth was preserved against the will of Enlil. He and Ninmah also preserved the seed of life by saving DNA extract of every living creature.

The gods decided to abandon Earth. They realized that not even their advanced technology was able to stand against the flood. They saved themselves in their chariots, orbiting Earth. Neither Marduk's wife Serpanit, nor the wives and children of the Titans were welcome to their chariots!

> The Igigi who Earthlings espoused must between departure and spouse choose: No Earthlings, Marduk's Serpanit included, to Nibiru to journey is allowed![5]

Serpanit, the mother of the Egyptians, 'was not worthy to be bestowed by lordship'. She was also explicitly mentioned as not welcome to Nibiru.

The Igigi were welcome to the chariots but not their earthly family members. This is witnessing that Enlil did have some respect for life as he invited his enemies to save themselves in the chariots. He also made a distinction between Nibiruan life and earthly life, witnessing of a man with racial beliefs.

In modern times some giant waves in the south hemisphere have broken down ships constructed of iron. Many people have wondered how the house-like boat of Ziusudra/Noah could manage to survive. It could for several reasons. It was built like a submarine. The boat was tight so that no water could slip in. Ziusudra had a navigator, also a son of Enki who certainly was a high-educated man as his name applies, 'Ninagal', Great lord of the waters (we assume).

> A boat that the watery avalanche can withstand, a submersible one, to build him {Ziusudra} tell, the likes of which on this tablet to you I [Enki] am showing; Let him in it save himself and his kinfolk, and the seed of all that is useful, be it plant or animal, also take;

* * *

> On the sixth day Ninagal, Lord of the Great Waters, to the boat came, a son of Enki he was, to be the boat's navigator he was selected.[6]

Marduk, the Igigi and their families, saved themselves on Mars. What they left behind, were only humans who knew nothing about the coming flood, except for Ziusudra.

The flood, although not caused by Enlil, it was welcomed by him. Many more people could have been saved, on mountaintops, if they had been warned. But Enlil forbade that 'by decree'. He can never escape the responsibility or the shame. Enki says:

> To let all happen as if by fate decreed, let it as Enlil's Decision be known, On Enlil alone let the responsibility forever rest! So did Enki to all pronounce.[7]

What Enki is talking about, is the moral responsibility. That suggests that Earth was under Nibiruan laws. Probably no Nibiruan could be accused for murdering a human, since our race is not represented on Nibiru. According to our laws, Enlil could be prosecuted and condemned as responsible for withholding information that could save millions of humans. His decision to forbid the gods to warn humanity can only be classified as a crime against humanity.

The Sumerian Deluge
Although the story of Utana-pishtim (even called Utnapishtim), is given to us in the Babylonian Epic of Gilgamesh, the hero Utana-pishtim, was a Sumerian wise king, and priest in the city of Shurupak. He was also grandfather of Gilgamesh. He was instructed by Enki to build a 'boat', and save himself, his family, and friends. A global flood caused the deluge too, and the god who wished mankind to be perished, was Enlil.

The Babylonian Deluge
One of these recorded stories found in the library of Ashur-bani-pal in Nineveh is an account of the Deluge. The tablets discovered in Nineveh by A.H. Layard and H. Rassam in 1851 CE, and brought to London 1854. George Smith examining these tablets, discovered, the story of the Deluge, the Legend of Gilgamesh, and a description of the Creation, among other important tablets.

In the Babylonian 'Atrahasis Epic', (from about 1700 BCE), the hero is Atrahasis, who was king in Shurupak. He too had been instructed by Enki to build a boat, and save himself and his family from the coming storm, followed by a great flood. Enki is supposed to have instructed Atrahasis standing behind a wall, thus not breaking the oath. In the 'Myths from Mesopotamia' by Stephanie Dalley, we read about that conversation:

> Wall, listen constantly to me!
> Reed hut, make sure you attend to all my words!
> Dismantle the house, build a boat, . . .
> Roof it like the Apsu
> So the sun cannot see inside it!
> Make upper decks and lower decks,
> The tackle must be very strong,
> The bitumen [a kind of tar] strong. . .

Prior to the deluge, the gods tried to decrease the population, according to the Atrahasis Epic. Enlil was alarmed by the fact that the humans increased in number. He tried famines and plagues, but Enki was always there to provide some help. Enlil was also angry because the humans disturbed his sleep. This does not sounds like a serious reason for exterminating the whole humanity unless there were some other reasons, as well.

> Twelve hundred years [had not yet passed) (when the land extended] and the peoples multiply. The [land] was bellowing [like a bull]. The gods were disturbed with [their uproar]. Enlil heard their noise [and addressed] the great gods. "The noise of mankind [has become too intense for me] [with their uproar] I am deprived of asleep."[8]

The intense uproar of starving humans, caused by famine and plagues, disturbed the Lord's sleep! The famines, and plagues had indeed great effects, but he was not satisfied with the results. They were not effective enough. Could he cause famines, and plagues at will? Someone could, probably his son Ishkur/Adad, by using chemical, and biological weapons. So they tried again and again, every time using more effective methods. People were dying because of the diseases, or starving to death. People turned to cannibalism. Ordinary, honest humans were neither ordinary nor honest any more, as starving people tend to have only one thing in mind, food. In 'Myths from Mesopotamia', by Stephanie Dally, we read:

When the second year arrived
They had depleted the storehouse.
When the third year arrived
The people's look were changed by starvation.
When the fourth year arrived
Their upstanding bearing bowed,
Their well-set shoulders slouched,
The people went out in public hunched over.
When the fifth year arrived,
A daughter would eye her mother coming in;
A mother would not even open her door to her daughter . . .
When the sixth year arrived
They served up a daughter for a meal,
Served up a son for food.[9]

Such inhuman circumstances were the result of destructive actions of the Grand Master of the Brotherhood of the Gold who later declared himself as God! To cause the whole population of Earth to be exposed to starvation is also a crime against humanity. We are not surprised to find humans, the bible believers, who justify such actions as being right. Could the reason be the influence of manipulative instructions, being in constant fear of punishment?

Then the flood came and destroyed everything except for the few survivors who had been warned by Enki. When Enlil discovered that there were indeed some survivors, (both men and women) he was angry because his plan to exterminate the human race failed. In the Epic of Gilgamesh, the part dealing with the deluge, the hero Atra-Hasis narrates the adventures of Gilgamesh seeking after the 'plant of immortality'. Atra-Hasis had been sent away by Enlil, in some faraway secret abode, not able to communicate with other humans. Eventually, Gilgamesh found him. Atrahasis says:

Now when Enlil came nigh
He saw the ship; then was Enlil wroth
And he was filled with anger against the gods, the Igigi
[saying]: Hath any being escaped with his wife?
He shall not remain alive, a man among the destruction.

Enlil, the God of the OT was angry because some managed to survive. He was ready to kill them in order to accomplish the destruction. Ninurta accused Ea for revealing the secret to the humans and helping them with the construction of the 'boat'.

> Who besides the god Ea can make a plan?
> The god Ea knoweth everything that is done.
> As for you I have not revealed the secret of the great gods. I
> made Atra-hasis to see a vision, and thus he heard the secret
> of the gods.

Despite the global catastrophe, the gods soon realized that the Gold Mission could indeed go on. The few survivors, against Enlil's will, were now an asset that could produce new gold miners and new servants. For the time being there were too many gods but not enough humans. Enki was forgiven and Uta-Napishtim was given long life!

> Formerly Uta-Napishtim was a man merely,
> But now let Uta-Napishtim and his wife be like unto us gods.
> Uta-Napishtim shall dwell afar off, at the mouth of the rivers.
> And they took me away to a place afar off, and made me to
> dwell at the mouth of the rivers.[10]

Enlil appears here to be good by giving Utanapishtim and his wife 'eternal life'. Nevertheless he was only interested in securing the future of his livestock. Note that neither Utanapishtim nor his companions were allowed to settle down at some place of their choice. 'They took me away' and 'made me dwell' witness of actions against his will. He had been sent to exile to some distant, mountainous place with no possibility to communicate with other people. Not even his children, who now were needed to populate Earth once again. He could not be allowed to reveal the truth about the actions of the gods at the time of the deluge. That was necessary in order to present the corrupted story of Noah.

The information about Utanapishtim/Ziusudra being exiled somewhere in a distant land is quite credible. In the 'Lost Book of Enki' by Z. Sitchin, we read that Gilgamesh, who was seeking after eternal life, managed at last to find Utanapishtim. It was however not Enlil but Enki who provided him with the plant, after the approval of Enlil, of course.

The events of the Deluge Ziusudra to Gilgamesh related, the
secret of long living to Gilgamesh he revealed: A plant in his
garden's well was growing, Ziusudra and his spouse from getting old prevented! Unique of all plants on Earth it was; by it
a man full vigor can regain. Man at Old Age Is Young Again!
This is the plant's name, Ziusudra to Gilgamesh said. A gift
of Enki, with Enlil's blessing, on the Mount of Salvation to us
was granted! [11]

The plant being a gift from Enki to Ziusudra could not had been
handled to him without Enlil's approval. Here we have two different
definitions of the gold powder elixir. When approved by Enlil, it is
called 'blessing', otherwise it is classified as 'sin'. Here we have
some additional information about the gold dust being consumed
through herbs. We are going to find the same information, later on,
concerning the Anakim where it is 'classified' as 'sin', against God's
will.

The Biblical Deluge
The deluge is also described in the bible, the book of Genesis. There,
the hero is Noah. According to this account, God decided to destroy
every living thing, except for Noah and his family. God is also a hero
since he saved some. Genesis 7:4:

> And yet seven days, and I will cause it to rain upon the earth
> forty days and forty nights; and every living substance that I
> have made will I destroy from off the face of the earth.

While the Sumerian, and Babylonia stories of the Deluge also point
out Enlil as the instigator, and Enki as the savor, the OT gives us a
corrupt version of the same story, where God is both instigator, and
savor. This is however not enough; we also read in the OT, that God
was right by doing so. Genesis 6:12:

> God looked upon the earth, and, behold, it was corrupt; for all
> flesh had corrupted his way upon the earth.

We find it difficult to believe that all corruptions were unintentional.
The scribes of the OT had not the knowledge needed for the pur-

pose. Some corruptions might have been presented to them by the Enlilite brotherhood.

Genesis does not supply any explanation about why the 'flesh' had been corrupted, or how. But despite the efforts of the Jewish scribes, under the Babylonian captivity, to distance this 'God' from the many other gods in their culture, the similarities between him, and the gods of the Sumerians are still there.

Since Enlil was responsible for the unnecessary death of millions of people and the god of the OT is none other than Enlil, then God has begotten a great crime against humanity. It is a crime never to be justified, or removed from the history records. This God is not a good one, as the Christian Cathars believed.

Since the calamity because of the Flood was global, it is not unexpected to find similar stories all over the Earth, from India to the Americas. Some scholars seek after similarities of these tales in order to justify the biblical story. Even when they discovered that other stories are older than the bible story, they do not admit that the story in the bible is but a copy of some older one.

Characteristics of the deluge
We find a similar story about a great flood that caused almost every living substance to perish, all over the world. This supports the thesis that the deluge was a global calamity, not a local one. If we look at the characteristics of the Deluge, irrespectively of the source, we find that:

There is always some god involved who wishes mankind to be perished. The same god, or another god saves some humans. Some other humans survived too, as they were wise enough to flee up to high mountaintops. The hero used some kind of boat, landed on a mountain, and then sent out some animals, often birds, in order to find out if the lands had become habitable again. After the Deluge, again some god, or gods were involved helping mankind to start all over again.

In addition Enlil/Yahweh promised not to destroy the world again. He wants us to think of that promise every time we look at the rainbow, so we would forget all about the destruction. He wants us to be thankful for not being destroyed once more!

There is an agreement in every source, except the bible, that the gods involved were humans, and yet not Earthlings. We know that the Anunnaki came to Earth, for incredibly long time ago, because of the Gold Mission. We also know that they probably left after the introduction of Islam. The bible does not supplies any information why God was here, or the Elohim, or his 'angels' (also gods), or for how long. There is no explanation why this god had to come down to Earth, transform himself into an old man, create humans, and then change his mind and try to destroy every one of them. For being God, his creation was far away from perfect. If he had known that, he would not have them created in the first place. After the work was accomplished in the end of the sixth day, God look upon his creation and, behold, it was 'very good' (Gen. 1:31). Yet, he decided to exterminate the crown of his creation. Unless, of course, it was somebody else who created man and woman, while he was busy with his gold-mining operations. The real reason why God wished mankind to be perished is to be found in Genesis 6:1–7:

> And it came to pass, when men begun to multiply on the face of the earth, and daughters were born unto them, that the sons of God saw the daughters of men that they were fair; and they took them wives of all which they chose . . . And the Lord said I will destroy man whom I have created from the face of the earth; both man and beasts, and the creeping thing, and the fowls of the air; for it repenteth me that I have made them.

The above expression is witnessing of a man of racial opinions. Additionally, we do not believe that the omnipotent God creates life and then repents!

The reason was, as we have seen, that the Watchers knew the secrets of the Gold Powder and passed the knowledge to their children. This knowledge was classified as top secret. So the only way to stop the knowledge to be spread all over the Earth was to exterminate all those who were in possession of that knowledge. Beside Enki, many writers of our time hold Enlil as responsible for the deluge too. Laurence Gardner says:

> The adapted Genesis version of the story tells that the Flood was an act of God's vengeance, but the Sumerian tablet explains that the great deluge was caused by Enlil and the Assembly of the Anunnaki. The decision was taken by way of a majority vote, but it was not approved by all concerned. Seem-

ingly, Nin-khur-sag, the Lady of Life, deplored the idea. In the event, Enlil's brother, Enki the Wise, made his own arrangements to save King Zi-u-sudra . . .[12]

Rand and Rose Flem-Ath say about Enlil:

> Three gods were of particular importance to the Sumerians. The first, "Enlil," was known as the "Lord of the Air" and the king of kings. He was the most worshiped and feared god for he had within his power the most destructive weapon: the power of the flood.[13]

Apparently, God/Enlil has always been underestimating our intelligence, because he wanted us to believe that he was the one who created mankind. That he was the one who saved a few of us. Didn't he think that one day we would discover the truth? Or have we? Our early ancestors were dumb enough to work without questioning or requests. At the same time, they were intelligent enough to perform the tasks assigned to them. We are certainly intelligent enough to accept that we have been manipulated and cheated. But we are not questioning his actions because of fear for punishment! It must be a suitable way for him, perhaps the only way, to dominate and direct our development during his absence, a development not in our interests but in his. The dogmas stated in the bible are not allowing us to think, only forcing us to accept.

---

[1]Zecharia Sitchin, The Lost Book of Enki, p. 224

[2]Ibid., p. 193

[3]Laurence Gardner, Genesis of the Grail Kings, p. 170

[4]Zecharia Sitchin, The Lost Book of Enki, p. 205, 206

[5]Ibid., p. 211

[6]Ibid., p. 219, 223

[7]Ibid., p. 214

[8]From http://home.apu.edu/geraldwilson/atrahasis.html, after article of Tikva Frymer-Krensky in Biblical Archaeologist December 1977

[9]Stephanie Dalley, Myths from Mesopotamia, p.25, 26

[10]The Babylonian story of the Deluge, Epic of Gilgamesh, from www.earthhistory.com by L.C.Geerts

[11]Zecharia Sitchin, The Lost Book of Enki, p. 294

[12]Laurence Gardner, Genesis of the Grail Kings, p. 94

[13]Rand and Rose Flem-Ath, When the Sky Fell, p. 54–55

Chapter 6

ISIS AND OSIRIS

The civilizers of Egypt

The story about Osiris, his wife Isis and their son Horus is one of the most beautiful and yet most tragic events in ancient times. It is also greatly misunderstood by most scholars.

They usually apply the ever going on method of classifying the gods by associating them with nature. Accordingly, Osiris is supposed to have been the god of fertility, symbolizing the rebirth of nature every year, since he died and 'resurrected'. He is also supposed to have been the god of the dead, and the god of waters, among other characteristics. Jesus being crucified and 'resurrected' can also be regarded as 'the god of fertility', if we apply a similar kind of logics. Isis is supposed to have been the Mistress of Words of Power, Goddess of Nature, Goddess of Wisdom, among other characteristics. She is also considered to have been the mother, sister or the wife of Osiris!

Many attempts have also been made to explain the meaning of their names. Similar attempts have been made by many authors to explain the building of the great pyramids at Giza by humans, since they cannot accept the only credible explanation that the builders were the gods themselves. It is not possible to give a meaning to the Greek name 'Osiris', since his real name was Asar. 'Isis' is also a Greek name, her real name being Asta. Since Asar was a son of Marduk and Asta a daughter of Shamgaz, both being alien from the

50

planet Nibiru, the most logical explanation is that their names too are alien names. We believe that 'A-Sar' means 'Prince of the Waters'. That could connect him to his grand father, the 'Water scientist' Ea. Among the many names of Osiris, we also find 'Asar Em Neteru'. The title 'Neteru' was probably applied to his name later, after the confusion of the tongues by 'God' and it was just another name of the 'Igigi'. Asar-Em-Neteru is then equivalent to 'Asar the Igigi', or 'Asar the Titan'.

What we know about this story comes to us from Egyptian stone-inscriptions, and from some ancient writers like Herodotus, Plutarchos, Pausanias and Diodorus Siculus, the Egyptian mythology and 'the Lost Book of Enki' by Z. Sitchin.

The story begins sometime after Osiris succeeded his father Marduk as king of Egypt. He and the queen Isis embarked a great program to civilize Egypt. They taught the people about agriculture, how to plant the seeds when the waters of the Nile had risen and then sunk leaving fertile mud over the fields. They taught them how to water the crops and how to cut the corn and make bread. They taught them how to plant vines and make wine. They also taught them how to live according to a code of laws and how to live peacefully together. Egypt became a land of plenty and peace, a civilized land. The reign of Osiris was a golden age in the history of Egypt, according to the Egyptians.

When this was done, Osiris left, leaving Isis to rule the country. He was to travel all over the world bringing useful knowledge to other humans too. He intended to civilize the whole world using, no commandments, no doctrines, but arguments and music. Isis was ruling the country, under his absence, in the same fashion. This was, however, against the will of Enlil. Osiris and Isis were passing more knowledge to the humans than Enlil was willing to allow. Osiris' brother Satu was making evil plans together with his father-in-law. It's not unthinkable that the Enlilites instigated the conspiracy. Upon Osiris' return the plans were put into motion.

Seth (Satu, Typhon in the Greek Mythology) invited Osiris to a feast, and then offered a nice coffin to whoever could precisely fit in it. The coffin being made after the measurements of Osiris fitted, of course. When Osiris tried, Seth and his fellow conspirators closed and locked the coffin. Then they threw it into the Nile. When Isis eventually found the body, Osiris was dead.

His son, Horus avenged his death and deposed Seth on the throne. The reign of Set was short and he is only remembered as the killer of his brother.

There are many similarities between the Osiris-Isis-cult and Christianity. Osiris was 'resurrected' like Jesus, and both are supposed to come back after the 'final battle', to rule the world. Isis with her child Horus has been venerated as 'the black Madonna'. The 'Notre Dame' image of Madonna in the French cathedrals, initiated and financed by the Templars, is connected with both Maria Magdalena and Isis. She was the sorrowful wife who lost her beloved husband. A devoted mother, who every woman can identify herself with; she has been the archetype of the cult practicing by the Christians to the present day. Isis and Horus or Maria and Jesus are equally respected and venerated. 'Sophia' the Hellenic 'Goddess of Wisdom' is also associated with Isis. She was also regarded as the Goddess of Marriage. The cult of Osiris and Isis was highly venerated by the Egyptians for several thousands of years, until the 6th century CE, when the last Egyptian temples of Isis closed. Her cult has been slowly and methodically replaced by Christianity and later by Islam.

In the cult of Osiris there is also a 'Day of Awakening' like in Christianity. It is supposed to be after the 'final battle' between Horus and Seth. At that day the tombs shall open up and all the dead will be judged. Osiris became judge of the souls of the dead with the power to grant life in heaven to those who lived righteously on Earth. Compare with Peter who is supposed to hold the keys to the Christian paradise. The Osiris temple in Abydos was dedicated to the 'Lord of Eternity', and was also called 'The House of Millions of years'. E. A Wallis Budge says:

> The belief that Osiris was the impartial judge of men's deeds and words, who rewarded the righteous, and punished the wicked, and ruled over a heaven which contained only sinless beings, and thus he possessed the power to do these things because he had lived on earth, and suffered death, and risen from the dead, is as old as dynastic civilization in Egypt. . . .[1]

Is nothing new under the sun? Had the Enlilites so great shortage of ideas that they had to imitate everything from the land of their adversary Marduk?

Life after death was expressed with the 'ankh' cross in Egypt. A symbol most venerated in Egypt, not only by gods, demigods and kings, but also by ordinary people. It's symbolizing strikingly the same as the crucifix of Jesus, symbol for 'life' after death. Another striking similarity between Osiris and Jesus is about his birth. From the Egyptian Mythology we read:

> When Osiris was born many signs and wonders were seen and heard throughout the world. Most notable was the voice which came from the holiest shrine in the temple at Thebes on the Nile, which today is called Karnak, speaking to a man called Pamyles bidding him proclaim to all men that Osiris, the good and mighty king, was born to bring joy to all the earth.[2]

At the time of Osiris' birth, the king of Egypt was Marduk. At least he was sincere enough to present Osiris as a king who would bring joy to the world, as he also did under his short life. This was probably a plan of Marduk concerning the humans and not some kind of 'prophecy'. Enlil/Yahweh announced long in advance about the coming of his son. At his birth, however, he said nothing.

As we have seen earlier, Marduk moved to Egypt after he married Serpanit. Most of the Igigi moved to Sinai with their leader Shamgaz, whereas some of them moved to Egypt invited to live there by Marduk. The significance of this invitation was much greater than it seemed to be. The Igigi (Titans) living at the site of Baalbek, and the Igigi living in Sinai, were holding the places by force as 'outlaws'. Those who moved to Egypt were living there legally, far away from the reach of the Enlilites, since Egypt was under the dominion of the House of Enki. Those rebellions hade become 'legal citizens'. A war between the 'outlaws' Igigi living in Sinai, and the 'legal' ones living in Egypt, could be good news for the Enlilites. Beside the writings of Plutarchos and other ancient writers, we also have some 'first-hand' information about this story from Enki himself, in 'The Lost Book of Enki' by Z. Sitchin.

Marduk was the master of Egypt, the domain given to him by his father Enki. Asar (Osiris) married Asta (Isis) and Satu (Set) married Nebat. Isis and Nebat were sisters, the daughters of Shamgaz. While Asar chose to settle down in Egypt with his father, Satu went to Sinai, the abode of his father-in-law. Shamgaz was a man with great ambitions. He was the leader of the Igigi who came to Earth from Mars, in order to marry earthly wives. He wished to bring the dictatorship of Enlil to an end, like Marduk and probably Osiris. The two of them, Marduk and Shamgaz, together with the rest of the Igigi and with the support of humans, would have had a chance against the Enlilites. Now their friendship and cooperation came to an end. The act of Shamgaz is very difficult to understand. It is most illogical too.

It is not known why he didn't move to some place away from Enlil. One would think that he could take some humans and start his own 'kingdom' somewhere, if the matter of a dominion of his own was that important to him. Was he really helping Seth to be the master of Egypt, or was he acting according to his own plans? It is, of course, possible that the conspiracy against Osiris (and Marduk) was not his idea, but someone else's idea. Whatever Osiris was teaching the humans it was certainly not approved by Enlil. The House of Enki was giving the humans more knowledge that Enlil wished. We are not stating that every bad thing that happened was the work of Enlil. On the other hand, a war among the Igigi in the domains of Marduk, would be most favorable to the Enlilites alone.

There are no evidence of such cooperation between Enlil and Shamgaz, but it would probably explain the sudden hostile action against Egypt where his own daughter was the queen, and against his own friend, Marduk. The man was willing to sacrifice his son in law in favor of another son in law. He was willing to replace the queen of Egypt, his own daughter, by another daughter if his. He wanted to hinder one of his daughters to be the queen of an united kingdom of Egypt for the other daughter. The reason for his action was so unexplainable, so illogical that it is only reasonable to assume that he probably had some other hidden reasons as well. Like a promise to Enlil, for example, to saw enmity among the members of Marduk's family, and spoiling Egypt, in exchange for something. After that event, there are no signs of Shamgaz.

This was the war of the Titans. As we have seen in an earlier chapter, among the instructions given by Enlil to his sons about the punishment of the Igigi and their offspring was the following:

> . . . send them one against the other that they may destroy each other in battle . . .

For the time being, this was the only suitable solution to his problems, according to the principle 'divide and rule'. According to

Greek Mythology, Typhon unsuccessfully fought Zeus in an attempt to replace him as the chief of the gods on Earth.

Enki, being there himself witnessing the death of his grand son and the serious wounding of another grandson, gives us first-hand information.

> Asar the one called Asta chose, Satu the one called Nebat be-trothed. Asar with his father Marduk in the dark-hued lands to abide chose, Satu near the Landing Place, where the Igigi dwelt, with Shamgaz his dwelling made. About the domains on Earth was Shamgaz concerned: Where shall the Igigi the masters be? . . .

> By staying with his father, Asar the successor alone shall be, the fertile lands he will inherit! So did Shamgaz and his daugh-ter Nebat to Satu day after day say. How the succession in the lands of Satu alone to retain, father and daughter schemed.[3]

Then Enki describes how Shamgaz and Satu invited Asar to a banquet where they offered him 'an admixture of wine' that made him first glad and then unconscious.

> They Asar to another chamber carried, in a coffin they him laid, The coffin with tight seals they closed, into the sea they threw it.[4]

After Asta had been informed about what happened, she applied to Marduk for help. After a long searching, they found the coffin, but Asar was already dead. Asta applied again to Marduk for revenge. She also asked for a heir by his own seed, as the custom was among the gods. That would make it possible for the lineage to survive, something that was of immense importance to them.

> This, alas, cannot be done! Enki to Marduk and Asta said: The brother who killed, the brother's brother must be the keeper, for this Satu must be spared, by his seed an heir to Asar you must conceive! . . .

> Before the body of Asar was wrapped and in the shroud in a shrine preserved, From his phallus Asta the life seed of Asar

extracted. With it Asta herself made conceive, an heir and
avenger to Asar to be born.[5]

Isis was then forced to hide away from Satu/Seth. She named the
child Horon (Horus). She raised him to avenge his father. The boy
was in a way adopted by his uncle Gibil, who educated him and also
taught him how to make weapons of iron. Gibil prepared Horus for
the coming battle with Satu. Horus summoned an army of humans,
the first one to do that and the first one to use arms made of iron.

For him Gibil winged sandals for soaring fashioned, to fly like
a falcon he was able;[6]

Horus and his army marched against Satu in the Sinai. That means
that the throne of Egypt was 'empty' under that time. Osiris was
often represented in hieroglyphics as a bearded man with long hair,
(compare with Jesus), an eye, and an empty throne. Horus challenged Satu.

The battle took place in the air between the two. Satu had a 'whirlwind', while Horus could fly across the sky aided by the 'winged
sandals'. In the Greek mythology, both Athena and Hermes were
using such flying sandals. Even Perseus could fly through the sky
using winged sandals provided to him by the nymphs. We are not
laughing any more at the 'whirlwinds' described in old documents
since we ourselves have been able to manufacture helicopters. But
we still laugh at 'the flying sandals', at least, until the day we can
produce such things too. The fight of Horus for justice and punishment was the concern of many of the House of Enki. Everybody
tried to contribute with something, supporting Horus with help and
advises. Except for Nergal, the son of Enki who married Ereskigal,
the grand daughter of Enlil. He was the only one to side with the
Enlilites in almost every conflict between the two clans. The battle
took an end when Satu managed to hurt Horus with a poisoned dart.
Asta applied to Ningishzidda/Thoth for help.

With magic powers Ningishzidda the poison to benevolent
blood converted. By morning was Horon healed, from the
dead was he returned. Then with a Fiery Pillar, like a heavenly
fish with fins and a fiery tail, Ningishzidda to Horon provided,
its eyes from blue to red to blue their colors changed.[7]

'From the dead was he returned' is not supposed to be understood literally, but as 'he would have died' without that 'magical' help. At the next battle Horus was doing much better. Satu was hurt but alive. He was now a captive of Horus and brought to the council for judgment.

> They saw that he was blinded, his testicles squashed, like a discarded jar he stood. Let Satu, blind and heirless, live! So did Asta to the council say. To the end of his days as a mortal, among the Igigi, the council his fate determined. Triumphant was Horon declared, the throne of his father to inherit: . . . Having lost both sons, in each other Marduk and Serpanit solace sought. In time to them another son was born; Nabu, Prophecy Bearer, they named him.[8]

The council found that Horus was indeed the legitimate heir of Osiris. The decision made it possible for him to ascend the throne of Egypt. 'To live as a mortal' can be understood as 'he was deprived of the right to use the gold-powder elixir'. A rather credible story with many details about Osirs and Isis has been left to us by Plutarchos (ca 45-125 CE) in the book containing 78 essays, known collectively as 'Moralia'. Plutarchos confirms the good character of Osiris and his wise wife, Isis, stating:

> One of the first acts during his was to deliver the Egyptians from their destitute and brutish manner of living. This he did by showing them the fruits of cultivation, by giving them laws, and by teaching them to honor the gods. Later he traveled over the whole earth civilizing it without the slightest need of arms, but most of the peoples he won over to his way by the charm of his persuasive discourse combined with song and all manners of music.

The benevolent actions of Osiris established him as a peaceful king, who taught humans useful knowledge. Both Osiris and the queen Isis were two of the most sympathetic characters in the history of humanity. Osiris was the son of a god, Isis was a 'child of the rocket ships', and both devoted themselves in the service of humanity. Their gifts to mankind were of such vital importance that we believe that the development of mankind could have been faster and more successful, had their reign been allowed to continue. An envious brother and an ambitious Igigi-god, Shamgaz ended their reign. It is possible that the Enlilites were acting behind the lines.

Enlil became alarmed because of several things happening in Egypt. We know from several documents that he was always observing the developments on Earth with great interest, always ready to act and put an end in every action not serving the purpose of his Gold Mission. The demigods of Egypt were consuming 'ambrosia', the gold dust. They were also supplying the humans all over the world with knowledge that, in time, would cause serious problems. From a military point of view, the army that Horus summoned and armed with weapons made of iron was unforgivable. An army of humans was now a new factor in the relationship between the gods and the humans. Horus showed that the support of the humans, depending on good treatment, was to be of vital importance in the future.

Do we have any evidence that the demigods of Egypt knew about the gold powder and even how to consume it? Indeed we have. Plutarchos states that when Isis was searching for the coffin with her husband's body near the land of Byblos, (Phoenicia) sitting by a spring with tears on her face:

> She [Isis] exchanged no words with anybody, save only that she welcomed the queen's maidservants and treated them with great amiability, plaiting their hair for them and **imparting to their persons a wondrous fragrance from her own body** [emphasis added]. But when the queen observed her maidservants, a longing came upon her for the unknown woman and for such hairdressing and for a body fragrant with ambrosia.

Ambrosia was the food of the gods, according to the Greek mythology, the same as the Egyptian 'what is it'.

As we shall see later on, the energy from a 'shining body' can be transferred to other bodies. The energy is so benevolent that it can cure diseases and even bring high spiritual awareness. By consuming gold powder the body loses weight and eventually the energy is visible as light around the body.

Jesus is often depicted with an aura around his head or his body. Was it an artistic invention of later times or was he really consuming gold powder sanctioned ('blessed') by Yahweh? Laurence Gardner about Isis:

It is a well-established fact that the familiar image of the White Madonna is founded upon the depictions of Isis, the nursing mother. It was she too who inspired the mysterious Black Madonna, of whose image there were nearly 200 in France by the 16th century.[9]

All the scriptures we have about this drama, witness of good things that Osiris and Isis have done with the blessings of Marduk, and other members of the House of Enki. The enmity already established between the House of Enlil in Mesopotamia, and the House of Enki in Egypt, was now developing into dramatic proportions. Things could not be solved in good understanding any more, but by wars.

Osiris was the first demigod being killed by another demigod. It was a dramatic event caused by political, economical, social, and even military reasons, worthy an epic film. The consequences on human civilization have been enormous. The old Egyptian civilization, later on destroyed by both Christianity and Islam, has been a great lost for humanity. Osiris was not to be the only victim of the struggle about power among the gods.

Osiris' passion to civilize the humans was equally dangerous to the Enlilite brotherhood, as Marduk and the Igigi. Remember the words of Enlil in a previous chapter: 'the murder of their beloved ones shall they see'.

The Enlilites might have been acting behind the lines in the war among the Titans/Igigi. Soon there would be more events of dramatic character in Egypt and this time the Enlilites would act openly and more warlike than any time before.

---

[1] E.A. Wallis Budge, Osiris and the Egyptian Resurrection, p. 337

[2] April McDevitt, the story of Isis and Osiris from www.egyptianmyths.net/mythisis .htm

[3] Zecharia Sitchin, The Lost Book of Enki, p. 244

[4] Ibid., p. 244, 245

[5] Ibid., p. 245

[6] Ibid., p. 246

[7] Ibid., p. 247

[8] Ibid., p. 247,248

[9] Laurence Gardner, Bloodline of the Holy Grail, p. 104

Chapter 7

THE DEATH OF DUMUZI

The first war and the birthright of Marduk

Inanna was a great grand daughter of Anu and granddaughter of both
Enlil and Enki. Dumuzi was a grandson of Anu, son of Enki. She, of
great beauty, spoiled by everyone during childhood, frustrated about
the fact the men always were observing her body qualities, tired of
the patriarchal governing which prevented her from being assigned
a dominion of her own. Ambitious and avaricious, she had to try any
possible way to 'make herself a name' among the Anunnaki.

As Aphrodite, she was, and still is the Goddess of love, an epithet
she probably does not deserve. She was a good pilot and as good
warrior as any man. She must have been very clever too; otherwise
it wouldn't have been easy to combine such different properties as
love and war. Actually she was more famous as a war goddess. Since
she had an attack aircraft, 'sky bird' of her own, it is very likely that
she made flights all around the eastern Mediterranean region. It is
possible that she landed on the waters in the south of Cyprus directing the aircraft toward the land. It could look as she was coming up
'through the foam of the sea', hence the meaning of her name in
Greek.

Dumuzi appears to have been a cool young man, well educated in
farming. He fell in love with her because of her exceptional beauty,
or perhaps because of some other qualities of her, unknown to us.
We don't know either, why she fell in love with him. Perhaps be-

cause she knew that the man loved her, or was easy to control. Or it may have been an easy way to get control over a dominion, his dominion in Africa.

In the 'Queen of heaven and Earth, her stories and myths from Sumer', by Wolkenstein and Kramer, we read that Inanna was persuaded by her twin brother, Utu, and her mother Ningal to meet Dumuzi, since she was not interested, as she said. Her mother's interest was probably bringing the old strife between the two houses to an end. This is, however, not credible enough, since her marriage, a daughter of Enki, with Nannar, a son of Enlil, didn't affect the relationship between the two clans in some positive direction. But she was certainly hoping that it could, at least bring some peace, as Enki was hoping. There are several hymns to Inanna and Dumuzi, about their first meeting, their love, and also their marriage, uncertain if it really took place. To begin with, she had no interest in meeting him at all. We quote www.piney.com/Bab-Courtship.html: Inanna says:

The shepherd? I will not marry the shepherd!
His clothes are coarse, his wool is rough.
I will marry the farmer.
The farmer grows flax for my clothes,
The farmer grows barley for my table.

Then Dumuzi spoke:

Why do you speak about the farmer?

*   *   *

What does he have more than I do?

Inanna replied to that:

Shepherd, without my mother, Ningal, you'd be driven away, without my grandmother, Ningikuga, you'd be driven away into the steppe, without my father, Nanna, you'd have no roof, without my brother, Utu . . .

After these arguments, Dumuzi made his standpoint clear: 'Inanna, do not start a quarrel.

My father, Enki, is as good as your father, Nanna.
My mother, Sirtur, is as good as your mother, Ningal.
My sister, Geshtianna, is as good as yours.
Queen of the palace, let us talk it over.

Although the royal lineage was very important, it is possible that
they, at last, fell in love with each other. It is nothing wrong in helping someone to find a partner; yet, here we find suspicions that some
other reasons contributed to the arrangement.

Any way, beside the young couple, there were a lot of other people involved. Was it real love, or based on some calculations, it was
dominated by politics, domain interests, intrigues, and the ever going on struggle between the House of Enlil and the House of Enki.

It seems that Marduk had nothing against this marriage, until he
heard about Inanna's ambitions, and plans concerning Dumuzi, his
dominion in Africa and their common future. He probably became
aware that there were some political and territorial interests. After
all, he was the one who always defended the interests of the House
of Enki. Probably, he could not trust any of the Enlilites. Inanna
would, through the marriage, practically gain some partial control
of the lands solely dominated by him and his brothers. The lands
included the whole of Africa except for the mines in South Africa
that were under the administration of his half brother Nergal, and his
consort Ereskigal, sister of Inanna.

The two sisters were of quite different character. While Ereskigal
was satisfied pretending being the queen of the mines (the underworld), Inanna had much greater ambitions. She wished, at least, a
dominion of her own, as a first stage of her career. To prevent that
the domain of Dumuzi in Africa would fall under the control of the
Enlilites, Marduk wished to stop a new liaison with an Enlilite. He
instructed his sister, (probably a half sister) Geshtinanna, to mate
with Dumuzi in order to have a heir to his African domain from
the proper bloodline. A heir by a half sister would precede a heir
between Dumuzi and Inanna. Those were the rules and ethics of the
Anunnaki. Enlil distanced Enki in that matter, because he was the
son of Anu with a half sister, whereas Enki, the first born, was a son
of Anu with his first wife. Geshtinanna agreed to that, and it appears
that Dumuzi agreed to that too.

After the mating, she told Dumuzi that Marduk intended to arrest
him accusing him of raping her. If she was instructed by Marduk

to do that, or if it was her own idea, only she knew. The accusation sounds very unexpected because the only one who could accuse Dumuzi for raping her, or free him from such an accusation was, of course, Geshtinanna herself. But, somehow, she wanted him to believe that the accusation was true. She too, was probably interested in stopping the marriage. That was a serious accusation that would send him into exile to some distant land, and make the wedding between him and Inanna impossible. That was probably not the plan of Marduk, since for him it would be enough if Dumuzi could get a heir by his sister. Dumuzi, not able to think clearly, ran out in the darkness in the middle of the night, certainly full of anger, fell and hurt himself so badly that he died. It was a tragic accident, of course, but still an accident.

He was the youngest son of Enki, probably relative young, without much experience of life or of political intrigues. Enki says:

As the custom was, to perfume and clothe Inanna a sister of
   Dumuzi was sent,
Geshtinanna, a sister-in-law-to-be, was her name.
To her Inanna what was in her heart revealed, of her future with
   Dumuzi to her she said:
A vision of a great nation I have, as a Great Anunnaki Dumuzi
   there shall rise.
His name over others shall be exalted, his queen-spouse I shall
   be.

* * *

Inanna's visions of rulership and glory by Geshtinanna to her
   brother Marduk were reported.
By Inanna's ambitions Marduk was greatly disturbed; to Geshtinanna a secret plan he told.

* * *

My brother, with you I will lie down! Bridegroom, with you a
   peer to Enki we shall have!
So did Geshtinanna to Dumuzi whisper, a noble issue from her
   womb to have.[1]

Dumuzi's body was brought to the land of the mines, the abode of his brother Nergal, and Inanna's sister Ereskigal in South Africa.

It is unknown if there was any particular reason for that. Inanna's 'descent to the underworld' to get Dumuzi's body, is full of mythical elements, but the story is not mentioning the real reason of her visit. The reason would probably have been to mate with Nergal in order to get an heir by Dumuzi's older brother. As we have seen in the case of Isis and Osiris, that was usual among the Anunnaki.

An heir by Nergal would give her access to Dumuzi's domain. She seemed to be unaware of the mating between Dumuzi and Geshtinanna. It is also possible that this was Nergal's intention, and it was he that probably ordered that the body should be brought to him. But he didn't count with the reaction of his wife. Nergal's wife, Ereskigal, was not prepared to share her husband with Inanna. Her reaction however could have depended on some other reasons too. In fact, she appeared to be very surprised by Inanna's visit. She wondered what brought Inanna to her, and why. She made no mention about Dumuzi's body, assuming that Inanna's purpose was something else, somehow hostile. So she treated Inanna as an intruder. After Inanna was forced to hand over her weapons, and everything else she had, including her clothes, she was imprisoned by Ereskigal. Some believe that Ereskigal killed Inanna and Enki brought her back to life again. However that would be most strange, if Enki could resurrect Inanna but not his own son Dumuzi. Enki helped however to get Inanna out of her sister's prison.

Anyhow, the 'resurrected' Inanna accused Marduk as responsible for Dumuzi's death. Enlil and his sons, decided in council to make war against Marduk. Things were developing very quickly. They did not demand any negotiations, not even some kind of explanation. Inanna demanded that Marduk would surrender, and be punished as responsible for Dumuzi's death. Enki could not accept Inanna's demand, since he didn't consider Marduk as responsible for Dumuzi's death. The Enlilites never said that they intended to bring Marduk to trial. They immediately decided to make war. They planned to kill Marduk. The fact that they were not interested in bringing justice, strengthen the suspicion that the marriage had some political background.

> Of secret words between Marduk and the Igigi exchanged, Utu
> to them reported.
> Of Marduk, an evil serpent, Earth must be rid! Enlil with them
> agreed.[2]

What kind of secret words Marduk exchanged with the Igigi, we never know. This information is witnessing about Marduk, and probably many others, being wired by the telecom-specialist Utu. There were no investigations, no negotiations, and no warnings, just war.

Inanna assisted by Ninurta, attacked by air destroying many dwellings all over Africa. A lot of innocent humans lost their lives because of a war among the gods. A war they had no idea what it was about. Marduk not able to defend himself against the aerial attack was forced to hide himself in the great pyramid.

The sudden attack by the Enlilites surprised all of the House of Enki. It all seemed as they had been waiting for some excuse to put Marduk out of action, and they now had one. No contacts were made. The war began without any warnings, and was also directed against all the Enkites as well as the people of Egypt.

With a Weapon of Brilliance, by a horn directed, Inanna the hiding place attacked. Horon (Horus) to defend his grandfather came; by her Brilliance was his right eye damaged.[3]

Young Horus, who was the king of Egypt by now, had, of course, the right to defend his country and his grand father. The damaged eye of Horus can be found in many Egyptian depictions. The struggle between Enki and Enlil was now spreading, through their children, to their grand children. Anyone who hoped that it would some day come to an end, had been miscalculating.

As Enlil stated 'Marduk, an evil serpent, Earth must be rid'! So the purpose of the Enlilites was to neutralize Marduk, or even better, to kill him. Since they didn't succeed, they closed the exit to the chamber he was hiding. Without trial, food and water, Marduk was facing a certain death.

This is another evidence that the Enlilites was the only group with weapons, advanced weapons, like the 'weapon of brilliance', which can be understood as some kind of missile firing weapon. The Enkites, not able to defend themselves, could only observe the hostile actions. From a military point of view, the Enlilites were victorious.

Under different circumstances they wouldn't care even if every single one of the sons of Enki had been killed. Now they made war because they considered Marduk as responsible for Dumuzi's death. Did they have a case? Dumuzi's death seemed to have been an accident. If Marduk instructed his sister to mate with Dumuzi, that was not a crime. Not by their rules. On the contrary, it was often practiced by all of them. Ninurta was himself the result of such a mating between Enlil and his half sister Ninmah. If Marduk had instructed her to accuse Dumuzi of raping her, that would of course have been a crime of some minor character, and the two of them would be equally responsible. The punishment for such a crime was certainly not death, if that was a crime at all.

But the Enlilites didn't demand a trial that would have been the right thing to do, as in the case of Cain, after he killed his brother Abel. From 'The Lost Book of Enki' we read that Ninurta was the mentor of Cain, and Marduk was the mentor of Abel. Ninurta taught Cain about metallurgy whereas Marduk and Dumuzi, taught Abel about farming. Cain was brought to trial where Marduk first demanded the penalty of death for Cain, and later accepted that Cain should be sent to exile to some distant land. This time, the Enlilites demanded Marduk's death without trial. Had they any other purpose? Indeed they had. We know that Marduk claimed to succeed Enlil on Earth. But nowhere it is mentioned that Marduk had that right. That is why he was considered to be a rebellion striving for power. Was he claiming the Command over the gods on Earth without having that right? Was he a freedom fighter demanding a new administration for gods and men, or was he a troublemaker? Was his friendship with the humans and his ability to summon human armies a threat to the whole Gold Mission? Probably yes. As we have seen, nobody could threat the outcome of the Gold Mission unpunished. Marduk (and the Igigi) had already done that without success. Perhaps Enlil wished to bring an end to Marduk's ambitions once and for all. So when Ninurta's mother, Ninmah/Ninkhursaq came to make peace between the two clans, she proposed:

> Let Marduk in exile live, the succession on earth to Ninurta submit! Enlil by her words was pleased and smiled: Ninurta was his son, of Ninurta She was the mother!

> If between succession and life the choice is, what can, a father say? So did Enki With heavy heart answer.[4]

Marduk's right to succession could be submitted to Ninurta in exchanged for his life! Here we have the real reason of the war. Now

how could Marduk submit a right he didn't have. The demand to release the right to Ninurta is witnessing that Marduk had indeed that
right. They didn't ask Marduk if he was willing to give up his right.
Enki was to decide about the agreement, although in reality it was
not an agreement at all, but real blackmail. Enki was to decide what?
To deprive his son of his right without trial, without justification,
even without asking him, or leave him to die slowly without food
and water? What a choice for a father indeed! The man who once
was deprived of the right to succeed Anu, because of alternation
of rules, was now forced to accept that his son was deprived of the
same right on Earth. Not because of alternation of rules this time,
but because of superior power. In 'The Lost Book of Enki', Zecharia
Sitchin says in the Synopsis of the 11th Tablet:

> Fearing the consequences (of Inanna and Dumuzi falling in
> love with each other), Marduk causes Dumuzi's death.

Nowhere in the text of the eleventh tablet is there any evidence of
that. In most of Sitchin's books, Marduk is always 'the bad guy'
and Enlil/Yahweh the good one. However Sitchin never supplies any
evidence of such a stand point of view. No evidence of bad deeds
made by Marduk. No evidence of good deeds made by Enlil/Yahweh.
Unless the destruction of the Tower of Babili and the confusion of
the tongues are regarded as 'good', as it is stated in the bible.

Marduk was humiliated once again by the Enlilites. Not because
he was 'a bad guy', but because the Enlilites trusted more in power
than justice. They had the power and they used it. Marduk was deprived of his right by force and without even being informed in
advanced, without trial too, in exchange for his life. Who decided
about that? Ninurta and his father and mother! The god who was
against the Gold Mission could not be allowed to succeed Enlil.

But that was not enough. Enlil demanded that the Igigi/Titans
had to abandon Baalbek. They were allowed to settle down in Sinai
among the other Igigi. The purpose was to bring them all to the same
place.

The results of this 'peace' were all in favor of the Enlilites. Ninurta granted the Enlilship powers, to succeed Enlil and to be his
fathers surrogate in Ki-Engi (Sumer), the lands of the Enlilites.

Ishkur/Adad, another son of Enlil, was granted the Landing place
in the Cedar Mountains (Baalbek in Lebanon), now freed from the

Igigi, and the lands northward. He was to control the Hittites later on and the area of Asia Minor. South and east of the domain of Ishkur, the Igigi and their offspring were permitted to spread i.e. in Canaan, and the Master Enlil/Yahweh would not forget their location. It was still a state of war between the Enlilites and the Titans. The Place of the Chariots in the Sinai Peninsula and the lands thereof were given to Nannar/Sin, who gave his name to 'Sinai', also a son of Enlil. Utu, a son of Nannar/Sin and twin brother of Inanna, became the Commander of the Place (of the Chariots in Sinai) and the Navel of the earth (Nippur).

Egypt was for a while a land occupied by the Enlilites. Their power replaced justice and could dictate conditions of life and death. It was also a demonstration of power. The future of the Gold Mission was not negotiable! The victorious Ninurta entered the pyramid chamber and found some very advanced installations made by Ningishzidda. There he ordered the destruction of almost everything. Anything he didn't wish to destroy, he ordered to be dismount and taken away to be used somewhere else. Enki states that the pyramids were built to support the direction of the chariots to the landing place, (Sippar) which was something of vital importance to the Enlilites. Yet, such a marvelous creation was destroyed because of ignorance, fear, and hate. Enki says:

> Through the horizontal corridor to the Ekur's vulva he [Ninurta] went.
> In its east wall, in the niche artfully fashioned, the Destiny Stone a red radiance was emitting.
> Its power to kill me grabs, with a killing tracking it me seizes! Ninurta inside the chamber cried.
> Take it away! To obliteration destroy it! to his lieutenants Ninurta shouted.

* * *

> Its Gug Stone, that directions determined, Ninurta ordered to be taken out, to a place of his choice carried.

* * *

> To the Apex Stone his attention he turned; his enemy's epitome it represented.

With his weapons he shook it lose, to the ground in pieces it
toppled.
By this the fear of Marduk is forever ended! Ninurta, victorious,
declared.[5]

History is full of barbarians who have declared themselves victorious by destroying irreplaceable treasures. Ninurta was not even able
to appreciate the value of what he destroyed. It is possible that the
unbelievable installations inside the great pyramid at Giza served
some other purpose than just directing the chariots. Otherwise Ninurta would not feel that 'the fear of Marduk ended'. But we never
know, unless Ningishzidda left behind some information still under
the Egyptian desert.

Ningishzidda, a man of science and peace, was accepted as Lord
over the Land of the Two Narrows (Egypt). Inanna alone opposed to
that claiming, either the domains of Dumuzi, or some other domain
for herself. She might have been in love with Dumuzi, but his domain in Africa was not without interest to her either. Both her hate
against Marduk and her love for Dumuzi, would last 'for ever', and
direct her future actions as the goddess of War and Love.

Marduk, angered and humiliated was sent to exile in the Land of
no Return, (probably Mexico in the Americas), with his wife Serpanit, and their little son, Nabu. Exiled with no return, means that
it was not possible for him to return without help. The help would
arrive when the time of the exile had come to an end.

It is possible that magnificent citadel at Teotihuacan, Mexico,
was built by Marduk, and the pyramid of the Sun was the family
dwelling. It is not known how long his exile lasted, but long enough
for Serpanit to die there. At that time, the native population of South
America was collecting gold for Viracocha. There are no records
that Marduk was using the native people of Central America for the
same purpose.

Much later, Marduk honored Dumuzi in Babylon with the name
of a month, Tammuzi. In human traditions Dumuzi (Tammuz) was
venerated as the god of fertility. The name of the fourth month of the
Jewish calendar is also 'Tammuz', which the Jews introduced after
their return from the Babylonian captivity. Another important consequence of that war was the decision by the Anunnaki to establish
common settlements for themselves and the Earthlings. They also

decided to make use of a new title, 'god' that could easily enable them to maintain control over mankind. The Sumerian and Egyptian civilizations started at about that time. Soon thereafter, the gods abandoned the counting in 'shars' for the more practical counting in earth years, at about 3760 BCE, some 7200 years after the Deluge. Enki says:

> How over mankind lofty to remain [the Anunnaki], how to make the many the few to obey and serve. [6]

'To obey and serve', that was mankind's mission! That was the reason behind the creation of Man! Now with the rebellious Marduk away from the scene, and the equal rebellious Igigi away from the Landing Place, and under some control for the time being, the Enlilites were to govern Earth as 'The Gold Company (Earth)'. No opposition was allowed. More gold was needed as well as human gold miners. The future of the Gold Mission, more important than anything, was secured by using power.

But Marduk was to come back, and challenge Enlil once again. The Igigi affair was not ended either. However they just could not be permitted to continue guiding the humans. In fact, the Igigi and their descendants could not be permitted to live at all. Would they permit Marduk to live?

---

[1] Zecharia Sitchin, The Lost Book of Enki, p. 252
[2] Ibid., p. 256
[3] Ibid., p. 258
[4] Ibid., p. 260.
[5] Ibid., p. 262, 263
[6] Ibid., p. 265

Chapter 8

THE SUMERIAN CIVILIZATION

The beginning of human history

History began at Sumer, according to a book by Noah Samuel Kramer, one of the first to study and interpret Sumerian texts. The Sumerian civilization appeared suddenly, at about 3700 BCE. It had not passed through the usual steps like the Stone Age, the Bronze Age and the like. On the contrary, this civilization had almost everything from the very beginning. They had the plough, the wheel, schools, the calendar, astronomy, mathematics, medicals and much more. The Sumerians are considered to have had most of what was needed in order to live as civilized humans. Ass we have seen earlier, the purpose of the initiation of settlements was to exercise control over humankind fast increasing in numbers.

The Sumerians stated that the Anunnaki gods established their civilization and that the first human beings were slaves with the sole purpose to serve them. We are not allowed to ignore this information, because this is the explanation why the Sumerians didn't achieve much. The whole society was, not only controlled by the alien rulers, it was owned by them. The society's attainments and wealth were directed by the aliens to be at a level suitable to serve them, no more than that. The Anunnaki called themselves 'gods' but to the Sumerians, they were not 'gods' at all, but real people who acted as powerful masters and slave owners.

Ironically, people who do not recognize the involvement of the Anunnaki in our history, they indeed believe in them without knowing they are doing so. The Lord Yahweh of the bible was just another Anunnaki as well Christianity's several 'angels'. The Anunnaki were as real to the Sumerians as their own families. Laurence Gardner says about the Anunnaki:

> The Anunnaki presence may baffle the historians, their language may confuse linguists and their advanced techniques may bewilder scientists, but to dismiss them is foolish. The Sumerians have themselves told us precisely who the Anunnaki were, and neither history nor science can prove otherwise.[1]

Indeed, the Anunnaki, have been dismissed by most historians, scientists, archaeologists, and many others, and they still are. There are many books and studies trying to explain, through imaginative theories, how humans built the two great pyramids in Egypt, or some megalithic structures, just to mention a few examples. Since they exclude the most important guideline involved in these works, the alien gods and their advanced tools, they can never fully understand or explain the purpose of those buildings, or how they were built.

According to the Sumerians, kingship was lowered from heaven, i.e. from the Anunnaki gods who came from heaven. For not so long ago, there have been kings believing that kingship was an appointment from God! The first kingdom on Earth after the Deluge was the kingdom of Kish, in the land of Sumer. Some Anunnaki of the House of Enlil used to choose suitable kings, and all of them had to be approved by Enlil himself. The first king was appointed by Ninurta, a son of Enlil. The kingly title was 'Lu-Gal' meaning 'Great Man'. By doing so, the Anunnaki created a governing form that was under their control, in contrast to democracy, which would bring forth leaders selected by the people. When a king diverged from the instructions being given to him, was immediately replaced. The death penalty was usual.

Almost all the kings of Sumer, and the pharaohs of the Egyptians of the olden times, were gods or demigods. In Sumer there were several city-states, but only one could house a king, and the 'Heavenly Bright Object'. That object could have been some energy device, supporting the functions of the temple with power, as well as several weapons and guarding equipment. Although a physical device, or a group of devices, it was loaded with high symbolic value as well.

The Sumerians were not allowed to decide about matters concerning foreign affairs or war and peace. They were exclusively up to the gods to decide, even if the wars were to be executed by the humans.

The social life in Sumer may have been better, at that time, than any other place. They had for example schools at a time when other people had no organized societies at all. They practiced astronomy, and mathematics. They had a calendar, and some kind of 'Code of Law'. They practically had everything that characterizes a civilized and well-organized society. It was a gift from the gods who needed security, and security was easier to maintain in an organized society.

The most famous gods of the Sumerians were Enlil, his consort Ninlil, his sons Nannar and Ninurta and his grand children Inanna and Utu. Even Enki was popular in Sumer, living from time to time in Eridu, a city he built together with members of the first crew that arrived to Earth. After death, the Sumerians believed they would descend into the underworld and live there as Ghosts. The knowledge about the underground gold mines contributed to associate their afterlife with the underworld. They had been manipulated to believe that the gold miners were spending their lives there as dead.

The adobes of the gods, situated at the top of ziggurat pyramids, were called 'Temples' by the humans. The ziggurats (from Akkadian zaqaru, 'build high' or built on a high place) were pyramidal structures in multiple levels, often two to seven, surrounded by adobes for the service personnel. They were designed by the gods and built by humans after precise instructions. It was usual with landing platforms for helicopter-like vehicles. The Temple-adobe offered security because of its high location and its limited accessibility through the stairway. Only divinities, and the high priest or priestess, had access to the dwelling place of the god. The word 'Temple' was loaded with fear, respect and mystical powers, contributing to increased security. A temple was the very center of the city, surrounded by human habitations.

'Hierodule' means 'temple servant', often female, but there were male hierodules too. 'Hieron', from Greek, means 'holy' which refers to the temple as a holy place and to hierodule as 'holy prostitute'! The word 'hierodule' has been beautified in the same manner as 'angel'. Neither of them should be connected to anything 'holy'. Here we see how the Anunnaki, by calling themselves 'gods' managed to implant respect, not only for themselves, but even for prostituting servants. The temples were no more holy than the gods themselves. Scriptures about gods are called 'holy scriptures'. 'Hieros gamos', Holy wedding between a deity and an earthling, is another example of misusage of words. There was not a single temple without hierodules, and no god (of some importance) without messengers.

So the Sumerians were given everything needed to maintain an organized society in the service of the gods, but no more than that. In fact, the knowledge was censured in order to keep the humans depended of them and make them willing to serve them. The Sumerians knew that they had been created to serve the gods. They were free citizens or slaves. In fact, even the free citizens had a labor duty whenever the gods wished. They could, however, free themselves from the labor duty if they could pay in silver!

The gods were not interested in the advancements of the society. Producing food and serving the gods in several ways was just enough. This is why the Sumerian civilization was in about the same level at 2000 BCE, as it was at 4000 BCE. Fear, obedience, control, and punishment, by the gods, were so effective that status quo was better than to strive after advancement. The Sumerian civilization was the creation of the House of Enlil. Even the Egyptian civilization was the creation of the gods, the House of Enki, although more freely administrated. This was the great difference between the Sumerian civilization and later civilizations created by humans.

The Sumerian women had jewels and nice and practical houses, but the society was lacking of dynamics. Creativity was not encouraged. It was a society totally controlled by the gods of Sumer, who had their own agenda to follow. The most we know about Sumer comes from the Sumerians themselves who wrote down, in cuneiform, the history about gods and men.

The Sumerian language belongs to no known group and it may well have been the gods' own language. As the creation of the gods, the whole humanity was of one language. Later, Enlil assigned different languages to different groups and spread them all over the world, as stated in the OT. Not as a gift but as a punishment. Probably the Sumerians were not among those groups because they didn't participate in the building of the Tower of Babylon. Any attempt to connect the Sumerian language to other language groups has failed. The Sumerians used to add words to each other to create new words in the same way the Anunnaki did. We have, for example, 'Bab-Ili' meaning the gateway of the gods, 'En-Gal' great master, 'Shar-Gal' great Prince and the like.

The Sumerian pantheon didn't squirt out of the imagination of the people. From the beginning, it was not even a pantheon loaded with religious attributes, but a Council of powerful rulers, as real as the Sumerians themselves. While the gods felt safer being surrounded by civilized humans, the Sumerians were proud being under the protection of the gods, as in the following hymn to Enlil as quoted by N. S. Kramer.

> Without Enlil, the great mountain, no cities would be built, no
>   settlements founded
> No stalls would be built, no sheepfold established,
> No king would be raised, no high priest born... [2]

Even the Egyptian, Akkadian, Babylonian, and Assyrian empires, although founded by Anunnaki, created their independence from time to time, and made achievements not ascribe to the gods but to their own citizens.

The gods of Sumer were friendly to people as long as their instructions were followed, as long as their security was guaranteed, as long as the humans provided food and services. If not, they could punish a king or a whole society. Everybody was expendable.

Although all of them came to Earth for the same purpose, to obtain gold, they soon became divided in two clans, the Enki-clan and the Enlil-clan, or as they also were known, the Enkites and the Enlilites. Enki had been deprived of the right to succeed his father because of changed rules. Enlil was the new crown prince. Enlil became the High Commander on Earth replacing Enki who was the first Commander. The struggle between the brothers was later transplanted among their children.

The members of the House of Enlil (also referred to as 'the Enlilites') were strongly devoted to the Gold Mission. The crown prince of Nibiru couldn't afford to be unsuccessful and the Mission had to be completed by all means, no matter the cost. The members of the House of Enki were less interested in the gold. Eventually, since several of them were demigods not allowed to live on Nibiru, they considered a future on Earth, and consequently the future of humanity as of greater interest.

In order to complete the Mission, the Enlilites founded a secret brotherhood, the Brotherhood of the Gold. Its purpose was to promote the Mission without the involvement of some of the members of the House of Enki. The brotherhood was often acting secretly avoiding entrusting any important task to non-member, much like secret brotherhoods of modern times. It was also forbidden to pass knowledge to humanity except for disinformation serving their mission. It seems that the Enkites also founded a brotherhood, the Brotherhood of the Serpent. The purpose was quite the opposite, to bring knowledge promote civilization of mankind.

What happened then, is our history, dictated by the antagonism between those two brotherhoods, the Brotherhood of the Gold and the Brotherhood of the Serpent. Every important event on Earth, from the incident of the Tower of Babylon, to the introduction of Christianity and Islam, was the result of the struggle between the two brotherhoods and their relation to the gold.

A Sumerian woman to her husband:

"Dear husband, since we expect another child, we would need more space. As a bricklayer you could easily build one." The man could not avoid comparing a little room for his children with the enormous temple he was working at.

"As soon as my labor duty to the gods is over for this time, I will take care of it," he said.

Enlil went down the steps leading to the lowest level of the E-Kur to speak to the thousands of workers who were about to complete his temple, the E-Kur.

"There shall soon be other projects too. You shall come to perform your duty whenever my messenger calls for you. I am the god from the kingdom of heaven. Those who refuse will be sent all the way down to the mines of the underworld wherefrom no return is possible."

---

[1] Laurence Gardner, Genesis of the Grail Kings, p. 83
[2] N. S. Kramer, History begins at Sumer, p. 92

Chapter 9

THE TOWER OF BABILI

The revolt of gods and men

When his exile ended, Marduk returned to Egypt with his now grown up son Nabu. Serpanit died in the land beyond the oceans. A new decision by Enlil, intentional or not, was to be yet another humiliation for Marduk.

Enki says:

> When the time term of Kishi (Kish) shall be completed, to Unug-ki (Uruk) kingship shall pass! So did Enlil declared.[1]

That was the beginning of the first dynasty of Uruk. According to the Sumerian king list, the dynasty reigned for 2,310 years, the first king of Uruk being Mesh-ki-ang-gasher of E-ana, son of Utu, who reigned 324 years. Among the kings of the first dynasty of Uruk, we find Lugal-Banda, (Great Man Banda), and his son, Gilgamesh, two of the most well known kings of that dynasty. Most of the kings of those times had names that are not telling us anything at all, because they were titles, meaning something only in the language of the Anunnaki. Their reign periods were more like 'Anunnaki-periods' than 'human-periods' that sometimes lasted for more than a thousand years.

Uruk (Erech in the bible) was the 'city' of Inanna. It was not really a city. A temple had been built to honor Anu and his spouse

77

Antu when they visited Earth. But since Inanna became Anu's beloved, he gave her the temple as a gift.

Now, if kingship was to be passed over to Uruk (together with the 'Heavenly Bright Object') that would transform the little place to a great town under her dominion. Inanna was getting her own dominion, Marduk not. This is not easy for us humans to understand why it was so important to them to have their own dominion. It seems to us that, although they came to earth for a very important mission, for some of them was an excellent opportunity to make a career. For some leader-subjects, it appeared as necessary to prove their skills as great administrators. Additionally, the dominion had to be assigned to them by the High Commander. Kingship and the 'Heavenly Bright Object' could only be transferred to officially assigned cities. The kingship was never transferred to the dominion of Enki in Africa.

Anyhow, it seems that Marduk had enough. But what was he supposed to do? He could not demand back his lost rights by legal means, since the Enlilites, who were in majority, controlled the council. Was he to start a war? He had no weapons that could match the weapons of the Enlilites either. But he had the support of the Titans/Igigi, and then he could always count on the support of the humans. His grand son Horus proved that the human factor was indeed something to count on. Would he dare challenge the High Commander? He did.

Nabu summoned the people of the rocket ships, the offspring of the Igigi and Earthly women, together with humans from several lands and followed Marduk into the heart of the Enlilites lands. There he planned to build a landing place for the chariots of his own. A tremendous project which he would never be able to accomplish without human labor. But why build a landing place for the chariots? Was he planning to send the gold from his own landing place? How could he possibly redirect the chariots from the landing places of the Enlilites to his own? In order to succeed with that, he would be forced to neutralize, or get control of the other landing places as well. It seems that this was only the beginning of some great changes. The god, who could control the flow of the gold to Nibiru, could also have it stopped. He could be, de facto, the King of Earth. It was not only an attempted coup, but also a vengeance for his lost rights.

Let us keep in mind that the sons of Ziusudra/Noah were not allowed to settle down at any place of their choice. Enlil allotted specific lands to them. Ham was not among them who Enlil allowed to live in his lands. Therefore Ham was living in the lands of Enki in Africa.

According to the bible, the rebellious king Nimrod, a grandson of Ham, was the builder of the Tower together with other humans. Genesis 11:4:

> And they said, Go to, let us build us a city and a tower, whose top may reach unto heaven; and let us make us a name, lest we be scattered abroad upon the face of the whole earth.

Why would they be scattered all over the earth unless they made themselves a name? Would they feel safer if they were famous?

Was it because the Enlilites could send whomever they wished to the underground gold mines? Perhaps. Probably they would indeed be safer living by a landing place controlled by a god.

As Z. Sitchin points out, the word 'shem' means both 'name' and 'rocket', so they didn't plan to make themselves a name, to be famous, but to build a landing place for the rocket ships. As we have seen earlier, the Igigi descendants were called "the people of the rocket ships." The Watchers (Titans/Igigi) were people working with rocket ships, suggesting that they had great skills in the field, like engineers and service personnel.

The event took place in the year 3453* BCE, and it may not be confused with the building of the city of Babili (Babylon), which was built some eleven hundred years later, around 2350 BCE. Neither with the Esagil, the temple of Marduk, which was built at the same time as the city.

We use information from 'The Lost Book of Enki', in order to establish some important dates in the history of humanity. Ningishzidda left for 'the lands beyond the oceans' after 350 years of quarrel with Marduk. There he introduced his own counting. We assume that the counting introduced by him, is the same as the Mayan Long Count calendar, which began in 3113 BCE. We also assume that this introduction happened the same year he left Egypt. Going back 350 years, we arrive at

3463, which was the year Marduk left Egypt and began the building of the Tower. Marduk returned to Egypt after the destruction of the Tower. At the time of Ningishzidda's depart, i.e. 3113, the counting was 650 years.

Going back 650 years from 3113, we arrive at **3763**, as the year the counting in earth years began.

The demolishing of the Tower by the Enlilite air force happened 310 years after the counting in earth years, in 3453. The starting year of the building of the Tower was then **3463** BCE, and the destruction, ten years later, in **3453** BCE. Naram-Sin died 1500 years after the counting began, in 2263, the same year as Agade was destroyed. According to N.S.Kramer, The reign of Naram-Sin lasted for 56 years. Three kings reigned before him, Manishtushu, 15 years, Rimush 9 years, and Sargon I, 56 years.

If we count back, we find that Naram-Sin reigned between 2319–2263. Using the same way, we find that Manishtushu reigned 2334–2319 BCE, Rimush 2343–2334 BCE, and Sargon I 2399–2343 BCE. Both Agade, and Babylon, were built under the time of the reign of Sargon I, 2399–2343 BCE, although by different people, and because of different reasons.

According to Torskild Jacobsen, Naram-Sin reigned from 2390–2334 BCE.

Zecharia Sitchin counts 3760 BCE as the year when kingship began in Kish. That does not contradict our calculations since the year when kingship began could be the same, or probably, some time after the beginning of counting in earth years. The start of the Jewish calendar is the year 3755 BCE.

The choice of the location was without doubt meant to challenge Enlil and Ninurta. In Marduk's opinion, the right to succeed Enlil had been unrightfully shifted over to Ninurta. Since the shifting of his right was based on power, he was now using power himself to get his rights back.

The building is always referred to as 'the tower of Babel'. Since we consider the name 'Babel' to be a great insult against humanity, as we shall soon see, and an even greater insult against the men and women who lost their lives working to achieve a common task, we are here using the original name of the city, Babili, despite the fact that the city of Babylon had not yet existed. According to old descriptions, the E-temen-an-ki, as the tower was called (Heavenly Foundation House on Earth), was a ziggurat pyramid, some 92 meters high in seven levels, beside the base level.

Z. Sitchin states in his book 'The wars of Gods and Men' (p.199), the following about the event:

> By this attempt, however, [the building of the tower] Marduk started a chain of events replete with tragedies.

Marduk's action was against the 'agreement' between the House of Enlil and the House of Enki, about the dominions of each clan. It is, on the other hand, a fact that the 'agreement' was engineered and forced on the House of Enki by the Enlilite clan. The House of Enki had no other option but to accept. It was an agreement based on power, not on negotiations. Our opinion is that the act, which started 'a chain of events replete with tragedies', was when the Enlilites deprived Marduk of his rights in exchange for his life. Marduk's decision to build the tower-landing place was just the reaction of that. In addition, the action of the Enlilites, to deprive Marduk his right was neither democratic nor just, but a demonstration of power, and an act of extortion.

Marduk taught his followers how to make bricks and how to burn them on fire. Then the structure began to rise up to the sky. It was a colossal project with several hundred, perhaps several thousands of people working together for a mutual goal. Such a big project must have been well organized in order to achieve the goal, and at the same time support the people with tolls, building material, food, water, dwellings, and a lot of other services.

Nowhere do we find any mention of force. It seems that everybody was supporting the project out of free will. A great project, in fact, one of the greatest in human history. Nowhere do we find that humans ever supported Enlil/Yahweh in a similar way, out of free will. The hostile action was that the building was located in the lands of the Enlilites and leaded by the adversary of Enlil. Another fact that disturbed the Enlilites was the great human support from the whole area. In fact, the supporters were so many that the only humans left were the Sumerians.

According to the bible it was Nimrod who built the tower. According to Sumerian and Babylonian texts, it was Marduk aided by Igigi and humans alike.

In the Lost Book of Enki we read that Marduk's action was 'unpermitted', and that he was entrusting the building to the Earthlings. 'It was not permitted' means that it was against the rules about domains, and that Marduk was acting as an intruder by building the tower in the domains of the Enlilites. Nobody knows how the Enlilites would react if Marduk had built the tower in Egypt. Would they still consider it as 'unpermitted'? The Enlilites attacked Egypt, Marduk's domain without permission too. Both acts were acts of war, and in case of war one does not ask for permission to attack. Neither they asked Marduk if he was willing to submit his rights to Ninurta. They just did, and Marduk was now acting in a similar way.

The Enlilites became alerted, not so much because of a landing place in their domains, but by the fact that humans were acting in unity, supporting a man who challenged the High Commander and the whole Gold Mission. This was the second time they became worried concerning the power of the humans. The first time was when Horon (Horus) summoned the first earthly army in order to fight against Satu, (Seth) and his allies. The message from Nabu and Marduk was clear. We are the protectors of the humans, the new factor in the history of the Gold Mission.

The new human specie on Earth proved to be more intelligent, energetic, dynamic, curious, and thirstier to learn than the Brotherhood of the Gold could ever imagine. Genesis 11:6:

> And the Lord said, Behold, the people is one, and they have all one language; and this they begin to do: and now nothing will be restrained from them, which they have imagined to do.

Here we have the explanation why Enlil confused the tongues of the people. They 'had all one language' so they could communicate with one another. 'The people is one', they acted in unity and were able to achieve great things. They were on the move thirsting for development, but also to fight Enlil's administration. The human actions were bad things according to Enlil, who wanted the humans either as slaves or under his totalitarian control. The decision to stand up against a powerful dictator couldn't have been easy. The humans, as well as Marduk, must have been aware of the risks. But it seems that the humans were well informed about the purpose of the undertaken action. And they decided to side with Marduk against Enlil. It was perhaps the first democratic decision on Earth. Their decision and their unity were however, a threat against the High Commander, and his mission. He could not allow them to do 'which they have imagine to do'.

By this, Enlil exposed his real character and his relationship to the humans. He proved that the gold mission was so important that it should continue at the expense of human development. The attack against the Tower is witnessing about the importance of the event. Marduk, the Igigi and the humans, all working together, they threaten the continuation of the Gold Mission. But we do not understand the character of the scribe of the OT and his totally manipulated opinion. Nevertheless, it would have been more understandable if the attack had been directed against Marduk, and not against the humans who certainly knew nothing about the original reasons of the conflict between the two gods. In 'Marduk and Monotheism' by Dr M. D. Magee we read:

> There was a grave doubt about the justice of the gods. A poet in about 1000 BC wrote 'I will praise the Lord of Wisdom' a work declaring that humans simply can never get to know what gods want of them, and therefore necessarily suffer whatever they do. All they can do is worship nevertheless.[2]

How could these humans, guided by the skills of Marduk, Nabu and some Igigi, happy to be united, and of one language, trying to achieve some security for themselves and their families (not to be scattered again), be wrong and wicked? How could the Master Enlil/Yahweh and his family members, who only wanted mankind's knowledge to be at a level just suitable to serve them, be right? How can even one human agree with the scribe of the OT! We must keep in mind that the version of the event given in the OT is the version of Enlil/Yahweh. If there had been a Babylonian version, describing the event in completely different manner, it is not known. We also must keep in mind that it was he who wanted mankind perished in the great flood, and that it was Enki (the Lord of Wisdom) who saved a few of them.

Was Enlil/Yahweh angry because Marduk challenged him by attempting to build a gateway in the domains of the Enlilites? Of course he was. But he was equally angry because the supporting humans were operating in unity and after their own choice.

> If this we allow to happen, no other matter of Mankind shall be unreached! This evil plan must be stopped! Ninurta said; all with that agreed.[3]

'This evil plan' he said. This was a quarrel between two gods. Who of them was right, and who was wrong, we can only have our personal opinion about. But these Enlilites called everything and everyone who was against them 'as evil'. That ought to be their personal opinion too. But unfortunately it is not, thanks to a long and systematic indoctrination of the biblical scribes. Their enemies, even good ones working for the benefit of humanity, are given the epithet 'evil' throughout the whole bible. They adopted the same characteristics about Marduk as Enlil/Yahweh ordered. Otherwise it is not possible to understand their point of view. Otherwise it is not possible to understand why a human would have the same opinion about this matter as Ninurta. As it is not possible to understand why the plan was 'evil'. It was evil to the Enlilites all right, and to the scribe of the OT. It is probably to the letter-believers of the bible too. They all have the right to have their own opinion, although it is probably an opinion based on fear and manipulative doctrines than on free will. But we cannot find anything 'evil', whatsoever, for the accounts of humanity. On the contrary, the action to destroy the Tower, and to confuse the tongues, was the real evil action, an attack on humanity itself and its future. Genesis 11:7-9:

> Go to, let us go down, and there confound their language, that they may not understand one another's speech. So the Lord scattered them abroad from thence upon the face of the earth: And they left off to build the city. Therefore is the name of it called Babel; because the Lord did there confound the language of all the earth: and from thence did the Lord scatter...

The Lost Book of Enki' by Z. Sitchin states:

> It was night time when the Enlilite Anunnaki came, From their
> sky ships havoc upon the rising tower, fire and brimstones they
> rained; To the Tower and the whole encampment a complete
> end they made . . .

> Until now the Earthlings one language had, in a single tongue
> they speak; . . .

> In each region and every land the people a different tongue he
> [Enlil] made to speak, A different form of writing thereafter to
> each was given, that one the other will not comprehend.[4]

It was an attack from the air that destroyed the building and the
encampment. They won through destruction and killing, using advanced alien weapons, like firebombs and missiles directed against
a building and its builders. How can it be possible to justify this
action? It seems that Marduk had not anything that could match the
aerial attack; otherwise we would read about some aerial battle. His
supporters might have had bows and perhaps spears. Marduk had
nothing we could call 'plan B'. The defense of the Tower and the
people was quite chance less against an aerial attack.

   In the book of Jasher, 9:38, we read that the attack had come from
the heavens too.

> And as to the tower which the sons of men built, the earth
> opened its mouth and swallowed up one third part thereof,
> and a fire also descended from heaven and burned another
> third, and the other third is left to this day, and it is of that
> part which was aloft, and its circumference is three days'
> walk.

The education and ethics of some of the scribes of the OT is highly
questionable. It is doubt if they actually wrote history or just forwarded their personal opinions, or the opinions of the enemies of
humanity. Were they historians or agents? Where they friends, or
betrayers of humanity? Are they reliable? St. Jerome (347–420 CE),
had been asking himself the same question.

St. Jerome, when translating the OT from Hebrew into Latin
in the 4th century, complained that many of the narratives
were 'rude and repellent'. From medieval times, Jewish rabbis
and Christian bishops have opted for selective teaching, and
interpretation rather than accurate reporting, while they have
justified the obvious scriptural anomalies with the unqualified
dogma that God's logic is impeccable; only man's understanding is wanting.[5]

By justifying his actions as God's actions, even destroying and killing, the scribes sided with a destroyer instead of their fellow humans. But if the scribes of the OT were manipulated agents, what
can we say about the believers in them. We do not believe that any
freethinking person can worship this god, unless, as a result of a
long time of manipulative doctrines and fear for punishment.
    The scribe of Genesis 11:9 didn't know that the tower already
had a name.

> Therefore is the name of it called Babel; because the Lord did
> there confound the language of all the earth: . . .

First, he confused the Tower with the city of Babili (Gateway of the
gods), which was not yet to be built in another thousand years.
    Secondly, he assumes that the name derives from the fact that
the Lord there did confuse the languages of all people of the earth,
and he is making fun of the most tragic event in human history. No
human could do such a thing unless he was manipulated, and highly
indoctrinated agent. Every human being should feel offended by the
name used in the bible. As a human using one of those 'made up'
languages forced on my ancestors as a punishment, I feel pity for
the character of the scribe of Genesis 11:9. Only a real manipulated
agent would speak the words of Enlil/Yahweh as stated in Deuteronomy 18:18 'will put my words in his [the prophet's] mouth;'
    The confusion of the languages so that they could not understand
one another any more, was part of the 'divide and rule' policy, although more effective in the long run.
    How did the Lord confuse the languages? Did he manage that
by some kind of spiritual intervention or some kind of magic? Did
he make the people forget their own language by some miracle, and
then in some similar way made them speak another language? Or

did he force them to learn a new language in the classrooms of some special change-your-language-school? In The Lost Book of Enki we read:

> In each region and every land the people a different tongue he [Enlil] made to speak.[6]

'He made to speak'. He made them, means that it was done without their actual participation and thus, against their will. That means that they could speak a new language without remembering the language they spoke before and probably were unknowing of what had happened. The old language had been erased; otherwise the people would be able to speak at least two languages. In our opinion, Enlil's scientists must have been using some kind of electronic device to partly erase the memory, or perhaps the whole memory, and then in some similar way 'implant' a new language in their head, by using computer programs to create new languages at random.

It must have been a huge task for the scientists of Enlil. Despite the help from the computers and the electronic devices, the whole operation must have been carefully organized. The humans were forced to sit down for a while with some cables and other equipment mounted on their head. The administration of the whole operation must have been enormous. First the erasing of their memory, and then the downloading of a new language, different for each group, and even a different form of writing. That could keep a lot of gods busy for several days.

Each group had to be prepared and treated individually. They certainly couldn't recognize their family members or friends after the treatment. Neither they knew what actually happened. Then, after the operation had been completed, the Enlilites had to transport different groups to different locations, both in the neighborhood and to distant lands of 'no return'. They also must have been in possession of some big aircrafts in order to be able to transport thousands of people. The whole operation may have taken considerable time to accomplish. Meanwhile, they must have had some extensive logistic program to provide food and water to thousands of people. Or perhaps they didn't. If some hundred people died waiting to be 'reprogrammed' or transported, it certainly didn't matter! The forefathers of the Alaskan Eskimos, the Japanese, and even the Egyptians have been transported to where their descendants live now, according to their mythology.

In fact, the Eskimo mythology tells us that their forefathers had been transported there inside 'big metal birds'. When the Anunnaki leaders decided to appoint a Third Region to Inanna in the Indus valley, Enki was asked to create yet another language for the people of the area.

> As by Enlil's decree required, the Lord Enki, Lord of Wisdom, for the Third Region a changed tongue devised, a new kind of writing signs he for it fashioned, A tongue of man heretofore unknown, for Aratta Enki in his wisdom created;[7]

There are no records about the other languages, if they also were created by Enki or by computers. 'Created by Enki' does not exclude the use of computer-like devices.

Enki was certainly not as rebellious as Marduk was. If he refused, then somebody else would have done the job. On the other hand, 'by Enlil's decree required' means that any eventual refusing would have been regarded as 'crime' according to their laws. By the way, it has not been possible to decode this language of the Indus valley (Aratta), despite serious scientific attempts under the last decades.

The language of the Aymara Indians, in the area of Tiahuanacu in Bolivia, maybe of these computer-made languages that have been almost unchanged during the ages.

> In the 1980s Ivan Guzman de Rojas, a Bolivian computer scientist, accidentally demonstrated that Aymara might be not only very ancient but, significantly, that it might be a 'made-up' language—something deliberately and skillfully designed. Aymara could easily be transformed into a computer algorithm to be used to translate one language into another:' The Aymara algorithm is used as a bridge language. The language of an original document is translated into Aymara and then into any number of other languages.[8]

Master Enlil had been challenged by another god, Marduk. Enlil could have done in the same way as his father Anu, who challenged Alalu in wrestling. Anu, the winner took the kingdom of Nibiru. Enlil had to deprive Marduk of his power, his human supporters. They ought to forget everything Marduk and the Igigi taught them. The winner was Enlil and the brotherhood of the gold. The losers were Marduk and the whole of mankind. That was a real Machiavellian technique. Niccolo Machiavelli (1469–1527), described how several Italian rulers could maintain control over a population by using techniques, like creating disputes, disarming, or creating disunity and conflicts.

Here we see that the Master Enlil and his sons, alias Yahweh and his angels, needed to hold back any advancement among the humans to freely exploit the gold of the Earth by using them as labor.

The description of this event in Genesis 11, as if the people did something very wrong, and the Lord did something right, is actually a disgrace for everybody believing that the god of the OT is faultless. The confusion of the tongues is certainly one of the most tragic events in human history. Only one person was happy about that, the scribe of Genesis 11 who joyfully forwarded the malicious pleasure of the destroyers. The development of mankind was thrown back thousands of years. The destruction of the Tower and the confusion of the tongues by Enlil/Yahweh ought to be classified as a crime against humanity too.

Although we are not conscious of that in our everyday life, this event has been the most effective way to slow down human development. We only need to think about numerous books we are not able to read because of the language used. Or the great amount of clay tablets stored in many museums waiting for someone to find the key that could make it possible to interpret them. Conflicts and even wars started because of miss understandings, caused by insufficient translations. Even the bible we read in our tongue is a result of several interminable interpretations. The result is that no bible-version is completely in accordance with any other.

There is always some dispute among scholars about the meaning of some particular word, phrases or 'names'. Like the word 'Nahash', translated from the Hebrew into 'serpent', but according to Zecharia Sitchin in his book, 'Genesis revisited', it could also mean 'he who knows secrets' and 'he who knows copper'. Enki's used the entwined serpents as his emblem. The word 'messenger' has been wrongly translated to Greek as 'angelos', while the correct word should have been 'angelio-foros' meaning 'message-bearer'. 'Angelos' then became 'angel' and the like and even corrupted in order to describe some 'godly beings'. Consider the difference between 'God and his angels' and 'Enlil and his messengers'! It is worthy to think about the consequences of the translation of just one word. It is no doubt that there is an agreement among all humans that understanding between people would highly approve, by using the same language. But people use to be proud of their own language because they believe that it is their own creation. Nobody knows, or wish to know that each language is allotted to different people by random. Not as a gift, but as punishment for our great creativity, by an enemy.

Computer programmers have to follow some rules in creating programs. By alternating some of the rules, the outcome too becomes different. It is as easy as that to explain why some languages belong to the same group with similar characteristics. Then we have languages that sound more poetic; some are more suitable for science, mathematics, or technical expressions. It is not far fetched to claim that different languages are directing development into different paths. Some are easy to learn, some not. Some are more attractive to students than others. By directing development into different paths, through something as simple as a language, the timing of development becomes unevenly matched among the people of the Earth. It was a genius tug indeed, in diversifying the development with respect to both people and time.

More than five millennia and a half later, we are not acting as 'one people', and we do not 'speak the same language'. Presumptions needed to achieve whatever we can 'imagine to do', according to the god of the OT. A common language was a great invaluable asset.

Deprived of his supporters and humiliated once again, Marduk returned to the Land of the two Narrows, or Magan, as the name was now in the new Egyptian language. The 'House of Enki' was now called the 'House of Ptah'. 'Enki' meaning 'Master of Earth' and 'Ptah' meaning the 'Developer', supports the idea that the humans who previously knew Enki had now no idea who he was! The humans knew nothing about Marduk any more, nothing about the struggle among the gods, and nothing about the revolt against the alien dictatorship.

As we have seen earlier, the ruler of Egypt, after Marduk was sent to exile, was Ningishzidda. Now with Marduk back, the two brothers had a lot of different opinions. One of those was the moon-calendar, introduced by Ningishzidda and based on the orbit of the moon. Marduk was insisting in the Sun-calendar, based on the orbit of the Earth around the sun.

For three hundred and fifty years was the land in chaos, between the brothers it was split;

Then Enki, their father, to Ningishzidda said: For the sake of peace, to other lands depart!

To go to a land beyond the oceans Ningishzidda chose, with a band of followers thereto he went.

Six hundred and fifty Earth years was at the time the count,

But in the new domain, where Ningishzidda the Winged Serpent was called, a new count of its own began

* * *

Marduk/Ra the two lands, of the North and of the South, into one crown city united. A king, an offspring of Neteru and Earthling, he there appointed; Mena was his name'.

'To benefit the second region, Ptah [Enki] to Ra all manner of ME he gave'.[9]

Neteru was the new name of the Igigi after the confusion of the tongues. The incident of the Tower was not the first one in a sequence of dramatic events that would direct the future actions of Enlil and Marduk, not the last one either. This incident, as well as their consequent actions, would also affect human history in every possible way, even to this very day. The struggle between them, although it was concerning the post of the High Commander on Earth, also exposed how they felt about the gold and the Earthlings. The Earthlings and their fate were valuated as dispensable by Enlil, while Marduk regarded them as friends and equals. We do not know if some of the gods devoted any thoughts for the thousands of human victims, uprooted from their homes and dispersed all around the world. They certainly applauded enthusiastically the tragic event, like the biblical scribe did.

Although the struggle was about the supremacy on Earth, the biblical scribes managed to turn it into a matter of religious character. That would facilitate for humans to choose side and even scare the life out of them.

Marduk's return to Egypt was not without problems either. After 350 years of quarrel, Ningishzidda gave up and went to 'the lands beyond the oceans' (in 3113, 3452 minus 350) with some followers.

The year 3113 BCE is also the start point of the Mayan Long Count calendar. There we shall meet him again as Quetzalcoatl, the peaceful god who taught the natives of Central America how to live in a civilized society, also against the will of Enlil/Yahweh. As the administrator of Egypt, Ningishzidda-Thoth transferred more influence and responsibilities to the Egyptians. They soon became the motive power behind the achievements of the Egyptian civilization. Here we see that lineage and succession were of great importance to the Anunnaki. As the firstborn of Enki, Marduk took over the administration of Egypt, despite the fact that Ningishzidda was better educated and a great administrator. Walter Emery, University of London states:

> At a period approximately 3400 years before Christ, a great change took place in Egypt, and the country passed rapidly from a state of Neolithic culture with a complex tribal character to one of well-organized monarchy.[10]

After deposing Ningishzidda, Marduk established himself as Ra, the Sun god, who was to become the great god of the Egyptians

---

[1]Zecharia Sitchin, The Lost Book of Enki, p. 281
[2]Dr. M.D. Magee, Marduk and Monotheism, www.askwhy.co.uk/judaism/0235Marduk.html
[3]Ibid., p. 282
[4]Ibid., p. 282, 283
[5]Laurence Gardner, Genesis of the Grail Kings, p. 111
[6]Ibid., p. 283
[7]Ibid., p. 287
[8]Graham Hancock, Fingerprints of the Gods, p. 91
[9]Zecharia Sitchin, The Lost Book of Enki, p. 284, 285, 286
[10]Walter Emery, Ancient Egypt, p. 38

Chapter 10

VIRACOCHA AND QUETZALCOATL

The god of gold an the god of peace

Two of the most important gods of central and South America are known by the name Viracocha and Quetzalcoatl. What we know about them comes to us from various Indian tribe-myths, and from some Spanish writers.

Some scholars make no distinction between the two, merging their properties and presenting them as if they were one and the same person. Still, others use to confuse Quetzalcoatl the god, with some kings who used the 'name' as a title. The same name was also in use by the Aztec high priests. The Christian oriented Spanish writers were more interested in finding similarities between the Aztec, Toltecs, Inca, and Maya religions with Christianity, rather than study their history and culture. It might be unkind to note that the Spaniards seemed to have been more interested in the Mayan gold, than the culture of those people. Ironically enough, the great amount of Indian gold collected by the Spaniards and brought to Spain, spoiled their own economy, since it was used very quickly outside the boundaries of economic plans. They perhaps directed by Dominican traditions, destroying everything that seemed to be anti Christian in their eyes. We must keep in mind that Spain was one of the greatest advocates of the Inquisition.

Robert Sharer says:

Knowledge of Maya writing did not long survive the Spanish
Conquest, owing to the diligence of church and government
officials who rooted out any manifestations of this visible
symbol of "paganism." Diego de Landa, in a passage that ironically accompanies his invaluable eye witness description of
Maya writing, described his own role in its suppression "We
found a large number of these books in these characters and,
as they contained nothing in which there was not to be seen
superstition and lies of the devil, we burned them all, which
they regretted to an amazing degree and which caused them
great affliction."[1]

Was Diego de Landa (1524-1579 CE) some uneducated soldier?
Not at all, he was educated in the Christian dogmas and doctrines.
He was bishop of Merida, Mexico, born in Cifuentes, Guadalajara,
Spain. His actions were actions of a fanatic rather that the actions
of an ignorant. The burning of non-Christian books in Europe and
Middle East, initiated by agent Constantine, was to be repeated in
the Americas 1200 years later. The destruction of the native civilizations was not the work of barbarians. It was the work of people
practicing instructions stated in the Bible. The sign of the cross, first
used by Constantine, was once more conquering lands in the name
of Enlil-Yahweh. Fortunately today, the heritage of the native people
of the Americas is valuated higher.
 Spanish missionaries believed that Quetzalcoatl was the Apostle
St. Thomas who had come to convert the Indians to Christianity.
Cortez was supposed to bear the spirit of St. Thomas! The result of
the Spanish writings about the Indians and especially their gods has
been most confusing. There are many different versions of Indian
beliefs, all influenced by Christian values. Who was then Viracocha
and who was Quetzalcoatl?
 According to legends of the Aymara Indians, Viracocha, the creator god, appeared at Lake Titicaca during the time of darkness to
bring forth light. He created the earth, the sun, the moon, the stars
and even mankind. Inca legends claim that Viracocha came to the
Andes after the great Flood to restore civilization. The first humans
had survived the flood hiding in a hollow up on a very high mountain peak.

According to the Creation myth, Manco Capac and his sister and wife Mama Ocllo, together with his brothers and their wives, founded the city of World Pole in the name of the Creator god Viracocha and the Sun god Inti. In-ti (probably meaning 'bearer of life') gave them a golden stick for testing the land for cultivation and helped them find a suitable place to settle down.

Viracocha was worshiped as the Creator god, the Sun god and even as the Storm god. He was of medial length, white-skinned and bearded, wearing a long white robe and sandals. He taught people astronomy, agriculture and other arts to improve life.

The Incas considered him as their progenitor and the preserver of the Inca race. Although he was the most powerful god of the Incas, only the priests and the Inca leaders worshiped him. For ordinary people, his name was not to be uttered. Rather strange indeed, since 'Viracocha' was not his real name. 'Yahweh' was neither the real name of Enlil, nor a name at all, but is still taboo.

After Viracocha left the land, now called Peru, he told the people about things that would happen in the future. He said that if some other came claiming to be Viracocha, they should not believe him. Why was he assuming that some day, someone would do that? It was a remarkable warning indeed.

Then Viracocha and his two servants went traveling over the waters as if it was land. Therefore they named him Viracocha, which means 'the foam of the Sea'. Compare with the tale of Inanna/Ishtar whom the Cypriots named Aphrodite, meaning 'rise from the foam of the sea'. At another occasion, Viracocha summoned many people at a place now called Tiahuanaco (or Tiwanaku) in Bolivia, gave each one of the tribes a name and ordered them to go by a different road and people the country. In Huari where he was worshiped too, his characteristics were apparently more militant.

In the province of Cacha, Viracocha called the people of the area to come forth. They did, but they came forth armed. Either they didn't know who he was, or perhaps they did but didn't like to be commanded by him, or perhaps, they just didn't wish to deliver the gold. They rushed to him with their weapons raised, ready to kill him. As he realized the serious situation, 'he caused fire to fall from heaven' burning everything around them. When they saw that, they realized his power and feared that they would die in the fire. They threw their weapons to the ground and went to him and kneeled themselves before him. Then he told them that it was he who had created them!

We know from 'The Lost Book of Enki' that at least four Anun-naki were in Mesoamerica at different times. It is not surprising to find the characteristics of some of the protagonists of the near East gods in the personalities of some of the gods of Mesoamerica. The first to make observations in the 'land beyond the great ocean', after the Deluge, was Ninurta. His father Enlil ordered him to search the continent in order to find gold deposits. He found more gold that they could imagine. He also found some survivors. Both discoveries were good news for the Anunnaki. Almost the whole humanity was gone, yet they could continue the Gold Mission as if nothing hap-pened! Like in the old times.

> From that land, on the other side of Earth, astounding words he [Ninurta] delivered:
>
> From the mountainsides uncounted gold, in nuggets large and small, to the rivers below fell down, without mining can the gold be hauled! . . .
>
> Gold, pure gold, refining and smelting not requiring, all about was lying! . . .
>
> Now who could collect the nuggets, how to Nibiru they will be sent? The leaders each other asked.
>
> Of the first question, Ninurta had the answer:
>
> In the high mountain land on this side of Earth, some Earth-lings have survived! Descendants of Cain they are, with the handling of metals they are knowing: Four brothers and four sisters are their leaders, on rafts they themselves saved, Now their mountaintop in the midst of a great lake is an island. As the protector of their forefathers they me recall, the Great Protector they call me!

* * *

> Even Enlil, who the end of all flesh planned, was no longer angered.
>
> It is the will of the Creator of All! To each other they said.[2]

So there was a lot of pure gold, even nuggets large and small ready to pick up. But who would do that? As usual, the Anunnaki were lucky. Enlil, who planned the destruction of the whole mankind, was once again glad that there were some survivors. Why? Because these few survivors would soon multiply and begin to collect the gold nuggets, delivering it to places pointed out by their 'creator' god Viracocha. The gods also believed that it was the will of God; both the fact that some humans survived and the plenty of gold!

Besides, those humans were in possession of knowledge about metals. Cain had been educated in metallurgy by Ninurta. Then he was exiled to the lands beyond the ocean after he killed his brother. It must have been hundreds of generations between Cain and his descendant Manco Capac; the mentor (and slave owner) was however, still the same!

It is interesting to find similar lies and the same policy as in Near East. Ninurta was willing to lie in order to convert the independent natives to be his servants. He said 'he was their creator'. He said that he made 'the sun, the moon and the stars to come forth'. The three main islands of Titicaca Lake are probably named after that as the island of the Moon, the island of the Sun and the island of Amantari.

How could he make the Sun, the Moon and the stars to reappear? According to the natives, Viracocha came under 'the time of darkness', just after the deluge. He knew that the sky would 'open up' again very soon. This knowledge however, could be used to manipulate the native people to believe in him as the creator.

Ninurta was not there to establish a new Region of civilization. It is worthy to note that the first three major civilizations of the old world (Mesopotamia, Egypt and Indus valley) were established in fertile river valleys. This is not the case with Mesoamerica. The civilizations that arose around the Titicaca Lake and in the area of Tiahuanacu were not based on agriculture since these areas are rather inhospitable. On the other hand they were rich in gold.

We know from the Lost Book of Enki that the Anunnaki established a landing place not long from lake Titicaca.

Thus was the secret mission in the hands of Ninurta entrusted;
In the mountain lands beyond the oceans, beside the great lake, A new Bond Heaven-Earth he was setting up, within an enclosure he placed it; At the foot of the mountains where

the gold nuggets were scattered a plain with firm ground he chose; on it the ascent and descent markings he made. Primitive are the facilities, but the purpose they will serve! So did Ninurta to his father Enlil in good time declared:[3]

The landing place could be at the site of Ollantaytambu, between Cuzco and Machu Picchu in Peru, or at the site of Tiahuanaco in Bolivia. The structuring and building of the landing place, as well as the whole gold expedition in the land beyond the oceans was carried out by the Enlilites alone, leaded by Ninurta. None of the House of Enki was participating, they didn't even know about it.

This secret could be the reason why Viracocha warned the people of the coming of some other god claiming to be him. Anyone could disturb his plans and therefore the future of the Gold Mission. Would Marduk do that or Ningishzidda? If someone wished to do that, the only reason would have been to urge these people not to collect gold for the gods, that they should not be depended on Viracocha. None of them would certainly pretend to be Viracocha unless they wished to take hold of the gold. It seems that some other god, perhaps Marduk, could have done that but he didn't. This is another evidence that they had different opinions about the gold.

By helping the natives of South America to improve their lives, Viracocha was actually promoting the Gold Mission.

It seems that the Enlilites never did anything not connected to the Gold Mission. We find a parallel in the bible where Jesus warned the people about the coming of other prophets, and that they should not believe in them.

At Tiahuanaco there are four interesting structures. The Akapana pyramid, which could serve as the residence of Viracocha, the Kalasasaya platform, which could be the landing place, a subterranean Temple, (which could be the landing place too, in an enclosure), and the Puma Punku structure which could be a storehouse for the gold.

One block of this building weighs more than 400 tons according to several estimations. The city of Tiahuanaco existed long before the Inka culture, according to the Inkas themselves. Another connection of the Inka and Aymara cultures in South America with the Enlilites is the Illapa, or Tunupa, the Storm god, the 'Flashing one' associated with storms and thunders in the same manner as Enlil and his son Adad. Ishkur/Adad was the Storm god of the Assyrians and the Hittites. Although there are no records about Adad being in the lands beyond the oceans, it is possible that he was one of the followers of Viracocha, occasionally helping his brother. It is also possible that the properties of all three of them, Enlil, Ninurta and Adad, were merged into one personality, Viracocha.

Ninurta knew how to administrate the humans to gain control over them. He gave names to different groups of people and told each one of the tribes to go by a different road. The purpose was of a double nature. Spreading themselves in different parts of the land they would be able to find more gold. They would also create different cultures and having different tribe-names, it would be more difficult to understand one another. In fact, they would easier fight one another, despite the fact that only a few generations earlier, they all were brothers and sisters. The parallel with the confusing of the tongues after the incident of the E-temen-an-ki is obvious. In the Americas too, the Enlilites used their weapons, fear and threats in order to exercise dominion over the humans. Here are some important similarities between Ninurta and Viracocha.

- Both provided useful help to the survivors of the great flood.
- Both had military experience and powerful weapons.
- Their followers were messengers and soldiers.
- The megalithic structures built by Viracocha appear to have been landing places, storehouses and installations suitable for the Gold Mission. Ninurta too was the chief of the metallurgical establishments in Bad-Tibira and responsible for the supplies of gold.
- Their greatest interest was the gold.
- Both were great conspirators against humanity by sowing the seed of conflicts among different tribes.
- Both demanded gold and labor in exchange for providing help.

We have now enough evidence and indices to merge these two characters into one and the same, Ninurta/Viracocha. By teaching people things necessary to improve live, they assured themselves that the humans would in turn provide them with help in their mission. Help in the form as it always had been, to continue to perform their task as 'primitive workers'.

Not long after Ninurta, Marduk too went to 'the land behind the great ocean'. Not by his own free will but as a punishment after

Dumuzi's death. He was exiled there together with his wife Serpanit and his son Nabu. Not much is known about his deeds in those lands. But some information about Viracocha is in conflict with his character. It is possible that Viracocha was venerated as 'the Sun god' for a while, as he 'made the sun to reappear in the skies'. The 'Gateway of the Sun' in Tiahuanaco could probably be the work of Viracocha himself. But the Kulkulkan pyramid/temple at Chichen Itza in Yucatan, Mexico, the pyramid of the Sun in Teotihuacan, Mexico, the pyramid of the Moon, and the whole citadel, are probably the works of Marduk and Quetzalcoatl.

Quetzalcoatl was the other great god of most of the people of the Americas. According to Andrés de Olmos, he never admitted sacrifices of the blood of humans nor of animals, but rather of bread, flowers, roses and perfumes. He watched and prohibited with much efficacy wars, thefts, murders and other harms, which they did to one another. Whenever wars were mentioned before him, or other evils concerning the wrongs of men, he would turn his face and cover his ears so that he would neither see nor hear them. He too was a white bearded man. He too promised to return. He was considered as the Sun god too, and was given a yellow beard like the rays of the sun.

So, while Cortez and most of his men who landed in Mexico were dark-haired, Cortez's second in command, Pedro de Alvarado was a white-skinned man with yellow-red beard. This fact made Moctezuma hesitate in inviting resistance as he thought of him as a descendant of their god Quetzalcoatl. Otherwise they could easily win the battle against the small force of the Spaniards. Ironically, Pedro de Alvarado showed up being the most notorious for his cruelty towards the Indian population of Mexico. Ironically enough, the Aztec civilization was much superior in many sense, than that of the Spaniards. The legends of Quetzalcoatl acting in Mexico and not in South America are in accordance with the fact that Mexico was the place where Marduk had been for many years, while South America was the base of the gold operations of Ninurta/Viracocha.

In the history of the Olmec, Mixtec, Toltecs, Atzec, and Maya, one name and one epithet appears often, Quetzalcoatl—the Winged Serpent. Kulkulkan was another name of his also meaning 'Plumed', or 'Feather Serpent'. The Aztec also considered him as the god of light. He arrived to Central America in a boat, with some followers. According to Maya legends, he founded cities, gave them the calendar, laws and magical herbs. He taught men science too, and devised ceremonies. He presented corn to them and all good aspects of civilization.

Ningishzidda/Thoth went also to the big continent after an advice from his father Enki, as we have seen. Ningishzidda was the man who built the two great pyramids in Egypt. He was also the man who, assisted by Ninurta, built most of the megalithic creations in the world to observe the coming age of the Ram, at about 2000 BCE.

The departing of Ningishzidda to the land beyond the oceans took place after the incident of the Tower, the E-temen-an-ki. That happened, as we have seen, in 3463. Ningishzidda left Egypt 350 years later, in 3113 BCE. This is also the starting point of the Mayan Calendar.

The Mayan calendar includes the Tzolkin calendar with a cycle of 260 days, the Haab calendar with a cycle of 365 days, and the so called Long Count, where the smallest period is a kin, equal to one day, and the greatest a baktun which equals to 144,000 days, or 394 modern years. The previous Long Count lasted from 8238–3113 BCE, which is equal to 13 baktuns, and the present count is expected to last from 3113 BCE–2012 CE (21 December), assuming that it also endures over 13 baktuns. Now these four digits, 2012, have become something of a strange phenomenon. There are books and articles, and several theories about what is going to happen at that day. People believe that almost everything is going to happen. From World war III, and the end of the World, to a new era and a higher level of consciousness. What certainly is going to happen is that the sun will raise to conjunct the intersection of the Galaxy and the plane of the ecliptic, which happens once every 25,920 years. This is also the end of the time of Pisces and the entering of the constellation of Aquarius.

Almost certainly, the introduction of the calendar used by the Mayans, beginning in the year 3113 BCE, was the work of Quetzalcoatl. The twelve Houses of the Zodiac (25,920 years) observed by Enki, were of course known to Ningishzidda. But nobody knows why he introduced a 'count of his own', or why he chose the length of the 13 baktuns as the length of the Count. Perhaps he was trying to tell us about the coming celestial phenomenon of the year 2012, or some event of the year 8238 BCE, or both.

Quetzalcoatl was a man of science and the builder of megalithic monuments. He was a man of peace too and the 'Feather Serpent' of the Toltecs and the Aztecs, the Plumed Serpent of the Mayas. The

'Winged Serpent' mentioned by Enki as an epithet of Ningishzidda, could not have been fabricated by him. It was most likely part of information 'beamed' to him by his son in the faraway land. Here are some important similarities between Quetzalcoatl and Ningishzidda-Thoth-Hermes.

- Both were men of science who willingly shared their knowledge with the humans.
- Both were constructors of pyramids and other megalithic monuments.
- Both provided mankind with knowledge without demanding anything in exchange.
- Both were rather uninterested in gold.
- Both were men of peace.

We have now enough evidence and indices to proclaim Quetzalcoatl as the same man/god as Ningishzidda-Thoth-Hermes. Thoth himself would have said 'As in the near east, so in the Americas'. He was the very contrast of Viracocha/Ninurta. It is only logical to state that the followers of the scientist Quetzalcoatl/Ningishzidda also were men of good education and friendly to mankind. In fact, we have two more bearded white gods in Central America. Votan, who was considered as a great civilizer, and Itzamana, who had great medical skills. They could have been two of the followers of Thoth or some other of the House of Enki.

What happened to Quetzalcoatl? While Viracocha was seen to leave walking on the waters with his servants, we have no records about Quetzalcoatl leaving the area. Except for some Mexican legends. They tell us that the era of the Plumed Serpent was brought to a sudden end by some other god called Tezcatilpoca. His name means 'Smoking Mirror'. He was a malevolent god who demanded human sacrifices. Tezcatilpoca forced Quetzalcoatl to leave the land. There are no other records confirming this information, but we know for sure that he did return to Egypt.

We know from The Lost Book of Enki that by the time around 2000 BCE, both Enlil and Ninurta were in the Americas. That happened after Marduk had replaced Enlil as the Supreme god on Earth, 2027 BCE. Ninurta was often there to send the gold collected by the natives to Nibiru. The new landing place was a secret among the Enlilites. None of them had the authority to send away Quetzalcoatl, since by that time the Supreme god of the gods was Marduk and not Enlil. It is unlikely that Ninurta would force Ningishzidda away, although he had the power to do that. The two of them, Ninurta and Ningishzidda were cooperating at several occasions and there is no record about them being enemies. In fact, there is no record that Ningishzidda had been in conflict with any other god, except for Marduk. The reason of their quarrel was about the organization and ruling of the Egyptian region. Enlil however, had all the interests in the world to bring an end to Quetzalcoatl's teachings about peace and useful knowledge, independent if that occurred before, or after the time of Marduk's supremacy. Like Prometheus had given the gift of fire to the humans, Quetzalcoatl was giving them equal important knowledge to make them able to manage themselves. Zeus/Enlil had punished Prometheus according to the Greek mythology. It is possible that Enlil himself had driven Quetzalcoatl away from the land. He had the power (the weapons) to do that and certainly a lot of reasons too, mainly, the continuation of the Gold Mission.

As Enlil was leaving the scene of the Meddle East, and after he had accused Marduk as being the reason for everything bad that happened, he says to his brother Enki:

Let Marduk over the desolation in the Regions his supremacy declare!

As for me and Ninurta, we will in his way no longer stand.

To the Lands Beyond the Oceans we will depart, what we had all had come for, The mission to obtain for Nibiru gold we will complete![4]

Still after the nuclear disaster in the Near East, the Gold Mission was indeed the most important task to complete. While Enki spent many years helping people who suffered from radiation after the use of the nuclear-like weapons, Enlil was making plans how to complete the Gold Mission! As for the promise that they (the Enlilites) would no longer stand in Marduk's way, we know by now that the promise was of no value, as we shall soon see in the chapter, about 'the wars of Enlil' against Babylon and Egypt.

Perhaps it's time for us humans to stop seeing the megalithic works all over the world with wide, open eyes, as they were miracles or the works of gods. They simply were the works of men with some advance knowledge. After all, everything is possible with the right knowledge and the right tools. It's time for us to see the cross-symbols curved in stones in many places in Mesoamerica, particularly in Puma Punku, long before the time of Jesus, as the 'logotype' of the alien rulers, the symbol of their own planet, with no association to Christianity. The confusion of these two symbols was the intentional work of Enlil/Yahweh and his sons. For the same reason he didn't want to reveal his name to Moses, he wanted to obliterate every connection to his own planet.

The Serpent is today associated with medical science, as it had been from the beginning, used by Enki, Ninmah and Ningishzidda. The Serpent of the Bible associated with something evil does no longer deserve any credibility. The evilness lies in the mind of the scribes and not in the Serpent, the symbol of Wisdom. This is a hopeful beginning, a new era for humanity, perhaps the era of revising our ancient history and the works of the alien gods. Good and evil alike.

[1]Robert Sharer, The Ancient Maya, p. 513
[2]Zecharia Sitchin, The Lost Book of Enki, p. 233,234
[3]Ibid., p. 249
[4]Ibid., p. 316

Chapter 11

BABILI–THE GATEWAY OF THE GODS

Marduk's new attempt to replace Enlil

The constellation of the Bull, from about 4380 BCE to about 2000 BCE, dedicated to Enlil, was nearing to its end. The coming age of the Ram, dedicated to Marduk, became a new starting point of a chain of challenges and hostilities that would continue under the next 2,000 years.

Some scholars believe that the cause of these events was Marduk's demand of supremacy over the other gods. We know by now that Marduk had that right, but it had been taken from him through power and extortion. Marduk neither forgot nor was he willing to give up. He was once again claiming his right, better prepared than any time before. He was not only the adversary of Enlil; he was against the Gold Mission and the whole Brotherhood of the Gold. Marduk declared:

The one who is without equal, the great solitary and sole one!

So did Marduk, as Ra, above all other gods himself emplace,

Their powers and attributes to himself he by himself assigned:

As Enlil I am for lordship and decrees, as Ninurta for the hoe and combat; As Adad for lighting and thunder, as Nannar for

illuminating the night; As Utu I am Shamash, as Nergal over
the Lower World I reign; As Gibil the golden depths I know,
whence copper and silver come I have found; As Ningishzidda
numbers and their count I command, the heavens my glory
bespeak!

'By these proclamations the Anunnaki leaders were greatly
alarmed.[1]

Some scholars believe that Marduk, by the above declaration, was
intending to introduce some kind of monotheism. However, declar-
ing himself 'above all the other gods', is not supporting this idea.

What we can read from the above lines is that Marduk wished
to replace them all. They were not needed any more. Probably, this
could be the end of the Gold Mission. He was announcing the transfer of their authorities to himself. He was convinced that he had that
right. All his descendants, being not welcome to Nibiru, since they
were not 'gods', he certainly was more interested in their future,
than the future of the Gold Mission. The fanatic supporters of the
Gold Mission, the Enlilites, oppressed not only the humans, but also
his own children. Probably he wanted the gods to 'go home' leaving
Earth to the humans alone.

Once again was Marduk challenging the Enlilites. Once again
Enlil and his sons were unwilling to release the power to him. We
are not surprised. Enlil could not agree to be replaced by Marduk,
because that would also have been the end of the Gold Mission.
What was their reaction to Marduk's declaration? They all said that
the time had not yet come!

Its worthy to note that nobody denied Marduk the right to succeed
Enlil. They were surprised as to the time of Marduk's proclamation,
but not to the proclamation itself. On the contrary, everybody was
telling him that he must have been miscalculating. The sign of the
Bull was still visible in the heavens. He had to wait for the sign of
the Ram to appear.

This is evidence enough that they knew that the supremacy was
about to be shifted to Marduk. That he had that right, but not yet.
They could not avoid the unavoidable, but they could push it a bit
forward in time. In order to prove that Marduk had been miscalculating, all of them began to make calculations and observations of
their own. Enki says:

To Ningishzidda the Anunnaki leaders appealed, how to the
people the skies to observe to teach. In his wisdom stone
structures Ningishzidda devised, Ninurta and Ishkur to erect
them helped. In the settle lands, near and far, the people how
to observe they taught, that the Sun in the Constellation of the
Bull was still rising To the people they showed.[2]

They didn't attack Marduk this time, but were very eager to present
some evidence to convince him. They calculated with instruments,
they built megalithic structures (like possibly the Stonehenge, and
other structures in the Americas and elsewhere), to show the people
that Marduk had been miscalculating.

The sons of Enlil were helping Ningishzidda (the most well educated Hermes) to erect the megalithic structures. So they could cooperate when they could find it convenient.

But why teach the people how to observe the skies? Why show
the people that the sign of the Bull was still visible? Wasn't it enough
to present the evidence to Marduk? He had no reason to misbelieve
Enki, or Ningishzidda. Since then were the Enlilites aware about
ordinary people's opinion? Apparently they became aware of that
now. It was clearly obvious that they would need people's support.
They had to show even to Marduk's supporters that they had to wait.
Marduk was not the only opponent to their policy. From now on,
they could not ignore the human factor. From now on, any war between them was to be carried out by human armies. Marduk had,
through his son Nabu, summoned a strong army of humans. Since
the gods were few and the humans many, the gods knew by now
their power was depending on how great the support of the people
was. Although the Enlilites had advanced weapons, they too needed
an army of humans to defend themselves from Marduk's army. Marduk was threatening Sumer from the North, while Nabu was waiting in the West. Of course, they could use their advanced weapons
against the humans, but that would not be a war, not even a battle,
but a slaughtering. And then, some twenty or thirty years later, Marduk could summon a new army again. They would need to exterminate all humans to deprive Marduk of his power. That was however
not a good option since they, themselves needed human labor. The
situation was not in the Enlilites' favor. It was necessary to show
Marduk and his supporters evidence that the age of the Ram had not
yet come. For the first time ever, the Enlilites were using arguments,

with the help of the Enkites, instead of power. The question was, for how long?

At the same time, they had to bring up some army to stand against Marduk's pressure. They needed to secure Enlilstan (Sumer); the only place on Earth they still had some support. Enlil appointed Inanna to find a suitable man to unite the cities of Sumer into one kingdom. A united Sumer could have a chance to defend itself against Marduk and his human supporters. Or, so they thought.

Inanna chose the demigod Shar-ru-kin, probably meaning 'The Earthly Prince'. He is known in history books as Sargon I. After he became her lover, she presented him to Enlil, who appointed him as king. Sargon was the first king to found a dynasty and an empire. He reigned for 56 years (2399–2343 BCE), and was succeeded by his two sons, Rimush (2343–2334 BCE), and Manishtushu (2334–2319 BCE). He built a new capital, Agade (Akkad) from which the name of the Akkadian empire derives. He expanded the Akkadian empire from the Persian Gulf to the Mediterranean Sea, by using some alien weapons. Later on, the Assyrians were to appear as a power in the north of Sumer. And Babylon, the city, would become the Babylonian empire.

In the text 'The Legend of Sargon' he tells his personal history which is rather remarkable.

> Sargon the mighty king of Agade, am I. . . .
> My mother, the high priestess, who conceived me,
> In secret she bore me.
> She set me in a basket of rushes, with bitumen sealed the lid
> She cast me into the river, it did not sink me.
> The river bore me up, it carried me to Akki the irrigator. . . .
> Akki, the irrigator, as his son made me and reared me.
> Akki, the irrigator, appointed me as his gardener . . .
> While I was a gardener, Ishtar granted me her love . . .

In another document, Sargon says that Inanna accompanied his warriors in battle, bearing her 'weapons of brilliance'. He was also very proud participating in banquets arranged by gods and drinking beer with Utu.

The fact that his mother was a high priestess, a hierodule, along with the fact that she bore him in secret, and then cast him in the river, witnesses that his father could have been some of the Anunnaki leaders. The story has many similarities with the story of Moses, also being sailing in a basket as a baby. Demigods were in great demand, since they were few, and destined to play some important role. It was certainly not by chance Inanna found him. While building his new capital, Agade, Sargon moved sacred soil from the place where Marduk and his followers attempted to build the Tower, to Agade.

What 'sacred soil' really was, nobody knows. It must have had some important significance, however, which Sargon knew, or perhaps he was just imitating the gods. Since kingship was alternating among different cities from time to time, the 'Heavenly Bright Object' was also moving around, implanted outside (or in) the Palace. The soil could have had some special properties, or perhaps, they were just superstitious. No city could be assigned kingship without that object, and no Temple was built without 'sacred soil'. Sargon's action, however, started some serious nuisance, had it been his intention or not. First to be alarmed was Marduk.

> Enraged did Marduk to the first region rushed, with Nabu and followers to the tower's place they came . . . .
>
> Dikes and walls in the place of the Tower they raised, the Esagil, House for the Utmost God, for Marduk they built;
>
> Babili, the Gateway of the Gods, Nabu in his father's honor named it, In the heart of the Edin, in the midst of the First Region, Marduk himself established.
>
> Inanna's fury no boundary knew, with her weapons on Marduk's Followers death she inflicted.
>
> The blood of people, as never before on Earth, like rivers flowed.[3]

That was the starting point of the foundation of the city of Babylon. If Earth had been ruled by democratic principles, then Marduk and the humans would have the power to rule since they were in overwhelming majority. Since the Enlilites governed by means of power, Marduk too, used his power by establishing himself, as the 'Challenger-Supreme god', in the heart of their domain.

Nobody knows if Marduk had plans to build a city at the same place where he earlier built the Tower. Probably he felt forced to do something after the 'steeling of sacred soil' by Sargon, the soil being symbolic or not. And so the city of Babylon and his temple, E-sag-il, (House of the Head God) made their sudden appearance in the lands of the Enlilites. The city was built sometime under Sargon's reign (2399–2343 BCE), approximately 2370 BCE. It must have taken sometime to complete the buildings, and some advanced installations in the Esagil performed by Marduk. But, as once before, his action was considered as hostile against the Enlilites. Although, neither Enlil nor Ninurta were intended to use their weapons against the city, somebody else wished to kill the supporters of Marduk, and destroy the city from the air, using missiles and fire weapons.

This time it was the goddess of war, Inanna, who decided to act. After all, Marduk was the man she hated most. Probably Marduk's feelings about her were of a similar character. If the other Enlilites did not want to demonstrate their powers once again, then she would. According to the 'Lost Book of Enki', she alone attacked Babylon from the air. By using some advanced weapons against the supporters of Marduk, she spread death and destruction around her. There was no battle, no war, only pure slaughtering of humans by alien weapons. It was a crime against humanity, this time begotten by Inanna-Ishtar-Aphrodite. The reason? She had a lot of strong feelings against Marduk.

Marduk's brother, Nergal, persuaded Marduk to leave Babylon for the sake of the people, and wait until the Constellation of the Ram was visible in the sky. Nergal/Erra was a betrayer of his Enki-family, and a real supporter of the Gold Mission. In fact, he was more 'Enlilite' than the Enlilites themselves.

Marduk had constructed some installations under the Esagil, probably some security or defense installations. They were supposed to prevent anybody from seizing the Esagil and the city of Babylon, perhaps a lesson he learned after the destruction of the Tower. That could be the reason why Inanna used her weapons instead of an army. Nergal promised Marduk not to remove or damage the installations, whereupon Marduk agreed to leave Babylon. He must have been convinced that he had been miscalculating and left. He intended to travel around the world watching the skies, waiting for the constellation of the Ram. So he became unseen to his people

in Egypt, he became 'Amun', the Unseen One. Here we have parts
of the conversation between Marduk and Nergal.

> On the day I step off my seat, the flooding shall from its well
> cease to work . . . the waters shall not rise . . . the bright day to
> darkness [shall turn] . . . confusion shall arise . . . the winds of
> draught shall howl . . . sickness shall spread.

> . . . he [Nergal/Erra] assured Marduk there was nothing to
> worry about: he (Erra) would enter Marduk's House only to
> "erect the Bulls of Anu and Enlil at thy gate."

> Marduk heard this; The promise, given by Erra, found his fa-
> vor. So did he step down from his seat, and to the Land of
> Mines, abode of the Anunnaki, he set his direction.

> . . . But no sooner he had done that than Nergal broke his
> word.

> . . . and there Erra caused its "Brilliance" (radiating source of
> energy) to be removed. Thereupon, as Marduk had warned,
> "the day turned into darkness," the "flooding was disarrayed,"
> and soon "the lands were laid to waste, the people were made
> to perish.

> All of Mesopotamia was affected, for Ea/Enki, Sin and
> Shamash, in their cities, became alarmed: "with anger [at
> Erra] they were filled" . . .

> Ea, Erra's father, reproached him: "Now that Prince Marduk
> had stepped off, what have you done?" . . . "Go away!" he
> ordered Erra. "Take off to where no gods ever go!"[4]

The actions of Nergal against his brother Marduk witness that he too
was against the idea of Marduk becoming the Supreme god. Marduk
had the support of Enki, who became very angry because of Nergal's treachery. There are no records, no proclamations about what
Marduk planned to do if, and when he would become the supreme
god of the gods. Except for the fact that he planned to be the king

of the Earth and absorb the authorities of the other gods. As a friend of the Igigi he would probably allow them to stay, but he would certainly expel all the other gods. He would then stop the deliveries of the gold to Nibiru, or circumscribe the flow. The gold would stay on Earth. That must have been the reason why the Enlilites, and even his own brother were not willing to accept his supremacy. This theory is supported by the fact that, if Marduk had the intention of continuing the Gold Mission without changes, neither the Enlilites, nor Nergal would have some real reason to oppose him. The man, who wanted our gold to stay on Earth, became 'the evil one' in the scriptures of the OT. The man, who was steeling our gold, became 'God'. Are the scriptures serving the interests of humanity or the interests of Enlil/Yahweh?

By destroying the installations in the Esagil, Nergal and the Enlilites were calculating that Marduk should be unable to return. This time it was them who were miscalculating.

After Manishtushu, Naram-Sin, (Beloved by Sin, the father of Inanna, 2319–2263), ascended the throne of Akkad. Inanna commanded him to seize all the lands. She was now cooperating only with her father. With Ninurta and Marduk absent in the First and Second Region, Inanna saw her chance to seize all powers. While Marduk wished to be 'the King of Earth', Inanna's plan was to be 'the Queen of the gods'. For the time being, nobody could stop her. She had both the weapons and a strong army. The only power left in the area was Nabu. But he too, like his father, was waiting for the sign of the Ram to appear.

Marching against Egypt, Naram-Sin passed the Fourth Region, the Landing Place, which no humans were allowed to enter. Enlil hearing this put a curse on Naram-Sin. 'To put a curse' on someone was a popular thing to do for Enlil. We do not know the real meaning of the 'cursing', but it appears often in the bible too. It could be just words, or it could be some power if his. It could also be as simple as putting a price on Naram's head, that it was not enough to replace him, he would probably be killed. Anyway, the following year, (2263 BCE) Naram-Sin died of a bite of a scorpion, which could have been a murder looking like an accident! By Enlil's command, Agade was 'wiped out off the face of the Earth'. 'Wiped out' means just that, as it had never existed. The whole city, with people, and everything disappeared. Neither the ruins nor the location of Agade have been found.

He, or probably Ninurta, also ordered the Gutaeans from the Zagros Mountains, northeast of Sumer, to invade and destroy Akkad, the empire they, themselves created. Everybody was expendable. This act explains why the Enlilites never had any faithful supporters. They could however, summon armies by giving the king weapons, or by using threats and force. Whenever those kings and their people had the opportunity to diverge from the path, they also did. The Gutaeans were under the influence of Ishkur/Adad, who could hold them or release them at will. They were powerful for a while, ready to march at his command. The only city spared by them was Lagash, the city of Ninurta. The Gutaeans ruled Mesopotamia for 91 years. All these destructions and punishments because of Naram-Sin passed through the Fourth region. The importance of this place, which was also some kind of military base, was great, as we shall see. Anyone who mastered this place could master the world.

The bible has only evil things to tell us about Babylon and its god, Marduk, but there is no information about what these 'evil things' were. Without any supporting facts, it can only be regarded as the propaganda of the agents of Yahweh. Except from the fact that the city was built by an adversary of the god of the OT. It was an 'evil deed' according to Yahweh, but certainly not according to anyone else. Fortunately, historians have completely different opinions about that.

Babili, (Babylon) the gateway of the gods, the hated city in the bible, the hated city of the Enlilites, built by Marduk, Nabu and their human supporters, made her sudden appearance in human history. In several history books we find the name 'Babylon', a new city, never heard of before. All of a sudden, Babylon was there, beautiful and powerful. A city probably supposed to be 'the capital city of the King of the Earth', Marduk.

Could the Enlilites allowed that? Marduk's second serious attempt to gain supremacy ended with tragic events too, also at the same location as the time before. He was not present when the Enlilites decided to transfer his right to Ninurta. He was not present when Nergal destroyed the installations under the Esagil. But he would not give up this time either. The Esagil and the city of Babylon was founded and destined to affect the future for a long time. The city was also destined to direct the actions of the Enlilites as long as the city existed. Marduk was just waiting for the sign of the Ram to make its appearance in the sky. Babylon was destined to become a great city, for more than two millennia, despite the plans of Enlil/Yahweh. As Laurence Gardner says:

> . . . Marduk gained new support from the incoming Amorites in Babylonia, and he instigated a revised building program of such magnitude that Babylon soon became the key power-center of the following era.[5]

The Persian king Artaxerxes IV (338-336) decided to restore both the E-temen-an-ki and the Esagil temple. According to the Greek researcher Herodotus of Halicarnasus (fifth century BCE), the Esagil was still functioning in the first century CE. Alexander the Great ordered (323 BCE) restorations of the temple too.

Enlil/Yahweh could only watch how the city became an Empire with great financial and military power. He could only watch how Babylon became the center of the free world, the protector of humanity that could stand against the slavery created by the Brotherhood of the Gold. But he would not deviate from his plan to destroy Babylon either.

---

[1]Zecharia Sitchin, The Lost Book of Enki, p. 298–299
[2]Ibid., p.299–300
[3]Ibid., p.301
[4]Zecharia Sitchin, The wars of gods and men, p. 253, 254
[5]Laurence Gardner, Genesis of the Grail Kings, p.115

Chapter 12

ABRAHAM AND NIMROD

Great Patriarchs on different paths

The Sumerian Patriarch Abraham was chosen by Enlil/Yahweh to be the father of the Jewish people. What plans had Enlil/Yahweh about these people? The Egyptian Patriarch Nimrod sided with Marduk in the struggle between Enlil and Marduk. Why? According to the bible, Abraham and Nimrod were contemporaries, the first being a servant of God and the latter being an evil king in the lands of Sumer.

A servant of God and a supporter of Marduk couldn't have been other than agents on opposite sides. This is why the bible has nothing good to say about Nimrod. Were they really contemporaries? Was Nimrod a king in the land of Sumer? Was Abraham an instrument in the hands of God while Nimrod was an enemy of God because he sided with Marduk? Very important questions indeed. The answers are also extremely significant, not only to the descendants of those two great personalities, but also to the whole humanity, as we shall see. Enlil/Yahweh sent Abraham to Canaan, a land between Egypt and Babylon, the strongholds of Marduk. According to the bible, Abraham acted after the instructions and orders of God, as stated in Genesis 11:31.

And Terah took Abram his son, and Lot the son of Harran his sons' son, and Sarai his daughter in law, his son Abram's

115

wife; and they went forth with them from Ur of the Caldees, to go into the land of Canaan; and they came unto Harran, and dwelt there.

Then some years later, God ordered Abraham to go south, for reasons not explained in the bible. Abraham was then seventy-five years old. In the Lost Book of Enki we read:

> By his father's word abiding, Nannar in the land of Arbakad the city of Harran established. To be high priest in its temple-shrine Tirhu he sent, his family with him;

> * * *

> Upon Ibru-Um, the eldest son of Tirhu, Enlil cast the choosing gaze.

> * * *

> To protect the sacred places, the chariot's ascents and descents enable, Enlil Ibruum to go commanded.[1]

Enlil ordered Terah (Tirhu) to leave Ur for the new city of Harran after the death of Ur-Nammu, the first king of the third dynasty of Ur, who reigned 2108–2090 BCE. Terah probably left Ur the same year Ur-Nammu died, i.e. 2090.

Abraham, whose original name was Ibruum, (Abram or Avram in Jewish) was the son of Terah, a high priest of Ur and later the high priest at the temple of Nannar/Sin in Harran. The 'High Priest' had no connection to any religious duties. It was a political authority much like a secretary. It was a misleading title applied to the highest authority in the temples of the gods. But since the temples of the old times were just the renamed adobes of the gods for security and domination reasons, the High Priest-title was also a title that demanded more respect and power than 'political secretary', or 'security minister'. Ironically, the Pope bears the title 'Pontifex Maximus', which was also an authority of political power and even the title of the High Priests of the temples in ancient Rome.

The god of Abraham was Enlil, who later refused to reveal his name to Moses and has been called 'Yahweh' or 'Jehovah' since then. The kings of Ki-Engi (Sumer) had the title 'Lugal' which means 'Mighty Man', or 'Great Man'. Lugal Banda was probably

the second king in Unug-ki (Uruk). He was a son of Emmerkar and
father of Gilgamesh. Some writers claim that the first king on Earth
was 'Lugal Banda' and ascribe the roll to Nimrod since Nimrod is
described in the bible as a 'Mighty Hunter'.

We know very little about Nimrod, although there are several
theories and speculations. He has been connected to several personalities, most of them without any supporting background. He
was supposed to have been Marduk, the Egyptian sun god Ra, or
Ninurta, son of Enlil/Jehovah, king Ninus, the husband of queen
Semiramis. Even the Mesopotamian demigod and hero, Gilgamesh
was supposed to have been the same person as Nimrod. Just to mention a few of them.

The most we know about Nimrod comes from the book of Yah-
weh. He is mentioned in the bible as a king of Babylon and both
Nimrod and Babylon are considered to have been 'against the Lord'.
In addition, Nimrod was a descendant of Ham whom Enlil/Jehovah
didn't permit to live in Sumer, so he settled down in Egypt with
Enki. Genesis 10:8–10:

> And Cush begat Nimrod: he began to be a mighty one in the
> earth'. He was a mighty hunter before the Lord. And the be-
> ginning of his kingdom was Babel, and Erech, and Accad, and
> Calneh, in the land of Shinar.

According to the first book of Abraham 2:7 Nimrod established
even the city of Ur. All the above cities, except Babel, were under
the control of the Enlilites. Laurence Gardner says about Ham and
Nimrod:

> Had Ham been correctly listed as the historical son of Tubal-
> cain, this subterfuge would not have been possible and Ham's
> important grandson Nimrod could not have been sidestepped,
> as he was, with just a passing mention (Genesis 10:9-10).[2]

Abraham was born around the year 2100 BCE, (several dates exist)
in the city of Ur, where his father was a high priest. Nimrod, being
a god, a demigod, or a human, he could not have been the builder of
the city of Ur, since Ur was a very old city by the time of Abraham.
Besides, the city had always been under the control of the Enlilite
gods. In all the history of the Sumerian kings, there is none with

the name Nimrod, not even some 'rebel' king who 'rose against the Lord'.

One wonders what sources these scribes of the OT and many of the scribes of the apocrypha have been using! The sources might have been right, of course, but they also have been intermixed with one another, even with other events, chronologies and persons, in order to establish a suitable propaganda. Concerning Biblical chronology Laurence Gardner says:

> What our schools teach in this regard [chronology] is not accurate history, but the propagandist ideal of a Church-led movement which is entirely dedicated to supporting its own mythology, irrespective of the historical truth.[3]

We know that they mixed up the two separate events of the building of the Tower, the E-temen-an-ki and the building of the city of Babylon. They also intermixed the first earthlings, Adamu (Adam), and Ti-Amat (Eva), with the first two Homo sapiens, Adapa and Titi, the parents of Cain and Abel.

Nimrod was also supposed to have tried to kill the Abraham child at his birth, in the same manner Herotes tried to kill the Jesus child. In the first book of Abraham 24:3–5 we read;

> And he said unto me, Abram, I am the God of thy fathers Peleg and Shem and Noah. It is I who preserved thy life when the wicked king Nimrod would have destroyed thee, for I softened the heart of thy father that he should hide thee away. This I did for I have a mighty work for thee to do in establishing mine order upon the earth, and, verily, I say unto thee, In the end, through thee shall this wicked Nimrod be destroyed from off the face of the earth.

Here we have some remarkable statements. First, Enlil says that he was the God of Noah. The meaning of this statement is very surprising. If he meant that he knew Noah and blessed him with long life, then it is true. But if he meant that Noah was worshiping him the same way Shem and Peleg did, then it is a remarkable statement indeed. Noah is the Hebrew name of Ziusudra, the son of Enki with an earthly woman. As a son of Enki, who saved himself and his followers from the great flood, he certainly knew that it was Enlil who wanted the destruction of mankind. He probably knew that a struggle was going on between Enlil and Enki.

As we have seen in an earlier chapter, Ziusudra/Noah was sent (by Enlil) to adobe in a mountainous land, isolated from the rest of the humans. Therefore it is not likely that he would change side and worship the man who didn't want him to live. Besides, there are no records about Ziusudra worshiping 'the one and only god', neither that this god of Ziusudra/Noah was the god Yahweh. The concept of the one god was invented much later promoted by the prophets of the OT, and applied retrospectively to the Jewish history. Ziusudra/Noah was neither Jew nor a worshiper of Enlil/Yahweh.

Secondly, 'I have a mighty work for thee' supports our theory that Enlil/Yahweh already had a plan! He could promise anything if only Abraham could provide some assistance!

Thirdly, at the time of the incident of the Tower, 3463–3453 BCE, there was not any king in Sumer with that name. Neither was Abraham born then. The kings of Sumer, all of them, were always appointed by some of the members of the Enlilite family, and were always approved by Enlil himself. If some king was not performing his tasks according to given instructions, then he was replaced and in some cases even killed. Now if Nimrod was a king in the Enlilite lands, then someone of the members of this family must have appointed him as king. And in that case they could easily remove him. If Nimrod was a king whom Enlil/Jehovah wished to replace but couldn't, then Nimrod must have been king somewhere outside his control. He must have been far away from the power of the Enlilites, under the protection of some other god. In that case, Nimrod could neither reach nor tried to kill the Abraham child in Ur. In the book of Jasher 7:39 we read:

> And when Nimrod had joyfully returned from battle, after having conquered his enemies, all his brethren, together with those who knew him before, assembled to make him king over them, and they place the regal crown upon his head.

Here we are informed that Nimrod was not appointed as king by some god, as the custom was, but was elected directly by the people. Something the Enlilites could not accept. Furthermore, Nimrod could have been some of the followers of Marduk in the story of the Tower; otherwise he could not have been king in Babylon (the beginning of his kingdom), in the lands of the Enlilites. The followers of Marduk in this, his first attempt to replace Enlil, must have been numerous and impossible to stop.

According to the book of Jasher (9:23) the people assembled to build the Tower were 'of about six hundred thousand'. Even if we include all family members, that was a considerable number indeed. If this figure is right, then it must have been most of the people of the whole area, leaving the Enlilites with just a minority of humans under their control. That would explain why Enlil could not stop neither the movement, nor the building of the Tower. He had to wait until the Tower was finished in order to destroy it. Enki says:

> To stop Marduk and Nabu in their endeavor Enlil did not suc-
> ceed, In Nibru-ki Enlil and his sons and grandchildren assem-
> bled; what to do they all considered. Marduk an unpermitted
> Gateway to heaven is building, to Earthlings it he is entrust-
> ing![4]

The entrusting of the building to the Earthlings was another act of Marduk Enlil could not accept. Both the bible as well as the Lost Book of Enki, agree that humans were involved in the building of the Tower. Now if Nimrod was a king who sided with Marduk, then Nimrod was also an enemy of Enlil/Jehovah. In order to choose side, he must have been informed about the struggle between the two gods. By choosing to support Marduk, he also chose to fight the slavery practiced by the Enlilites. That would make him the first hu-man (or demigod), hero on Earth.

There is another disturbing fact in the time given in the OT. It states that Nimrod was king at the time Abraham was born, in 2117 BCE according to our calculations. Most scholars agree that Abra-ham was born around the year 2100 BCE. The date given by Zecharia Sitchin is 2123 BCE. That would make Nimrod more than a thousand years old at that time. The building of the Tower started in 3463 BCE and ended with the destruction in 3453 BCE, as we have seen, while the city of Babylon was built under the time of Sargon, 2399–2343 BCE, in around 2370 BCE. This could be possible if some god (cer-tainly not Enlil/Jehovah) had 'blessed' Nimrod with long life. If not, then he couldn't possibly have been around at the time of Abraham. Besides, from 2199 to 2108 BCE, the land of Sumer was under the

Gutaeans. The Gutaean kings were all appointed/approved by the Enlilites.

The most plausible explanation seems to be that Nimrod was indeed a king directly elected by his people, and that he was a supporter of Marduk in his efforts to be the successor of Enlil. That would make Nimrod a 'rebel' in the same manner as Marduk. A distinction has to be made between 'rebel against God' and 'rebel against Enlil'.

The picture we get of Nimrod is completely different from the picture the scribe of the bible and other apocryphal books bring about. Some passages have been edited according to the Lord's will, in order to present Nimrod as an evil man, some have passed through the censure unchanged, like the following in Jasher 7:41:

And he [Nimrod] placed Terah the son of Nahor, the prince of his host, and he dignified him and elevated him above all his princes.

Both the bible and 'The Lost Book of Enki' agree that it was Enlil himself who chose Tirhu (Terah) and not Nimrod.

Upon Tirhu and his sons, of worthy lineage descended, Enlil set his gaze:[5]

We do not know what Enki means with the expression 'worthy lineage'. If Terah was a demigod, then both he and Abraham must have been Anakim. Anakim were the descendants of Anunnaki and earthlings. That means also that, Anakim in the service of Enlil/Yahweh were considered as good people, while those who rebelled against him were considered as 'wicked'. It is worthy to note that Hagar, the second wife of Abraham and mother of Ishmael, is considered to be the daughter of a Pharaoh who was a descendant of Nimrod! Isaak was a 'gift' to Sara and Abraham by Yahweh. Before that, however, Yahweh persuaded Abraham to take Hagar as his wife for the purpose of having children with her. Yahweh also decided that Abraham would become 'the father of a multitude'! Were Ishmael and Isaac predetermined to be the Patriarchs of two different religions already scheduled by Enlil-Yahweh? Why did God wish Abraham to have a son with Hagar before he 'offered' him a son with Sara?

Terah being 'the Priest-Prince' of the Enlilites in the land of Sumer, and later in Harran, and 'the prince of Nimrod's host' are two statements contradicting each other. One of the sources, either Enki or Jasher, must be wrong. We choose to trust in Enki. Jasher 9:20:

> And king Nimrod reigned securely, and all the earth was under his control, and all the earth was of one tongue and words of union.

The above passage contradicts everything else about Nimrod in the scriptures. This was certainly a realistic picture of Nimrod. He was a king with great power reigning over all the people of the area, except, of course for the land of Sumer where the Enlilites had their own kings. 'And the beginning of his kingdom was Babel'. This sole fact would be enough to make Nimrod the enemy of Enlil/Jehovah. Babylon was a rebellion city founded by Marduk in his efforts to challenge Enlil/Jehovah. Then, every king of Babylon and supporter of Marduk would be qualified as an enemy of the Enlilites. 'Words of union' was another factor that disturbed the Enlilites.

'All the earth was of one tongue', was a fact. But 'words of union' could be understood as there was a movement going on, a movement striving to unite all the people of the Earth. Not only to unite the people, but unite them under the leadership of Marduk, Nabu, and Nimrod, against the slave-owner Enlil/Yahweh. An unified mankind was destined to perform miracles as Enlil/Yahweh says in Genesis 11:6.

'Being against the Enlilites', has been corrupted into 'being against God', in the bible. Babylon is not just a city in the bible. Babylon represents the coordinated actions by Marduk and earthlings to bring slavery to an end. Babylon was also governed by a king elected by the people. Nimrod became a rebellion too, by siding with the rebellion Marduk. Babylon represented the spirit of Marduk and the spirit of Nimrod. The authorized power was now shifted to the free world represented by Marduk and most of the earthlings.

In fact, we know nothing about any kings of Babylon before the first Dynasty of Babylon, that is to say, after Marduk became the Supreme god of the gods. The first known king of the First dynasty was Sumu-Abum (ca 1894–1891). From ca 2300–1900 BCE, there must have been some kings in that city, but there are no records since it was a rebel city in the lands of the Enlilites, but outside their control. The only king of Babylon mentioned in the bible at that time is Nimrod. A hostile king against Enlil/Yahweh in the Enlilite lands, or a king in a hostile land, not appointed by them, could only have been king of Babylon, as Genesis 10:10 states. And nobody could have been king of Babylon at that time without being appointed by Marduk.

Nimrod could thus, may well have been one of these kings and even the only one if had 'blessed' with long life. Such a 'blessing' would also classify Nimrod as 'wicked' as it was not approved by Enlil. As we have seen, Enki could provide Ziusudra/Noah with 'the plant of life' only after Enlil's approval. By being a king of Babylon, probably with a considerable army, and under the protection of Marduk, it was not possible for Enlil/Jehovah to get hold of him. The only kings Enlil/Yahweh could not replace were the kings of Egypt and Babylon. For that he would need some help from his human supporters. He turned to Abraham for assistance.

In the book of Jasher, Nimrod, king of Shinar, was a contemporary and allied of Kedorlaomer, the Elamite king who attacked Sodom and the cities of the plane, as it is stated in Genesis 14:1. The only difference, however, is that in Genesis 14:1 the king of Shinar is Amraphel and not Nimrod. At this time king of Shinar was Amar-Sin (2044–2035 BCE). However, as Z. Sitchin states, Amar-Sin and Amraphel could have been the same name in different languages, thank God for that! If Nimrod had been the same person as Amar-Sin/Amraphel, then Enlil/Yahweh would not need the help of Abraham to 'kill' him, since he could easily replace him, as he used too. A king who rebelled against Enlil could never continue to be king in the lands of the Enlilites. So Nimrod could not have been Amar-Sin or any other king in the lands of the Enlilites.

The following manipulative words of Enlil were passed down from Abraham to his descendants. They were as powerful as any order.

In the end, through thee shall this wicked Nimrod be destroyed from off the face of the earth.

Esau was hiding himself, waiting for Nimrod, who used to hunt in the wilderness, and without any particular reason, other than the manipulative words of Enlil/Jehovah spoken to Abraham, he jumped out from the bushes and killed him. It was a murder according to plan. It was a murder of a freedom fighter begotten by a man manipulated by Enlil/Yahweh through Abraham. Jasher 27:7–16 says:

> And Nimrod and two of his men that were with him came to the place where they were, when Esau started suddenly from his lurking place, and drew his sword, and hastened and ran to Nimrod and cut off his head. . . . and Nimrod died by the sword of Esau in shame and contempt, and the seed of Abraham caused his death as he had seen in his dream.

Did the scribe of this passage really know who Nimrod was? Probably yes. He knew that Nimrod was a great king who rebelled against the Lord. Did he know who the Lord was? If he did, then he was acting as a faithful agent of Enlil/Yahweh. Otherwise he was a victim of an artful manipulation. In the same manner as Esau was. The assassination of Nimrod by Esau reminds us of the killing of the Dragon (king) by St Michael. There was never a fight either, only a pure assassination. William Bramley says:

> It is easier for a religious person to kill someone if he believes that the victim is inherently sinful.[6]

The believers in the letter of the OT regard Esau as a hero, since they use to assert that Nimrod was the world's first tyrant. Esau acted according to God's instructions, i.e. he had license to kill! By justifying the terrible action of a murderer, they expose themselves as the real victims of the manipulative instructions of Enlil/Jehovah. They can't even answer the question why God so badly wanted Nimrod dead. They have no answer why God wished to kill the first king on Earth democratically elected by the majority of the people. They have no answer why God so desperately needed some assistance in murdering a human. They can't answer why God has to kill!

It is said that Nimrod persuaded the humans not to ascribe to god, in order to bring them into a dependence upon his own power. There is no support for that accusation. He might as well have been persuading them not to ascribe to god, in order to free them from the dependence of those extra terrestrials! Zeus punished Prometheus because he taught humans how to make fire. Prometheus also persuaded the humans not to offer to the gods. Enlil/Yahweh didn't want any god to give gifts to the humans, fire or freedom alike. We believe that not even God should have license to kill humans!

Enlil/Jehovah could manipulate humans to do his dirty work. Murder was no exception. Esau who performed the task knew certainly nothing about the reason Enlil/Jehovah wished the death of Nimrod. He certainly didn't know that Enlil/Jehovah was the persecutor of humanity, while Nimrod was a rebel fighting the extra terrestrial dictatorship on Earth.

Nimrod didn't die in shame and contempt. He died by the sword of a murderer. A murderer programmed by Enlil-Yahweh to kill. The world ought to remember Nimrod as the first freedom fighter. Esau, however, died because of grief, after he sold his birthright to his brother Jacob. He died in shame as a murderer.

Nimrod was probably the first human who rebelled against the foreign rulers, the Anunnaki. If that was the reason for the scribes of the bible to call him 'wicked', then any descendants of Nimrod, and every human who is against slavery and dictatorship ought to be proud of this man. Nimrod might have been the first great human hero on Earth, the first politician, and the first human who fought the alien slavery. The first king elected by the people. The first to observe that unity was the strength of humanity. He probably was the first to understand that the gold of Earth was worthy to fight for.

---

[1]Zecharia Sitchin, The Lost Book of Enki, p. 305, 306
[2]Laurence Gardner, Genesis of the Grail Kings p. 193
[3]Ibid., p. 85
[4]Ibid., p. 282
[5]Ibid., p. 304,305
[6]William Bramley, The Gods of Eden, p.124

Chapter 13

ENLIL DEPOSED BY MARDUK

Enlil authorized the use of nuclear-like
weapons before he stepped down

After the Gutaean occupation of Sumer, Ur-Nammu, (2108–2090
BCE) ascended the throne of Ur, which started an era of prosperity
and peace in Sumer. He was the founder of the third dynasty of Ur
that lasted for about a century. He called himself 'king of Sumer
and Akkad'. Enlil ordered the Sumerian Abraham to go to Harran
and there wait for new instructions. Sin, the moon god had already
established himself there and built a temple where Terah, Abraham's
father was to be his 'high priest' which was equivalent to minister
of security.

Ur-Nammu died in battle and was succeeded by his son Shul-gi
(2090–2044 BCE), chosen by Nannar/Sin. Shulgi too became Inanna's
lover. He expanded the empire to the west, passed through the Forth
Region with Elamite troops, and declared himself 'king of the four
quarters of the Earth'. This time Shulgi's passing through the Forth
Region didn't cause any curse from Enlil, as it did when Naram-Sin.
Mysterious are the ways of God (Enlil) indeed. Perhaps he couldn't
afford to lose a king at this time. Perhaps the 'crime' was after all
not a serious crime, or he had already decided about the future of
the place. Despite the Elamite mercenaries and the alien weapons he
was provided by the Enlilites, Shulgi was soon forced to build a wall
in the northwest, called the 'Wall of the Lands', to protect Sumer.

The lands of the Enlilites could no longer stand against the armies of Marduk. There were too many powerful gods but not enough human supporters. Other gods were just more popular. Shulgi says:

> I am the man whose name has been chosen by Nanna. I am the steward of Enlil's temple, the domestic slave of An. . . . Inanna, the queen of the gods, the protective deity of my power. . .

Shulgi was succeeded by his son, Amar-Sin (2044–2035 BCE). Enlil ordered General Abraham to move south (from Harran), into Canaan with his cavalry and all the members of his family, Genesis 12:4–5.

> So Abraham departed, as the LORD had spoken unto him; and Lot went with him: And Abraham was seventy and five years old when he departed out of Harran.

> And Abraham took Sarai his wife, and Lot his brother's son, and all their substance that they had gathered, and the souls that they had gotten in Harran; and they went forth to go into the land of Canaan; and into the land of Canaan they came.

Enki confirms the information too adding:

> Nabu, Marduk's son, was the people inciting; to seize the Fourth Region was his plan.[1]

> To protect the sacred places, the chariots' ascends and descends enable, Enlil Ibruum to go commanded[2]

Since Abraham was born in 2117, as we have seen, and was seventy-five years old when he left Harran, the year was then 2042 BCE.

Shu-Sin (2035–2026 BCE) succeeded Amar-Sin and built a new wall as a defense against the Amorites. The defense wall built by Shulgi was no more protective enough. The new wall was 275 kilometers long across the rivers Tigris and Euphrates. The situation for the Enlilites was now more than desperate. The pressure from the westerners Amorites and other supporters of Marduk was stronger than their kings could stand.

Marduk ended his wandering around the world and was back in Harran about the same time, still waiting for the sign of the Ram.

Nabu had summoned an army of supporters and allies in Canaan. He also gained the allegiance of the Canaanite cities Sodom, Gomorra, Admah, Zeboiim and Bela. The ring was closing against Sumer. It was now a matter of time until the Enlilites would give up. That could put an end to the hostilities between Enlil and Marduk and start a new era, hopefully an era of piece and prosperity for all the people in the area. Except that none of the Brotherhood of the Gold was willing to release the Supremacy to Marduk and give up the Gold Mission.

Inanna summoned an army of her own. It was an alliance among four kings leaded by the Elamite Khedorlaomer. He attacked the army of Nabu and the armies of the Canaanite cities. Since Ibruum (Abraham) was sent there by Enlil to defend the Landing place, it seems that Nabu, the Canaanite cities and Abraham together stopped and defeated the army of Khedorlaomer.

Although the battle is described in the bible (Genesis 14), the role of Abraham and his cavalry of several hundred men is not mentioned, until Abraham went after Khedorlaomer to free Lot who had been taken captive.

He succeeded in freeing Lot, which means that his forces were of considerable numbers and strength. It is logical to assume that Abraham did what he had promised, to defend the landing place, Genesis 14:1:

> And it came to pass in the days of Amraphel king of Shinar, Arioch king of Ellasar, Chedorlaomer king of Elam, and Tidal king of nations; And these made war with Bera king of Sodom, and with Birsha king of Gomorrah, Shinab king of Admah, and Shemeber king of Zeboiim, and the king of Bela, which is Zoar. All these joined together in the vale of Siddim, which is the salt sea.

The outcome of the battle, is somehow confusing, according to the bible. We read that the kings of Sodom and Gomorrah fled to the mountains. Then the kings of the East took Lot and his goods and all the goods of Sodom and Gomorrah and departed. Several theories have been presented about the reasons and purposes of this battle.

Since Enlil asked General Abraham for assistance to defend the Landing place, it is logical to assume that either Inanna, through Chedorlaomer, or Nabu were planning to seize the place. We assume that the place was still under the 'neutral' control of Nin-khursaq. By seizing the Landing Place and all the weapons therein, Inanna would have been so powerful that she could announce herself as 'The Queen of the gods'. She would the de facto High Commander. That would make it impossible for Marduk to announce himself 'The supreme god'. Either she had plans of seizing the place or just to prevent Nabu of doing that, she failed, thanks to the Canaanite cities, Nabu and Abraham.

Nabu, on the other hand, could seize the place after defeating Inanna's army but he didn't. Besides, Nabu and Marduk were certain that the age of the Ram had come and Marduk's demand to succeed Enlil would be accepted. They were holding their armies waiting for the announcement to come. Why then make battle to take the Landing Place if it was only a matter of time until the place would officially come under Marduk's authority. So it is possible that Nabu's intention was the same as Abraham's, to prevent Inanna of capturing the military base. This is strengthened by the fact that Enlil/Jehovah was satisfied with Abraham's role and rewarded him by giving him the Land. But the other allies of Abraham, Nabu and the Canaanite cities were not rewarded. On the contrary, they had to be punished. Why? According to the bible the inhabitants of those cities were wicked and sinful. The people of Sodom, for example, have been accused for homosexuality. This is done by intentionally misinterpreting some words in order to justify the destruction of the cities. The story has even given rise to words like 'sodomy', associated with homosexuality. Dictionary references says:

Sodomy was not known to be used in such context [homosexuality] until the 13th century CE.[3]

What? Obviously this invented excuse is an after construction some 3500 years later. Some messengers were sent by Enlil/Jehovah to inform Abraham about the coming punishment of the cities. Genesis 18:2:

And he [Abraham] lifted up his eyes and looked, and, lo, three men stood by him: and when he saw them he ran to meet them from the tent door, and bowed himself toward the ground.

Here we note two interesting things. First, they came from above because Abraham, sitting at the door of his tent, he had to lift up his eyes to see them. That means that they used some kind of mobile machine attached to them, if not some kind of helicopter. Secondly, they 'landed' at some distance from his tent, as he had to run in order to meet them.

Then, after they ate under the tree, (Genesis 18:8) and explained to him what they were about to do, they went to Sodom. Not walking we assume. One of them flew away in some other direction because only two of them (Genesis 19:1) visited Lot. According to 'the Lost Book of Enki', these two were Ninurta and Nergal. They didn't want the people of Sodom to know about their visit. And they needed both food and sleep under their time there. Genesis 19:4-5:

> But they lay down, the men of the city, even the men of So-
> dom, compassed the house round, both old and young, all the
> people from every quarter: And they called unto Lot, and said
> unto him, Where are the men which came in to thee this night?
> Bring them out unto us, that we may know them.

The people found out however, that some 'flying' people were in their city in the tent of Lot. It was quite natural for the citizens to investigate who the flying people were and why they visited a new-comer. Had they been messengers of Nabu, they would probably contact the council of the town. But these messengers were hiding in the tent of Lot, a foreigner. We have to consider that the strange visitors came just after the plundering of the city by Chedorlaomer. Naturally they were anxious to find out the intentions of the visitors. Besides, if the people of Sodom were sinful and not even a single one of them was a good being, why did Lot settle down there? He made his choice by himself before separating from Abraham. Genesis 13:10:

> And Lot lifted up his eyes, and beheld all the plain of Jor-
> dan, that it was well watered every where, before the Lord
> destroyed Sodom and Gomorrah, even as the garden of the
> LORD, like the land of Egypt, as thou comest unto Zoar.

It must have been easy to decide after observing that the plain was well watered. As we shall see, it was certainly of the same reason the Igigi/Titans also chose that place.

Those people were consuming gold powder and were unwilling to share with strangers. Lot pitched his tent toward Sodom, and he probably had gold of his own. Otherwise they would probably not welcome him to the city. We know that both Abraham and Lot left Egypt as rich men, although there are no records how. Genesis 13:1–2:

> And Abraham went up out of Egypt, he, and his wife, and all that he had, and Lot with him, into the south. And Abraham was very rich in cattle, in silver, and in gold.

For the people of Sodom, these 'flying men' were supposed to be 'the agents of Enlil' and they were not welcome. Being Igigi and Igigi-descendants, they had been in a war-like situation since their marriage with earthly women against the will of Enlil. The visit could only mean trouble. The inhabitants of Sodom were alarmed. They all came to the tent where the agents were hiding. They were young and old, men and women, from all the quarters of the city. Would the whole town come to be involved in sexual activities with the two strangers? The insinuation about homosexuality is a cheep 'cover up' argument with the characteristics of shamelessness. They also have been accused that they shifted their allegiance to other gods. This accusation is of great importance.

We know from exodus, that high walls surrounded the city of Jericho. Walls surrounded Sodom and the other four Canaanite cities too. This was unusual at that time (ca 2000 BCE). The first fortification of a place we can find in history was performed by the Igigi at Baalbek. There they were safe and no attempt to seize the place was made by the Enlilites. The walls of the Canaanite cities were built for the same reason. To defend the cities, from possible attacks from the Enlilites. These people were forced to hide behind high walls. It is very uncertain that they ever had been allies of the Enlilites, and therefore they couldn't shift their allegiance to Marduk.

What probably happened, was that Nabu managed to persuade them to choose side, which was certainly not difficult. The situation was in Marduk's favor. He had a strong army in the North while Nabu had a strong army in the West of Sumer. By choosing to support them, the people of Sodom and the people of the other Anakim cities of the plain, were now hoping that the struggle between

Enlil/Jehovah and Marduk would come to an end. If Marduk could be the winner, as they hoped, then life would be very different for them too. They would not need to hide any more and they could openly practice their knowledge concerning the gold powder. In fact, the Enlilites were now in trouble. They were on a path leading them to capitulation. That would probably be the end of the gold mission too. Surrounded by people who wished to free themselves from their cruel administration, including the Titans, and without enough support, they were already defeated. As they, themselves could not win, they decided that Marduk shouldn't win either.

According to different Jewish texts, those people had been exterminated because they were greedy and generally depraved. In the Mishnah (Judaism religious texts) we read that their sin was related to property. Now how could 'property' turn into 'homosexuality' is not for us to explain. The cities were rich but didn't treat visitors and foreigners well. It is understandable if they were suspicious. They also must have been egoistic in the manner that they were unwilling to share whatever they had with other people, especially visitors, and foreigners, who had heard about their wealth. But how cruel were they? Lot was a foreigner living there with his wife and daughters. If these people were so evil as some texts states, or sexual maniacs as the bible want us to believe, how could Lot, the worshiper of Jehovah, could live there? Most probably, the accusations about homosexuality were attached to them afterwards, just to justify the crime.

Flavius Josephus, (ca 60–100 CE) the Jewish historian wrote about the people of Sodom in his 'Jewish Antiquities', that the Sodomites were 'proud of their numbers and their wealth', that they hated foreigners and avoided any contact with others'.

> Indignant at this contact, God accordingly resolved to chastise them for their arrogance, and not only to uproot their city, but to blast their land so completely that it should yield neither plant nor fruit whatsoever from the time forward.

Note the words of Josephus. It was not enough, for God/Enlil/Jehovah to 'uproot their city'. He wished to make the place desolate for times to come. This is only possible by using chemical or nuclear weapons.

We know by now that the inhabitants of these cities were descendants from the Igigi (some of them could have been Igigi too), and knew the secret of the gold.

In the Babylonian Talmud: Tractate Sanhedrin 109a we read:

As for the earth, out of it cometh bread: and under it it is
burned up as it were with fire. The stones of it are the place of
sapphires: and it hath **dust of gold** [emphasis added]. . . .

They said [the men of Sodom]: 'Since there cometh forth bread
out of [our] earth, and it hath the dust of gold, why should we
suffer wayfarers, who come to us only to deplete our wealth.
Come, let us abolish the practice of traveling in our land.

Bread containing dust of gold. Here we have the real reason why
Enlil/Yahweh ordered the destruction of the cities.

Outside our cities of today, there is often a traffic sign welcoming
the visitors. The people of the cities of the plain, not wishing visitors
coming only for sharing their most valuable asset, probably didn't
exercise this custom, but quite the opposite. Something like 'Only
visitors in possession of gold are welcome'!

In the Sumerian myth 'Enki and the World Order' by Samuel
Noah Kramer, we read something similar about 'bread'.

Enki multiplied the heaps and mounds,
With Enlil he spread wide the abundance in the Land,
Her whose head and side are dappled, whose face is honey
covered,
The Lady, the procreatress, the vigor of the Land, the 'life' of
the black-heads, Ashnan, **the nourishing bread, the bread of
all,** [emphasis added] Enki placed in charge of them.

It is clear enough that these people knew about the gold dust. It is
also possible that the only way they knew the gold dust could be
consumed, was through herbs, or that was the most effective way.
The tree of life could equally be the herbs of life. Why had these
herbs the dust of gold? It is only logical to assume that these people
practiced a kind of advance agriculture by watering the herbs with
an admixture of gold dust and water. That is why Enlil/Yahweh had
to destroy both the people and the fields. The fact that they kept the
knowledge for themselves and allowed no one from the outside to
share it, does not justify their extermination and 'all that which grew
upon the ground'. Genesis 19:25-26:

Then the Lord rained upon Sodom and Gomorrah brimstone
and fire from the Lord out of heaven;

And he overthrew those cities, and the plain, and all the inhabitants of the cities, and that which grew upon the ground.

Obviously, it was important even to destroy the herbs to prevent
other people from eating, since the herbs contained 'the dust of
gold'. It was also necessary to make the fields unusable for some
time since the soil could still contain some dust of gold.

If the time of the Ram is coming, let us Marduk of the Bond
Heaven-Earth deprive! Enlil in anger proposed.

To obliterate the Place of the Celestial Chariots all except
Enki agreed;

To use therefore the Weapons of Terror Nergal suggested; only
Enki was opposed:

The evil thing to curry out Ninurta and Nergal were selected.[4]

The decision to 'punish' the Canaanite cities by destroying them
was taken by Enlil and his family (including Nergal) and was approved by Anu, only Enki opposed. The only purpose the 'Landing
place of the Chariots' was destroyed was to deprive Marduk of the
control of the place. Since Marduk used to cooperate with humans,
Enlil wished to deprive the humans too of any knowledge about the
Landing place and the advanced weapons therein.

Both the Landing place and the five Canaanite cities were wiped
out off the face of the Earth. The men who released the 'nuclear-like
bombs' were Ninurta, the son of Enlil and Nergal, the son of Enki.
The time of the Ram had come, yet Enlil/Yahweh refused to step
down.

According to 'the Lost Book of Enki', Anu gave his permission
to use the nuclear-like weapons to destroy the chariot's place. But
he also said to Enlil that the cities and people should be spared.
Enlil passed that information to Ninurta together with his wish that
Abraham was to be forewarned. They both forewarned Abraham and

saved Lot. Ninurta was supposed to inform Nergal but he 'failed' to do that, intentionally or not.

Enki was not alarmed about the decision to use the nuclear-like weapons. He knew that there were seven of them, brought to Earth by Alalu. Enki and Abgal hid them somewhere in the mountains in Southern Africa (Abzu). Only the two of them knew. What he didn't know was that Abgal had revealed the secret to Enlil.

Nergal activated the seven 'bombs' and gave each one a task name. The names describe the weapons destruction ability that should interest any scientist in the field.

> The One without Rival the first weapon he called, the Blazing Flame he named the second, The One Who with terror Crumbles he called the third, Mountain Melter the fourth he called, Wind That the Rim of the World Seeks he named the fifth, the One Who Above and Below No One Spares was the sixth, The seventh with monstrous venom was filled, Vaporizer of Living Things he called it. With Anu's blessing were the seven to Nergal and Ninurta given, therewith to destruction wreak.[5]

The 'bombs' were ready to be used to destroy the Landing place and the five Canaanite cities, ordered by Enlil and approved by Anu.

Meanwhile, Marduk returned to Babylon where he announced himself 'The Supreme god'. His waiting had come to an end; the sign of the Ram was now visible in the skies. The year was 2027 BCE; 1,736 years after the counting in earth years began (3763).

The same day Marduk proclaimed himself as 'the Supreme god', Enlil/Jehovah commanded Ninurta and Nergal to make use of the nuclear-like bombs. Enki describes the nuclear attack and the joy of the two men who dropped the first such bombs ever on human beings.

> Then the first terror weapon from the skies Ninurta let lose; The top of Mount Mashu with a flash it sliced off, the mount's innards in an instant it melted. Above the Place of the Celestial Chariots the second weapons unleashed, With a brilliance of seven suns the plain's rocks into a gushing wound were made, The Earth shook and crumbled, the heavens after the brilliance were darkened; With burnt and crushed stones was the plain of the chariots covered, Of all the forests that the

plain had surrounded, only tree stems were left standing. It is
done! Ninurta from the sky ship, his Black Divine Bird, words
shouted. The control that Marduk and Nabu so coveted, of it
they are forever deprived!

*   *   *

Over the five cities, one after the other, Erra [Nergal] upon
each from the skies a terror weapon sent, The five cities of
the valley he finished off, to desolation they were overturned.
With fire and brimstones were they upheavaled, all that lived
there to vapor was turned.[6]

Enlil/Yahweh avenged Marduk's challenge by depriving him of getting control over the weapons at the Landing Place. He punished
the cities because they supported Nabu and Marduk. Besides, they
were consuming gold dust that belonged to the Lord. Who was to
punish Enlil/Yahweh for this action? God perhaps, I mean the real
God. One would think that such a being or power does exist, since it
punished the Enlilites using their own destructive power.

A wind from the west drove 'radioactivity' to their lands, destroying the whole of Sumer. Ironically it spared Babylon.

Whatever it reached, death to all that lives mercilessly it delivered; From the valley of No Pity, by the brilliance spawned,
toward Shumer the death was carried.

From Eridu in the south to Sippar in the north did the Evil
Wind the land overwhelm; Babili, where Marduk supremacy
declared, by the Evil Wind was spared.[7]

The land of Sumer was unintentionally destroyed due to the use of
the advanced weapons ordered by Enlil. The Sumerians, under the
protection of Enlil, became the victims of his actions too. Laurence
Gardner says about Sodom:

It is possible therefore, that the Dead Sea centers of Sodom
and Gomorrah fell victim to a firestone radiation catastrophe,
when they were destroyed by fire and brimstone nearly two
millennia before Qumrân was settled in the region.[8]

The god of the bible has countless enemies, called evils, devils and demons as well as servants, people who helped him with his gold mission, the angel-gang. One of them who dropped the bombs from the air, Ninurta, is still 'flying' on the walls of Christian churches as the archangel Gabriel. He has never been tried for this criminal action. The people of the Anakim cities were annihilated, not because they were homosexual but because they were threatening Yahweh's Gold Mission by supporting his adversary Marduk. Had they been homosexual, this god would not yet have the right to exterminate them. He certainly wouldn't care. They just happened to be in the way in his efforts to take as much as possible of our gold. Although the bible states that it was Yahweh who ordered the destruction of the cities as a punishment, there is not a word about Marduk, the real reason behind Yahweh's action. Laurence Gardner says:

> The scribes recorded that it was he, the vengeful Enlil, who brought the 'great storm' which caused the annihilation of a people who had given their royalty to his nephew Marduk.[9]

Not long after this terrible disaster Marduk was officially installed as the Supreme god on Earth and recognized by all the other gods, including Yahweh. He had been deprived of the power the weapons of the place represented. In reality, his only power left, was the support of the humans.

> Let the rank of fifty, by me for Ninurta intended, to Marduk be given, Let Marduk over the desolation of the Regions his supremacy declare! As for me and Ninurta, we will in his way no longer stand. To the Lands Beyond the Oceans we will depart, what we had all had come for, the mission to obtain for Nibiru gold we will complete! So did Enlil to Enki say; dejection was in his words.[10]

Enlil was forced to step down from the 'throne' because of the strong armies of Earthlings Marduk and Nabu had summoned. Not because of some kind of democratic process. He seems to be glad, Enlil, over the desolated regions he and the other Enlilites left for the new Supreme god. Since Enlil had no reason to be happy, he could, at least, feel happy because of Marduk's setback. Marduk became, at last, the king of the gods. He has always been the Supreme god of Babylon and the main god of the Egyptians. In the jubilee chapel of Pharaoh Senusret I (ca 1965–1920 BCE), Amun (Marduk) is described as the king of the gods. Under the Ptolemaic era he was worshiped as the king of the gods too, not as Zeus but as the equivalent of Zeus/Enlil. But, without the destroyed military base, his supremacy was indeed only a matter of formality.

Enlil on the other hand, had his own Landing Place in Meso-america, as we have seen. The flow of gold to Nibiru was still under his control.

One expects that the struggle between Enlil and Marduk had come to an end now. Unfortunately it was not. Although Enlil says that he and Ninurta would not stand in Marduk's' way any more, the struggle continued for another 2000 years. Either Enlil changed his mind and decided to fight Marduk in all the way, or he was not telling the truth in the first place.

From about two thousand BCE until the time of Cyrus the great (ca 539 BCE), we have a lot of wars against Babylon and Egypt, initiated by Enlil and his sons. We shall keep in mind that the Enlilites were always the ones who still had some powerful weapons under their control. The supporters of Marduk, both in Egypt, (Ra/Amun), and in Babylon, were unwilling to shift their allegiance to other gods. In Akkad, Assyria and the Hittite empire, the kings were supporting the Enlilite gods, only if, and when it was suitable to them, or just because of fear. Enlil's plan was to spoil everything positively connected with Marduk. Wars against Babylon and Egypt were combined with incredible propaganda and theatrical performance by the angel-gang, in order to undermine any possible resistance. What was life in Babylon like under the leadership of the 'Supreme god'? A Babylonian text says:

Marduk was one of the main deities worshiped by Hammu-rabi, as stated in the preambule to the famous Code of Laws of Hammurabi. The growth of Marduk's cult among the people is one of the most fascinating religious aspects of the Second Millennium, and His popularity was mostly because He is seen as a approachable deity, who cares about human beings and their suffering.[11]

Also from the Phoenician letters:

The civilizing power of Marduk: See in the streets of your city a man and a maid. He shines before the people as a sun in splendor, she as the moon keeps her face to her lord. As they pass, old men sitting in their doorway smile. Old women cease to scold and the soldiers do not jostle. See in the market as they move, ripples of smiles upon the face of the people, spreading amongst the throng. Such is the power of Marduk. See you that **golden glow that wraps them as one that is the mark of his power** [emphasis added]. It is not the power of Ishtar, much more fiery and passionate. Marduk's power spreads peace in man.[12]

In the bible, Babylon is described as a sinful city, and the Babylonians as a sinful people. Does the above description fit? This is indeed not a picture of a sinful people, or a sinful city. On the contrary, it is a picture of happy people living in a free world. The 'golden glow' is witnessing about something important. Did the people of Babylon know about the gold powder? Only the consuming of gold powder can explain the 'golden glow'. 'The mark of his power' was probably the characteristic of the power of Marduk and his relation to the humans. A power Enlil/Yahweh didn't want anybody to practice on Earth. He wanted the secret of the gold to be preserved in the heavens. That would explain why Enlil wished not only to defeat Marduk, but also destroy the city of Babylon and its inhabitants. That would explain why he instigated a war program of such magnitude that would go on until Babylon was no more.

The 'sins' of the people of Babylon was then nothing else, than the consuming of gold powder, the same 'sin' as the people of the Canaanite cities of the Anakim. But while 'the golden glow' of the Babylonians was considered as evil, the 'golden glow' that wraps Jesus and his mother is considered as something godly. In fact, the cause could have been the same! The life of the free and happy citizens of Babylon is witnessing of a different world that the one created for us by Enlil/Yahweh. Unfortunately, we are unknowing of why we are deprived of that world and by whom!

As we have seen, these Anunnaki people had no democracy on their own planet, not on Earth either. Like the humans still solving most of their problems by using power, so did the gods themselves.

A Babylonian woman, around the year 2000 BCE, said to her husband:

"Dear husband, since we expect another child, we would need more space. As a bricklayer you could easily build one."

"In the name of Marduk and Nabu, I will take care of that," the husband said.

Marduk stepped down to the lowest level of the Esagil to speak to his people.

"We, the gods of Babylon, and you the free citizens of Babylon, have together established freedom, the very foundation for a bright future."

---

[1] Zecharia Sitchin, The Lost Book of Enki, p. 304
[2] Ibid., p. 306
[3] http://dictionary.reference.com/search?r=67&q=sodomy
[4] Zecharia Sitchin, The Lost Book of Enki, p. 307
[5] Ibid., p. 309
[6] Ibid., p. 310–311
[7] Ibid., p. 312
[8] Laurence Gardner, Lost Secrets of the Sacred Ark, p. 196
[9] Ibid., p. 114–115
[10] Ibid., p. 316
[11] From 'www.gatewaytobabylon.com/gods/lords/marduk1.html'
[12] From the same website 'Phoenician letters'

Chapter 14

DESTROY BABYLON

The Wars of Enlil

'By Enlil was Shar-ru-kin empowered; Inanna with her
weapons of brilliance his warriors accompanied'
Sargon I

Under some 1800 years, from ca 2300 BCE until ca 500 BCE, the whole area from the Mediterranean Sea to the Persian Gulf was in war in the name of the gods. Kings and Empires succeeded one another through divine aid. One after another the empires of those times were exchanging borders, capitals and gods. Sometimes, even language and culture. The boarders of the city-states of Sumer, which later became Akkad, the borders of the Babylonian and Assyrian empires, and the borders of the Hittite empire, were under continual floating. Under the Babylonian era of greatness, the Assyrians became 'Babylonized', while under the Akkadian era of greatness, Akkadian language was the 'diplomatic' language of the time.

Directly after the appearance of Babylon, about 2370 BCE, one of the main targets of the Enlilites was to destroy the city and everything it stood for. There was a systematic order in the attacks. Not only according to the law of action-reaction, but according to the plan of Enlil/Yahweh. We humans are of course able to start wars for reasons like the control of natural resources, borders, independence and many other things. One would think that the wars of those times started because every king or emperor, with strong enough army,

141

wished to test his power, expand his county's borders, answer for some attack, or to secure some trade routes. The problem has always been that any victory or defeat, was leading to a future victory or defeat.

Historians always try to find some reason for the wars of those times, which is always an easy thing to do, even if there is no obvious reason of the kind we are used to. It is difficult to believe that most of those wars, perhaps every one of them were initiated and directed by the Anunnaki. Since we use to exclude this reason, we are unable to understand the events of those times. We are unable to believe that some king would start war against another city, or another country, because some god ordered him to do that. Yet, the wars we refer to here were all well planned in advanced, and ordered by the alien Anunnaki. In fact, many wars were scheduled hundreds of years in advance, which is not easy for us to understand. Helping a king to organize, reorganize, unity, or just create a new kingdom to use the military powers of the kingdom in fifty, or hundred years or so, is quite normal for the 'immortal' Anunnaki. For us on the other side, such a long time constitutes an obstacle because such long-term projects have a very different meaning, as they are limited to the boundaries of our lifetime.

All Anunnaki, including Enlil, had to accept Marduk's Supremacy (2027 BCE) since the event had been approved by Anu. As the Supreme god of the gods, Marduk was also the king of Earth. Earth was considered as a Nibiruan colony.

For some of the gods it must have been hard to accept. In addition, they had to obey the man they had been fighting for a long time. Now it was a time of cooperation, if they liked it or not. All of them had to contribute with whatever they could, to make a good start for the human civilization. Probably ordered by the king of the gods. If they really cooperated for some common purpose, then this was the last time they did so. From now on, they would rather make plans about how to destroy one another.

Hamurrabi, the Babylonian king who is most known for his famous 'Code of Laws', is supposed to have reigned between 1792–1750 BCE. Hammu-rabi, or Hammu-rapi means probably 'Kinsman healer'. As a son of Marduk, 'the seed was implanted in his mother by the Sun god', Hamu-Ra-Bi could mean 'The son of the bright father'. The first known Babylonian king, if one does not count Nimrod, was Sumu-abum 1894–1881 BCE. Although the dates are highly uncertain, the reign of Hammurabi is closed enough to the time Marduk's Supremacy began. In his declaration of the intro-duction of the 'Code of law', he had some very interesting things to say. His extremely accurate description of the character of some gods, witness that he, either knew them personally, or he had a very good knowledge about them. We quote the epilogue of 'Hamurrabi's 'Code of Laws' by Phillip Martin.

> Hamurrabi is a ruler, who is as a father to his subjects, who holds the words of Marduk in reverence, who has achieved conquest for Marduk over the north and south, who rejoices the heart of Marduk, his lord, who has bestowed benefits for ever and ever on his subjects, and has established order in the land . . .

The new order in the land was probably meant to expand all over the world. Although Serpanit, the wife of Marduk, died in the Americas long before the time of Hammurabi, it seems that Marduk had some image of her in the temple. It was a sign of veneration and love. A good wife with a very short life compared to his. Hamurrabi con-tinues:

> When he reads the record, let him pray with full heart to Mar-duk, my lord, and Zarpanit, my lady; . . .

The 'Code of Law', was a contribution by Utu/Shamash, and was a part of a great civilizing program, launched by Marduk.

> Hamurrabi, the king of righteousness, on whom Shamash has conferred right (or law) am I.

Then Hammurabi goes on to describe how the particular gods would punish his successors, or some other ruler, who would distance him-self from the law.

- If this ruler do not esteem my words . . . if he destroy the law which I have given, corrupt my words, . . . may the great God (Anu), the Father of the gods, who has ordered my rule, with-draw from him the glory of royalty, break his sceptre, curse his destiny.

- May Bel, the lord, who fixeth destiny, whose command cannot be altered,, who has made my kingdom great, order a rebellion which his hand cannot control: . . .
- May Ea, the great ruler, whose fated decrees come to pass, the thinker of the gods, the omniscient, who maketh long days of my life, withdraw understanding and wisdom from him . . .
- May Shamash, the great Judge of heaven and earth, who supporteth all means of livelihood, Lord of life-courage, shatter his dominion, annul his laws . . .
- May Sin (the Moon-god), the lord of Heaven, the divine father, whose crescent gives light among the gods, take away the crown and regal throne from him; may he put upon him heavy guilt, great decay, . . .
- May Adad, the lord of fruitfulness, ruler of heaven and earth, my helper, withhold him rain from heaven, and the flood of water from the springs, destroy the land by famine and want; . . .
- May Zamama, the great warrior, the first-born son of E-kur, who goeth at my right hand, shatter his weapons on the field of battle, turn day to night, and let his foe triumph over him.
- May Ishtar, the goddess of fighting and war, who unfetters my weapons, my gracious protecting spirit, who loveth my dominion, curse his kingdom in her angry heart; . . .
- May Nergal, the might among the gods, whose contest is irresistible, who grants me victory, in his great might bum up his subjects like a slender reedstalk, cut off his limbs with his mighty weapons, and scattered him like an earthen image.
- May Nin-tu, the sublime mistress of the lands, the fruitful mother, deny him a son, vouchsafe him no name, give him no successor among men.
- May Nin-karak, the daughter of Anu, who adjudges grace to me, cause to come upon his members in E-kur high fever, sever wounds, that cannot be healed, . . .[1]

Hammurabi succeeded to supply a lot of information in a few words about the characteristics of some gods. The most important statement is that Anu had ordered his rule. The fact that Hammurabi was appointed by Marduk, the legal King of Earth and approved by Anu, the King of the gods, makes any attack on Babylon illegal. Consequently, the wars of the Enlilites against the Commander Marduk were as illegal as the wars of Marduk against the Commander Enlil. We also note that the gods cooperated to establish a righteous world kingdom, contributing according to their skills, and powers. The punishment they eventually would use, would also be according to their skills and powers. Here are some of their skills, and properties, described by Hammurabi.

Marduk: At the time, the king of gods and men.

Shamash (Utu): The lawyer of the Gold Mission.

Anu: Powerful father of the gods.

Ea: The thinker of the gods.

Nannar/Sin: He could put on, or take away the crown. It is witnessing of his great power in the former Enlilite lands.

Ishkur/Adad: Could withhold rain, and destroy lands by famine, certainly through using some advance chemical weapons. Famine could also due to natural circumstances. But there are a lot of examples in the bible where Enlil/Yahweh used both famine and plagues directed, at will, at both certain locations and people.

Zamama (Ninurta): The great warrior with powerful weapons.

Ishtar: The goddess of war. She had access to all advanced weapons of the House of Enlil.

Nergal: Mighty avenger with mighty weapons.

Nin-karak (Nin-khursaq): Could cause high fever and wounds because of her advanced medical skills; fever and wounds that could not be healed.

The above descriptions are well in accordance with their deeds on Earth. Another important information given by Hammurabi, or actually, not given by him, is the absence of Enlil. He is not mentioned here at all. Perhaps he only needed to accept Marduk's supremacy, but could not be forced to cooperate with him. His absence could also mean that he was not interested in establishing an everlasting kingdom that eventually was to be taken over by the humans, despite his promise that he and his son, Ninurta, would no longer stand in Marduk's way.

Another missing important personality is Ningishzidda/Thoth. The reason could have been his aversion to participate in politics and conflicts, or perhaps he had already left Earth.

Babylon was not just a city. It was the capital city of the world. It also represented the united spirit of gods and men against the Gold Mission.

Although the master Enlil/Yahweh threatened Babylon at several occasions, and sent many armies against the city and its gods, he never explained what 'evil' things they had done. We can, however, read between the lines.

The Assyrian empire raised with the support of Adad, a son of Enlil/Yahweh. The Assyrians, like the Gutaeans before them, were powerful long before they attacked Sumer and Babylon, at the command of Enlil. Of the 86 kings of Assyria, from the Old Assyrian period, ca 1900 BCE, through the Middle Assyrian period, to the Neo Assyrian period, and its last king, Ashur-uballit II, (609 BCE), 56 of them had names associated with Enlil, Ashur (Enlil), Sin, Adad, Ninurta, and Ishtar. Names like, Enlil-Kabkabu, Ashurbanipal, Nasir-Sin, Eriba-Adad, Tukulti-Ninurta, Ibqi-Ishtar, and the like.

Of the 35 known-by-name kings of the Akkadian Empire, the name of 19 of them was associated with Ashur, Sin, and Adad. Kings we know were elevated to power by the Enlilites, like Sargon, and some others, not counted. It was also usual that some gods fathered many of those kings through mating with hierodules. Those 'related' kings were all devoted to Enlil and his family members. Not all of the priestesses, however, wished to have children with the gods. Being the hierodules of the gods, they certainly wished that their children, whom, in many cases, were conceived against their will, would be sent free, like in the case of Sargon I. Despite his mother's efforts to hide him away from the gods, he was later found by Inanna and appointed as king of Akkad.

The names of most Babylonian kings are associated with Marduk and Nabu, like Eriba-Marduk (769–761 BCE), or Nabu-shuma-ishkun (761–748 BCE). But since Babylon had, at different times, been under Assyrian and Akkadian dominance, there had been several kings with names like, Enlil-nadin-apli, Adad-apla-iddina, Ninurta-kudurri-usur, or Shamash-mudammiq. Although many 'nations flowed together in Babylon', according to Yahweh, the human defenders of Babylon could not always stand against the angel warriors of Yahweh, and their 'weapons of brilliance'. Despite the fact that Anu himself appointed Marduk as the king of the gods on Earth, recognized by all the gods, the Enlilites launched a long-term program of wars against him. Probably Marduk had not even the technical equipment needed to 'beam' the news to Anu. The Enlilites could broke the 'covenant' since they alone had such equipment. They could send a message telling Anu something like, 'From earth nothing new', while they were in the move to destroy the basement of the human civilization.

The wars of Enlil/Yahweh were always directed against Babylon and Egypt. His agents/prophets were very happy about the threats against Babylon and Egypt, like Isaiah 13:19:

> And Babylon, the glory of kingdoms, the beauty of the Caldees' excellency, shall be as when God overthrew Sodom and Gomorra.

Despite the fact that Babylon was regarded as 'the glory of kingdoms', and a beautiful city, the scribe of Isaiah is full of joy regarding the destruction of the city. The same applies to Ezekiel 29:9.

> And the land of Egypt shall be desolate and waste; and they shall know that I am the LORD: because he hath said, The river is mine, and I have made it.

He would destroy Egypt too. 'The river is mine'? He also said 'the gold is mine'. We wouldn't be surprised had he said 'the Earth is mine'! We know, on the other hand, that Earth was administrated by the alien colonial power, the Kingdom of heaven! He says that he could also direct Babylon and Egypt against each other, according to Ezekiel 29:25–26:

> But I will strengthen the arms of the king of Babylon, and the arms of Pharaoh shall fall down; and they shall know that I am the LORD, when I shall put my sword into the hand of the king of Babylon, and he shall stretch it out upon the land of Egypt.

> And I will scatter the Egyptians among the nations, and disperse them among the countries; and they shall know that I am the LORD.

There was never any legal right allowing him, or anybody else, to bring destroy people and their habitations. The reason, according to him, was that they would know that 'he was the Lord'. They would be forced to accept him as Lord, even through criminal actions! Assyrian kings marched against Babylon, Akkadian kings marched against Babylon, the Hittites marched against Babylon, the Kassites and other people from the Zagros-mountains marched against Babylon. What was so important about Babylon for the attackers?

The Enlilites had elevated many of the kings of those empires to power, with the sole purpose to destroy Babylon. Many of them did sack Babylon too, while others became conquered by Babylon's beauty and the Babylonian civilization. The second target of those wars was always Egypt. Most of the wars against Egypt, were the wars of the gods, planned, initiated, powered when needed, ordered by them and executed by humans. The well-organized wars of Enlil/Yahweh against Babylon and Egypt have all the characteristics of organized terrorism.

Babylon was forced to defend itself against the surrounding enemies. If there was an original plan ordered by Anu, to cooperate with Marduk for the benefit of the human civilization, that plan was not followed any more. The task to defend Babylon was enormous, even for a well-organized army. Even for people and soldiers who had something valuable to defend. But neither the Babylonians, nor Marduk, could stand against some kings who were armed with powerful and effective weapons, given to them by the Enlilites. Obviously, that was the only way to defeat the Babylonian army. Such weapons were used at several occasions.

Some of those kings declared proudly by themselves, or through their official secretaries, that they had the support of some gods, in several ways. Here are some of these declarations.

Sargon I, (Shar-ru-kin, means probably 'The Earthly Prince'), king of Akkad, (2399–2343 BCE), the first to unite the Sumerian cities, the founder of the Sargonite dynasty of Akkad, and the builder of a brand new capital, Agade, says:

Sceptre and crown Enlil him gave, Sharru-kin, Rightenous Regent, Enlil him appointed . . .

By Enlil was Sharru-kin empowered; Inanna with her weapons of brilliance his warriors accompanied.[2]

Appointed by Enlil, powered by Enlil, and accompanied by the goddess of war, Inanna. Certainly there was not any army on Earth that could stand against the alien 'weapons of brilliance'. Such weapons must have been as effective as the name suggests. Sometimes the gods were desperate enough to use such weapons against humans armed with bows or spears. Many of the wars were also the desperate wars of the Enlilites and their increasing desperation. All of them could be classified as 'unpermitted' wars against Marduk, just to use the same word Enlil/Yahweh used to describe Marduk's building of the Tower. Without those 'weapons of brilliance' they would lose, forced to give up the gold mission and go home. Human freedom fighters, like Nimrod who probably knew about the gold mission, and devoted their lives to stop it, would become humanity's heroes. Humanity would have a 'General Code of Law' instead of 'Holy Books'.

The gods could also replace a king as easily as elevating him on the throne. There are several such examples.

Naram-Sin, (2390-2334 or 2291-2235 BC), a grandson of Sargon I, committed some 'sacrileges', although ordered by Inanna, and had been punished by Enlil. The Fourth region was a place of the Celestial Chariots in Sinai, accessed only by the gods. Enki says:

> The sacrilege of an Earthlings' army through the Fourth Region passing Naram-Sin committed, Magan he invaded, the sealed Ekur, House Which Like a Mountain Is, to enter he attempted.

> By the sacrileges and transgressions Enlil was infuriated; upon Naram-Sin and Agade a curse he put:

> By a bite of a scorpion did Naram-Sin die, by the command of Enlil was Agade wiped out.[3]

Ur-Nammu (2112–2094 BC) king of Akkad appointed by Enlil's son Nannar/Sin. In a text named 'Atigi to Enlil for Ur-Namma' from earth-history.com we read:

> Lord Nunamnir gave to my king the lofty mace which heaps up human heads like piles of dust in the hostile foreign countries and smashes the rebellious lands; he gave to the shepherd Ur-Namma . . .

'Heaps up human heads', they were quite destructive weapons indeed. The conclusion is that, without those weapons, human history would certainly have taken other paths of development. Perhaps paths that would have lead us to healthy lives through the consuming of the gold powder. Something Enlil/Yahweh was intended to stop at any cost. Even by 'heaping up human heads'.

Shulgi, (2094-2046 BC), king of Akkad, son of Ur-Nammu, was appointed by Nannar/Sin and installed himself as king in Uruk. In the 'Hymn of praise to Shulgi' by N.S.Kramer, we read:

> He who was blessed by Enlil am I, . . .
> The mighty king of Nanna am I, . . .
> Shulgi chosen for the vulva of Inanna am I, . . .
> With virile Utu, my brother and friend,
> I drank beer in the palace founded by Anu, . . .
> Anu set the holy crown upon my head,
> Gave me to hold the scepter in the lapis lazuli Ekur, . . .
> Exalted there the power of my kingship,
> So that I bent over all the foreign lands,
> made secure the Land of Sumer [4]

Do we need to comment the statement 'exalted there the power of my kingship, so that I bent over all the foreign lands'?

The Hittite Empire in Eastern Anatolia was first under the influence of Ishkur/Adad, and later under the influence of Nannar/Sin. Adad, the Storm god, was the supreme god of the Hittites by the name Teshub, meaning 'storm god'.

The Hittite king Murshilis, (1620–1590 BC), attacked and plundered Babylon in 1595 BC.

He explains here what kind of help he received from the gods, some of them participating in the battles. In 'The Wars of Gods and Men' by Z. Sitchin, we read:

> The Mighty Storm god, my Lord ' [wrote the king Murshilis], 'showed his divine power and shot a thunderbolt' at the enemy, helping to defeat it. Also aiding the Hittites in battle was the goddess ISHTAR, whose epithet was 'Lady of the battlefield'. It was to her 'Divine Power' that many a victory was attributed, as she 'came down [from the sky] to smite the hostile countries' [5]

Enlil's son Ishkur/Adad and Enlil's granddaughter Inanna/Ishtar participated in battles, according to Murshilis, and even used air-crafts and advanced alien weapons against human armies. Inanna, the goddess of war, must have killed more humans than anyone else of the Enlilites. Her killings can also be classified as murders, since she pointed and fired her advanced weapons against human soldiers, armed with bows and spears, and even against civilians. Murshilis had no problem in acknowledging that it was indeed 'the thunder-bolt' that 'helped him to defeat his enemy'.

Shalmaneser III (859–842 BCE), son of Ashur-nasirpal, stated that he was an instrument in the hands of the gods and owed his victories to the weapons provided by Ashur and Nergal.

I was acting only upon the trustworthy commands given by Ashur, the great lord, my lord who loves me. . . .

I fought with the Mighty Force which Ashur, my lord, had given me; and with the strong weapons which Nergal, my leader, had presented to me.[6]

Esarchadon, (681–669 BC), king of Assyria, recounting his deeds against his enemies says: 'upon the trustworthy oracles of his lord Ashur'. He also received a trustworthy command from the gods say-ing:

Go, do not delay! We will march with you![7]

Both Esarchadon and his son and successor Ashurbanipal attempted to advance against Egypt. Both were in possession of 'Weapons of Brilliance'.

The terror-inspiring Brilliance of Ashur', Ashurbanipal wrote, 'blinded the Pharaoh so that he became a madman.

* * *

Ishtar, who dwells in Arbela, clad in Divine Fire and sporting the Radiant Headwear, rained flames upon Arabia'. [7]

'We will march with you'. They certainly marched with him. And with other kings as well. With 'weapons of brilliance' and many others advanced weapons. Those gods who killed more humans than any human ever did, are justified in the OT (Enlil/Yahweh and his angels) as doing right and their victims as doing wrong. Many writers, and the readers of their books, are now supporting the theory that Enlil/Yahweh and his messengers/angels have been manipulating us through the eons. Many of the victories described in our history books were, in reality, the victories of the alien gods and their alien weapons.

Ashurbanipal (669–627 BCE) king of the Neo-Assyrian period, son of Esarchaddon, was also a king supported by the Enlilites. Here is what he said:

> When Ashur, who selected me, who made my kingship great, entrusted his merciless weapon into my lordly arms, I verily struck down the widespread troops of Lullumu with weapons, during the battle encounter. As for the troops of the lands of Nairi, Habhu, Shubaru, and Nirbu, I roared over them like Adad the destroyer, with the aid of Shamash and Adad, my helper gods.[8]

The merciless and other advanced weapons, provided by the gods to several kings, were not only very effective weapons, but perhaps also weapons of mass destruction. Ashurbanipal is also known as the king who created the Royal library in the palace in Nineveh. He sent scribes to ancient places to make copies of the ancient works preserved there. He was also a well-educated man who says that he 'understood the wisdom of Nebo'. That means that the reputation of Nabu, the son of Marduk, was known widely outside the Babylonian Empire. The question is if Ashurbanipal knew that his wars were also directed against Nabu.

Enlil used 'prophecies' as parts of his plan, like the announcement that he would cause Babylon to dry up. Jeremiah 51:36, 44 informs about some plans of Yahweh concerning Babylon and Bel (Marduk).

> Therefore thus saith the LORD; Behold, I will plead the cause, and take vengeance for thee; and I will dry up her sea, and make her springs dry.

> And I will punish Bel in Babylon, and I; and the nations shall not flow together any more unto him: yea, the wall of Babylon shall fall.

The Assyrian king Sennacherib (6th century BCE), after the Babylonians revolted against Assyria, responded by opening the canals around Babylon (built by Marduk), which supported the city with water. The city was forced to starvation and surrender. It dried up. Most of its inhabitants were scattered. He also razed the walls, palaces and temples to the ground. The destruction of Babylon by Sennacherib had chocked the whole area around Mesopotamia, even the Enlilite cities of Sumer. Sennacherib was murdered some years later, probably by one of his sons. His successor, Esarhadon, rebuilt the city and made it the capital of the Assyrian/Babylonian Empire.

In order to understand this information, two options are available. Either the scribe of the book of Jeremiah was ordered by Enlil/Yahweh to reveal the plan in advance, or the story was written after the destruction of Babylon. The latter is witnessing that Jeremiah was just forwarding a historical fact within the boundaries of the same systematic propaganda aimed to ascribe almost every historical event as 'the work of Yahweh'.

Of great interesting is the statement 'and the nations shall not flow together any more unto him'. The only way it can be understood is that Marduk/Bel and his policy was popular among the humans. Not because he was powerful, but because he was a friend of the humans, treating them as equals. Marduk's popularity and power was expanding and the nations wished to establish good relations with Babylon. Enlil/Yahweh's power was much greater, but his popularity among the humans was quite absent.

The allegiance of so many nations was unacceptable to Enlil/Yahweh. Neither gods, who decided or forced to stay on Earth, nor humans would be allowed to consume gold powder. Enlil would 'bring forth out of his mouth (Marduk's) that which he hath swallowed up'. But he was not intended to fight Marduk on some ideological level. Neither was he intended to use civilized methods to win the sympathy of the Babylonians, and other people. Enlil was intended to use alien advanced weapons to brake down Babylonia and its god. Marduk was not to be allowed to rule Earth.

These are just a few examples of witnesses by the kings elevated to power by the Enlilites. The kings, or their secretaries had passed the above historical declarations to us, in order to show their greatness to their people, unknowing of the fact that they also left evidence behind them. They were proud as being selected by the great gods. They just knew no better. Do we?

The 'gods of war', the Enlilites, is not something we invented. It's history! Ishtar, the goddess of war and Ninurta-Ares-Mars, the god of war were highly real. The warlike character of them, in the wars against Babylon and Egypt, is not different from the character of the deities of the OT. We are able to compare them, thanks to documented evidence left behind by their own kings and their own agents.

The wars of those times were the wars of gods and men. Initiated by the gods and executed by humans. If you wonder why Assyria, or Akkad, or the Hittites so badly wanted to destroy Babylon, the answer is because Enlil/Yahweh ordered them to do that, in the same way he ordered the Jews to hate Babylon, Egypt and their gods. He chose the kings. He instructed them. He powered them. He directed them. He sent his warrior-angels, his children and grand children, to march with them, because he wished to neutralize Marduk's program and human development.

Marduk and his family members could not be allowed to supply the humans with gold powder. Enlil/Yahweh had other plans. No more than that? It was more.

As we shall soon see, there were wars, manipulations, establishing of religions, genocides and much more. Those historical events were directly connected with the Gold Mission of Enlil/Yahweh on Earth. From now on, he would also erase any sign of their Mission on Earth. He does not want us to know that any gods ever been here except the one and only God. He would confuse our memories so that we wouldn't be able to distinguish between god and God. A God, that according to the Cathars, and probably the Templars too, was not 'a god one'. Have we always been able to make war, or are we just imitating the gods of war?

---

[1] www.phillipmartin.info/hammurabi/hammurabi/_epilogue.htm
[2] Zecharia Sitchin, The Lost Book of Enki, p. 300
[3] Ibid., p. 302
[4] www.gatewaytobabylon, Hymn of praise to Shulgi by N.S. Kramer
[5] Zecharia Sitchin, The wars of gods and men, p. 5
[6] Ibid., p. 14
[7] Ibid., p. 18, 19
[8] www.metmuseum.org/explore/anesite/html/el_ane_inscript.htm by Samuel M. Peley

Chapter 15

EXODUS—THE APPEARANCE OF YAHWEH

The Army of God and the genocide of the Anakim

The exodus of the Hebrews from Egypt is regarded as, either history or mythology. The event, first described in the OT, has, during the last hundred years been deeply studied in hundreds of books. The time of this event has constantly been discussed, as well as the 'manna' and the Ark of the Covenant. According to Laurence Gardner in his excellent book 'Genesis of the Grail Kings', the exodus occurred during the reign of Amenhotep IV (1367–1361 BC) who succeeded Amenhotep III by marrying his half-sister Nefertiti. Amenhotep IV then changed his name to Akhenaten IV and he was indeed no other than Moses himself.

Interesting to note that the father of Amenhotep III (1405–1367) was Tuthmosis IV (1413–1405) who says have founded the Brother-hood of the Snake. There is no supporting evidence that the brother-hood of the Snake, or the brotherhood of the Serpent, as the original name was, was founded by Tuthmosis as it was of much ancient origin. However, Tuthmosis might have corrupted the brotherhood according to some instructions by the new god, Aten, probably just another name of Enlil. The House of Enki/Ptah had been using the serpent as an emblem, thousands of years earlier and probably founded the brotherhood too, with the purpose to handle knowledge to the humans.

155

Since the brotherhood had a good reputation, Enlil-Adon-Aten decided to make use of it. But first it had to be corrupted and cleared of such elements like 'Enki/Ptah', 'Thoth' or 'gold dust'. The corruption by Tuthmosis was intended to spread disinformation instead of useful knowledge.

Another important fact, about two centuries before the exodus, was the invasion of Egypt by Semitic people, probably from Canaan and Syria. They have been called the 'Hyksos' by Manetho and for some reason also 'the shepherd kings'. Their dynasty held Egypt for five hundred and eleven years, according to the Jewish historian Flavius Josephus (37–100 CE). They accepted the Egyptian ways of life but didn't succeed to be integrated into the Egyptian society. Probably because they were cruel, burned down the cities and destroyed the temples of the Egyptian gods. That could have been the main purpose of the invasion. Their last king, Khamudi, had been forced to withdraw his army, from the capital of Avaris, to the east.

Manetho, who wrote a complete account of the Hyksos in his book 'Aegyptiaca' (about Egypt), was an Egyptian priest who was commissioned by Ptolemy II to write down the history of ancient Egypt. Flavius Josephus quoted many passages from Manetho concerning the Hyksos. One of these passages in Book I 'Against Apion', he says:

> Under a king of ours named Timaus God became angry with us, I know not how, and there came, after a surprising manner, men of obscure birth from the east, and had the temerity to invade our country, and easily conquered it by force, as we did not do battle against them.

Was Marduk, the god of the Egyptians, angry or was he unable to stop the attack of those 'obscure people' that Enlil/Yahweh might have sent. Manetho says that those 'men of obscure birth' came from 'the east', most likely, the lands of the Enlilites. We shall now take a look at some important facts of that time never being the main theme of any book.

1. The God of Abraham, Enlil/El-Shadai, was responsible for the 'immigration' of the Hebrews into Egypt. The God of the Israelites, Enlil/Yahweh was the main protagonist under their 'emigration' out of Egypt.

2. The introduction of the new god, Aten in Egypt, sometime before the exodus, also initiated by some deity after a 'vision' in the sky.
3. The 'borrowing' of gold by the Hebrews just before their departure, ordered by Enlil/Yahweh.
4. The mysterious 'wandering' in the desert under forty years, demanded and administrated by Enlil/Yahweh.
5. The genocide of the population of the cities of Jericho, Ai, Ashdod, Gibeon and other cities, also ordered by Yahweh.

The God of Exodus
The God of the Israelites was the same as the God of Abraham, i.e. the chief deity of the Sumerian pantheon, Enlil.

Long before Moses, Enlil informed Abraham about the exodus which was to happen in the future. Since not even Enlil had the ability of foreseeing the future, the only logical explanation of 'how he knew it was going to happen' is that he was the one administrating the happenings. So not only the exodus of the Hebrews out of Egypt but also the 'immigration' of them into Egypt, was a work of his and his companions, according to plan. An evil plan, one could say, but a plan successfully executed, step by step, aided by fear, promises, threats and superior power demonstrations. Genesis 15:13–14:

> And he [the Lord] said unto Abraham, Know of a surety that thy seed shall be a stranger in a land that is not theirs, and shall serve them; and they shall afflict them four hundred years; And also that nation, whom they shall serve, will I judge: and afterward shall they come out with great substance.

We understand from the above that it was Enlil/Yahweh who influenced some Jews to immigrate to Egypt. It was he who decided how long they would stay there. It was he who decided that they, when leaving, would 'borrow' as much gold and silver as they could.

Moses, being a wise and well-educated man, saw that this god, who was eating and drinking and had a terrible temperament, was a human being, naturally he asked him: 'what is your name?' Enlil, who didn't want to reveal his name, answered 'YHWH'. The mystical 'name' was not to be uttered and thus easier to associate with God. Perhaps he wished to say something like 'don't bother about my name'. The 'no-name' became indeed a name, 'Yahweh' or 'Jehovah', which the Israelites were forbidden to utter. This word 'YHWH' is supposed to be in Hebrew, meaning 'I am that I am', but it is doubly that Enlil could speak Hebrew. In fact it is more likely that the demigod Moses could speak Enlil's own language. This is strengthening by the fact that Enlil never spoke directly to the Hebrews, but always through Moses or through messengers.

What was the purpose of the exodus out of Egypt? It seems that the main purpose was to free the Jews from the Egyptian slavery. It seems so, yes, although one of the real purposes of the drama was to hurt Egypt. We shall soon see which was the other one.

Egypt was the domain of Enlil's adversary Marduk. Enlil and his clan were in war with Marduk and his followers. Babylon was also Marduk's city. As we have seen, all the wars initiated by Enlil/Jehovah and his clan, were against Marduk, against Babylon and against Egypt.

In order to take the Israelites out of Egypt and spoil Egypt at the same time, he had to take them there in the first place, and wait until they multiplied enough and be an important factor in the Egyptian economy. At the same time, they would be customized to the Egyptian culture, knowledge and traditions. Plagues were also used to spoil the economy of the Egyptians, as Exodus 11:1 states.

> And the Lord said unto Moses, Yet will bring one plague more upon Pharaoh, and upon Egypt; afterwards he will let you go hence: when he shall let you go, he shall surely thrust you out hence altogether.

The god of wonders, the all-powerful god, wants us to believe that he had to destroy much of the life supporting resources of the country, kill numerous innocent people, in order to get some other people out of there. The plagues sent by God at different times, in different places, did indeed great damage, by killing people, animals, destroying herbs and waters. It was certainly the work of the 'Storm god', Ishkur/Adad, a son of Enlil/Yahweh. His temple was called 'the house of the seven storms'. Is it possible that a single man could cause storms, plagues, or withhold rain from falling down to earth? Why did those people associate Adad with storms? Unless they knew that it was some special ability of his through using chemical weapons. In that case, the plagues, and the storms were mass destruction chemical, and biological weapons.

Enlil/Yahweh and his messengers may have been in a warlike situation with Marduk, but they were not in war with the Egyptians. Then, the desolation of the land through mass destruction weapons and the killing of innocent people could be classified as acts of terrorism. In the OT, 'terrorism' is regarded as 'divine punishment'. The word 'terrorist' is just another word for 'evil'. Marduk was a terrorist according to the Enlilites. Had Marduk been successful in fighting Enlil/Yahweh, he would be called freedom fighter and liberator while Enlil/Yahweh would be called terrorist.

Here are some of the evil actions against the Egyptians at the time of exodus. In the 'Admonitions of Ipuwer' 1 that is supposed to have been written at that time (several dates exist), we can find remarkable parallels to the biblical passages. Exodus 7:21 and 9:6:

And the fish that was in the river died; and the river stank, and the Egyptians could not drink of the water of the river; and there was blood throughout all the land of Egypt.

. . . and all the cattle of Egypt died: but of the cattle of children of Israel died not one.

Admonitions of Ipuwer 2:5–6 and 2:10:

Plague is throughout the land. Blood is everywhere.

The River is blood.

Although it sounds like a miracle that all the cattle of the Egyptians died but not the cattle of the Israelites, this is another evidence that they could control the use of the chemical and biological weapons.

The plagues of Egypt are often connected to the volcanic explosion on the island of Thera. The results of this enormous explosion certainly devastated the Knossos civilization on Crete and stroke Egypt too. But it is supposed to have happened at 1628 BCE while the exodus of the Israelites occurred sometime around the year 1350 BCE. We often seek explanations caused by nature, although sometimes the reason is the very nature of Yahweh.

The time of the exodus was also carefully selected. Although the time varies from 1447 BCE to 1250 BCE, the most common opinion is that the exodus started about 1350 BCE. In any case, the exodus occurred between two other significant events, the Argonautic Quest and the Trojan War, where Enlil/Zeus was involved too. At this time, we find 'Enlilite' kings in the whole of Middle East.

Babylon was ruled by the Kassite dynasty from ca 1570–1153 BCE. Kadashman-Enlil was king of Babylon 1377–1361 BCE. Ashur-Uballit was king of Assyria 1353-1317 BCE, succeeded by Enlil-Ninari 1317-1307 BCE. Murshili II was king of the Hettites 1375–1358. Akhenaten was ruling Egypt. All of them were appointed by the Enlilite brotherhood. That means that Marduk was not able to defend neither Egypt nor Babylon at that time. The Enlilites ruled everywhere aided by the 'Weapons of Brilliance' and the angel-gang.

Aten, a New God in The Egyptian History

Egypt's great god was Amun/Ra, the Sun god. In Babylon, after Marduk was declared and accepted as the Supreme god, he assigned himself the attributes of all the other gods. Probably was Enlil/Jehovah doing the same thing in Egypt by introducing Aten, or Aton, (Phoenician Adon 'my Lord'), who was supposed to replace Marduk-Amun-Ra. Akhen-Aten (means 'Servant of Aten') IV (1350–1334 BCE), declared Aten as the sole god of the Egyptians, a concept that later spawned both Judaism and Christianity. In order to make the introduction of Aten easy to accept, Aten was attributed with the sun disc, the very symbol of Ra.

Amenhotep III had a daughter with the queen Sitamun, Nefertiti, and a son named Akhenaten, with the second queen Tiye, who was a descendant of a Hebrew tribe. He was 'a prince from among the Egyptians' as Enlil/Yahweh said to Abraham hundreds of years earlier. Akhenaten was able to succeed his father by marrying his half sister Nefertiti. After he moved the capital of the country from Thebes to El-Amarna, he then ordered the destruction of the temples of Amun/Ra, his statues, and all the worship sites. This was not popular however, since Amun/Ra had been the great god of the Egyptians for ages, and the priests of Amun were very loyal to him. In order to lessen the political power of the priests of Amun, he declared that he was the sole link between the new god Aten and the people.

How could that happen? It is said that he was guided by a vision to introduce a new god in Egypt. The vision he observed in the skies was a sun disc between two mountains. He thought that Aten was guiding him to build a new capital between two mountains, El Amarna. The Temple of Akhenaten at El Amarna had the shape of a cross, the symbol of the home planet of the Anunnaki, later also adopted by Christianity. He does not say how he knew the name of the god. It is not far fetched to suspect Enlil/Yahweh or some of his 'angels' for the 'projection' of the vision. When it comes to the introduction of new gods, or new prophets, and the like, the vision-technique was both popular and effective. It was to be used more often in the future.

Akhenaten's introduction of 'the sole god' was not without opposition. The priests of Amun refused to accept him. They considered him as an intruder in the Egyptian pantheon. He was, finally, forced to abdicate in 1334 BCE, and succeeded by Smenkhare (1336–1334 BCE) who was supposed to have been, either a son of Akhenaten with another wife, or his cousin. It seems that there were two Pharaohs at the same time, between 1336–1334 BCE. While Akhenaten was still formally the Pharaoh, Smenkhare was the de facto Pharaoh. Akhenaten was then somewhere else under those two years, perhaps administrating the exodus as Moses. That could also explain the fact that Akhenaten's son, Tutankh-Aten, became Pharaoh first after his father abdicated. The young Tutankh-Aten, (1334–1325 BCE), changed his name to Tutankh-Amun (or Tutankh-Amon), partly to calm down and please the priests of Amun, but also because Aten was a completely unknown god. There was never any reason for the Egyptians to replace their great god Amun with a new one that meant nothing to them.

The capital was again moved to Thebes, and the Egyptians turned back to their old familiar gods. Tutankh-amun's generals, Ay and Horemheb, re-established the temples of Amun, and selected priests from the military to keep tighter control, and hinder that it would happen again. Almost all memories of Akhenaten were destroyed and attempt was made to erase even his name. Order was reestablished and the attempt to capture the Egyptian kingdom from the inside was ended in failure.

The man who instructed Akhenaten could have been Enlil/Yahweh. He was about to start the exodus of the Jews from Egypt. If he could get control over Egypt, get the Jews out of the land and spoil Egypt at the same time, then it would be only one task left for him to do, as we soon shall see. The same attempt was to be repeated later in Babylon by his son Sin, where he tried to replace Marduk with himself. The introduction of Akhenaten could be related to the emerging of the exodus. There are no records that Marduk was involved in the fall of Akhenaten, although not impossible. As we have seen earlier, many events in the human history were directed by the conflict between Enlil/Yahweh and Marduk/Amun.

Just before the Israelites left Egypt Enlil/Yahweh punished the Egyptians by killing the first born of every family. That means that he killed adults, teenagers and children, men and women. It is not possible for anybody, Christian or not, to accept that the benevolent almighty God killed innocent people. Exodus 12:29 and 12:30:

> And it came to pass, that at midnight the LORD smote all the firstborn in the land of Egypt, from the firstborn of pharaoh that sat on his throne unto the firstborn of the captive that was in the dungeon; and all the firstborn of cattle.

> . . . There was not a house where there was not one dead.

Admonitions of Ipuwer 4:3:

> Forsooth, the children of princes are dashed against the walls.

The hands of the alien warriors of Yahweh, and their advanced weapons were upon the children of Egypt.

By our laws, and surely by the Egyptian laws of that time, the penalty for such a crime, would certainly be the death penalty.

We have to understand that human life was not high valuated by this man. The action of killing so many innocent people seems to us very unnecessary. Since the Egyptian Pharaoh, Akhenaten, was his agent, there should not have been any resistance against the exodus. According to Immanuel Velikovsky in his book 'Ages in chaos', 'the killing was much more extensive'.

> According to Haggadic tradition, not only the firstborn but the majority of the population in Egypt was killed during the tenth plague.

The plagues were certainly caused by mass destruction weapons. It was certainly nothing 'divine' about the plagues. It was simply a war dominated by dirty weapons against civilians. Soldiers and murderers have always justified their killing by citing such statements in the bible. World leaders and church leaders have also searched justification of their actions in the bible. The bible has been a great source of manipulative inspirations for two millennia. Then, as the commander of a fleet of flying vessels, he gave the Israelites aerial guidance day and night.

Gold and Silver
In the book of Exodus, the word 'gold' occurs 105 times, silver, brass and jewels uncounted. Why the need of gold? To spoil the Egyptians does not appear as a good argument. Rather like an under cover operation. Exodus 3:22 and 11:2 state:

> But every woman shall borrow of her neighbour, and of her that sojourneth in her house, jewels of silver, and jewels of gold and raiment: and ye shall put them upon your sons, and upon your daughters; and ye shall spoil the Egyptians.

> Speak now in the ears of the people, and let every man borrow of his neighbour, and every woman borrow of her neighbour, jewels of silver, and jewels of gold.

'Speak in the ears of the people' means 'must be kept as secret'. He said, he wished to spoil the Egyptians. Comparing with the plagues, and killing of young men, this was a minor hit. The word 'borrow' is quite interesting. To borrow something while knowing they would never return the jewels was not a nice thing to do. But the commandment of the Lord could not be ignored. Then again the covering of the real purpose of 'borrowing' the jewels. The gold was smelt into a calf by the Israelites, and then transformed into gold dust by Moses, and Enlil/Jehovah. Moses himself tells the story in the passage below. The jewels were to play a major roll in this story, a roll that is directly associated with the Gold Mission. Exodus 32:20:

> And he took the calf which they had made, and burnt it in the fire, and ground it to powder, and strawed it upon the water, and made the children of Israel drink of it.

The gold calf didn't become powder by chance. The gold was indented to play a major roll from the beginning. That was the reason Enlil/Yahweh needed Moses, who had the knowledge 'of the metals of the earth and how to work them'. Enlil/Yahweh was using Moses, a man that knew how to transform gold into gold dust, although not at all as easy as it is described above. Moses had certainly access to advanced labs provided by Yahweh. The real reason was the extermination of the Anakim who also had that knowledge. Deuteronomy 9:21 says:

> And I took your sin, the calf which ye had made, and burnt it in fire, and stamped it, and ground it very small, even until it was as small as dust: and I cast the dust thereof into the brook that descended out of the mount.

The Wandering in the Desert

Enlil/Yahweh forced thousands of men, women and children to spend forty years in the desert. What was the reason? Exodus 20:2 explains:

> I am the LORD thy God, which have brought thee out of the land of Egypt, out of the house of bondage. Thou shall have no other gods before me.

The reason was to establish himself as 'Yahweh', whatever the word means. When he says 'I am the only god', he means 'I am the only god you are allowed to worship'. He was aware that people knew there were other gods as well. Exodus 18:11:

> Now I know that the LORD is greater than all gods: for in the thing wherein they dealt proudly he was above them.

Now consider Exodus 18:11 in modern words:
   'Now I know that this god has a higher position than all of them: for in the aircraft they act from he is the Commander'.
   He demanded total obedience to him and only him. For the Israelites there was no any council of Justice, no participation in any decisions, no possibility of choice. There was only one authority dominating their lives, the authority of Yahweh. Enlil/Yahweh became the only authority allowed. Laurence Gardner says:

> In the tradition of old Sumer, the Anunnaki gods sat in council at Nippur and decided all important matters by majority

vote. . . . From the dawn of the subsequent Hebrew culture, however, everything changed as Jehovah became ever more rationalized as an individual absolute-a unilateral overlord of all things.[2]

This was the price the Israelites had to pay for being helped out of Egypt. But that was not enough. He planned to use them for his own purpose. But first they have to multiply even more. He needed two new generations of young men. Young people are easier to manipulate. There are, of course, no other records concerning the forty years in the desert except for the OT. The scribes used to count forty years for every generation. By counting in this way, forty years are enough to raise not one but two generations. Exodus 22:29:

Thou shalt not delay to offer the first of thy ripe fruits, and of thy liquors; the firstborn of thy sons shalt thou give unto me.

It is easy to miss the essential part of the above passage as it is 'covered' by fruits and liquors!

The sons had to grow up like gods, eating of the ambrosia, the food of the gods, the gold dust, the bread they called 'manna'. By eating/drinking the gold powder for forty years, two new generations of young men were supposed to be something like the descriptions we already have seen. The manna could sustain a human for several days without food. The losing of weight could make a soldier much more effective. The high-spin of mind could make one to think faster. And of course they could live a bit longer. All appear to have been fine gifts from God. But they were no more gifts than the food provided to slaves, which was necessary in order to be able to perform the tasks assigned to them. The slave owner needed to feed his slaves as much as the slaves needed the food.

The gift of long life, was, however, not given to Moses. Yahweh denied that gift to the man who probably made the whole operation possible. It seems strange that Moses would die before they came into possession of the 'promised land'. Strange for us may be, but not for Enlil/Jehovah. Moses was not needed any more. What Yahweh needed now, was a fast army of young people leaded by a young man who would totally obey him, in contradiction to Moses who often disagreed with him.

The Israelites however, were complaining being in the desert for so long time. We are not surprised, the conditions in the desert must have been miserable and no one could understand why they had to stay there for such a long time. No complains however were allowed. When so happened, the punishment was always cruel as in Numbers 21:5–6:

> And the people spake against God, and against Moses, Wherefore have ye brought us up out of Egypt to die in the wilderness? For there is no bread, neither is there any water; and our soul loatheth this light bread. And the LORD sent fiery serpents among the people, and they bit the people, and much people of Israel died.

Could the Lord afford losing people at this stage of the operation? Obviously he could. We assume that the 'fiery serpents' were sent to kill ordinary people, not his soldiers. Besides, total obedience was more important. It was a cruel punishment indeed for such a complaint. The 'light bread' is of great interest here. Note that they said that they had **no bread except for the 'light bread'.** They made a distinction between ordinary bread and 'this light bread', which they found out of favor. Probably baked out of gold dust. From the gold they 'borrowed' from the Egyptians.

Another cruel action of Jehovah was the killing of Natab and Abihu, the sons of Aaron. Leviticus 10:1-2 says:

> And Natab and Abihu, the sons of Aaron, took either of them the censer, and put fire therein, and put incense thereon, and offered Strange fire before the LORD, which he commanded them not. And there went out fire from the LORD, and devoured them, and they died before the LORD.

'Fire from the Lord', the fire came from his gun, attached around his waist, not unlike movie stars. The offering of incense or adulating with smoky incense was (and still is) a tradition in many countries. The brothers had certainly no intention to offend the Lord, but probably to honor him. As priests, it was their duty to offer incense. Remember that the three wise men offered incense to Jesus. Here we have the same purpose, showing some appreciation. But what kind of incense was that? They probably used gold dust, instead of the usual incense, or a mixture of the two. The incense does not make 'a strange fire', only smoke. Nobody knows if by putting gold dust on coals of fire the result would be 'a strange fire'. But it is possible and would explain why the Lord became so angry and fired his weapon against them. They had an unauthorized knowledge, about gold dust. Both Moses and Aaron knew certainly the secret, but they would soon die while Aaron's sons were to live much longer. The secret of the gold had to be preserved in heavens.

Monatomic elements, like gold, silver, rhodium, iridium and some other precious metals are non-metallic. They can be found in herbs as well as in volcanic soils, and in seawater, although in very small quantities.

Monatomic gold transforms into gold dust in the volcanoes. Gold dust has none of the metallic properties of gold. Gold dust is a super contactor with a single frequency light, and does not allow any voltage potential to exist within it. David Radius Hudson claims that he has successfully transformed gold into gold dust. He calls the product ORME, Orbital Rearranged Monoatomic Element. Here is his description:

Monoatomic gold is much more powerful, as in a fuel cell . . .

The gifts that go with this are: perfect telepathy, you can know good and evil when it's in the room with you, you also can project your thoughts into someone else's mind. You can levitate, you can walk on the water, because it's flowing so much light within you that you literally don't attract gravity. . . .

I haven't achieved everything yet, but it miraculously cured every disease that we've tested on thus far.[3]

At this point nobody knows if David Hudson's gold dust has the properties described above. Since he considered himself to be restrained by some authorities, he decided to go public and reveal the 'secrets' of his research. There are many web sites about the subject, and the number is increasing. Products of gold colloid can be found in the market today, both in liquid and in tablet form. For human use as well as herb watering. But they are not monatomic. Perhaps D. Hudson has opened a door unknown to science. Government organizations may curry on his research, but the results may be preserved inside the doors of these organizations, like the secrets of the metals of the Earth 'were preserved in heavens'.

The Army of the Desert

This Israelite army, created from scratch in the desert by Yahweh and his military experts, must have been something unique. Never before had it been an army with such properties as described above. Besides, they had the Ark, assembled after precise instructions, probably for military use. Shining was the only lacking characteristic of the Israelite soldiers. The gods marching for battle were often 'shining'.

Do we have any evidence that the Israelites had some group of soldiers that could be classified as an organized army? Indeed we have, organized by Yahweh himself, as in Exodus 18:21:

> Moreover you shall provide out of all the people able men, such as fear God, men of truth, hating covetousness; and place such over them, to be rulers of thousands, and rulers of hundreds, rulers of fifties, and rulers of tens:

This is a military organization with commanders on several levels. In addition, the leaders should be men who feared God. That was the only way he could count that they would execute his orders. The Israelite army counted hundreds of thousands of men according to the OT, but the figures are much too high to be credible. We assume that both the population and the army were of considerable numbers.

Was Joshua the chief of the army? Or was this special army, created by Yahweh, entrusted in the hands of some god too? In Joshua 5:15–15 we read:

> And it came to pass, when Joshua was by Jericho, that he lifted up his eyes and looked, and, behold, there stood a man over against him with his sword drawn in his hand: and Joshua went unto him, and said unto him, Art thou for us, or for our adversaries? And he said, Nay; but as **captain of the host of the LORD** [emphasis added] am I now come. And Joshua fell on his face to the earth, and did worship, and said unto him, What saith my Lord unto his servant? And the captain of the LORD's host said unto Joshua, Loose thy shoe from off thy foot; for the place whereon thou standest is holy. And Joshua did so.

Note that Joshua assumes that the man was one of his own, or perhaps one of his enemies. But nay, he was the commander of the army, immediately accepted by Joshua! This is yet another evidence that the Anakim were not giants as the Bible claims but perfectly ordinary looking people. Although he informs Joshua that the place is now 'holy', he does not explain why, and Joshua takes off his shoes! The captain of the army of God (Israel means 'Soldiers of God) is probably the archangel Michael, the architect behind the Christian religion too. Yahweh provided one of his sons to lead the army. He became 'archistrategos' in the Greek Bible, meaning the highest chief of the army!

One could ask why they shouldn't have a regular army. After all, they were about to conquer the land promised by Enlil/Jehovah. But he had already given the land to Abraham. Did all the descendants of Abraham go to Egypt? Not likely. Some of them ought to have been in the country already. In fact, it is more likely that there were more Jews/Hebrews in the country than those who now left Egypt. Yet, Enlil/Jehovah promised them the land once again and he needed a special army for the purpose. What options did Enlil/Jehovah have in order to keep his promise?

In fact, he had a lot of options. He could for example 'softened the hearts of the inhabitants' of the cities of Canaan so they would accept the Israelites as co-habitants, or surrender to them. He could have given them some land with none or few inhabitants. He could easily have made peace with all the people living there. After all, many of them were Hebrews. But he didn't because he was interested in something else. He needed a war. Giving the land to the Israelites was just an undercover operation in order to hide the real purpose of the war.

And he had prepared the war very carefully. He had the patience to wait forty years to raise the most superior army ever, fed with gold powder. Whom was this army going to fight? What kind of people was living in Canaan at the time?

He probably had some 'weapons of brilliance' left. Enlil/Jehovah could easily deliver some great weapons to the Israelites in order to conquer the land, as the Enlilites used to do. Or he could use the weapons by himself, as he had done earlier at several occasions. But this was not his purpose. By helping the Israelites to conquer the land, the Israelites were in fact helping him, unknowing that the purpose was to slaughter a certain kind of people.

Was God planning a war using the Israelites as his soldiers? Indeed he did. 'Israel' means 'Soldiers of God'. He introduced even the name. He needed them as much as they needed him. Otherwise he would never care about educating them under the forty years in the desert, train them and, of course, manipulate them. The question is: Had he liberated the Israelites or were they his captives. Or was he the shepherd, driving and directing his sheep's in a way most suitable to him? Was he a liberator bringing peace or war? Exodus 15:3:

The LORD is a man of war: LORD is his name.

The Genocide
According to the Old testament, the people living in the area at that time were Canaanites, Amorites, Hittites, Perizittes, Jebusites, Hivites and Anakim among others. Some were descendants of Abraham, some not. The Anakim were, as we have seen, the Igigi/Titans and their descendants. Most of them moved to that area after they revolted against Enlil and married Earthly wives. He decided to exterminate them long ago. The time had now come. Most Anakim died at the destruction of Sodom and Gomorrah, but most of the population of Jericho, Ai and some other cities, were still Anakim.

This was the real purpose of the adventures of the Israelites. They emigrated to Egypt, had been in bondage, left Egypt, lived in the desert for forty years just to come home again. Why? That was what the Israelites believed, what they had been manipulated to believe. The real purpose was to do a dirty job for Enlil/Jehovah, to slaughter the descendants of the Nephilim, the Anakim. In order to get them to perform the task, he had of course to promise them something. Even if what they got was not exactly what he had earlier promised Abraham. Joshua 1:4:

From the wilderness and this Lebanon even unto the great river, the river Euphrates, all the land of the Hettites, and unto the great sea toward the going down of the sun, shall be your coast.

This great amount of land, from the Mediterranean Sea to the Persian Gulf, had now become a small area where the Anakim happened to live. Enlil and his angels were to participate in guiding the

Israelites and even participate in battles. Just to be sure that Joshua didn't let anyone to escape. Exodus 23:23:

> For mine Angel shall go before thee, and bring thee in unto the Amorites, and the Hettites, and the Perizzites, and the Canaanites, the Hivites, and the Jebusites: and I will cut them off.

Just replace the word 'angel' with 'warrior', or the alien 'chief of the army', reread and consider the result!

Remarkably enough, the Anakim are not mentioned here. At this stage, nobody knew if some of those people were to surrender or make any resistance. Despite that, he decided to 'cut them off'. Nowhere in history is there any record about slaughtering every living soul, men, women, children and animals, as in Jericho and the other Canaanite cities. Joshua 6:21:

> And they utterly destroyed all that was in the city, [Jericho] both man and woman, young and old, and ox, and sheep, and ass, with the edge of the sword.

After the destruction of Jericho, the people of the surrounding cities were alarmed. Many of the cities wished to offer Joshua capitulation and peace. Joshua had no reason to refuse their offer. The war and the butchering could be avoided had he been allowed to make the decision. He could then be master of the land, without any more killing. But the decision was already taken by Enlil/Jehovah. Joshua was what we could call today 'programmed' to perform a specific task.

Since Enlil/Jehovah didn't want anybody to surrender, he manipulated the people of the cities not to surrender and at the same time, he made it clear that Joshua had to kill everybody who didn't surrender. Joshua obeyed. Machiavelli could easily have got the idea concerning his theories from the bible! Joshua 11:19:

> There was not a city that made peace with the children of Israel, save the Hivites the inhabitants of Gibeon: all other they took in battle. For it was of the LORD harden their hearts, that they should come against Israel in battle, that he might destroy them utterly, and they might have no favor, but that he might destroy them, as the LORD commanded Moses.

Joshua 6:24 says about the destruction:

> And they burnt the city [Ai] with fire, and all that was therein:
> only the silver, and the gold, and the vessels of brass and of
> iron, they put into the treasury of the house of the LORD.

How could the inhabitants of Ai make peace when the Lord manipulated and perhaps promised them some help to make the battles
possible!

After the job was done, he ordered them to bring the silver and
the gold to him. No gold was needed anymore for the 'manna' or
for the construction of the ark. This time the gold would directly
be accumulated in the stores waiting to be transported to Nibiru.
The lord knew that the Anakim had a lot of gold. The same strategy
continued from city to city, until all the cities of the Anakim had
been destroyed. It is logical to assume that not all the inhabitants of
the cities were Anakim. It could have been Jews as well and other
people. But why take the risk! Kill them all. Joshua 11:21:

> And at that time came Joshua, and cut off the Anakim from the
> mountains, from Hebron, from Debir, from Anab, and from
> the mountains of Judah, and from all the mountains of Israel:
> Joshua destroyed them utterly with their cities.

Many managed to flee from the slaughtering and the superior army
of Joshua. Joshua had already defeated them. Now they ran for their
lives. But they were not allowed to live. Since Joshua's army could
not reach every fleeing soldier, old or young, woman or child, some
of them could indeed manage to survive. But that was not a problem,
because the Lord could reach them all. Following the battles from
the air, Yahweh could intervene whenever it was necessary. Yahweh
decided to participate in the battle by hunting the fleeing people
from the air. Not one of the Anakim was allowed to escape. The real
slaughtering was, in fact, exercised by Yahweh. Joshua 10:11:

> And it came to pass, as they fled from before Israel, and were
> in the going down to Bethhoron, that the LORD cast down
> great stones from heaven upon them unto Azekah, and they
> died: they were more which died with hailstones than they
> whom the children of Israel slew with the sword.

If we ought to call things by their right names, then 'the hailstones from the Lord' were nothing else than the 'missiles from Enlil', fired from some airborne vessel.

Enlil/Jehovah managed to exterminate his enemies in Canaan and at the same time managed to manipulate the Jews and the Christians to believe that the gold-dust consumers Anakim were the enemies of the Jews and even the enemies of mankind. God is always right even when he kills innocent people! The appearance of Anunnaki-flying-objects in the skies is not restricted to some religions or the pages of the bible. His son Ninurta had his own 'black bird' and even his grand daughter Inanna had her own 'attack sky-bird'. Some two thousands years earlier, Enlil became furious about the fact that the Igigi revealed the secret of the gold dust to their offspring.

As we have seen in the Book I of Enoch, he promised to kill the descendants of the Igigi wherever they lived. More than two thousands years later he was in the position to do that. As we have noted earlier, it is not easy for us, living some 75 years, to understand plans extending over thousands of years, not to mention remembering! It is worthy to repeat the words of Enlil as in Enoch Book I chapter 12:6:

. . . and inasmuch as they delight themselves in their children, **The murder of their beloved ones shall they see**, [emphasis added]

The extermination was now completed. The Igigi 'saw the murder of their beloved ones', as the Lord said!

The results of the whole operation, including the migration of some Hebrews to Egypt and the return of their offspring to the land he had promised Abraham, were several. He instigated and helped to complete the genocide of the descendants of the Igigi. He manipulated the Israelites, to obey him in every aspect.

He created conflicts in Canaan still going on. He introduced the conception of the 'only God' in the desert, that later became the highest authority in the land. He managed to establish himself as Yahweh despite people's resistance. The land of 'honey', promised to Abraham and his descendants, became 'Yahweh-stan', a land entirely controlled by fear and punishment. As if that was not enough, he demanded to be paid too, in silver and gold. Archaeological discoveries of the last century have unearthed the remains of metallurgical establishments in Jericho. Beside violence and intimidation, he could be deceitful in order to establish himself as God. Exodus 20:22:

> And the Lord said unto Moses, Thus you shall say unto the children of Israel, Ye have seen that I have talked with you from heaven.

Enlil/Jehovah's plan seems to have been both primitive and sophisticated at the same time. In fact, this evil plan could have been the masterwork of the devil, elevating Machiavellian intelligence to new heights. Three millennia and a half later, the Israelites, 'soldiers of God', and the Palestinian soldiers of Allah are fighting each other for the same land! What other plan could get the soldiers of Enlil to fight the soldiers of Enlil!

The military victory of Nannar/Michael, the chief of the army of God (archistrategos), has been poisoning human relations since then.

The lord Yahweh and his angels could now update the chart of the plan. One more point on the agenda was now marked 'executed'. The Anakim-affair was now brought to an end. The seed that would create conflicts for times to come was now sown in the Promised Land! The brotherhood could now move to the next point of the agenda in order to complete the plan and secure the future of the Gold Mission. Unless there were some rebellious Igigi-descendants left somewhere, or some managed to escape.

---

[1] The Plagues of Egypt, Admonitions of Ipuwer from: www.mystae.com/restricted/streams/thera/plagues.html
[2] Laurence Gardner, Genesis of the Grail Kings, p. 136
[3] www.halexandria.org/dward467.html

Chapter 16

THE TROJAN WAR AND THE TROJAN GODS

'In this way, the counsels of Zeus were fulfilled'
Homer

The most we know about Troy (Troia or Ilion in Greek) comes from
the great storyteller Homer (9th century BCE). He wrote about the
Trojan War that probably occurred at the 11th century BCE, in 'Iliad',
'about Ilion'. He also wrote about Odysseus' adventures on his way
home from Troy, the 'Odyssey'. There are also some other ancient
writings about the Trojan War, like 'The Library of Greek Mythology' by Apollodorus, (100 CE), the 'Aeneid', by Publius Vergilius
Maro, (70–19 BCE) and 'The fall of Troy', by Quintus Smyrnaeus
(400 CE).

According to Greek mythology, Teucrus from Attica (some say
from Crete) founded a colony in Phrygia, Asia Minor, and the people of the colony were called Teucrians.

Dardanus, a son of Enlil/Zeus, had two sons with his first wife,
Chryse, Idaeus who emigrated to Phrygia with his father, giving
name to the mount Ida, and Deimas who succeeded Atlas as king
of Arcadia. Dardanus had a brother, Iasion, who had been killed by
Zeus by a thunderbolt. He left the Island of Samothrace and sailed
away to the opposite mainland in order to avoid being killed by Zeus
too. Was there some kind of plan from the very beginning? Dardanus married Batia, a daughter of Teucrus and became king of the
land Dardania, named after him.

175

Dardanus succeeded by his son Erichthonius, who was succeeded by his son Tros, who called the land Troad and its inhabitants Trojans after himself. Ilus, son of Tros, founded a city too named after him, Ilion (Ilium), better known as Troy.

Laomedon succeeded his father Tros but was killed by Heracles, also a son of Zeus, when he destroyed the city of Troy prior to the Trojan War. Somehow Priam, the young son of Laomedon, survived the destruction and managed to restore and fortify the city of Troy. At the time of the Trojan War, Troy was a great city with broad streets and beautiful buildings. Note that until the time of the Trojan War, all known fortified cities were inhabited by Titans and Anakim. If some of them were living in Troy, then it was as certain as anything that their presence here would not be without trouble!

Another son of Tros, Assaracus became king of Dardania. He succeeded by his son Capys who was the father of Anchises, who was the father of Aeneas. Since Anchises was crippled Aeneas was ruling the country of Dardania. Aeneas was the leader of the Dardanians, who sided with the Trojans and he became the second in command of the Trojan forces. He was married to Creusa, a daughter of king Priam of Troy. He was also the son of the goddess Inanna/Aphrodite.

That was a very short story of Troy prior to the Trojan War. Since there were gods and demigods involved from the very beginning, it is not farfetched to claim that they also were involved in the Trojan War, a Homer stated. Aphrodite, Ares, and Apollo sided with the Trojans, while, Zeus, Hera and Athena sided with the mainland-Greeks.

This information, if true, is quite interesting because we find members of the same family on both sides. Ninurta/Ares was always 'working' together with his father. Not in this case, however. By supporting both sides, they wished to be sure that the war would break out. It seems that neither Ninurta/Ares, nor Inanna-Aphrodite had any closed bands to the Trojans, except from the fact that Aphrodite was the mother of Aeneas. Perhaps they just wished to encourage them to participate in the war. Unlike many other wars fought between Enlil and Marduk, it seems that this one was a war among the Enlilite themselves. We assume that they were just pretending being in war with each other in order to involve the Trojan-Igigi into a war the Trojans could not win.

Here we have the Igigi/Titans, demigods, Enlil-Zeus and many of his family members, in fact every ingredient needed for a war, except for Marduk. Do we need a beautiful woman too?

Was the Trojan War a war between a colony and the metropolitan states of Hellas? Colonies at that time are not to be compared with colonies of modern times. In modern times, European countries declared most of the counties of Africa as their colonies. Sometimes it was enough if they could maintain a small military force in some strategic city. Sometimes the colonial powers needed strong forces in order to hold a colony. These colonies were in fact occupied by foreign powers forcing their own administration, language and often religion on the inhabitants. The colonial powers used the colonies as trade centers, military bases of strategic significance, or simply as a market for their own products. Most of those colonies won their independence after bloody wars against the colonial powers.

The colonies of the old times were quite different. They were establishments in foreign counties with no inhabitants, at least not in the neighborhood. The colonists were pioneers who started a new life and could develop a colony into a rich and important trade center. Since there were no other people than the new settlers, the development of a colony was depended on the colonists alone. Many colonies provided civilization and development to places where civilization would have come much later if it hadn't been for the colonists.

The Phoenicians spread their culture by establishing colonies across the southern cost of the Mediterranean Sea, while the Greeks did the same on the northern cost of the Sea.

Wars were often fought among major colonies, as between the Greek colonies of Sicily and The Phoenician Carthage. The reasons were always the control of sea routes as well as the control of trade. No war was fought, neither before nor after the (Trojan War) because of an apple or a single woman, even if she was quite beautiful.

The colonies in the Troad and Dardania became rich because of the location, which permitted them to control the passage of merchant ships from the Aegean Sea to the Black Sea. Their riches were not however the reason of the Trojan War. According to Homer, the gods themselves instigated the war through manipulations. The War occurred, by coincidence or not, not long after the exodus of the Israelites from Egypt and the genocide of the Igigi-Anakim in Canaan.

The story began at the wedding between the mortal Peleus and the goddess Thetis, the parents of Achilles. Eris, the goddess of discord, was angry because she was not invited. Has there ever been any god or goddess of unity? Eris visited the wedding banquet and threw a golden apple onto the table. She said that the apple belonged to 'Kallisti', the Fairest. The apple was supposed to have been one of the golden Apples of the Hesperides (was it made of gold or gold dust?) presented by Gaia to Zeus after his marriage with Hera. All the gods were present. Since Athena, Hera, and Aphrodite, each one considered herself to be the fairest, they asked Zeus to judge. Zeus, however, proclaimed that Paris, the Trojan prince, who also was a beautiful man, would act as judge. The prince had been raised up as a shepherd, excluded from any involvement in the affairs of the state, because of a prophecy that he would cause the downfall of Troy. Now Enlil/Zeus invited this shepherd to participate as a statesman! Somebody has to promote the fulfillment of the prophecy, a process that would be enormously successful in the future! All three of the Goddesses tried to influence Paris to judge to their favor. Athena promised him wealth, Hera promised him power, and Aphrodite promised him the most beautiful woman, the wife of king Menelaus of Sparta. The fact that she was already married didn't bother her. Paris judged in the favor of Aphrodite and then he managed to abduct Helen from Sparta while Menelaus was hunting.

The story is still fascinating people around the world. It has all the ingredients of a love story, a high level of political and military conspiracy, and of course, treachery and war. But was the 'apple to the fairest ' the real reason of the war, or was it just another 'undercover' operation for something more important than to restore the honor of the king of Sparta? Why dishonor him in the first place? Here is what Homer has to say in the beginning of the Iliad, about the instigators of the war:

> Sing, goddess, the wrath of Peleus' son Achilles, that brought endless harm upon the Achaeans. Many brave men did it send down to the Underworld, and many heroes did it yield a prey to digs and vultures. In this way, the counsels of Zeus were fulfilled, from the day on which Agamemnon—king of men— and great Achilles first fell out with one another. And which of the gods [emphasis added] was it that set them on to quarrel?

Indeed which of them and why?

Since several gods were involved, we believe it must have been something much more important than with whom the fair Helen would live with, or who of the three goddesses was the fairest. We know by now that beside several gods, there were also some demigods involved. It is also possible that several other gods and demigods were among the inhabitants of Troy.

According to Greek Mythology Zeus believed that the Earth was overpopulated by humans and especially by demigods and started the war as a means to depopulate it.

Depopulate the Earth and especially exterminate the demigods! That is precisely what he did in Canaan! We are not surprised to find Enlil/Zeus having similar targets here too. It is rather interesting that Zeus wanted the Trojan prince Paris to act as judge. Aphrodite, mother of another Trojan prince, Aeneas, a cousin to Paris, sided, as expected, with the Trojans in the Trojan War. Helen was from the mainland of Hellas. Was the intention to create war between Troy and the city-states of Hellas? Then one might wonder why. The Enlilites might have had interests in seeing Troy growing into a strong power that could face their enemy Babylon. It seems that the Trojans were not interested in expanding their territory. And probably the Enlilites could not even force them to make war at all. It seems that the Trojans, gods, demigods and humans had no intention of being directed by the gods. However, if the Trojans were unwilling to go to war, they could always be forced to defend themselves against invaders. Here are some significant characteristics of this war.

1 It was not really a traditional war with two armies facing each other. The city was under siege for nine years. Under that time there had been fights among 'heroes', occasionally skirmishes, but no real battles between the two armies. Then we have some strange events, like Achilles visiting a Trojan princess under a truce, or the war taking a break for some days in order to give the Trojans the opportunity to bury their hero, Hector.

2 The involvement of gods before the war, under the war and even after the war. The whole Enlilite family was involved with several members on both sides. Some other gods, probably Igigi with their families were also living among the Trojans.

3 The involvement of the 'mystical divine object', called the Palladium, although made by Athena it was supposed to protect Troy.

The Palladium

These Anunnaki gods and demigods living in the city of Troy were probably doing so against the will of Enlil, like the Anakim of the Canaanite cities. Tired of wars and the old struggle between Enlil and Marduk, they settled down in Troy to create a life for themselves and their families on Earth. Some of them could have been survivors from the Canaanite cities seized and destroyed by Joshua and the 'soldiers of God', the Israelites. They had the Palladium that was supposed to protect the city against anybody. It is said that nobody could take the city as long as that object remained there.

According to Greek Mythology, the Palladium was a wooden statue made by Athena and thrown down from the heaven by Zeus, as a gift to Ilus, the builder of Troy. Ilus built then a city on the same spot the fallen Palladium had landed and also a temple for it. Other sources state that Ilus moved the Palladium from Dardania to Troy. Another remarkable fact about this object is that it was not to be looked upon by any mortal. Ilus was blinded when the Palladium fell down but later recovered. We have a parallel in the Sumerian king-cities protected by the 'Heavenly Bright Object', always moved to the city of kingship. It was used to legitimate the kingship of the city but also as a defense power too. The appearance of such an object strengthens the idea that several Anunnaki gods were indeed living in Troy, and that the Palladium was some kind of defense weapon.

The characteristics of the Palladium are quite significant too. The object was of divine nature. It was made by gods and not available to humans unless approved by some gods. It was directed down to a hill from the sky.

It was emitting 'strong brightness', some kind of energy rays, much like the Sumerian 'Heavenly Bright Object'. It was also re-minding of the divine 'weapons of brilliance' given to some kings by the Enlilites. Were the emitted rays able to influence human minds or bodies?

It had a great protecting power although no one knows how. The Palladium could have been something similar to 'Heavenly Bright Object', perhaps stolen, perhaps manufactured by some Anunnaki-Igigi to defend the city.

Beside the gods involved in the war, there have been several sons of Zeus too, acting according to his directions. We have yet another significant event that took place in the area. It is the story of the Argonauts who were sent by Zeus to Colchis, the mountain land at the border of the Black Sea, to bring back the 'golden fleece'. The event, associated with gold, is supposed to have taken place before the Exodus of the Israelites, sometime between 1400 and 2000 BCE.

The Golden Fleece

Worthy to note that the name 'golden fleece' suggests of something made of gold. This is, however, an insufficient translation due to the confusion of the tongues by Enlil/Yahweh! The name in Greek is 'chrysomallo deras', which means 'golden-haired skin'. The skin was not made of gold. As skin was also used as parchment, the name was probably supposed to apply to some (sheep) skin with inscriptions of, or about gold, which leads us to a parchment describing the secrets of the gold. The same secrets that Azazel revealed to the humans about 'the secrets of the metals of the Earth and how to work them'. The connection of the skin with knowledge of the gold dust is supported by the fact that Hermes (Trismegistos-Thoth) was also involved in hiding away the parchment that Enlil so desperately wished to destroy! It is also possible that it was some of his Hermetic Works, (the Emerald Tablet of Hermes) about gold dust and longevity. That would explain the great efforts made by Zeus/Enlil to get it back. Some of the 'heroes' of the expedition were the sons of Zeus too.

In the story of the Argonauts we find a very important event that strengthen the theory about the gold dust and longevity. Medea was the daughter of the King of Colchis, who helped Jason to take the Fleece and became his wife. After a request from Jason, she was able to 'add' some years to Aeson, the old father of Jason. After she did that, Aeson is supposed to have said 'I am young again'. No matter what one believes, the gods, gold dust and longevity always make their appearance throughout the history of gods and men. The event, although recorded as Mythology, is probably a real historical fact.

The ship 'Argo', of the Argonauts, was supposed to have been built by Argus, under the supervision of Athena, (the daughter of Zeus). Athena also ordered that among the timbers used, one of them would have a 'speech devise' build-in. It was called the 'speaking timber'. Why was it necessary to communicate with the ship's crew? In modern words we would call it a communication devise mounted on, or inside a timber. Things become more understandable if we take some 'ancient' information seriously and use the right terms.

Otherwise we have golden apples, speaking timbers, Golden Fleece, whirlwinds, burning bushes, or illustrious angels that remain unexplainable to us.

The shipbuilder Argus was also called 'Panoptes', meaning 'the all-seeing', which is equivalent to 'Watcher', another name of the Igigi/Titans. The 'heroes' participated in the Argonautic expedition had been used by Enlil/Zeus in the same manner the Israelites had been used by him. The fate of the Golden Fleece is unknown, probably destroyed, after orders or manipulative instructions by Enlil/Zeus, as so much other ancient knowledge about gold powder.

The Igigi/Titans Once Again

The whole Trojan War too, appears as another undercover operation. The real reason was to destroy the Anunnaki Igigi gods and their descendants, who revolted against him and his mission to make a peaceful home for them and their families on Earth. Were the participating gods on both sides really fighting each other or were they just 'helping' both sides in order to bring about destruction and suitable results? We do not believe they were really fighting each other. According to Iliad by Homer, Aphrodite used to return to Olympus with her horses after each battle at Troy. Zeus, Hera and Athena were 'stationed' at Olympus according to Greek Mythology. They sided with the mainland Greeks, while Aphrodite sided with the Trojans. Why then return to Olympus, the 'headquarter of her 'enemies'? Or was it a common War-head-quarter? Once again, we see that undercover operations manipulated by the gods are preventing us from understanding our own history.

There is a parallel to the Trojan colony too. It is the myth about Atlantis, the Nibiruan colony on Earth. The story is supposed to have been told to Plato by an Egyptian priest. Although this short story, no more than a few pages, has been written down by a single writer, it has been fascinating writers and readers since then. Atlantis could have been a colony established by some Anunnaki-Igigi gods, who rebelled against the Commander Enlil.

It is unknown if the colony had been sank under the deluge-flood or destroyed after orders from Enlil. In any case, the gods were not willing to talk about. Not a single word about Atlantis is to be found in 'The Lost Book of Enki'. The reason could be that either Atlantis has never existed or the destruction of this civilization is a shame on them. Enki/Poseidon is associated with both Atlantis, and Troy. He

is supposed to have given name to the capital of Atlantis, Poseido-
nis. He is also supposed to have built the defending walls of Troy.
We believe that neither the Trojans nor the Atlanteans (if they have
been real) were any supporters of Enlil/Zeus.

We know that Enlil didn't want that any Anunnaki should stay
on Earth. He didn't want Anunnaki knowledge to be passed over
to humans. In fact, he destroyed every single society of them and
their descendants. Was the destruction of Troy the work of Enlil/
Zeus too? Was the undercover story to bring back a woman to her
husband, while the real reason was to destroy the Anunnaki-Igigi
gods of Troy?

One could ask, if the Trojans, gods, demigods and humans,
had the Palladium and some godly knowledge, why were they defeated?

They were not actually defeated in battle by means of power, but
by means of cunning and resourcefulness, which says a lot about
us humans. Any way, the information about the Palladium is various. According to Homer, Odysseus managed to infiltrate the Trojan
defense and then stole it and that was the reason they could take the
city. It is also said that Athena offered the men hiding in the wooden
horse ambrosia (gold dust) to eat. Some say that Diomedes brought
it to Attica, then it was brought to Argos by Erginus, descendant of
Diomedes and then again to Sparta. Other writers claim to have been
Heracles, a son of Zeus, who removed the object when he captured
the city sometime before the Trojan War. This information is greatly
significant because, if true, then it could have been the first step of
the Trojan War, which, in that case, was planned long before it happened. Pausanias, 2nd century CE, a geographer who wrote the first
'tourist guide' 'Periegesis Ellados' (Tour around Hellas) claimed
that Aeneas brought the Palladium to Italy. Others again, claim that
the Palladium must have been removed from Troy before the fall of
the city. Otherwise it would have prevented any one from taking the
city.

The Aftermath of the War

The Trojan War was very real to people of ancient Hellas. In fact it
still is. Alexander the Great believed he was a descendant of Achilles, one of the great heroes of the war. He also visited the site, in
334 BCE and made sacrifices to the tombs of Achilles and Patroclos.
The story of the war is still closed connected to the old gods of the

Hellenic Pantheon. We prefer to believe that neither the Trojan War nor the participation of the gods was fabricated. The same gods who are still forming our lives, either we believe in them or not. The war ended thanks to Odysseus and the wooden horse. The men hidden inside the wooden horse opened the city gates after the Trojans took the horse into the city, believing that it was some kind of gift from their enemies who pretended sailing away.

What happened to the people of Troy after the war, humans, gods and demigods alike? Snorri Sturluson, (1178–1241 CE) the Icelander poet, historian and mythographer, says in 'Prose Edda' that Troy was 'Asgard', the home of the Norse gods. Some of them (or all the survivors?) went north after the war and eventually found their way to Scandinavia. He believes that the fallen Troy was 'Ragnaroek' which these gods survived. In Norse mythology those gods are collectively called 'Asar' gods and their chief deity was Odin. They are supposed to have come to Scandinavia from the South. Asar is neither a Scandinavian nor a Greek name. In fact it is not an earthly name at all, but Nibiruan. Marduk named one of his sons 'Asar', Osiris in Greek. The group of gods and demigods that managed to survive the war and wandered north to Scandinavia, through Russia, leaded by someone called 'Asar' was probably the real reason of the war. By wandering north they came away from the epicenter of the ever going on wars and quarrels between the gods and their instruments, the manipulated humans.

Another demigod, Aeneas, survived the war according to Rome's greatest poet, Publius Vergilius Maro. Aeneas and his followers left Troy in 20 ships. Then they must have been at least several hundred of them. It is interesting to see that Aeneas and his followers, trying to find a new home, were continuously directed from one place to another in order to find the final destination decided by Enlil/Zeus.

In Thrace, a ghost of Polydorus, son of Priam, warned them that the Thracian king Polymestor was not to be trusted and advised them to find a new home in the land of their 'ancient mother' Crete.

In Crete they found that the island was suffering from a famine and left again. Could it be famine of the kind Canaan suffered forcing Abraham and later Jacob and his relatives to move into Egypt? Somebody wished to encourage Aeneas to continue the journey in the same way Jacob was 'encouraged' to immigrate to Egypt.

In Epirus, in northwest Hellas, Helenus the seer, another son of Priam, informed them that their final destination was Italy. Consider many parallels in the OT where the agents/prophets of Enlil/Yahweh used to inform the people about the 'future plans of his'. 'Seer' means 'prophet' in Greek.

Aeneas and his followers continued to the Phoenician colony of Carthage where the queen, Dido welcomed them and offer them to stay. She fell in love with Aeneas and they lived for several months as a couple. All the Trojans believed that this was their new home marking the end of their journey. Aeneas too was willing to stay. After all, he found a new queen and a new kingdom. Why shouldn't he? Juno/Hera/Ninlil, the consort of Jupiter/Zeus/Enlil was pleased because she wished that Aeneas would forget all about his destiny in Italy. Why she had another opinion than her husband in this matter, nobody knows.

As everything seemed to be just right for everyone in Carthage, Jupiter/Zeus sent a message to Aeneas, through some airborne angel, we presume, ordering him to leave Carthage for Italy. If Aeneas could disobey the order of the 'king of the gods' without any consequences or not, nobody knows. Jupiter/Zeus had already made preparations for his arrival to Italy. Here we see that despite the fact that Marduk was the official 'King of the gods' on Earth, this was not known everywhere because Enlil/Yahweh/Zeus was still acting, as the king of the gods, thanks to the power of the weapons the Brotherhood of the Gold possessed.

Latinus was the king of Latium ruling from the city of Laurentum. He was a descendant of the god Saturn/Cronus, the father of Zeus. The demigod Latinus and his wife Amata had a daughter, Lavinia whom many young men wished to marry. One of them was Turnus, handsome and strong, king of the city of Ardea. But Latinus was against every one of these suitors because he witnessed, in several 'oracles', that his daughter was pre-determined to marry a foreign prince. That according to the king's own prophet! He announced the coming of a foreign prince, all according to some divine vision. Why are we not surprised? There are more 'oracles as in a dream' and divine visions to come! Although Aeneas and his followers had found suitable places to settle down, their steps were indeed directed to Latium by Enlil and Ninurta.

When Aeneas arrived in Laurentum, Latinus welcomed him, believing he was the foreign prince of his oracles. He permitted him to marry his daughter, despite the warnings that a war between the Latins and the newcomers would break out, as it also did. This is another evidence that the Trojans must have been of considerable numbers as they could make war against the Latins. A war Aeneas won with the help of the Etruscans. After marrying Lavinia, he is considered as the king who founded first Lavinium and later Alba Longa, the city the Romans thought of as their mother city.

A logical question is why Enlil/Zeus/Jupiter, or Ninurta/Ares/ Mars, helped Aeneas to found a new empire, while both of them participated in the destruction of Troy and the destruction of Aeneas' own kingdom. Was it just in case they would need them, or were they performing some actions already included in their plan? We believe that they rather acted according to some plan, than just taking actions in random. We also know that they probably never did anything not promoting the Gold Mission.

If the Palladium was moved to Italy by Aeneas and was kept there in the temple of Vesta in Forum Romanum, then one would expect that the next world power would be the city of Rome. It was also rumored that the Palladium was later transferred to Constantinople by Constantine and buried under his forum. This object being symbolical or not, its power being true or not, both Rome and Constantinople became world powers under a very long time.

Aeneas and his descendants would never forget the destruction of Troy. They would some day take vengeance. Vengeance is a human weakness, as certain as to hear 'Amen' in the church. They would march eastward, first to Hellas and then all the way to Egypt and Babylon. It would take some hundred years of course, but Enlil-Yahweh-Zeus-Jupiter could wait. Time was never a problem for him. And neither the Roman descendants of Aeneas nor the Greek descendants of Agamemnon and Achilles would remember the real reason. Time has always been loaded with dissimilar significance for gods and humans. Enlil had many unfinished affairs to complete. To his help he had architects for structuring the plans, warrior-angels for executing his orders and delivering his messages, agents-prophets to manipulate people, and human kings and emperors with armies to curry out the necessary wars. After the Meddle East, it was now Europe's turn to be ruled by Enlil and Mars, and their martial laws.

The Roman writer Marcus Porcius Cato (234–149 BCE) stated that Aeneas founded Alba Longa.

The Greek writers Hellanius of Lesbos and Damastes of Sigeum, (5th century BCE) both wrote that Aeneas was the founder of Rome.

According to Roman legend, Romulus and Remus were the sons of Mars/Ares and Rhea Silvia, also called Ilia, whom he seduced while she was asleep. By the way, the baby brothers, Romulus and Remus were abandoned on the banks of the river Tiber in the same way as Sargon the Great and Moses before them. Surprised? According to others, Romulus was a great grand son of Aeneas and Ilia. Romulus founded the city of Rome. The reason we mention Ares/Mars here is because he appeared to play an equal important role in Rome as in Troy. Other sources claim that it was Ascanius, also known as Iulus, a son of Aeneas and Creusa who founded Alba Longa.

More than a thousand years later, both Julius Caecar (100–44 BC) and Gaius Octavius (54 BCE–14 CE), who later changed his name to Augustus, traced their lineage to Aeneas through Ascanius/Iulus.

Since all things under the Sun are related to all other things, we find more connections to the Trojans as well to Jason, the leader of the Argonautic expedition.

Many writers find parallels between Jason's quest and Columbus expedition to the new world, but while everybody is happy that Columbus found land beyond the ocean, we wish that Jason had never found the Golden fleece. Duke Philip III of Burgundy founded in 1430 CE 'The Order of the Golden Fleece' with the purpose to defend the Roman Catholic Church and reward nobles who participated in the Crusades. The order is reserved for the highest nobility of Europe. The Golden Fleece was also the emblem of the House of Habsburg. The Holy Roman Emperor Charles V (1530–1556 CE) was considered himself as a descendant of Aeneas. Aeneas considered himself as a descendant of Jason! He was also a son of Inanna-Aphrodite. Just heave a thread and you find some god at the other end, as if the whole humanity was entangled in their toils! Since Enlil/Yahweh, the persecutor of humanity, was involved in the Argonautic expedition, the Trojan War and he even directed Aeneas's steps to Italy, any imitation of those events (in his name or not) is evidence enough that his influence on human affairs is still very strong.

The Romans marched eastwards as it was expected. Aemilius Paullus defeated Perseus (the last Macedonian king) at Pydna 168 BCE. Perseus died in captivity. Julius Caesar conquered Egypt 48 BCE. Neither Babylonia nor the city of Babylon was a world power any more. According to 'Historia Regum Britaniae' by Geoffrey Monmouth (1090 (?)–1155 CE), the first king of the Britons and the one who named Britain after himself, was Brutus, a great grand son of Aeneas.

It is well known that the Romans, after they defeated Hellas, they brought every kind of art and other valuable items to Rome. The rest they copied. After some years, Rome became a beautiful city built and decorated in the Hellenic style. They also copied the Greek pantheon and replaced the Greek names with their own. Despite the fact that Jupiter was the king of the gods, like Zeus in the Greek mythology, it was Mars-Ares-Ninurta, the son of Enlil-Zeus-Jupiter, who was worshiped as the greatest god by the Romans. He was the most venerated god, the god of war, the avenger. Perhaps a coincidence, or perhaps the very ground of the Roman Empire was the work of Mars who turned the rather peaceful Trojans to a warlike, martial army. Mars is considered the father of the Roman people as well as Aeneas.

Other theories are connecting the Trojans with the Cathars of Gaul and the Merovingians. That would explain the plethora of Greek names in France, such as Troyes, Paris, Cathars (from katharos, meaning pure) and many others. If all these theories are true, or at least some of them, then it was a remarkable achievement indeed, of the survived demigods of the defeated city of Troy. It would have been impossible without some divine aid. The Greek names in France could, however, derive from the old Greek colonies in the south of France, such as Nikaia (Nice), Antipolis, Massalia (Marseille), Emporion, Agathe (Agde).

It is also a well-known fact that some gods begot 'demigods' with the sole purpose to elevate them to kings. But not all of them were willing to be subjected to the gods. That would explain the tales of the Asar-gods of Scandinavia, who fled as long away as possible from the center of a world dominated by the warlike Enlilites. Some other Trojan gods and demigods could have wandered eastwards. That would explain some advanced technical achievements of the old times, by such demigods in far away lands like India and China. Their only chance to survive was to hide away in some distant lands. The reason the whole Earth was declared as a restricted area was the knowledge of the gold dust, which the Brotherhood of the Gold wished to remain top secret only known in 'the kingdom of heaven'. The Trojan War grounded the beginning of the Roman Empire, which in turn grounded the end of the Hellenic era. The extermination of the Anunnaki-Igigi-Titans-Anakim was now completed, save the few who probably managed to escape to distant lands. The plan was progressing; the flow of human blood was continuing as well as the flow of gold to Nibiru.

Chapter 17

THE CORRUPTION OF THE EARLY HUMAN HISTORY

Gods, Lords and Serpents

At the time of Nebuchadnezzar II (605–562 BC), Babylon was still
powerful, beautiful, and a great center of trade and culture. Despite
the wars of Enlil/Yahweh and his sons against Babylon, most of
its conquerors adapted Babylonian customs. Under the Kassite Dynasty, for example, (Third dynasty of Babylon from around 1550 to
1150 BCE, the Kassites ordered the copy of the classical Babylonian
texts, propagated the cult of Marduk and adopted most elements of
the Babylonian culture. But their attempt to change the name of the
city to 'Kar-Duniash' was unsuccessful.

Other conquerors made Babylon the capital of their empire. But
the adoption of the Babylonian culture and the Babylonian gods was
not according to plan. The intentions of Enlil/Yahweh were to spoil
Babylon and her gods, as it is stated in the bible. Surprisingly, Marduk always managed to stand against the attacks of the Enlilites, and
even turning military defeats to his advantage. Marduk's program of
good relations with the humans was the winning concept. Enlil/Yahweh
became more and more isolated, supported, at this time, only by his
'chosen' people.

Now Enlil/Yahweh needed some assistance for a specific task in
Babylon. The most suitable for the tasks were the Jews scribes who
had been an instrument in his hands for a long time. He used them
although they had no idea why. Almost all of them were normal

people who had only one interest, to make a good living for themselves and for their families. However that was before the advanced manipulation program started. The program that turned them into fanatic supporters of Yahweh. After that, even the most peaceful scribe, even the most free thinking one, could only speak the 'words put in his mouth' by Yahweh and his messengers.

Some of them, being employed by him, like the prophets Daniel and Ezekiel, had probably being ordered to copy the old Sumerian and Babylonian documents. The Babylonian Captivity is mentioned in the bible several times. Jeremiah 25:8–9 says:

> Therefore thus saith the LORD of hosts; Because ye have not heard my words, Behold, I will send and take all the families of the north, saith the LORD, and Nebuchadnezzar the king of Babylon, my servant, and will bring them . . .

The most interesting expression here is 'my servant'. How could Nebuchadnezzar, king of Babylon, servant of Marduk and Nabu be the servant of Enlil/Yahweh? As the name implies, Nebu-chadnez-zar was probably appointed king of Babylon by Nabu, the son of Marduk. Despite that, Enlil/Yahweh knew that Nebuchadnezzar would take 'all the families of the north' as captives to Babylon. That was something no king exercised before. Enlil/Yahweh could not have known unless he had some agreement with Nebuchadnezzar. In that case the Jews were sent to Babylon by Enlil/Yahweh in order to perform a specific task. Even their comeback had been scheduled in advanced in the same way as the come back of the Israelites from Egypt. Taking captives by victorious kings and generals was not unusual however, especially young men and women. Esarhadon, king of Assyria, (681–669 BC) summoned ten kings from Cyprus and twenty kings from Hatti and brought them to Nineveh to use as 'building material' for his palace.
Nebuchadnezzar would have taken captives anyway, but here we suspect that he had already promised Enlil/Yahweh to do that. The captives taken from Jerusalem were men, women and even children. It was as that part of the population was planned to live a normal life somewhere else. They were also treated well in Babylon, witnessing about Marduk's respect and friendship to all humans. There they became part of the society, in fact so well integrated that when the

Persian king Cyrus the Great (550–530 BC) allowed them to return, (539 BC) many of them chose to stay in Babylon. Jeremiah 25:12:

> And it shall came to pass, when seventy years are accomplished, that I will punish the king of Babylon, and the nation . . .

First Nebuchadnezzar was supposed to take captives from Jerusalem as a service to Enlil/Yahweh, and then some other king of Babylon would be punished for that. Indeed mysterious are the ways of this god!

The captivity lasted from 586–539 BCE, which makes 47 years, not seventy as the lord said. Why? Was Enlil/Yahweh miscalculating or did something happen that changed the time line of this part of the plan? A lot of articles and even books are dealing with the problem of the 70 years. They try every kind of arithmetics in order to make the 23 missing years (70–47) to reappear, just to show that God is always right even when he is wrong! A Chinese proverb says:

> Prophecy is extremely difficult—especially with regard to the future!

In fact, two important things happened. 'The Chronicle of Nabonidus' and 'The Verse Account of Nabonidus', give us contemporary information about the situation in Babylon and Persia. Cyrus the great (559–530 BCE) entered the throne of the united Persia after defeating his adversaries.

First, Nabonidus, (555–539 BCE), the last king of the Neo-Babylonian Empire, attempted to replace the gods of Babylon, Marduk and Nabu, by introducing Sin, the moon god, son of Enlil, as the new god. This was in reality, an attempt, by the Enlilites, of kidnapping the whole kingdom of Babylon. We have already seen a striking parallel of this story in Egypt, where Pharaoh Akhenaten IV declared Aten as the sole god, in an attempt to replace Amun/Marduk.

'The Stela of Nabonidus' (British Museum ANE 90837) says:

> He [Nabonidus] was not a member of the royal family but came to the throne after the legitimate ruler had been murdered. . . One of his projects was in the city of Harran where the temple of the god Sin was rebuilt. He appears to have been

devoted to this god, and it is probable that his mother had been a priestess of Sin in Harran.[1]

Again, we are not surprised. It sounds like Nabonidus was an agent of Nannar/Sin from the very beginning, probably his son too. It is also possible that the murder of the legitimate ruler had been ordered by Sin. Nabonidus appears to have been a well-educated agent with instructions to deliver Babylon into the hands of the Enlilites by the means of a coup. Sin was the powerful god of Harran since the time of Abraham. His symbol was the crescent moon that later became the symbol of Islam. He was the god of the Harranians, a tribe from the Harranian Mountains that practiced sacrifices in large scale. The fasting of Ramadan was practiced by the Harranians long before Islam, and was introduced to Arabia by them. Sin is regarded as the architect behind many important events in the area, including the genocide of the Anakim and the introduction of Christianity and Islam. The information about Nabonidus' plan to replace Marduk by Sin, is described in 'The Verse account of Nabonidus' by a Babylonian priest of Marduk

> A weakling [Nabunaid or Nabonidus] was installed as the king of his country; the correct images of the gods were removed from their thrones, imitations were ordered to place upon them . . . The worship of Marduk, the king of the gods, he changed into abomination . . . He tormented its inhabitants with corvée-work without relief, he ruined all . . . .

> He made the image of a deity, which nobody had ever seen in this country, he introduced it into the temple, he placed it on the pedestal; he called it by the name of the Moon. It is adorned with a necklace of lapis lazuli, crowned with a tiara, its appearance is that of the eclipsed moon . . .

> Nabonidus said: 'I shall build a temple for him, I shall construct his holy seat. Yet till I have achieved this, till I have obtained what is my desire, I shall omit all festivals, I shall order even the New Year's festival to cease! . . . When I have fully executed what I have planned, I shall lead him by the hand and establish him on his seat.[2]

Nabonidus made an image of a deity never seen before in the land. Whoever made the image, it must have been approved by Sin. This is interesting because Enlil/Yahweh forbade the Israelites to make any images of him. Probably Sin considered it as necessary to present an image that would make it possible for him to be distinguished from Marduk. Nabonidus, like Aten in Egypt, never invited the inhabitants of Babylon to make a choice, but he forced them to accept the new god. That was also according to some plan of his as he said, 'when I have fully executed what I have planned'. The question is if it was Nabonidus' own plan or part of the 'Machiavellian' plan of the Enlilites.

Nabonidus' devotion to the moon god Sin is a historical fact, proven by an inscription found in Harran, 1956 CE. Harran was the city where Abraham was instructed to go, by Enlil, and there await further instructions.

Nabonidus is, according to the Babylonian priest, considered as a tyrant whose religious ideas were not shared by the inhabitants of Babylonia. Again we are not surprised. Several hundreds of years later, Constantine would force Christianity on every citizen of his empire. After a few generations, any fraud transforms into an accepted truth.

The attempt to replace Marduk from the inside was not successful. It appears somehow strange that both kings entrusted to replace Marduk in Babylon and Egypt, Nabonidus and Akhenaten, were suffering of bad health. Was it a coincidence or the result of some kind of treatment for keeping them under control?

Secondly, Marduk helped Cyrus to unity Persia. Probably he was away from Babylon under sometime. Then he delivered Babylon into the hands of Cyrus. Probably Cyrus would have been successful without the help of Marduk, as the Persian army leaded by Cyrus was the strongest army of the time. But, because of Marduk's help, things were developing faster than the Enlilites had calculated, hence the difference of the 23 years.

Cyrus himself declared some important events, according to the 'Cyrus cylinder' discovered in 1879 CE, now in the British Museum, London. Here are some lines from Cyrus' decree in Babylon, which is regarded as the first declaration of human rights.

I am Kurash ['Cyrus'], King of the World, Great King, Legitimate King, King of Babilani, King of Kiengir and Akkade,

King of the four rims of the earth . . . . When I entered Babilani
as a friend and when I established the seat of government in
the palace of the ruler under jubilation and rejoicing, Marduk,
the great lord, induced the magnanimous inhabitants of Babilani to love me, and I was daily endeavouring to worship him
. . . I also gathered all their former inhabitants and returned
them to their habitations. Furthermore, I resettled upon the
command of Marduk, the great lord, all the gods of Kiengir
and Akkade whom Nabonidus had brought into Babilani to
the anger of the lord of the gods, unharmed, in their former
temples, the places which make them happy.[3]

The texts tell us that Cyrus knew that Marduk was the supreme God,
'the lord of the gods', and not only the supreme god of Babylon.

It is also telling us something important about the character of
the two gods, Enlil and Marduk. While Enlil said 'I am the only
god', Marduk sent back the images of the Enlilite gods, to Ki-engi
(Sumer) and Akkad, whom Nabonidus had removed, meaning that
people were free to have whatever gods they liked.

Cyrus says nothing specific about the exiled Jews in Babylon
but we assume that the expression 'I also gathered all their former
inhabitants and returned them to their habitations' applies to them
too. The return of the Jews is a historical fact that couldn't happen
without the permission of Marduk. It appears as if Cyrus' deeds in
Babylon were commanded or recommended by Marduk. This is not
contradicting the picture of Cyrus as a righteous king, even if he
somehow was acting according to a divine mission.

The Jews were free to go after 47 years and not seventy as Enlil/
Yahweh had 'foreseen'. The seventy years might have been the time
needed to replace Marduk by Sin, through Nabonidus, according
to their own calculations, and perhaps the time needed for Cyrus to
unite Persia and march westward. In both cases, Marduk's intervention disturbed the calculations of the Enlilites. As usual, the Enlilites
presented 'the future' to their agents as a prophecy. The returning
of the images of the gods of Sumer (Kiengir) and Akkad, could
have been a message to the Enlilites that their attempts to replace
him were unsuccessful. The real losers, however, were the inhabitants of Babylon during the time of Nabonidus. If the return of the
Jews also was a similar message, then it was Marduk who was mis-
taken this time, because the Jewish scribes already had done the job

expected from them. They had already made copies, corrupting the old Babylonian and Sumerian texts. Something that Marduk seems to have been unaware of. In the OT, we read that it was the god of the Jews who helped Cyrus to conquer all the lands. Ezra 1:2 about Cyrus the great:

> Thus saith Cyrus king of Persia, The LORD God of heaven hath given me all the kingdoms of the earth; and he hath charged me to build him a house at Jerusalem, which is Judah.

How easy Marduk, 'the lord of the gods' according to Cyrus, became 'the Lord God' according to the book of Ezra. According to Ezra 1:4, Cyrus also ordered the Babylonians to give the Jews silver and gold, although no reasons for that are supplied.

Enlil/Yahweh said 'I am the only God, and no other gods before me'. It was not an easy task for the Jews to abandon their other gods and even the consort of Yahweh, Asherah. Gods worshiped in the Canaanite city-state of Ugarit, were El Shadai, El Berith and El Elyon, all of them used by the scribes as applying to Yahweh.

Ugarit was unearthed in 1928 CE by a group of French archaeologists. There they found art works from Egypt, Phoenicia, Cyprus and Mycenae, and in 1932 CE a collection of tablets in cuneiform script. Inscriptions found at Kuntillet Ajrud from about 800 BCE, and at El Qom state:

> I bless you through Yahweh of Samaria, and through his Asherah!

> Uriyahu, the king, has written this. Blessed be Uriyahu through Yahweh, and his enemies have been conquered through Yahweh's Asherah.[4]

She was not only Yahweh's wife but also participating in battles. The worship of Asherah by the Yahwists until the 3rd century BCE is also known from the Elephantine papyri.

The adopting of the names and titles of different gods by attributing them to Yahweh was just an attempt by the Jews to eliminate these gods in favor of Yahweh. It was an attempt to assign the attributes of these gods to Yahweh only. Several prophets made attempts to deprive Yahweh of his wife, which was not an easy thing to do.

In fact it was as difficult as the command not to make images of him. In the temple of king Solomon there were a number of different images, among them El and the Serpent. The Jews brought back from Babylon even the Babylonian god Tammuz and applied the name to Yahweh too. This is another evidence that the scribes under the Babylonian captivity operated according to instructions and had only evil to say about Babylon, while ordinary people adopted Babylonian gods and culture.

So, with most of the Jews back at home, what was the result of this exile-undercover-operation? It could not have been the captivity itself as a punishment. He had always the opportunity to punish them at home.

The Jews had, under their captivity in Babylon, written down the human history in all honesty, from available Babylonian and Sumerian records. That was the real purpose of the 'captivity'. 'In all honesty' means that the scribes had no intention of corrupting any record. Neither they had the required knowledge to do that. The corruption, however, unintentional as well as inevitable, was the result of the cemented rules of their religion after several centuries of manipulations by Enlil/Yahweh. Not only the present but also the past had to be falsified in order to fit into the limited world of the doctrines of Yahweh.

Their religion didn't permit them to use the names of the various gods of the stories copied by them. According to their doctrines, there was only one god, the God of heaven, the God of the great Mountain, alias Enlil. He became God, or Lord in their interpretations. In some cases, Enki too was interpreted as 'the Lord' but in most passages both Enki and Marduk became 'the evil Serpent'. Asherah couldn't be interpreted as 'Goddess', not even as the consort of God. Did they knew that he raped her before she accepted to marry him?

The hero of the deluge, Enki who saved Ziusudra and his family, became 'Lord' because it was not possible to assign any bad attribute to the god who saved humanity from total extermination. That is why we have both 'God', and 'Lord' and even 'Serpent' in the OT. The words represent 'god Enlil', 'Lord Enki' and 'Enki the god of wisdom', the 'wise Serpent'. It is the interpretation of the Anunnaki gods having nothing in common with God. Because of the merging of the names Enlil and Enki into God and Lord, we have the illogical statement that it was God who decided to exterminate every living thing on Earth and God who saved a few of them. That is why we also have 'Elohim' which means 'gods'. For the normal reader of the OT there is no possibility of 'knowing good and evil'. Enlil/Yahweh knew that the interpretation would follow his doctrines that began with Abraham. Once again Enlil/Yahweh punished the Jews, or so he told them, for exegetical reasons. Once again, they accepted the punishment without protests. Once again they had been used, without their knowledge, to corrupt the early human history.

Some corruptions are indeed laughingstocks, like the operation in the 'House of Life' where God is creating a woman from the rib of Adam. It is the work of scribes exposed to advanced manipulations, but, without the necessary education!

The results of this operation have been much malicious than one might think. Although the Sumerian and Babylonian stories are the original and true stories about the early history of gods and men, the corrupted copies of the OT have been the only allowed since then. Laurence Gardner says:

> What actually transpired was that the original Mesopotamian writings were recorded as history. This history was later re-written to form a base for foreign religious cults—first Judaism and then Christianity. The corrupted dogma of the religions then became established as 'history' and because the contrived dogmas (the new approved history) was so different from the original writings, the early first-hand records were then labeled 'mythology'.[5]

Another consequence of the corruption of the early human history was the retroactive introduction of the conception of Yahweh as the Biblical God. Although the Sumerian Enlil was operating the Gold Mission for the benefit of the aliens, Yahweh is supposed to have been here for the benefit of humanity, something not supported by any source except for the OT. Laurence Gardner again:

> . . . we are now far wiser than our parents and forebears, for we now have to hand the Sumerian and Akkadian documentation which enabled the Captivity Jews to complete their ancestral story. What we now know is that their biblical account was not an accurate transcript of ancient records, but a strategically compiled set of documents which distorted the

annals of the original scribes in order to establish a new cultural and religious doctrine. This was the doctrine of the One God, Jehovah-a doctrine born out of fear, that was contrary to all tradition and historical record in the contemporary and preceding environments.[6]

A dirty task was once again completed, designed by Yahweh, and executed by his agents. The corruption has deprived humanity of its true history, independently of the intentions of the scribes.

---

[1]The Stela of Nabonidus, translation by A. Leo Oppenheim (British museum)

[2]The Verse Account of Nabonidus translation by A. Leo Oppenheim (British Museum).

[3]The Kurash Prism Iran Chamber Society, edited by Charles F. Horne

[4]www.theology.edu/ugarbib.htm

[5]Laurence Gardner, Genesis of the Grail Kings, p. 78

[6]Ibid., p. 150

Chapter 18

ALEXANDER THE GREAT AND THE SEVEN WHO JUDGE

Alexander's invisible enemy

As we have seen, Cyrus the great proclaimed himself as king of Babylon assisted and approved by Marduk. Assyrian, Akkadian and Hittite kings were assisted and approved by the House of Enlil, or at least, controlled by them from time to time. Nobody could become king in these lands without being appointed by these gods. A remarkable thing about Cyrus is the fact that he is referred to as 'the anointed' in the bible, and the servant of Enlil/Yahweh.

The Persian Empire was the greatest at the time, and Babylon could feel secure under the Persian protection. That was obviously Marduk's plan. Marduk could relax. Neither Akkad or Assyria, nor the Hittites had any power to help the Enlilites against the Persians. Marduk and Cyrus created an empire that was calculated to last for a long time. The Enlilites appeared as defeated. Probably Marduk thought so too. In fact this is the last time we hear about him on Earth. Did he depart for Nibiru feeling secure that the Babylonian civilization, his own creation, and the Egyptian civilization would survive? On the other hand, he would never depart leaving the Enlilites alone on Earth. Did he die on Earth or been assassinated? We shall come to that later. There is no information about Enki either, short after the installation of Marduk as the Supreme god. He must have been rather old at that time, and may have returned to Nibiru in order to 'stop' aging as fast as on Earth. Enlil being in the Americas 'to complete the gold mission', and Marduk being the chief of the gods, may have affected such a decision. With both Enki and Marduk gone, only the Persian Empire alone was standing in the way.

But only ca two hundred years after Cyrus and while the Persian Empire was still very strong, something unexpected happened. A young king, Alexander (356–323 BCE), from Macedonia in Northern Hellas, made his appearance in Asia Minor. The reason was the Persian presence in the area and the fact that the Persians earlier tried to conquer Hellas. Alexander, although he was the son of a relatively powerful king, Philip, rose suddenly and unexpected out of the blue, without being selected or appointed by neither Marduk nor the Enlilites. This was only allowed for small kingdoms without any influence outside the limits of their dominions. Cyrus was the first king ever to conquer Ki-Engi, against the will of the Enlilites. Soon thereafter, Alexander conquered Ki-Engi too without their approval either. Was he assisted by Marduk, as Cyrus, or was he just an outsider?

A lot has been written about Alexander's farther. Some scholars can't drop the idea about some deity being his father. Both Amun, the Egyptian High god, and Zeus, the chief god of the Greek pantheon have been named. Yet, others are merging these two deities into one and the same. Herodotus (5th century BC) wrote that the Greeks had taken many of their gods from the Egyptian pantheon, which is correct with respect to some of them. However gods like Inanna/Ishtar (Aphrodite) was never a deity in Egypt. Neither was Enlil-Yahweh-Zeus.

Zeus was the chief god of the gods, like Enlil. When Marduk replaced Enlil-Zeus as the Supreme god, Zeus was still the chief deity of the Greek pantheon. The confusion might have come from the fact that Marduk/Amun was the chief deity of the Egyptians.

Here are some reasons why Enlil/Zeus couldn't be the same person as Marduk/Amun.

Enlil/Zeus' spouse was Ninlil/Sud, according to the Sumerian pantheon. The Jews called her Asherah and the Greeks Hera. Marduk/Amun married Serpanit, an earthly women whose name is not mentioned in the Greek mythology at all. After her death there is no record about any other woman in Marduk's life.

Aries/Mars, the god of war of the Greeks and Romans, was son of Zeus/Jupiter, like Ninurta, Enlil's' hero and foremost warrior was son of Enlil. Marduk's sons were Osiris, Seth and Nabu and none of them was regarded as 'god of war'.

Zeus was known to use lighting weapons and thunders like Enlil, who also provided the Akkadian, Assyrian and Hittite kings with such weapons, as we have seen. Such symbols or weapons were never associated with Marduk/Amun.

In the Greek mythology, it was Zeus who decided to destroy mankind using the flood, like Enlil did, according to the Sumerian mythology. Zeus is also a brother to Demeter alias Ninmah/Ninkhursaq, the mother of the gods and the humans, like Demeter (Demetra), in the Greek mythology, which means 'double mother'. Poseidon, the god of waters in the Greek mythology, is the brother of Zeus. Enki was the brother of Enlil and the god of waters and father of Marduk/Amun.

Having separated Enlil-Zeus from Marduk-Amun, let us continue with the interesting case of Alexander. It is rather remarkable that scholars who consider the Anunnaki as mythical characters, they do accept the 'flying angels' of the OT. Scholars who do not accept Homer's information than the Trojan War was initiated by some gods, who also participated on both sides, also claim that someone of those gods was the father of Alexander.

Although it was usual that gods fathered many men with the sole purpose to use them as kings, there is no evidence that this was the case with Alexander.

He could not have been fathered by Amun, neither selected by him, for the task of defeating the Persians and conquering the world, simply because Marduk/Amun didn't need to replace the protecting empire of the Persians by another one. In fact, Marduk was the one who had reason to be worried by the rising of yet another empire. That is to say, if he was still around. Any attack on the Persians was not good news for him, neither for Babylon. On the contrary, he might have had some suspicions that Alexander could be an agent of the Enlilites. Was he to act or wait and see?

We have some information about Alexander visiting the temple of Amun at the oasis of Siwa. Yet, there is no evidence that Alexander was worshiping this god prior to his visit in 331 BCE. According to Arrian's story, Alexander visited the oracle because he wanted to imitate his ancestors, the heroes Perseus and Heracles. This was also a political gesture to the Egyptians that he respected their god. For him, Amun, the chief deity of the Egyptian pantheon was equivalent to Zeus, the chief deity of the Greek pantheon.

It was nothing unusual with that visit. He never asked the priests however he was a son of Amun or not. It is generally accepted that the priests told Alexander what they thought he wanted to hear. Since his visit to Heliopolis and Memphis, and since he had been declared as Pharaoh, he was symbolically regarded as 'the son of Ra', as all the Pharaohs before him, which he exploited out of political reasons. 'The son of Ra' was equal to 'the son of Amun' and since the highest god of the Greek pantheon was Zeus, it had been customized as 'the son of Zeus'.

Alexander also declared that the gods were not only the rulers of Earth but also the fathers of the human race. Did he know anything about Enki, the father of us all, or Enlil, the ruler of the world? Did he know anything about Enlil/Zeus real identity? In that case, it is only logical to assume that he must have known that Enlil/Zeus was the great persecutor of humanity and that a great struggle was going on among the gods. We do not believe that he knew that much. The people of that era knew that some god, or some gods were ruling the Earth, visible or invisible. They also knew that the gods had powerful 'lighting' weapons and even some elixir, by the name 'elixir of life', 'water of life' and the like. Of much greater importance about Alexander's Egyptian affairs, is the fact that the Egyptians welcomed him as a liberator and the founding of the city of Alexandria, destined to be a great center of education and trade in the eastern Mediterranean.

How did the Enlilites react about the new situation created by Alexander? They must have been surprised and very confused. Probably alarmed too. Surprised, because an outsider was playing a roll, quite unexpected and not assigned to him by them. Confused, if they were thinking that Alexander was, in a way, an instrument in the hands of Marduk. Why would Marduk replace the strong Persian Empire under his influence with another one? Nevertheless, the help to bring down the Persian Empire was both unexpected and welcome to the Enlilites alone.

By 323 BC, the new king of the world was back in Babylon after his return from India, which was almost regarded as the end of the world. We still have no sign of Marduk, but if he was alive, he must have been glad to hear that Alexander, planned restorations of

204 Planet of Gold

his temple Esagil, as Cyrus did before him. Some uncertain sources speak of plans to rebuild the E-temen-an-ki (the Tower) as well.

Much has been written about the character of Alexander. Most of it has been written long after his death. Alexander himself had a good sense of history. He appointed professional history writers to follow his route. There is an almost total agreement about his military genius, which stands out above all others. Alexander never lost a battle. By conquering the east, he extended culture (not only the Greek culture) and civilization. Those who describe him as brutal and megalomaniac are often the same writers who support the idea of Alexander being the son of some deity. What the critics of him do not realize is that he cannot be judged by the standards of our time. In many biographies about Alexander one can read more about our own time rather than the age they are supposedly depicting.

Although not a son of Amun, Alexander attained the status of a demigod, and he continues to fuel the imagination of the humans more than two thousands years after his death. He is one of the very few persons mentioned in all three holy books of the three religions established by Enlil/Yahweh/Allah, the Jewish bible, the Christian bible and the Islamic Koran, as well as in the apocrypha first book of Maccabees. There are, of course no words of unity concerning Alexander in those books. The verses referring to Alexander in the 1st book of Maccabees could as well have been written by Enlil/Yahweh himself. They deserve no credibility.

Alexander had, like Cyrus, understanding and tolerance for other cultures allowing every people to worship whatever gods they liked. This was in accordance with Hellenic traditions and Marduk's principles, but very much contradicting the fundamental policy of Enlil/Yahweh. Alexander's multi culture ideas were unpopular even among his own officers and friends. He has been accused as being much too favorable to other cultures at the expense of his own.

It is also said that Alexander became changed and corrupted by power. Here we have a young man of age 33 (in 323 BC) who was regarded as 'king of the World', the greatest conqueror of all times, even being worshiped as god. Wouldn't that change anybody? It should be more remarkable if he hadn't been influenced by his experience and the enormous power as king of the world.

Since we are not intended to examine Alexander's character and military campaigns in this book, we quote some of the many writers who have studied this remarkable man.

Dr. Agnes Savill:

> Plato described the Ideal Commonwealth, but never persuaded
> any people to make use of it. Alexander, building over seventy
> cities among the barbarous nations . . . weaned them from
> their wild and former savage mode of living . . .
>
> But if the deity that sent down Alexander's soul into this world
> of ours had not recalled him quickly, one law would govern
> all mankind, and they would look toward one rule of justice as
> though toward a common source of light. [1]

Pseudocallisthenes:

> It is said on good authority, that Alexander was the first to
> declare that God was not only the ruler but also the father of
> all men.

Pseudo-Callisthenes (Exploits of Alexander), are some legends
with no prove they have been written by Callisthenes, the historian
who followed Alexander. One of those legends is about Alexander's
search after the 'water of life', like Gilgamesh sought 'the plant of
immortality' he believed existed somewhere and could make life
healthy, younger and longer. Some rumors say that he finally did
find that 'water'.

N.G.L.Hammond:

> Alexander's military conquests are just one part of his timeless
> allure. He transcended the inevitable brutality of war though
> the study of philosophy and poetry and through not subjugat-
> ing his vanquished but elevating them, letting them continue
> to govern themselves, letting them continue to worship their
> gods as they saw fit.[2]

Dr. Ranajit Pal:

> Alexander had dreamed of a Brotherhood of Man in a world
> torn by conflicts. This may forever remain an unattainable
> goal but he remains the finest symbol of our vision of a United

Nations. It was due to his initiative that East and West first met and the myriad effects of this fraternization are beyond any estimate.[3]

'Letting them continue to worship their gods', reveals an important aspect of the character of Alexander. The man could not have been in the service of Enlil/Yahweh, that's for sure.
'A brotherhood of Man'! Surely that would have been in the interests of humanity. A Brotherhood of Man against the alien Brotherhood of the Gold!

Here we are more interested in the mystical death of Alexander. We shall therefore contribute with a new theory about the consequences of his deeds, more specifically, the consequences of his plans, had he been allowed to live.

Babylon was at that time still a great city, the capital culture-city of the world and a great trade center. A new era of architectural activity, which started under Nebo-Polassar (626–605 BCE) after the fall of Nineveh in 612 BCE, and continued under his son Nebuchadnezzar II (605–562 BCE), established Babylon as one of the wonders of the ancient world. That might have influenced Alexander in his decision to make Babylon his residence, or at least the Capital of the East in his new empire.

Babylon was also the hated city of the Enlilites and of the Jewish scriptures. Babylon was a symbol for the fight the alien rulers. There are no records at all suggesting that the Babylonians were less good than any other people. Babylon being beautiful and important culture and a great trade center is, evidence enough that the scribes of the OT were not expressing their own opinions but the 'words put in their mouth' by their master Enlil/Yahweh. By founding over seventy cities, from Egypt to Afghanistan, Alexander created some kind of Commonwealth 2300 years before the European union.

The consequences of Alexander's campaigns were dramatic but expected. The great Persian Empire was not destroyed but replaced by an even greater one. Marduk's city had again a strong protector against the Enlilite enemies. We shall keep in mind that, despite the fact that Alexander was an outsider, selected neither by Marduk nor by the Enlilites, his deeds were not without significance or consequences to them. The ruling of the whole area, from Egypt to Persia under 1500 years, was dictated by the struggle between Marduk/

Amun and Enlil/Yahweh. They were involved in almost everything that happened there, having the whole situation under their control.

Then suddenly there was a young man who was the master of an even greater area. A young king who didn't have to report to them! For the first time ever, since they came to Earth, Ki-Engi 'the land of the Master Watchers' was under the control of an earthling, without any approval by any god. The master was now the king of the world, who allowed the conquered people to live in peace in a multi culture era, worshiping whatever god they liked. The Hellenic culture was greatly enriched by assimilating the best essences of the cultures of the east.

The new king of the world was there, in Babylon, and neither Marduk nor Enlil could replace him as they used to. In a short period of ca ten years, they witnessed the greatest and fastest changes in the history of Ki-Engi, never happened before in such a short time.

At this time the Enlilite-Elohim must have called the Council of Seven to discuss the new situation. The Council could decide about anything concerning Earth. A decision could be executed immediately or a thousand years later, when the right occasion appeared. Alexander knew nothing about the council, neither about its existence. Yet, it was his greatest enemy, an enemy he couldn't fight because it was invisible. The new enemy of the Enlilites was neither god nor demigod, but an earthling. The new empire was bigger and stronger than the one before. Was Alexander a new servant of Marduk? In that case Marduk was a bigger problem than they thought. If not, what was the man up to? He dreamed to unite the world like Nimrod, against their will. Alexander was about to build something that was 'unpermitted' by the Brotherhood of the Gold. Then something was very wrong. For Marduk however, the situation was hopeful. If the humans could unite themselves and go their own way, without the influence of the gods, then he had achieved his goal. Enki too would be glad to hear.

Even more important than what Alexander had achieved, was what he planned to do. That would seriously disturb the Enlilite brotherhood. How could the Lofty Lords, who could not accept to be defeated by another Lofty Lord, accept to be defeated by an earthling?

What was Alexander planning then? We know that any major changes in the earthly affairs had to be approved and in agreement with the plans of the Brotherhood of the Gold, or traversed by them

if not approved. Non-developments were better than anything else. They would never approve any development of any kind, initiated by humans or gods, if it was disturbing their plans. They had stopped such plans earlier and they were prepared to do it now too.
We have Alexander's plans from the Greek author Diodorus of Sicily in his 'Library of World History', here after a translation by M.M.Austin.

> He was intended to build 1,000 warships larger than triremes, in Phoenicia, Cicilia and Cyprus for the expedition against the Carthaginians and the other inhabitants of the coastal area of Africa, Spain and the neighbouring coasts as far as Sicily; to build a coastal road in Africa as far as the Pillars of Heracles [Gibraltar], and, as required by such a large expedition, to build harbours and shipyards at suitable places;

> In addition, to settle cities and transplant populations from Asia to Europe and vice versa from Europe to Asia, to bring the largest continents through intermarriage and ties of kingship to a common harmony and feeling of friendship.

Very ambitious plans indeed. Certainly very disturbing and contradicting the Enlilite plans. It would not be easy to approve any part of the plan. Like 'to transplant populations from Asia to Europe and vice versa'. It is not easy to imagine the consequences of such an operation. However the important thing here is not our opinion about the plan, or anyone else's opinion, but how it would affect the plans of the Enlilites and even Marduk's situation. If the plan was able to materialize or not, is without significance too, as the important fact was what the Enlilites thought about its possibilities to succeed. We like to remind the reader the words of Enlil when he saw the Tower of Babili, 'and now nothing will be restrained from them, which they have imagined to do'.
    We do not believe that the Enlilites laughed at this plan. The man who conquered the word and built seventy cities in a very short time was certainly capable to achieve these goals too, or at least, some of them. Why would the Enlilites be alarmed by this plan? What do we make out of such tremendous plans? Let us suppose that he didn't die that day, (11th of June 323 BCE) and that he was able to materialize the plan or part of it. Let us take a short look, at the consequences

this would bring upon mankind, as seen from the point of view of the two men who dictated human history and development under long time, Marduk/Amun and Enlil/Yahweh.

From Marduk's point of view, it seems to have been wonderful news. The man who started the building of the Tower of Babylon, together with humans striving after unity, was now witnessing a similar repetition. The world would have seen a unified kingdom from India to Gibraltar. A world trade using the same coin 1500 years before the 'note of hand' of the Templars and 2300 years before the introduction of the Euro in Europe. Was that possible after such a 'short time'? Only some 3000 years, after the incident of the Tower, was really a short time by Anunnaki means.

In time the whole world would speak the same language too. That too, would be a quick restoration from the great tragedy that hit mankind after the confusion of the tongues. The astronomic knowledge of Babylon, the medical science of Hellas, the mathematic science of India, the sacred geometry of Egypt and much more would become common knowledge in the whole empire. There would not be any doubt that the promotion of science would have the highest priority, instead of the promotion of religious doctrines. One does not need to have a decree in economics in order to calculate the effects on development in such a society. Not to mention the escalation of the development.

Ordinary people and traders always valuate a stable economy. Good, effective and profitable trade, has always been of greater importance than whose image was printed on the coins they used. Jobs and food for the family was more important than the name of the emperor. Hopefully, mankind would come under unity, prosperity and development. The humans would govern themselves and make it impossible for the few gods to be around. The most important prerequisite for the survival of the Gold Mission was to be able to control the humans. If they couldn't they would be forced to leave. Then the world would be on the high way of development without any stops for such things like Christianity or Islam. The very strives of Enki and Marduk. The civilization would have been based on science and brotherhood. Not on doctrines and fear, still highly honored in the pages of the OT.

From Enlil/Yahweh's point of view, that would represent everything he so desperately tried to avoid. Especially the unification of the humans that was a postulation of human development. He formally lost his Supremacy because of Marduk, now he would de facto lose his power because of Alexander. The humans had now a good chance to unite themselves once again, under the flag of Alexander, the sixteen-pointed star, which could easily be confused with the symbol of the Sun god, Marduk himself.

The first time mankind was on a program of unity, was when they helped Marduk to build the E-temen-an-ki, only some 3000 years earlier. Should he, the man who destroyed the Tower, confused the languages and scattered the people all over the earth, allow that to happen again? Should he allow mankind to unite itself and strive along a common goal? Should he allow that the E-temen-an-ki would be rebuilt? Why would he, if he had the power to put an end to such a development? Ironically, once again, for the third time in history, the events were taking place at the same location, the beautiful city of Babylon, which Alexander planned to make his residence.

Would the Council of Seven send some 'sky birds' armed with missiles to destroy Babylon and kill Alexander? Not likely. They introduced a new policy, which they had practiced for sometime now, acting behind the lines.

Did they send some messengers in the middle of the night to poison Alexander? Perhaps. They could kill anybody threatening the gold mission. Were the Enlilites about to put an end to this 'Tower' too? Except that the Tower this time was not a building, but another kind of structure. This time the 'tower' was a political-economical structure of global proportions. It would be the beginning of a unified humanity, free from the bondage of the Anunnaki. To stop what was to be the greatest threat ever against the gold mission, they only had to destroy the head of the 'tower', Alexander himself.

The starting point of this short presentation of Alexander's life, so far, has been some facts that almost all writers agree to. About his death, however, there are a lot of theories. Historical records inform us about some unknown kind of fever as the reason of his death. Some equally unknown poison could have caused the fever. Now we have a hypothesis suggesting that some agent operating according to instructions from the Brotherhood of the Gold poisoned Alexander. We have indices but not evidence, yet it is as good as any other theory, as long as contradicting evidence are not presented.

The only certain thing about Alexander's death is that it was caused by fever. Although his physicists (doctors) had not the knowledge the doctors of today possess, most of the diseases of the time were indeed familiar to them as well as most types of fevers. That was not the first time Alexander was struck by fever. His physicists had a lot of effective anti-pyretics and a lot of experience. In this case, however, they were unable to even determine the cause of the fever. As we have seen from Hamurrabi's declaration, the Anunnaki had very advanced medical knowledge. Ninkhursaq was able to cause fever.

> May Nin-karak, the daughter of Anu, who adjudges grace to me, cause to come upon his members in E-kur **high fever, sever wounds, that cannot be healed**, [emphasis added] . . .

'High fever and sever wounds that cannot be healed', leading to death, but still seems like an ordinary fever. Naram-Sin, king of Sumer, died by a bite of a scorpion after he had been cursed by Enlil. Was it an accident, or an assassination looking like an accident, after somebody put a price on his head?

The greatest motive to poison Alexander was to keep mankind divided, unknowing of human history, manipulated about good and evil, unknowing of the secret of the gold powder. That was the motive of the Brotherhood of the Gold. Yet, perhaps not the only one. If Alexander found the secret about the gold powder, independent if the name was 'water of life', 'plant of life' or whatever, then his assassination was only a matter of time. The Brotherhood of the Gold never allowed anybody with such knowledge to live. Laurence Gardner, citing R.S. Loomis, says:

> Alexander the Great of Macedonia (356–323 BC) was said to have owned a Paradise Stone which gave youth to the old.[4]

This only information, if true, would be enough for the brotherhood of the gold to put a price on his head.

It is rather remarkable to find Alexander mentioned in the OT. The book of Daniel is supposed to have been written sometime in the 2nd century BCE, i.e. after the death of Alexander. On the other hand, it is supposed to be based on Daniel's experience under the Babylonian Captivity, some two hundred years before the death of Alexander. It is also regarded as less credible than other books included in the OT. Daniel had many visions and some encounters with some of the alien gods. One of them is concerning Alexander.

If all the deeds of Daniel and the efforts by the Enlilites to assist him attain some disturbance in the palace of Nebuchadnezzar are true, then Daniel must have been a real top agent in the service of Enlil/Yahweh. Daniel 8:16–22 says:

> And I heard a man's voice between the banks of Ulai, which called, and said, Gabriel, make this man to understand the vision. So he came near where I stood: and when he came, I was afraid, and fell upon my face: but he said unto me, Understand, O son of man: for at the time of the end shall be the vision. Now as he was speaking with me, I was in a deep sleep on my face toward the ground: but he touched me, and set me upright. And he said, Behold, I will make you know what shall be in the last end of the indignation: for at the time appointed the end shall be.

> The ram which thou sawest having two horns are the kings of Media and Persia. And the rough goat is the king of Grecia: and the great horn that is between his eyes is the first king.

> Now that being broken, whereas four stood up for it, four kingdoms shall stand up out of the nation, but not in his power.

The scribes of the book of Daniel may have written down events that were history already, in order to elevate the reputation of their god. It's also possible that Gabriel was informing Daniel about future events they would cause to happen, according to plan. Then another question arises. How could they have known about the rise of the Persian and the Hellenic empires? Although it seems like they were foreseen the future, it was nothing like that. They were just simulating, using parameters known to them from observations. A computer simulation program could calculate future possibilities according to information available at the time. Then how could they have known that the first king of the Hellenic empire would be 'broken' down, unless they already had decided to bring him down? All kings, even the most successful have to die some day. But the king mentioned here neither died in battle, nor of a natural death but had been 'broken'.

Besides, Alexander was the product of the Hellenic civilization that was just as dangerous and rebellious to them as Marduk was.

It was based on science and freedom instead of religious bondage. While the Greeks philosophers discussed ideas like the existence of God or not, Daniel and the other agents of Enlil/Yahweh were not allowed to utter the name of their god. It seems that Daniel was unable to understand what the Enlilites wanted him to understand. But that was never a problem, because they provided 'understanding' too. Sometimes they used even drugs (Ezekiel 3:2) to help them understand and remember the message. In Daniel 9:22 we read:

> And he [Gabriel] informed me, and talked with me, and said,
> O Daniel, I am now come forth to give thee skill and under-
> standing.

Once more, we can see how easy it was for the Enlilites to manipulate individuals to be their faithful agents.

Another remarkable fact, about the plans of the Enlilites, was the time they selected for the coming of the Messiah. One could wonder about the significance of that time, time zero of the Christian counting. Why didn't they start that part of the project under the Persian time, or under the Hellenistic period, or any other time? Had they planned to introduce the Messiah particularly under the Roman occupation? Were they afraid that if Alexander had conquered Europe, as he planned to do, then it wouldn't have been any Roman empire? Was it a coincidence that Ninurta/Ares was on the Trojan side during the Trojan War, and Enlil/Zeus directed Aeneas (the ancestor of the Italians) and his followers to Italy? Was it a coincidence that Ninurta/Ares was the great god of the Romans? Was it a coincidence that the death punishment by crucifixion used by the Romans was practiced only by them? Who introduced that kind of death punishment in Rome?

What if Jesus had lived before the Roman occupation of Palestine? Had he been condemned to death under the Persian or the Greek occupation, he would have been executed by the using of spear or the sword. Would the symbol of Christianity have been a spear or a sword? Or, is the confusion of the crucifix with the cross symbol of the home planet of the Anunnaki intentional and planned in advance too? By the way, the symbol of Christianity from the beginning was the fish. The man who replaced it with the cross was, as we shall see, Constantine the great agent and servant of Yahweh.

Even the birth of Jesus was planned long in advance, as Gabriel says in Daniel 9:25:

> Know therefore and understand, that from the going forth of the commandment to restore and to build Jerusalem unto the Messiah the Prince shall be seven weeks, and threescore and two weeks . . .

Gabriel could know the exact time in advance, only if the operation was already planned.

But if Jesus had existed and died under the new era of a united world, then it would be much easier for Christianity to establish itself as the great, and perhaps, the only religion in the world. How very true. Then Enlil/Yahweh would have contributed to another kind of unification, through a common religion. He could not do that, of course. That was against everything he believed on. The man who bombed the Tower, confused the languages and scattered the people all over the Earth, had no wish, whatsoever, to create a world religion. For him, it would be enough with a rather local religion, important enough to be a factor in world's affairs, but small enough to be exposed to the competition of other (already planned?) religions. The Brotherhood of the Gold could, of course, have killed Alexander some ten years earlier, why wait? Because they needed a common language in order to promote Christianity. The man, who didn't want the humans to be able to communicate with one another, was now in need of a common language!

There was really nothing good to expect from God. He might as well have decided to assassinate Alexander. The plans of Alexander and the plans of the Brotherhood of the Gold were just in conflict! They couldn't let an earthling to decide about human affairs. The Enlilites had the motives, a lot of motives, they had the means, some advanced kind of poison, and they certainly had the opportunity. Really, the Enlilites were the only winners by destroying the Tower as well by putting an end to the plans of Alexander the great.

Ironically, the man the Greeks are venerating as God is the same man who probably ordered the murder of their greatest hero. They are worshiping the man who brought an end to unification and common progress of the people of the Earth. The man who also initiated the destruction of their great ancient civilization and did everything he could to neutralize the influence of science and philosophy. By judging his actions, we find that he has no right to demand any glorification from us.

These warrior Enlilites, these conspirators against mankind are the real characters behind God and his angels in the holy book of the Christians. As we have seen, Enlil/Yahweh was morally responsible for the murder of Nimrod. He could be equally responsible and suspected for the murder of Alexander the great.

A Greek woman, in the meddle of the first century CE, said to her husband:

"Dear husband, since we expect another child, we would need one more room. As a bricklayer you could easily build one."

"I will take care of it as soon as the harvest fest is over, and gods willing," the husband said.

---

[1]Dr. Agnes Savill, Alexander the Great and his Time p. 187 Citing Plutarch of Chaeronea (46-122 CE)

[2]N.G.L. Hammond, The Genius of Alexander the Great

[3]www.geocities.com/ranajitda 'Alexander's dream of a United Nations, by Dr. Ranajit Pal

[4]Laurence Gardner, Genesis of the Grail Kings, p. 178

Chapter 19

THE SON OF GOD OR THE SON OF YAHWEH

Arriving over the clouds

According to the first book of Abraham, God visited him in Egypt at the end of the seventh year. God changed Abram's name to Abraham, meaning 'bright shepherd father', and Sarai's name to Sara, meaning 'princess'. He had already introduced a new 'name' for himself! He informed Abraham about the coming Moses, 'a prince from among the Egyptians' and the coming of the Messiah. First book of Abraham 77:5:

> Moreover, from the loins of thy heir shall precede the Messiah, even the Son of God, who shall work upon the Earth . . .

Luke 1:26:

> And in the sixth month the angel Gabriel was sent from God unto a city in Galilee, named Nazareth, to a virgin espoused to a man whose name was Joseph, of the house of David: and the virgin's name was Mary.

Luke 1:31:

> And, behold, thou shall conceive in thy womb, and bring forth a son, and shall call his name JESUS.

Mathew 1:23 says:

> Behold, a virgin shall be with child, and shall bring forth a
> son, and they shall call his name Emmanuel.

Much was decided in advance, even his name(s)! What a fate for a
child! We find a parallel in Islam. There too is Gabriel acting, according to the instructions of 'the Lord of the Throne' (Enlil). There
too he decided the name of the new religion, which was to be 'Islam', meaning 'Surrender'. Surrender to the will of Enlil alias El,
Elon, Eloh, Ila, Ilu, Elil, Elloh, Allah, in the same way the Israelites
were commanded to total obedience to Enlil/Yahweh.

Suppose Mary had been informed about what was going to happen to her son. Would she still have accepted the offer? Or would
she place him in a basket and put him on the waters like the mother
of Sargon and the mother of Moses before her?

If Luke is telling us the truth, then Jesus was the result of an artificial insemination of a demigoddess, with the seed of some Anunnaki. There is nothing supernatural about that.

Now, Mary, the mother of Jesus, was conceived in a similar way.
While conceiving by the natural way, (is called 'sinful' in the holy
scriptures), the sex and other properties of a child are determined at
random, by artificial insemination, (is called 'pure' in the holy scriptures), it is possible to decide such values in advance, even the color
of the child's eyes. Enlil/Yahweh having children of his own, by the
usual way of mating, we presume, was also practicing 'the sinful
way'. And the girl Mary, born by Anna was taken to the Temple, at
the age of three, and her parents left her there for some nine years.

The Apocrypha Gospel of James, the brother of Jesus, also known
as Protoevangelion (the first gospel), states in chapter 4:

> And behold an angel of the Lord appeared, saying unto her:
> Anna, Anna, the Lord hath hearkened unto thy prayer, and
> thou shalt bear, and thy seed shall be spoken of in the whole
> world.

And then in 8:1:

> . . . And Mary was in the temple of the Lord as a dove that is
> nurtured: and she received food from the hand of an angel.

Both the birth of Mary and the birth of her son were scheduled long in advance. Was the 'food provided to Mary by an angel' ordinary food, or some gold powder? Mary being a child of Anunnaki seed, and an earthly mother, was then a demigod (50% Anunnaki and 50% earthling), which makes Jesus extraterrestrial up to 75%. William Bramley says:

> The only stipulation for this honor was that Joachim and his wife must surrender their child to be raised by the priests and angels at a temple in Jerusalem.[1]

The 'Messiah' project was just a continuation of a plan that started by selecting Abraham to be the father of people with total obedience to Yahweh.

At the time of the birth of Jesus, there were signs in the heavens. The bible says that a bright star guided three wise men from Persia to Bethlehem and back again, which excludes any natural phenomenon. In fact, there are striking similarities between the birth of Jesus and the birth of Abraham. In Abraham book I 22:1 we read:

> On the night that I [Abraham] was born, there were great signs in the heavens, and when Nimrod's astrologers saw them, they were astonished and they spoke evil of me to the king, saying that surely I should overthrow his kingdom.

The Indian 'Messiah' Krishna was also born by a virgin, his earthly father being a carpenter too. A star in the east also announced his birth. Theologians and bible believers think of Jesus as the Son of God, while others believe in Jesus as the good teacher with no divine inheritance. Additionally, others believe that he never existed.

According to Daniel 7:13–14, Jesus was to be 'arriving over the clouds, the triumphant son of man coming with power'. Zecharia 9:9 states that 'he will be riding on a donkey'.

The expectations among the Jews were also various. He would throw out the Romans and restore Israel in all the ways. Others believed in cultic reforms and a true interpretation of the law.

Neither Enlil/Yahweh nor his 'angels' made any announcement of the type 'this is the Messiah I promised you', or 'this is the king', or 'this is the teacher', or 'Savor', or 'my son'. Why not? Because they didn't know, at the time that Jesus would pass the test. They had raised up kings in the past, educated them, prepared them for the task, but we do not know how many of these demigods and humans never came that long as to be kings. Surely some of them didn't 'passed the final test', or didn't wish to serve the gods. What should become of Jesus was depended on the environment around him, the education he was supposed to receive, the kind of his character and his own expectations, certainly all these factors that form the character of any human being.

That means that Enlil/Yahweh had to wait and see if Jesus was to be trusted the job. It was just an investment with uncertain outcome. According to a well-supported theory, Jesus had a twin brother by the name James (Jacob). If Jesus was conceived by insemination, then the twins could have been according to plan rather than by chance. James could represent 'plan B' in case Jesus failed.

What do we know about Jesus' life? There is not much information about his life, in fact, so little that there is a doubt about his existence. St Epiphanius claimed that Jesus was born during the reign of king Alexander Jannaeus (103–76 BCE). Irenaeus (130–202 CE) claimed that Jesus was more than fifty years old when he died. Many writers support the idea of Jesus being a member of the Essenes, which was one of the three major religious sects, the other two being the Pharisees and the Sadducees. The Essenes were also in possession of great medical skills originated in Egypt. Their symbol was a coiled serpent around a staff, the very symbol of Enki, the 'Wise serpent'. The Greek Asklepios of Thessaly (c. 1200 BC), the great father of medicine, had a serpent coiled around a plant as his symbol. The same symbol as used today by several medical societies.

It is possible that Jesus was sent to some Essene monastery from the age of 5 until 12, as it was common among the Essences, for the purpose of education and practice, like his mother. Then he made an appearance in Jerusalem at the age of 12, only to disappear again until the age of thirty. Now, if Jesus was planned to be the Messiah promised by Enlil/Yahweh, then it is only logical to assume that they provided him with a great lot of education. He seems to have been an intelligent man with the ability to consume all they had to offer him, perhaps even more than they planned to. Then what? What was he supposed to do next? Was he supposed to go out announcing that he was the expected king who would restore Israel?

It is not without interest to recall the announcements made by several kings, appointed and supported by the gods, as presented in a previous chapter. Many of them announced that the kingship had been handled over to them by some god. The gods also used to call these kings as their 'servants', at least, as long as the kings acted according to instructions given to them.

Jesus said nothing about being 'the Messiah' or 'appointed by God'. Neither did Enlil/Yahweh nor Ninurta/Gabriel. Instead, suddenly and quietly he began to practice peace instead of war, love instead of hate, understanding instead of violence, free will instead of obedience. Why?

Should they accept that the man they educated for a specific purpose, supposed to be given 'great powers', preached love and peace? Or should they wait and see? Enlil/Yahweh never practiced love and peace. Was he currying out the task assigned to him or had they raised a rebellion that had no fear or respect for their great powers?

What kind of education had Jesus? A lot we might think. He knew all about Abraham, Moses and the history of the Israelites. Probably he knew most of the secrets of the Anunnaki, including the 'secret of the gold powder'. He was probably consuming gold dust, which would explain the story of 'walking on the waters'.

We have reasons to believe that a disagreement took place between Enlil/Yahweh and Jesus, at the time Jesus should be ready to undertake the task assigned to him. We have reasons to believe that Jesus was in serious trouble, according to our theory. We believe that the conflict between them was about the nature of the mission. He could not serve these people because he knew about their mission on Earth. The mission they wanted him to perform was not for the benefit of humanity. Jesus cared about his people, they did not.

On the other hand, he could not refuse because he knew that they could replace him with someone else, probably his twin brother, in order to complete the task. Whatever the task might have been. So he had to convince them that he could reach the wanted results by going his own way. Did they believe him? Probably not, but they gave him a chance and at the same time, they laughed at him. After all, he represented a great investment to them. That is why they never said 'This is the Messiah I promised you'. They avoided to be connected with somebody who could turn up to be a rebellion. Somebody they could not really trust. That is why Jesus never said that he was 'the Messiah'. He was prohibited to do that. At the same time, he was hoping to be accepted as the Messiah by doing things in accordance with the Jewish prophecies, like entering Jerusalem riding on a donkey. That was much easier to fulfill than to 'arrive on the clouds'. He knew that by doing so, he was preventing Enlil/Yahweh to replace him.

So he went his own way for three years. Preaching a lot good things, like love and peace but also things imprinted to him under his education, like spiritual salvation was possible only after death. That was in accordance with Enlil's dogma 'An Earthling you are and an Earthling shall you remain'. That was also against Marduk's teachings to the Egyptians, that they could become spiritual beings because 'gold was the splendor of Life'. What knowledge could Jesus possibly have on this matter? Is there any man, or 'god', who knows that there is some kind of life after death, or what such a life is like? Jesus was also contradicting himself by saying that 'everything is possible if you believe'. How can then spiritual salvation under lifetime be impossible, if everything is possible?

Had Jesus any authority to give us spiritual salvation or to reveal the secrets of the gold powder, which is a part of spiritual salvation? He had been preaching, demanding, promising, and threatening for three years. By what authority was he doing that? According to Mathew 28:18 he had every kind of authority.

> And Jesus came and spake unto them, saying, All power is given unto me in heaven and in earth.

Yahweh used to call his father's kingdom on Nibiru 'the kingdom of heavens'. Was Jesus also speaking about the same kingdom? Why did he never mention 'Yahweh' by name? He was also contradicting some of the teachings of Enlil/Yahweh. Enlil/Yahweh in Exodus 21:23–25:

> . . . thou shalt give life for life, Eye for eye, tooth for tooth, hand for hand, foot for foot, burning for burning, wound for wound, stripe for stripe.

Jesus in Mathew 5:39:

> . . . ye resist not evil; but whosoever shall smite thee on the right cheek, turn to him the other also.

Enlil/Yahweh in Genesis 17:10:

> This is my covenant, which ye shall keep, between me and
> you and thy seed after thee; Every man-child among you shall
> be circumcised.

Jesus in Galatians 5:2:

> . . . if ye be circumcised, Christ shall profit you nothing.

There are a lot more contradictions between the two and even among
Jesus' own teachings. We believe the contradictions were on purpose
rather than by accident. We believe it is obvious that the purpose was
to distance himself from Yahweh. Three years was all the time he
got. Enlil and his angels decided to put an end to his deeds. He had
his chance. The results of his job were unacceptable. Put him on
trial. Put him to death. The man was cheating them. He might have
been more intelligent than they thought.

By putting him to death, despite the fact if he died on the cross,
or not, they discovered that they could make use of it, or perhaps
that was the real purpose. They could turn the whole thing to their
advantage. By using his death, which they, themselves caused, they
could indeed create a martyr, a Messiah. For the first time since Gabriel announced Maria that she was to bring forth the Messiah, they
made every effort to convince the disciples of Jesus that the man
was indeed the Son of God. They didn't need Jesus any more, but
they could use the consequences of the Crucifixion. The disciples
instructed to preach that everywhere, which they did. Christianity
was born. So was also another major factor for creating conflicts.
His chosen people, as well as the Romans have been accused as
responsible for crucifying Jesus, although the most probable can-
didate for that responsibility is Enlil/Yahweh himself. According to
Jesus it was Enlil/Yahweh, 'the ruler and his angels', who ordered
and planned the crucifixion.

Do we have any document supporting this theory? As a matter of
fact there is such a document.

'The Second Treatise of the Great Seth' is one of the documents
founded in Egypt in 1945. Among these documents, with the common name 'The Nag Hammadi Library' are The Book of James, the
Gospel of Thomas, The Gospel of Philip, The Gospel of Truth, The

Gospel to the Egyptians, The Hypothesis of the Archons, The Testimony of Truth and many others. Some of them are in accordance with the bible, some not. The scriptures were hidden in Egypt in the fourth century to avoid destruction. One of them begins with 'These are the secrets words which the living Jesus spoke, and which the twin, Judas Thomas, wrote down'.

'These are the secret words which the living Jesus'. The 'secret words' are highly troubling. Why 'secret words'? Was it because Jesus was forbidden to act publicly after the 'crucifixion'? Or was it because Yahweh sent him away (like he did with Ziusudra/Noah) to avoid that truth be known? He might have had no other choice either, than to go to exile in order to save his family. In fact, we know from many Sumerian texts that 'exile' was a common punishment practiced by the Anunnaki. We also know that Egypt was always the place the Jews chose to go when in trouble. Either we have the words of Jesus, or the words of some of his friends who fled away after the crucifixion fearing for their lives, the Nag Hammadi documents are both older, and much more credible than some of the gospels. It is, most likely, first-hand information, not passed through the later censure of the Nicaean doctrines.

'The Second Treatise of the Great Seth' talks about 'the archons'. The word (from Greek) means 'rich'. It also means 'powerful', and for that reason it has always been supposed to refer to wealthy people, the Jewish priests or the Roman occupants. But Jesus gives more information about them. He is also calling them 'The Ruler and his angels', 'the Cosmocrator' and 'those of the race of Adonaios'. He even makes a clear distinction between 'the race of Adonaios' i.e. the Anunnaki-Yahwists and 'those of the race that came down' i.e. the Igigi/Titans or Nephilim. 'The Ruler and his angels' couldn't be other than Enlil/Yahweh and his sons. This is also an obvious distinction between two races, the race of the gods and the human race. 'Cosmocrator' is equivalent to 'Pantocrator', meaning 'the ruler of the world' and the ruler of all' like 'Almighty'. Adonaios comes from the Phoenician Adon, a name the Jews applied to Yahweh.

In 'The Second Treatise of the great Seth' translated by Roger A. Bullard and Joseph A. Gibbons, we read what Jesus himself is supposed to have said about the plan of Enlil/Yahweh:

I visited a bodily dwelling . . . And the whole multitude of the archons became troubled. And all the matter of the archons, as

well as all begotten powers of the earth, were shaken when it
saw the likeness of the Image, since it was mixed . . . I did not
refused them even to become a Christ, but I did not revealed
myself to them in the love which was coming forth from me.

There was a great disturbance in the whole earthly area, with
confusion and flight, as well as (in) the plan of the archons.
And some were persuaded, when they saw the wonders which
were being accomplished by me. And all these, with the race,
that came down, flee from him . . . others also fled, as if from
the Cosmocrator and those with them, since they have brought
every (kind of) punishment upon me. And there was a flight of
their mind about what they would counsel concerning me . . .

'I visited a bodily dwelling'. If these are words uttered by Jesus,
which we believe they are, then he knew something about spiritual
salvation under lifetime.

'I did not refuse them even to become a Christ'. Think of it for a
while. That means that they asked him, or demanded from him to be
the anointed one, the Christ. If this is true, then Jesus is saying that
he was pretending to be the Christ, their agent.

The document also confirms a disagreement between 'the plan
of the archons', and 'the wonders accomplished by me'. Some of
the Igigi in the service of the Cosmocrator 'flee from him' i.e. they
disagreed about the plan. But this was not without consequences for
Jesus, because 'they have brought every (kind of) punishment upon
me'. As we understand, there is no doubt that there was indeed a
schism between the ruler Enlil/Yahweh, and Jesus. He took part of
the plan unwillingly. He didn't believed in the plan but he could not
refuse either.

'Ennoia' can be translated as 'Understanding'.

Jesus about Yahweh and his Plan

And then a voice—of the Cosmocrator—came to the angels:
'I am God and there is no other beside me'. But I laughed
joyfully when I examined his empty glory. But he went on to
say 'Who is man?' And the entire host of his angels, who had
seen Adam and his dwelling, were laughing at his smallness
. . . I placed the small Ennoia in the world, having disturbing
them and frightened the whole multitude of the angels and

their ruler. And I was visiting them all with fire and flame because of my Ennoia.

And everything pertaining to them was brought about because of me. And there came about a disturbance and a fight about the Seraphim and Cherubim, since their glory will fade, and the conclusion around Adonaios on both sides and their dwelling—to the Cosmocrator and him who said, 'Let us size him'; others again, 'The plan will certainly not materialize.

For Adonaios knows me because of hope. And I was in the mouth of lions. And the plan, which they devised about me to release their Error and their senselessness—I did not succumb to them as they had planned. But I was not afflicted at all.

For the Archon was a laughingstock because he said 'I am God, and there is none greater than I. I alone am the father, the Lord, and there is no other beside me. I am a jealous God, who brings the sins of the fathers upon the children for three and four generations' . . .

And he does not agree with our Father, for he was a laughingstock and judgment and false prophecy.

We never know about the details discussed at that meeting, or the fight about the Seraphim and the Cherubim. But still, we have a lot of useful information in the above text.

'Were laughing at his smallness'. We know from other documents that these gods saw man as a primitive creature with minor qualifications. Without activation of the spiritual body, the physical body is but 'flesh', as Enlil/Yahweh often used to say.

It must have been some violent discussion about the plan. They were frightened. There was also a disagreement among them. Some wanted to 'size him', and violently prevent him from going against the divine plan. Then others didn't believe that he would be able to carry out his own plan of 'love and peace'.

'For Adonaios knows me because of hope'. This only sentence reveals a lot about the relationship between Enlil/Yahweh and Jesus. He is telling us that Enlil/Yahweh needed him otherwise he would not even 'know him'. He was hoping that Jesus would carry out their plan. 'I did not succumb as they had planned'. He is telling us that they (the ruler and his angels) had a plan for him, which he rejected. 'Having disturbing them, and frightened the whole multitude of the angels, and their ruler', says that Jesus turned their plans upside down.

Jesus surrounded by angels in our churches, is a sharp contradiction to his words. The angels were never his 'friends' because they either wished to seize him or laughed at him.

They were his enemies, as well as the enemies of the whole humanity. They were the angels of Enlil/Yahweh, his messengers. Jesus said that the man is a laughingstock because he said 'I am God'. We believe that Jesus had a better knowledge about the god of the OT than we have.

Worthy to note is also the distinction made by Jesus between 'him' (Enlil/Yahweh) and 'our father'. What is obvious here is that 'our father' is certainly not Enlil/Yahweh, the God of the OT.

About the Crucifixion

Those who were there punished me. And I did not died in reality but in appearance, lest I be put to shame by them because these are my kinsfolk. For my death, which they think happened, (happened) to them in their error and blindness, since they nailed their man unto their death . . . Yes, they saw me; they punished me. It was another, their father, who drank the gall and the vinegar; it was not I. They stuck me with the reed; it was another, Simon, who bore the cross on his shoulders. It was another upon Whom they placed the crown of thorns . . .

They nailed him to the tree, and they fixed him with four nails of brass. The veil of his temple he tore with his hands . . . Therefore they knew what I speak of, for we took counsel about the destruction of the archons. And therefore I did the will of the father, who is I.

Here we do not know if Jesus speaks literal, or symbolically, about the Crucifixion. Perhaps both. What we do know however, is that he, (with some other persons, 'took counsel') wishing the destruction of the archons as being his enemies, and therefore even the enemies of humanity. It is possible that more scrolls about 'the destruction of the archons' had been written, and hidden somewhere in Egypt.

We have to keep in mind that all that is in our possession today in the form of scrolls, clay tablets or whatever, is but a minor part of what has been written down. 'The destruction of the archons' speaks certainly about some revolt. A revolt never developed because of the crucifixion. He also supports the information in the book of the Acts of the Apostles, even supported by several writers, that he was not crucified on the cross, but on a tree.

> The God of our fathers raised up Jesus, whom they slew and hanged on a tree.

The text connects Yahweh with 'the ruler and his angels', and also Jesus with Enlil/Yahweh, 'the God of our fathers', the god 'El-Shadai', or 'Ilu-kur-Gal'. This expression is more credible than 'God', and has been used to describe the god of his people, like 'the God of the Egyptians' or 'the God of Babylon'. The 'god of our fathers', referring to the Commander Enlil, is in conflict with the expression 'God'.

About the Gold

> For that which is not theirs and that which is theirs they use fearlessly and freely. They do not desire, because they have authority, and a law from themselves over whatever they will wish.

This is n amazing statement. They didn't ask for permission, they just took because they had the power. How very true! Now what did they take from Earth? There is no record whatsoever, that they have been taking anything else than **gold** (and other precious metals). And they used it fearlessly and freely. Another evidence that he was aware of the gold operations of the Ruler and his angels. He certainly knew how they used the gold powder too. The Sumerians, however, informed us that Enlil and the other gods came to Earth for the gold of the planet.

'The Hebdomad' (sevenfold), was probably the 'seven who judge', a council of seven judges on Nibiru, which they applied here on Earth too. 'The Hebdomad' was a group of executives deciding about all matters concerning Earthly affairs. Enki was one of them, but he alone could not make his voice heard, he was often in opposition to the majority of the council. The council had much to do with power, and less with democracy, or justice.

About the Agents
> Solomon was a laughingstock, since he thought that he was Christ, having become vain through the Hebdomad . . .

> The 12 prophets were laughingstocks, since they have come forth as imitations of the true prophets. They came into being as counterfeits through the Hebdomad . . .

> Moses, a faithful servant, was a laughingstock, having been named 'The Friend', since they perversely bore witness concerning him who never knew me . . .

We have stated here and there that the prophets were just the agents of Enlil/Yahweh. They were used by him like Moses was. 'They came into being through the Hebdomad', can only be understood, as they had been appointed by the council of the gods. They knew nothing about Jesus or the faithful Moses. What they said about him were just the words Enlil/Yahweh 'had put in their mouths'.

Jesus About Himself
> I am Christ, the Son of Man, the one from you who is among you. I am despised for your sake..

'The Son of Man' contradicts the church doctrine that Jesus was the Son of God. Jesus acting, as the advocate of humanity was despised because he didn't accept the mission they assigned to him. He couldn't accept because he knew the truth about the Gold Mission. Joseph A. Gibbons in 'The Nag Hammadi Library' says:

> There is no doubt that the Second Treatise of the Great Seth is a work that is both Christian and Gnostic . . . Knowledge is the means of salvation. **The God of this world is evil and ignorant, and can be identified with the God of the Old Testament;** [emphasis added] in addition all his minions are mere counterfeits and laughingstocks.

More opinions about the Nag Hammadi collection from Holy Blood, Holy Grail:

Taken as a whole, the Nag Hammadi collection constitutes an invaluable repository of early Christian documents-some of which can claim an authority equal to that of the Gospels. What is more, certain of these documents enjoy a claim to a unique veracity of their own. In the first place, they escaped the censorship and revision of later roman orthodoxy. In the second place, they were originally composed for an Egyptian, not a Roman, audience, and are not therefore distorted or slanted to Romanized ear. Finally, they may well rest on first-hand and/or eyewitness sources-oral accounts by Jews fleeing the Holy land, for instance, perhaps even personal acquaintances or associates of Jesus, who could tell their story with a historical fidelity the Gospels could not afford to retain.[2]

What are we to believe about Jesus? If he was 'the Son of God' as the Bible claims, then no human can identify himself with him, neither is it possible to imitate him. If he was the son of man, then he had some admirable qualities. In that case, he is not unique as there have been other humans who lived a pure life, performed 'wonders' and preached love and peace, like Apollonius of Tyana and the Indian Sages.

If he was the son of Yahweh, or the son of some other Anunnaki, as we believe, pretending to be their agent, and at the same time worked against them, then we ought to admire his courage and the information concerning the alien rulers he left behind.

Are we open to discuss alternative interpretations of the Bible, or are the powerful doctrines of Yahweh keeping us in a permanent state of mental status quo?

---

[1]William Bramley, The gods of Eden, p. 121
[2]Michael Baigent, Richard Leigh & Henry Lincoln, Holy Blood, Holy Grail, p. 381

Chapter 20

APOLLONIUS, PAULUS AND CONSTANTINE

Agents of different agencies

Christianity is a composite of Christian beliefs, practiced ancient traditions and older religions and philosophies, often associated with the Sun god. Therefore, Christ is often associated with old pagan gods like Osiris who is supposed to control the place of the souls, the child Horus, with Krishna, probably because of the similarity of the names, Apollonius of Tyana because of the similarity of the 'miracles' they performed and even with the Sun itself.

The most usual word in Christian liturgy, beside God, is 'Amen' meaning 'let it be according to Amun's will'. The first known Sun god was Marduk who declared himself as 'Ra' (Bright) in Egypt around 3450 BCE. He built Heliopolis (city of the Sun). He also built Babylon and became its Supreme god. He later became 'Amun' meaning 'the invisible'.

At around 1500 BCE he was the most famous god in the whole Middle East under several names, like 'Marduk', 'Bel', 'Ra', 'Amun', 'Sol Invictus' or 'Helios' and even as 'Mithras' in Rome. He was honored with great popularity among the humans, while Enlil/Yahweh was on a program to create his own supporters in the country he allotted to Abraham. According to the OT, (Jeremiah 51:44), Yahweh had always some plan how to hurt Egypt and destroy Babylon so that '. . . the nations shall not flow together any more unto him [Bel/Marduk]'. Those two gods were engaged in continual wars with each other using both powerful weapons and human soldiers. The struggle was, however, definitely not of some religious character. Since Marduk was the adversary of Enlil, who later became God, Marduk is supposed to be the adversary of God. Any adversary of God is supposed to be evil, although the adversaries of Enlil, gods and humans alike, were all friends and protectors of mankind.

At the time of Jesus there had been several famous religions, philosophy schools and famous individuals, attached to question about spiritual life and the relations between gods and men. Among the most known men and gods were the following:

Apollonius of Tyana and the Indian Sages

Apollonius, Jesus and Paulus (St Paul) were three contemporary individuals who in different ways influenced the future of mankind. Apollonius was famous in the whole Roman Empire. He was the most educated and traveled man of his time. The Christians have destroyed his works, as most of the ancient knowledge. Not surprisingly, the influence of Jesus and Paul began to expand thereafter. Some scholars claim that the Pauline 'epistles' are the work of Apollonius, or at least, that Paul must have been much influenced by him.

Both were born the same year (4 BCE) in Asia Minor by wealthy parents. Paul was supposed to have been in disagreement with Peter, the disciple of Jesus, just because of the influence of Apollonius' teachings and his Hellenistic education, except, of course, with regard to his opinions about the status of women. Note that the members of the Pythagorean schools, Apollonius was a Pythagorean, were both men and women, while Paul didn't consider women as worthy to participate in the affairs of the society. The inequality between men and women, introduced by Paulus, is still visible in the orthodox churches where different spaces are allotted to men, at the front part, and to women, at the back part of the church.

Apollonius is credited with pure life, numerous healings, and 'wonders' and both his life and his many journeys throughout the world, are considered as historical facts. He was most admired by ordinary people as well as by Emperors. One of his greatest qualities was his great understanding for other opinions not demanding from any one to follow his way of life. He too, was born under remarkable circumstances and disappeared at the age of 98, probably to meet again with the Sages of India, although nobody knows.

He visited the Master Brahmans, the Sages of India who were rather unknown in Europe at that time, except, perhaps, to the Pythagoreans. Who were those sages and what knowledge did they possess? Did they know what was going on in the land of Jesus? Was Apollonius their answer to the 'messiah project' of Yahweh, or was that project nothing to worry about? Did they assist him in finding that particular place?

> He saw before him a description of the exact spot which he had to reach, of the monastery among the ten thousand monasteries in India that was the adobe of the men who know Truth. Apollonius was to be the last Western emissary for centuries. After him the door was shut. Thenceforward it was to be possible to create light only from the almost vanished fragments of the ancient wisdom. Darkness was about to fall for centuries on the Christian world.[1]

We know a lot about Apollonius and the Indian Sages because of Damis. He was the disciple that followed Apollonius and wrote down everything concerning his life, journeys, and teachings. The most we know about Apollonius comes from the 'Life of Apollonius' by Philostratrus, the only book that survived the Christian mobs.

Apollonius had some remarkable things to say about the Sages of India. We learn that they lived in a castle, enveloped by clouds on the top of a hill defended on all sides by piles of rocks. They didn't need to fortify the place as it offered a natural defense. Coincidently, the Igigi/Titans used to fortify their cities as a defense against the attacks of the Enlilites. As we have seen, they did so in Baalbek, in Sodom, in Gomorra, Jericho and in Troy. The Sages were vegetarians and ate what they, themselves produced and of offerings from the people living in the valley. They didn't use alcohol, and could levitate themselves two cubits high from the ground. They had robots 'tripod' (moving on three feet/wheels) serving them food, thus avoiding servants. They called themselves gods because they were good men. Apollonius describes them as:

> Brahmas who dwell on earth, and yet are not on the earth; in places fortified, and yet without walls; and who possess nothing and yet all things.[2]

He was quite satisfied in meeting the Sages, and they seem to have appreciated his visit too. Before his departure, they gave him seven rings, named after the seven planets and told him to ware one for each day of the week. The rings were supposed to give him **health and long life**! Apollonius says:

> . . . they all curry both a ring and a staff of which the peculiar virtues can effect all things, and the one and the other, so we learn, are prized as secrets.[3]

It is understandable if they had secrets. We believe that their history was as interesting as their knowledge.

As we have seen in an earlier chapter, Marduk wandered all over the Earth. As he said, 'from where the sun goes up to where the sun settles down'. The last time, we know he traveled around the world was when he left Babylon around the year 2000 BCE waiting for the sign of the Ram to appear in the skies. We assume that he was not traveling alone but with some followers perhaps both Anunnaki/ Titans and Earthlings.

In the valley of Kashmir, not long from the castle of the Sages, there is a little town by the name Srinagar that means 'the home of Sri-Naga', the 'Serpent King'. The serpent was considered as a symbol of wisdom and it was associated with Enki and his son Ningishzidda.

The connection between the 'Nagas' (wise serpents, healers) and the 'wise serpents' of Egypt is not only obvious but also supported by Iarchas, the leader of the Sages at the time. He told Apollonius that the origin of their knowledge was Egypt. Marduk's brother Thoth was known in Mesoamerica as Quetzalcoatl, the 'feather Serpent' and we are not surprised to find the term 'Nagas' (healers) even in Mexico.

Not long from Srinagar, there is the ruin of the ancient Temple of the Sun. The temple was probably the work of Marduk (the sun god of the Egyptians) and his followers. Perhaps some of them chose to stay there and the Brahmans Apollonius visited could have been Igigi or their descendants. As we have seen, they were hunted and persecuted by the Enlilites. According to the Greek Mythology, the Igigi/Titans were defeated by Zeus (Enlil). Mythology is often mediating historical events!

Since Enlil/Yahweh used to chase them, provided that he knew where they lived, their only chance to survive was to hide away in distant lands out of his reach; like the 'Asar' gods who wandered northward to Scandinavia after the fall of Troy.

Did the Sages choose the location by chance? The place was very easy to defend, that was certainly one of the reasons. Another reason was that 'they regarded the top of the hill as the navel of the Earth'. Furthermore, their knowledge and their will to release such knowledge to humans was in accordance with the actions of the Egyptian gods, like Ptah, Thoth, Marduk, Osiris, Isis and the 'Brotherhood of the Serpent'. Marduk probably visited Japan too, under his wanderings around the world. The Sun goddess Amaterasu could have been a daughter of his. Her name in Japanese appears to mean 'Brightness of heaven'. In the tongue of the Anunnaki, however, 'Amat-E-Ra-Su' could mean 'House of the bright mother' or 'House of the Sun mother' which could be connected to the Sun god Ra-Marduk. The Japanese Emperors are supposed to be descendants of the Sun Goddess. There is no evidence, written or oral, that Marduk, in his wanderings all over the Earth, ever forced anybody to worship him, in contrast to Yahweh who said 'you shall not have other gods beside me'.

The presence of Anunnaki-Titans in India would explain, not only the advanced philosophical knowledge of the Brahman Sages, but also their advanced technology, allowing them to manufacture robots, like 'the serving tripods', the powerful rings, and the staff with properties we can't explain with other words than 'wonders'. The word 'miracle' was not known before Christianity and Apollonius never used the word. Perhaps because he knew that the 'magical' power of some staff was not magical at all. Our ancestors would certainly have regarded the power inside very small microchips of today as magical or even as 'miracles'.

The Sages being some Igigi/Titans, or some of their descendants who survived persecutions and genocides, or some of the followers of Marduk, they were friends of humanity still hiding in mountainous areas in order to escape from the Enlilite-persecutors. Their Goal was to help organize the humans under the **Brotherhood of Man,** against the alien tyranny of the Brotherhood of the Gold. Apollonius publicly denounced the reigning of tyranny which, we believe, was a result of the knowledge released to him by those peaceful gods.

The Sages also assigned some tasks to Apollonius, which he willingly accepted. Among the most important was to restore religions on the level they should be, to spread the ancient wisdom to the west, and traverse evil Roman Emperors. He considered himself as their emissary, which makes him the agent of those gods, in contrast to Jesus who had been forced to act as the agent of Yahweh.

Many historians and philosophers wrote about Apollonius but none of their works have survived, except for 'The life of Apollonius' by Philostratus. None of Apollonius' own works has survived either.

The Christian Church launched attacks particularly upon the life and work of Apollonius as a part of the great persecution of religions, philosophies, and science; only references to his books and life have survived.

Dion Cassius, Roman historian 155–229, stated that Emperor Caracalla (211–217) honored the memory of Apollonius with a temple.

Aelius Lampridius, 4-century, wrote that Emperor Alexander Severus (222–235) had the statue of Apollonius in his lararium.

Vopiscus, 3rd century, wrote that Apollonius was a manifestation of deity and no other than he was more holy, more venerable and more god-like.

Hierocles, 3rd century, wrote that the Christians did not have the exclusive right in 'miracles' as proof of the divinity of their master. He also claimed that the Christians created Jesus as a plagiarism of Apollonius. It was the two books of Hierocles (Truthful Words to the Christians) that caused Eusebius (275–339) to write his book 'Against Hierocles'. Eusebius denied that the wonderful things ascribed to Apollonius ever happened or, if they did, they were the work of daemons. The same 'wonderful things' ascribed to Jesus are supposed to be the work of God! Why the books of Hierocles vanished while the books of Eusebius have come down to us is a question for Christian theologians to answer!

St Jerome, 347–420, wrote that Apollonius found everywhere something to learn and something whereby to become a better man.

Marcus Aurelius (121–180 CE) learned (through Apollonius) freedom of will and understanding, steadiness of purpose and to look to nothing else, not even for a moment, except to reason.

By comparing the thoughts of Marcus Aurelius with those of Epiphanius of Salamis (315–403 CE) bishop of Cyprus, as stated in his 'Panarion 65' below, it becomes obvious that Marcus Aurelius was a freethinking man while Epiphanius was a captive of the doctrines of Yahweh.

We can tell the solution of any question not through our own reasonings but from what follows from the scriptures.

Some writers consider Apollonius as the prototype of Christ and even the man behind the Christian Jesus. We believe that even if Apollonius was more peaceful than Jesus, better educated, more traveled, and even if he performed more 'miracles' than Jesus, he was not Jesus. It is not known how much he knew about Yahweh, but he never mentioned him or Jesus, witnessing that they were unknown outside Jewish habitations. He would never accept Yahweh's doctrines, threats, or violence. Apollonius taught religious tolerance and subjection to science, things completely unknown to Yahweh and Christian beliefs.

Mithras/Sol Invictus

The Jews celebrated the seventh day of the week as the day of resting from labor, because God rested the seventh day, after all the work he had done! God had a human body, although very healthy because of the gold powder! The citizens of the Roman Empire celebrated the birthday of the Sun. The name of the cult was 'Sol Invictus' meaning 'the invisible Sun', a direct interpretation of 'Amun Ra'.

Emperor Constantine decided, in 321 CE, that the day of the Sun was to be the day of rest. The seventh day came to be the day of the Lord in many languages, and the Sunday, (day of the Sun) in English, has the same signification. The choice of Sunday was of a double character. The purpose was to distance this day from the Jewish Sabbath, and also make it easier for the Roman worshipers of the Sun to accept it as the day of God. Additionally, the 25th of December was the venerated day of the birth of the Sun, which the Christians adopted as the celebration day of the birth of Jesus. As god rather than mortal, Jesus could easily be associated with the Sun god. Despite that, Emperor Constantine and many of the emperors after him, had to use violence, threats and the death punishment to force the citizens of the empire to abandon their old beliefs.

The Old-Gods-religions

The old religions and the philosophical schools of ancient India and Hellas were characterized by religious tolerance and subjection to science. People had the freedom to worship whatever god they wished, and we find family members worshiping different gods. Different people worshiped almost every one of the old gods at different places. We find temples dedicated to Zeus, Amun, Artemis, Athena, Apollo, Asclepius, Dionysus, and many others. We believe that none of the worshipers knew the real identity of those gods or their real purpose on Earth.

Agent Paulus

Who was Paulus (St Paul), the man who more than others influenced the Christian religion? Some scholars claim that he has never existed. Others believe that the identity of Paulus is confused with the great personality of the time, Apollonius of Tyana. What we certainly know is that nobody knows who the writer of the Pauline letters was. Another annoying fact is that, at the time of Paulus (ca 50 CE), there were so few Christians that it is highly questionable if there were any "Christian congregations." It is more credible to assume that the "letters" have been written much later. The purpose was to establish the existence of such "congregations" at early times. It is also said that he was a persecutor of Christians. This information is highly questionable too. We know not of any persecution because of religious reasons before Christianity. Besides, by what authority was Paulus empowered to do that? There is no historical evidence that something like 'a Christian problem' existed at the time. He is supposed to have died the year 67 CE. Since he spent a great part of his life to preach the Christian message and traveled around, we do not understand when he could have had the time to persecute Christians. At the time around 50 CE there were barely any Christians outside Judea.

The reason, we believe, is to establish those imaginary persecutions as facts in order to justify the followed persecutions of non-Christians. Apollonius never mentioned the Christians, neither any persecution of them.

If we accept Paulus of Tarsus as a historical person, we find that he was a man with no religious tolerance, although he was living in a country where religious tolerance was something of a virtue. A great characteristic of the Hellenistic societies of that time was the subjection of religions to science and the absence of religious fanaticism.   Paulus was a Jew born and living in Tarsus, the same town where Apollonius of Tyana got his education. His name was Saul in Hebrew and Paulus in Greek. As he was of a wealthy family he could certainly afford education. He could speak Jewish and Greek and his education was probably the most usual education at the time, advanced reading of the classic Greek poets.

According to one theory, he visited Cyprus and presented himself as "Saulos" but the Cypriots found the name too difficult to pronounce so they called him "Paulos" in Greek and "Paulus" in Roman. According to another theory it was Apollonius of Tyana the Cypriots called "Paulos." However, there are no records concerning the historicity of the above theories.

It is most unlikely that Paulus didn't know about Apollonius being one of the most famous men of his time throughout the whole Roman Empire, and especially in Tyana and Tarsus.

The visits of Apollonius were big events everywhere. At his visits, the cities closed down, and the populace turned out to greet him and listen to him. One of those citizens must have certainly been Paulus.

At this time the role of Christians in the society was without trace. No historian or philosopher spoke or wrote about them. The few petty sects used to denounce each other as not following 'the right doctrines'. The only reason some of them became famous was their fanaticism and their refuse to accept any other authority than Yahweh. The symbol of Christianity was a fish and not the cross, which they adopted much later. Even their beliefs differed from place to place and even among individuals. One could not really speak about Christianity at the time.

When Paulus was on his way to Damascus, behold, a vision in the sky appeared. Was it a real vision, a natural phenomenon, or the imagination of his? The vision appeared in a very simple form, a strong light, and a voice. The voice is supposed to have said 'Saul, Saul why do you persecute me?' Paulus assumed that it must have been some "Lord" (god) speaking to him and replied 'Who are you Lord?' He had no reason to believe that it was the Lord Jesus. But as soon as he heard the 'voice' he became a Christian fanatic.

We know on the other hand that Enlil/Yahweh and his messengers had all the technical equipment needed in creating visions. They often used this kind of communication, as it was much effective. No human could see a vision in the sky without subjecting to its power. They all used to capitulate physically and emotionally completely convinced they were surrendering to the will of God.

The administrators of the project called "Christianity" could not possibly announce "we need agents, send us your CV." They had to locate suitable individuals and then easily 'convince' them, by using some technical equipment creating some imposing presentations, not unlike the technical effects in our films. This is the way they always used instead of arguments, from the appointing of Sumerian Kings to the appointing of prophets.

Daniel says (Daniel 10:15) after he saw a vision: 'I set my face toward the ground, and I became dumb'. We do not know if Paulus became dumb too, but he became blind for three days.

Paulus, as well as Apollonius, never married, but while Apollonius was dedicated to a pure life in all the ways, Paulus hated women and documented his feelings about women in the Christian bible. There are a lot more troubling questions about Paulus, like if he ever been in Canaan, how much he knew about Jesus, if he could speak Aramaic and much more.

After the "employment as agent", Paulus turned to be a fanatic Christian, not because of some arguments, but because of the imposing vision. Presentation of arguments was not a method used by Enlil/Yahweh. The vision was effective as any order. He was not persuaded to support Christianity; he was ordered to do that. He had been chosen by the Brotherhood of the Gold. To be chosen by Yahweh means that the man or the people of his choice were to be used by him according to his own interests. Some of the reasons could be his education, and the fact that he could speak both Greek and Jewish.

Many scholars state that Paulus, who later became co-apostle and even St Paul, either corrupted the teachings and letters of Apollonius by altering names and places, or he used them as a prototype to his own letters. He simply plagiarized Apollonius writings to produce something he never said it was his own. Even if he visited Jerusalem he could never have known much about Jesus as he asserts in his letters. There are no records that he could speak Hebrew or Aramaic. Since the vision came from the administrators of the Messiah project, the "ruler and his angels," then Paulus could be considered as the agent of Enlil/Yahweh and the "Brotherhood of the Gold," unless Paulus never existed. In that case Christianity presented Apollonius as being their agent, which is a fraud. Apollonius could never accept the doctrines of Yahweh! As their agent he had to promote the doctrines that re-enslaved mankind, provided to him in the same way as to the prophets. Deuteronomy 18:18 says:

I will raise them up a Prophet from among their brethren, like unto thee, and **will put my words in his mouth**; [emphasis added] and he shall speak unto them all that I shall command him.

Paulus was thus speaking the words of Enlil/Yahweh, the man whose greatest ambition was to rule the world.

The philosopher Apollonius, who fought non-Christian emperors for persecuting philosophers, became a victim of Christian persecutors. However, the teachings of Apollonius may have been saved, although corrupted and distributed, as the Pauline letters in the Christian Bible, like the Egyptian commandments that became the biblical commandments, or the early historical events that became the corrupted parts of the OT.

But while Apollonius was teaching religious tolerance and understanding, we have reasons to believe that he was an agent of the "Brotherhood of the Serpent," Paulus was teaching fanaticism and persecution of everyone not willing to surrender to the doctrines of Yahweh.

The Christian church succeeded even in erasing the memory of Apollonius for many centuries. Christianity could not accept him, as he never mentioned Yahweh. Jesus never did either, but the church assumes that he was referring to him by using the name 'father'. There is, of course, no support for this either. If Apollonius, this good, honest and sincere man, one of the purest that ever lived on this planet, is not worthy any admiration from the Christians, then who is? Almost two millennia later, Apollonius has once more made his appearance among us, trying to restore religion on the level it should be - that faith should be subjected to science and not the other way around. Today, we are able to speak about him only because some genius individual, by risking his life, managed to hide away the book of Philostratus.

Enlil/Yahweh said he would send his agents to different counties to deliver his message. Everybody has this right, even Yahweh. 'To subject people to doctrines by force' is quite different. Yet, this is what Christianity did. Paul traveled around in Syria, Asia Minor, Greece, Cyprus, among other countries bringing the message of Yahweh. The only certain about Paul's journeys however, is that they follow the same rout as the journeys of Apollonius. In the book of Isaiah 66:19 we read:

And I will set a sign among them, and I will send those that escape of them unto nations, to Tarshish, Pul, and Lud, that

draw the bow, to Tubal, and Javan, to the isles afar off, that
have not heard my fame, neither have seen my glory; and they
shall declare my glory among the gentiles.

It is worthy to note that until the time of Paulus, Yahweh was completely unknown outside Judea; nobody ever heart or wrote anything
about him.

Three hundred years after the crucifixion, the cult of Orpheus,
Dionysus, Apollonius, Sol Invictus, Ra and even Zeus/Enlil were
much more popular than Yahweh and Jesus. Some additional divine
aid to promote the new religion was necessary. Was it time for some
new vision in the sky? The recruitment of new agents was once again
unavoidable. Who was going to be chosen this time?

Agent Constantine
Was Emperor Constantine a Christian, a pagan who pretended to be
Christian for some reasons, or the agent of Enlil/Yahweh?

Three centuries after Jesus birth, Christianity was still a composite of small sects with different beliefs. Simply expressed, they
were divided in a Jewish faction believing in the personal God and
in Jesus as God too, and a Neoplatonic faction believing in the im-
personal Principle and in Jesus as a Man. The latter is also known
as the 'Gentile' group meaning citizens of other nations, non-Jews
Christians.

The Christians called the Roman citizens 'Pagans'. The word
probably derives from the Latin 'paganus' meaning 'people outside
the city walls' or 'country people'. The country people were supposed to be less updated about what was happening in big cities.
Most of the early church fathers and many Christian philosophers
were supporting either the Jewish faction or the Gentile faction. The
Christians of the first group were well organized and fanatics in their
beliefs, totally capitulated to the doctrine that they would inherit the
'kingdom of heavens'. They also declared that they were the only
group worshiping the 'true God' everybody should surrender to, in
contrast to the Pagans who were accused as exercising idolatry.
The most significant characteristic of Paganism was that those people really chose to worship whatever god they liked and exercised
great religious tolerance.

Except for the idea of a 'personal god' who eats, drinks and acts
violently most of the time, and the idea of Jesus being 'God', some

Hellenistic philosophers could accept Christianity because it consisted of many doctrines and ideas already exercised by most of the old religions. The Gentiles accepted the God of the Christians but they also knew which leg to stand on; they were not prepared to scarify science for the sake of religion.

While the Christians were accusing other religions for being false, and even one another for not practicing the 'right doctrines, they indeed used any kind of forgery in order to entice more supporters. They promised the 'Kingdom of Heavens' that attracted the heathens (poor country people). By the way, no rich or powerful people ever opposed Christianity in modern times. People who suffered injustice, slavery, or oppression could always hope for justice after death! In reality, Christianity sided with the powerful against the heathens. The heathens are persuaded to seek justice after death!

They promised remission of sins that fascinated people with blood on their hands. They threatened with hell that scared uneducated people. The only thing, they had to do was to be baptized. That could, however, wait until their last days, which was even better as it could cover even future crimes.

According to the Catholic Church, the archangel Michael is currying the souls to heaven. At the hour of death, he descends and gives each soul the chance to redeem itself independence of the crimes begotten!

Despite all that, the old religions were still practiced in the whole Roman Empire. At about the time of Constantine the Christians were ca five percent of the population of the empire. What the number would be in additional three hundred years nobody knows. The fact that the administrators of the Messiah project decided to intervene is witnessing about bad odds. The results must have been unacceptable. Who were the administrators? According to the Bible the grounders and administrators of Christianity were Yahweh, his sons Gabriel and Michael, and some other members and employees of the House of Yahweh, i.e., Enlil and the members of the Gold expedition on Earth, the Brotherhood of the Gold. What Christianity needed the most was some 'miracle'; otherwise the risk of being marginalized even more was great.

The time around 120 CE was a Golden Age. The Empire was in great wealth and Emperor Hadrian (117–138 CE) could celebrate the 150th anniversary of the grounding of the empire with special coins with the inscription 'saeculum aureum', Age of Gold.

In Rome he adopted Aphrodite/Venus as the patroness of the imperial family. In Hellas he ordered restorations of the temples of Zeus, Peseidon and other gods whoever they might be. He was welcomed around the empire as god and even with religious tolerance everywhere except in Antioch. The great city with a mixed population and culture, not far away from Tyana and Tarsus, the cities of Apollonius and Paul, was not a place of religious tolerance any more. The strongly manipulated Christians, by the doctrines of Yahweh and Peter, were not willing to let any other religion to co-exist with their own. Although nobody knows how much they knew about the scriptures that later became the OT, it seems that they were real slaves under the power of some doctrines. The intolerance of the Christians is grounded in many passages of the OT, like the following manipulative instructions in Deuteronomy 17:5:

> Then shalt thou bring forth that man or that woman, which have committed that wicked thing [worshiped other gods], unto thy gates, even that man or that woman, and shalt stone them with stones, till they die.

To enter the kingdom of heavens and the remission of sins was not enough for the worship of Yahweh and Jesus; the Christians must also follow the doctrines of the scriptures, like killing 'unbelievers'.

It all began with the death of St Stephan (34 CE) who is said to have experienced a 'theophany' (a vision of God). He was tried by the Sanhedrin and was stoned to death. Paulus of Tarsus is supposed to have been witnessing the event. The Jew with the Greek name 'Stephanos', meaning 'Crown', is supposed to have said before dying that he saw the Son sitting on the right hand of the Father. This started the doctrine of God and Son both being of the same essence. The 'Hole' Spirit and the 'Trinity' were to be invented later.

The Christian fathers of the first two centuries are supposed to have been bishops, while no churches existed, and theologians who wrote letters to Christian communities not existed either. The Catholic Church regards Peter as the first Pope while there were barely some Christians. Justin Martyr (ca 100-165), a Roman Christian Apologist, never mentioned Peter in Rome which some scholars use as evidence that Peter never been there.

During the three first centuries of the current era, we hear about Apollonius of Tyana in the whole empire, about temples of several gods, about the Neoplatonists, Pythagoreans and Asclepius practicing science, philosophy and religion and about some Christian sects not actually accepted in the societies because of their fanaticism.

The Greek philosopher Celsus (2-century), one of the opponents to the Christian beliefs, stated that 'Pagan gods offered better alternatives to an angry god who needs rest and has a mouth'. Since his works have not survived, all we know about Celsus comes from Origen in his work 'Against Celsus'. Not surprisingly, all the books 'against-Christianity' have perished, while the books and letters 'against-the-critics-of-Christianity' have survived.

Basilides, an early Christian teacher of Alexandria (2-century), is said to have written several commentaries on the Gospels. He claimed that the Crucifixion was a fraud, that Simon of Cyrene was used as a substitute, and therefore Jesus didn't die on the cross.
M. Blaigent, R. Leigh and H. Lincoln say:

> According to Irenaeus he [Basilides] promulgated a most heinous heresy indeed . . . Such an accusation would seem to be bizarre. And yet it has proved to be extraordinarily persistent and tenacious.[4]

As expected, the works of Basilides didn't survive. What we know about him comes from 'Against Heresies' by Irenaeus, which have indeed survived.

Sossianus Hierocles of Alexandria (284–305 CE), also a philosopher, wrote a two-volume work by the name 'True words to the Christians'. He found many Christian beliefs as illogical, since the miracle worker Jesus was considered as God, while the equally wonder worker Apollonius was considered as 'favored by the gods' and even as magician.

His works have not survived. The most we know about him comes from Eusebius and his work 'Against Hierocles'.

Porphyry (232–305) also criticized the conception of the 'Father and Son', meaning that God cannot have a son. He also objected to 'all things are possible for God' by claiming that in that case even lying was possible for God.

We believe that Porphyry had no idea about the real identity of the God of the Jews and the Christians. While Porphyry was speaking philosophically about God's ability to 'lie', we have shown that he was able to do much worse than that. The Christian Emperors Constantine and Theodosius II both ordered Porphyry's book to be burned on fire.

The Christian Emperor Julian (361–363 CE) converted to Hellenism and wrote a book 'Against the Galileans'. The book shook the Christians although Julian did not recommended violence against them. He was worrying that the study of Christian texts would make the children 'slaves'. Parents, the church, and schools have been turning the children into slaves since then. The fraud is still going on. Laurence Gardner:

> Even now, the dogma of contrived scriptural history is still taught in our schoolrooms and churches, while the original documents from which the scripture was constructed are ignored.[5]

Julian's program was to create an environment where all religions, including Christianity, would co-existence. A Persian bow ended his life much too early. Some rumors claim that the bow was directed against him from one of his own, a Christian soldier. The Christian bishops celebrated his death as 'an intervention from God'. Men like Nimrod, Alexander the great, Emperor Julian and other personalities that could have changed the path of history, have all been assassinated. We would not be surprised if some angel from the House of Yahweh, with license to kill, had been active behind the lines, as so many times before!

Perhaps the most important of the early church fathers, Christian or not, was the theologian Arius of Alexandria (250–336 CE). He was against the 'father and Son' doctrine meaning that the Son was not equal to the Father.

His teachings are known as 'Arianism' and the controversy involved philosophers, theologians and even ordinary people. Some Christian factions have evolved out of the ideas of Arius. Some are still existing in our times, others, like the Cathars, have been exterminated by the inquisition, as heretics.

At this time, the Christians had their own secret courts recognizing God as the highest authority. They were fanatics, unwilling to compromise about their beliefs, treating all the other citizens as unbelievers and ungodly! Christianity was not just a new religion; it was also a political movement striving to replace every other authority, political as well as religious, with the authority of the God of the OT.

Those were the circumstances at the time of Emperor Constantine. He is known as Constantine the great, even St Constantine, and the Roman Emperor who declared Christianity as the only official religion in the Roman Empire. He is also known as the emperor who moved his capital from the great city of Rome to the little colony known as Byzantium by the Black Sea.

According to Christian writings, Constantine had been 'chosen by God' to assist the new religion to establish itself as a world religion. He is supposed to have seen a marvelous sign, 'a vision in the sky' as many others did before him. The sign was supposed to represent a cross. Then, again at night, he saw another vision, as in a dream. This time it was Jesus himself commanding him to place the cross on his battle flag and march against his enemies to conquer lands for Christianity! Some 350 years later, Mohammed marched in the name of Allah, to conquer lands for Islam. For the first time in history, a religious symbol was marching in battle! That was the beginning of religious wars still going on today. Enlil/Yahweh managed to direct human armies to march against one another, using some of his different names.

Did Constantine actually see a vision, or was it fabricated by him? As we have seen, the visions were of immense importance to the administrators of the 'Messiah Project', and Constantine's actions bear witness that he was acting according to specific instructions. Apparently, Yahweh and his messengers could no longer just observe the development of the project that represented a big investment to them. The probability of ending up in failure was overhanging. They had to act, especially when they had the power to influence the development. It was time to select a human and direct him for the task. The Emperor of the Roman Empire was certainly the most suitable one. A new vision and perhaps some instructions was everything they needed.

Constantine was not emperor yet, but they could see to that too, by acting behind the lines. Ishkur/Adad, the physicist son of Yahweh who was an expert in the use of chemical and biological weapons, could easily arrange the vision. He is known as Raphael in the bible, the 'Healer of El'. The steps of Constantine could be directed in the same way as Enlil/Yahweh directed the steps of Abraham to Harran, or the steps of Aeneas to Italy.

The sign of the cross shown to Constantine and the words 'Εν τουτω Νικα' 'By this you conquer' were meant to stress him to do something. Constantine was a politician and many writers claim that his decision to declare Christianity as the official religion of the East Empire was pragmatic and meant to bring stability. The empire was a composite of many people and many religions. To declare the smallest and most violent of them as the only official religion was not an act destined to bring stability. It was an act according to plan. Besides, before Constantine, emperor Galerius declared (311 CE) toleration of all religions, including Christianity.

Nobody knows, of course, if Constantine was forced to cooperate with the Enlilites or if he accepted the mission willingly. On the other hand, it was unthinkable for any human to disobey a divine message. Only the sight of some 'shining angel' could bring humans (like the prophets) to dig their heads into the ground. Constantine was now on a program to establish the new religion as an agent of Enlil/Yahweh. The vision being real or not, he was probably approached by some 'angel' and given instruction on how to act.

First, in 324 CE, he declared Christianity as the official religion of the Roman Empire. The year after he assembled the synod of Nicaea. The purpose was to establish some kind of unity among the divided theologians.

It is said that Constantine was not even a Christian at that time. He was interested in promoting Christianity, which supports the idea that he was acting according to particular instructions. Another reason was certainly the fact that his crimes could be expiated through baptism. This was certainly the reason of his late baptism, just before he died. In this way, even more crimes could be covered. The remission of sins was a Christian specialty, something no other religion could offer.

Was the 'decision' at Nicaea religious or political? We never know. The decision was not democratic since the bishops did not vote. Even if they had, it would still have been undemocratic since only ca 300 of the 1800 invited bishops were participating. The decision is supposed to have been of a divine nature, emitting fear, as so many other things in Christianity, therefore not to be criticized. It could also be characterized as forgery since nobody knows what exactly happened.

Sabinus, Bishop of Heraclea, who was present at the Council, left the following description of the attendees and method used to determine which Gospels would be chosen to assemble the Bible:

With the exception of the Emperor [Constantine] and Eusebius Pampilus, these Bishops were a set of illiterate, simple
creatures who understood nothing.

* * *

The method used was determined to resort to 'miraculous intervention'.[6]

The Bishops put the books under the communion table in the church
and hoped that the 'right' books would appear on the communion
table the next morning. And behold, it happened accordingly. It was
a 'miracle' as it was expected. Miracles are up to this day a great
characteristic of Christian teachings!

If some of Constantine's men, some other person, or even some
'angel' of God had access to the church we never know. The practicing of the 'art of divination' that directed some books into the Bible
has also been used by the church to condemn and even burn thousands of people as sorcerers and witches. So far so good concerning
the credibility of the Christian scriptures!

We wonder if the whole performance was a play with words
since none of them could know anything about the character of the
essence of God! That was the first time in history a philosophical
dispute was solved through an Imperial decree. Despite the Nicene
Creed Constantine allowed Pagan practices to continue even after
325 CE. The dispute was however not ended. It continued to divide
the Christians for many years.

Julian succeeded Constantius II in 361. He declared that no religious branch should be favored over another and allowed the exiled
bishops to return. Other emperors after him continued to support
different factions at different times.

Constantine made the institutions of the Church permanent. He
even increased the number of Christians by offering gold to slaves
and pagans who could accept to convert to Christianity. They must
have been the luckiest slaves in history.

We do not believe that this was the intention of the two great
men that deserve the name 'Christ', Jesus and Apollonius. We do not
even believe that they wished to establish some new religion.

Constantine commissioned new versions of the Christian books
destroyed by Emperor Diocletian in 303 CE. M. Baigent, R. Leigh
and H. Lincoln say:

. . . it enabled the custodians of orthodoxy to revise, edit, and rewrite their material as they saw fit, in accordance with their tenets.

* * *

Of the five thousand extant early manuscript versions of the New Testament, not one predates the fourth century. The New Testament as it exists today is essentially a product of fourth-century-editors and writers-custodians of orthodoxy, "adherents of the message," with vested interests to protect.[7]

Once Christianity was legalized in the Roman Empire one would expect that persecutions and hostilities would cease. Verily I say unto you, nay, because that was the start point of the greatest religious persecution ever on Earth.

That was the start point of the destruction of the Egyptian, the Babylonian, the Hellenic, the Hellenistic, and the Helleno-Roman civilizations. Why did the Christians regard those civilizations as their enemies? Because they had been manipulated to believe that everything outside the small radius of the doctrines of Yahweh was ungodly. Any civilization exercising science and religious tolerance was the enemy of Yahweh and had to be destroyed.

Independent of which of the doctrines was the 'right' one, there is an aspect of the legalization of Christianity than no writer ever touched, the capture of the Roman Empire by the Christians. The new religion could now operate with the blessings of the empire and the power of its emperors. Constantine delivered the whole Roman Empire, the greatest power of the world, into the hands of fanatic Christians.

Christianity claims that Constantine chose God as the basement for his empire. In reality it was the other way around. It was God (Enlil/Yahweh) who chose Constantine and the Roman Empire to use according to his own plans. The next point on his agenda was the destruction of civilizations based on science. Eusebius believed that Constantine was a 'Pius Emperor'. The crimes of Constantine against people, science and cultures, constituting the criteria behind our own opinion, witness of a completely different person. However, we are not totally in disagreement with Eusebius. He claimed that 'Constantine was a Servant of God' while we state that he was the agent of Yahweh!

A great misunderstanding has been passed to us throughout the history books. It has always been stated that the Jews, the Hellenistic world, and the Roman Empire were the powers behind the establishment of Christianity. The Hellenes, the Romans, and other citizens of the empire never accepted Christianity by own free will. Only a few did, among them, some famous theologians, and poor people who hoped that private properties would now shift from the rich people to the poor, not unlike the doctrines of communism. The rest of the people resisted as long as they could. Finally, Christianity was forced on them by imperial decrees, Christian mobs, and military power. At the time when all the citizens of the east and the west empire could be counted as Christians, no temples of the old gods were left, no philosophers, no books or libraries, no statues or other kind of art. In fact, whole civilizations had vanished. Baptism was obligatory, law forbade the reading of books other than Christian and no other religion except Judaism was allowed.

The fanatic Christians could now, by using the power of the Roman Empire, replace the old civilizations based on science and religious tolerance by theocracy. The crimes begotten by Christian Emperors, Christian Bishops, Christian mobs, and Popes, after the legalization of Christianity, are countless. Those crimes created a world of violence, fear and destruction that are still visible today. They elevated theocracy to a cruel totalitarian dictatorship. It was a matter of life and death to speak against the 'Word'. Although it was impossible for any one to know anything about God, immortality, life after death, Holy Spirits and the like, the executives of the 'Brotherhood of the Doctrines' gave everyone the choice to accept them or die! The citizens of the Roman Empire became Christians by imperial decrees. Nevertheless, in their hearts, they were not. But that was a minor problem. In time, say after 2–3 generations, they would all feel like they had been Christians forever.

Later on, another 'Constantine', Clovis I and his wife Clotilde (475–545 CE) introduced Christendom in France. Clovis I is considered as the founder of the French state. He established the Roman Church as the supreme Christian authority in France. He was granted the title 'Novus Constantinus' and by establishing a bond between the Church and the state of France, he became the King over the 'Holy Roman Empire'. Without these two men and two women (St. Helena and St. Clotilde) Christendom would never survived as a major religion in the west.

The introduction of Islam put an end to the expansion of Christianity eastwards. At the same time, the nearer the Islamic threat came, the more, the citizens of the Roman Empire, who had been forced to accept Christianity, felt lucky about being Christians. The two religions were designed to balance each other's power and divide the world for times to come! The two religions, established by the same God, simply need each other in order to survive! A common religion has the ability to unity people the same way a common language does. Two or more religions, two or more languages, is an unavoidable invitation to division. The purpose was to prevent us from examining the reasons behind his actions.

The Byzantine Contribution
Constantine tog over Byzan, the colony founded by king Byzas and peaceful merchants, more than two millennia earlier. The Church states, quite proudly, that Constantine was the first to found a Christian empire. It is rather significant to note that both the emergence of this empire and its disappearance almost without trace, are coupled to Enlil/Yahweh.

A significant question is: What was the contribution of the Byzantine Empire to the world under its, more than a millennium, long existence? How had they been administrating the great knowledge they inherited from the Hellenic and the Hellenistic civilization?

The first Christian empire ever had the best economic, scientific and even technological prerequisites to succeed, than any other empire earlier. The Roman Empire (the Byzantine Empire as well as the Roman Empire of the west) was the sole heir of the Hellenic civilization of Hellas and the Hellenistic civilization based in Alexandria, Egypt. The new empire didn't have to invent the wheel again. They could take the high way of development inherited as a ready-made structure.

One would think that scientific attainments and practicable applications of already existing discoveries, would take giant steps and cause development to escalate. Even half of the achievements of the Hellenistic civilization would be enough.

At the time of the grounding of the Byzantine Empire (the time of Constantine) the Hellenic civilization had much knowledge to offer. Here is a short synopsis.

Anaximander (ca 610–547 BCE) said that "the Earth is like a globe and it is orbiting the Sun."

Pythagoras (580–520 BCE), not only accepted the teachings of Anaximander, he was also teaching about the discoveries of this great man.

Plato (427–347) BCE (several dates exist) was a philosopher who founded the Academy, the first university in Athens (388 BCE) that flourished for over 900 years. The Academy was closed after order from the Christian Roman Emperor Justinian in 529 CE. Plato was, like Socrates and Aristoteles, devoted to philosophy and science and ideas about moral.

Empedokles (494–434 BCE) said that the moon is orbiting the Earth and the moon "had no light of its own" but it is "borrowed."

Demokretos (460–370 BCE) about the dark marks on the moon: "They are the shadows of great mountains and valleys." Also that "in space, there are much more planets than we can see." He is also considered to be the father of the atomic theory.

Aristarchos from Samos (310–230 BCE) stated that not only the Earth was orbiting the Sun but also all the other planets in the solar system were doing the same. Earth was also rotating across its own axel, and that the distance between Earth and other stars, was great behind imagination.

Euclid of Alexandria (323–283 BCE) wrote the elements of geometry.

Archimedes (287–212 BCE) was a mathematician astronomer, engineer, philosopher, and physicist. It was probably in the library of Alexandria he invented the screw-shaped water pump, one of the very few inventions that survived the destruction by the organized criminality of the Christian mobs.

Heron of Alexandria (1st century around 62 CE, several dates exist) was a mathematician with great interests in engineering and mechanics. He constructed several kinds of "machines" for both civil and military use, of which the most known is the steam turbine called "aeolipile." His most famous work in mathematics was the Proposition 1.8 of his work "Metrica" known today as the Heron Formula.

The above is to give some idea of the world inherited by the Byzantine Empire. The philosophers of those times, and even earlier times, used to discuss their ideas with others of similar or competitive opinions. All of them had the freedom of thinking and the freedom of speech. That was a world of enlightenment that now had been replaced by a world dominated by darkness.

We find a few things the Byzantines are going to be remembered for. They destroyed the inherited knowledge and everything else not fitting into the doctrines of Christianity.

During the long Byzantine existence, Christianity flourished to unheard heights as it had the monopoly of religious doctrines. The Christian Church exercised a religious dictatorship using the imperial power delivered into their hands by the messengers and agents of Yahweh. Trade flourished too because of the strategic location of Constantinople between Europe and Asia. Knowledge was not flourishing at all. In fact, knowledge was completely suppressed because science could not support the doctrines of Yahweh.

The heritage of the Byzantine Empire can be summarized as follows: the development of church architecture, iconography, and church music. Many scholars claim that many ancient books had been preserved there and found their way to Europe after the year 1453 CE. The few ancient books that reached Europe under the renaissance came from Arab countries and from refuges. The books were hidden by individuals who risked their lives in order to preserve "forbidden knowledge." It's thanks to them, other individuals in Hellas and Alexandria and Arab traders we still have some copies of ancient books, not to the Byzantine Empire.

So the contribution of the greatest Christian Empire to the world, after more than 1100 years of Christian administration, was just something closely related to Christianity. Church architecture, church music, and religious paintings! No more than that? What a waste of time and knowledge! Architecture, music and painting witness that there was indeed a lot of knowledge, but they consequently avoided to apply any knowledge outside the boundaries of what was allowed by the religious doctrines.

In the year 380 CE Christian priests supported by a Christian mob closed the temple of the Goddess Demeter in Eleusis. The old hierophant Nestorius (95 years old), barely escaped the mob that tried to lynch him. He was forced to end the Eleusinian mysteries that started ca 1500 BCE, announcing that 'mental darkness was to predominate over the human race'. Unfortunately for his descendants, it has been fulfilled like a prophecy! Nestorius was not a prophet but an educated man who could see the alliance between Christian fanaticism and mental darkness. According to the Church, Nestorius's announcing was the speech of devil. The definition was based on neither scientific nor philosophical criteria, only on the authority of

254 Planet of Gold

the new religious super power. Had it been in the favor of Yahweh had it been called divine prophecy!

The world at the time of the fall of the Byzantine Empire was in much worst shape than the one they inherited. What they created, together with the Christian Roman Empire of the West, was a great darkness. The total absence of scientific and technological achievements was remarkable. One could say that it was mysterious too, following the mysterious ways of God. It is also understandable, as science was subjected to the doctrines of the new theology. Galileo Galilei (1564–1642) would rediscover what Anaximander stated 2000 years earlier. But while Anaximander could freely express his ideas, the Roman Church declared Galileo's theory as heresy, and sent him to prison. The Church forgave him in 1992 for being a heretic. That was some 2500 years after Anaximander!

Ironically the destruction of knowledge and the subjection of science by the Byzantines was the main reason of their military defeat. It was equally the main reason of their poor contribution to the world. Beside that the forces of Mehmed II massively outnumbered the imperial forces during the siege of the city in 1453, the Turks also used the greatest cannon in history. The Byzantines failed to construct defense weapons. They also failed to develop already discovered "military machines" by Heron. When they realized that the city of Constantinople (the last remains of the empire) was without hope, they put their destiny into the hands of God. Their God was, however, very silent, as he was later on under the persecution of the Jews too! The Byzantines paid the highest price as the supporters of Yahweh. The whole empire, the creation of agent Constantine, was exclusively directed by religious doctrines at the cost of scientific advancements.

Constantine put the sign of the cross on his flag in order to conquer lands for God. A few hundred years later Mohammed would launch a program to "conquer lands for Islam," in the name of another name of God.

According to one theory, Mehmed II who captured the city, saw the crescent moon all over the Earth, "as in a dream," and decided to put it on his flag. The cross and the crescent moon are just symbols, but the power behind them is real. The architect behind Christianity and Islam must have been genius. The origins of the cross and the crescent moon are to be found in Mesopotamia. Both are symbols associated with Enlil/Yahweh and the members of the alien Gold Mission.

[1]http://www.alchemylab.com/apollonius.htm

[2]Dr. R. W. Bernard citing Philostratus from: www.apollonius.net/bernard5e.html

[3]http://www.mountainman.com.au/atyana27.html

[4]Michael Baigent, Richard Leigh & Henry Lincoln, Holy Blood, Holy Grail, p. 379

[5]Laurence Gardner, Genesis of the Grail Kings, p. 6

[6]from www.ptet.dubar.com/bible-composition.html

[7]Michael Baigent, Richard Leigh & Henry Lincoln, Holy Blood, Holy Grail, p. 368, 369

Chapter 21

THE GOD OF FEAR AND THE CHRISTIAN ERA

Fear and Darkness, the companions of Christianity

Holy wars 'my-God-is-better-than-yours' could be classified as childish plays, if it wasn't for the bloodshed. The more, someone is manipulated in religious beliefs the more, fanatic is such a person fighting for them. We are unable to discuss 'God' without offending someone. Ironically, the ancients with their many gods could do that with much tolerance.

Judaism, Christianity, and Islam are powerful institutions that have been directing human development since they made their appearance on Earth; all three of them created by an alien man who said he was 'God'.

Christianity of today is not just a religion. It is a big, global, organization performing services of financial, social, political and religious character. Christianity, it is said, has been, and still is, one of the most important pillars of our civilization. Christianity is also the owner and the controller of millions of Christian souls, therefore carrying on the tradition of the first human civilization, which was built on slavery. Enlil/Yahweh was by then the slave owner, now he is the Chairman of the board of this global organization. He is the Grand Master of the religious fraternity administrating life and death. The church fathers claim to be his executives, his representatives on Earth, almost in the same manner as the high priests/security guards in his temples of the old times. The high priests and hierodules appointed by Enlil/Yahweh could never resign. They were his lifetime captives as the slaves he used in the gold mines.

Although he does no longer need any personal guarding, the priests are instead taking care of his reputation as God. The man, who, according to Jesus was a laughingstock, is indeed treated by us as God. By doing so we sided with Enlil/Yahweh against Jesus. In doing so, we are decreasing our intelligence to a level he wants us to be, easier for him to dominate us, easier to manipulate us. Like the native people of the Americas, who believed in Ninurta/Viracocha as God, because he said that it was he who made the Sun and the Moon to reappear after the deluge. It is indeed that easy to manipulate us. Ninurta, the man could hardly use them as gold miners, but Viracocha, the god could.

Although we are not any gold miners of his today, we are indeed collecting gold for him. And by doing so, we are making it possible for him and his likes to live a long healthy life. Something he denied us. Something he and the Brotherhood of the Gold denied the children of Earth who die because of lack of medical care. And we ourselves are equally responsible for the death of those children. We are responsible because we are storing the gold instead of using it to bring health to mankind. We are responsible because we do not want, or do not have the courage to question his doctrines. We do not question anything of what he said because of fear for individual or collective punishment. Because the church fathers are keeping telling us that it is sin to question God's actions. Is there anyone who can explain why we are not allowed to question God's identity, or criticize his actions when so needed? Any one who does not fear God's vengeance? Because of that, we are living under mental bondage like our ancestors were living under physical bondage. The slave owner is still the same. About fearing God, Laurence Gardner says:

> Upon their return to Jerusalem and Judea [from the Babylonian captivity] they had every reason to fear the retribution of Jehovah, but they turned this fear into outright veneration and absolute obedience-a veneration which set the scene for all that was to follow in the Jewish and Christian religions, whose disciples became classified as 'God-fearing'.[1]

Two millennia after the march of Christianity, we find political and religious leaders at different locations in Europe, persuading people to come together in church liturgies and prey to God for rain! We find companies marketing table water as 'blessed water'! We find priests, performing requiem (memorial service for the dead), persuading the relatives of the dead to go to church. The more relatives the more quickly and effectively the blessing is reaching the dead! Hypocrisy and holiness are walking down the street holding hands! Or?

The Christian Era
With Christianity a new kind of religion was born never seen before. The new religion has been built up around a false kernel; that Yahweh is God. The rest of it has been created through copying older religions and philosophical ideas, or corrupting real historical events to justify the kernel. It didn't make its appearance out of the blue, not by solely copying old religions either. It was the result after eons of manipulations, threats, punishments, and promises. Christianity used the same concept of commandments, threats, punishments, and promises as Enlil/Yahweh. They promised the poor justice after death. The promised the criminals remission of sins. They threatened ordinary people with punishment. The most famous promise was that of the 'kingdom of heavens'. Of course, they never had to explain what the kingdom of heavens really was, or how they knew about it. The most immediate threat was the 'stoning of unbelievers'. No other religion ever threatened people or promised things no man could possibly know anything about. No older religion or philosophy was prepared to meet such an enemy. The philosophers who used to discuss everything between heaven and earth were now murdered or forbidden to speak. No competition was allowed any more, no opposition to the doctrines of Yahweh was tolerated.

Despite the great efforts by Emperor Constantine, and other emperors after him, to force Christianity on everybody, Christianity was not really accepted until the appearance of Islam. The appearance of Islam established an effective barrier in Meddle East, so Christianity was forced to go west. Those two religions, as well as Judaism, have been exercising an almost totalitarian control, in every aspect of human activities. Only the last one hundred years or so, the pressure has been eased. From politics and wars, to science, development and social life, the church has been directing every aspect of development with the help of the world leaders and its own doctrines.

Something the Christians do not know, and do not want to think about, is that Christianity has slowed down the development in the west, by some 1500 years. From about 1850 CE, we have been forced to rediscover most of what had already been known to the ancients, thanks to the declination of the dominating power of the Church. The 1500 years are, however, lost forever.

Christian Versions
Christianity of today is divided in three main branches, the Orthodox Church of the East, the Roman Catholic Church and the Protestant Church. Each one of them is accusing each one of the others for being responsible for every evil thing that happened, both about actions against people and the administration of God's doctrines. Each one of them claims to be the right representative of God. Only this fact would please this Machiavellian Lord the most, since one of his special skills was to create conflicts. The power of the Church in the past appears to have been so great that any important decisions by kings, or emperors, had to be approved by the church. Especially in the west, the church leaders acted as if they were emperors. They had, occasionally, their own armies and a greater number of citizens under their authority than any emperor or king. Some emperors were even called 'Holy Emperors' since they had been elevated to power by the Popes. The Roman Catholic Church has often been accused of mass crimes against humanity.

The split of the original Orthodox Church occurred formally in 1054 CE. The legates of Pope Leo IX (1049–1054 CE) and Patriarch Michael I, (1043–1059 CE) excommunicated each other. The schism came after a quarrel between the Patriarch and the legates of the Pope, and was about the use of 'unleavened bread', the bread ordered to the Israelites under special circumstances by Enlil/Yahweh. What is the connection between the unleavened bread and Christianity anyway! What is the connection between the unleavened bread and religion? Is the unleavened bread baked of gold powder? In that case the church fathers had no idea about what they argued about. Other questions, that made the two Christian Superpowers to drift apart were about the creeds, some practices, differences in the practice of the liturgy, the use of icons and some other sources of different opinions.

Martin Luther

By the 16th century another split occurred when the Protestants went their own way, thus creating the Luther Protestant church out of the Catholic Church. The Protestants had been following the spirit of Martin Luther (1483–1546), who was a well-educated theologian and religious reformer. He is regarded as the man who created the modern German language by translating the bible. Not many Protestants do know, however, that Martin Luther was also the man who promoted anti-Jewishness to a level never before seen in Europe. Many scholars hold him morally responsible for the persecution of the Jews under World War II. Here are a few things Martin Luther wished to do about the Jews, as described in his book 'On the Jews and their Lies', translated by Martin H. Bertram, Fortress Press, 1955. As a true agent of Enlil/Yahweh, Martin Luther was pleading for actions against Yahweh's chosen people!

> My advise, as I said earlier is: [about the Jews] First, that their synagogues be burned down, and that all who are able toss sulphur and pitch; it would be good if someone could also throw in some hellfire . . . Second, that all their books—their prayer books, their Talmudic writings, also the entire Bible—be taken from them, not leaving them one leaf, and that these be preserved for those who may be converted . . . Third, that they be forbidden on pain of death to praise God, to give thanks, to pray, and to teach publicly among us and in our country . . . Fourth, that they be forbidden to utter the name of God within our hearing . . .

> They [rulers] must act like a good physician who, when gangrene has set in proceeds without mercy to cut, saw, and burn flesh, veins, bone, and marrow. Such a procedure must also be followed in this instance. Burn down their synagogues, forbid all that I enumerated earlier, force them to work, and deal harshly with them as Moses did . . .

Unlike Martin Luther, we do not put any label on the Jewish people or any other people. We have declared some individuals, like Abraham, Moses, Joshua, and the Israelites who were forced to live in the desert for forty years, as the victims of Yahweh. Yet, some other individuals, like the prophets, as the agents of Yahweh.

The fathers of the new branch used to adduce ideological and practical reasons for the splitting of the Christian Church, like the unleavened bread, or the use of the icons, or the color of the priests' dresses, or the remission of sins, although many ordinary Christians apprehend such reasons as ridiculous.

Now most of the Christians have no idea, whatsoever, about the reasons of the splitting of the Original Church, or about the time it happened. But all of them have certain opinions about their own church. The Catholics, for example, believe that they are members of a church that is more powerful and colorful than the Orthodox church of the East. The Protestants believe that their church is the most liberal, and the members of the Orthodox church of the East, believe that their church is the original and the most rightful one. Do the Christians need the Moslems to quarrel about things when they have each other? Our beliefs and opinions about other Christian branches or about Islam are, of course, cemented by the beliefs of our environment. This is witnessing of the great power of the doctrines. Had we been born in some other country our beliefs would differ too. And after the splitting of the Church, all the Christians of the world could live in a perfect religious world prepared and blessed by the fathers of their church, Amen! (be as Amun wishes).

Additionally, within these three main branches of the Christian church, we have a great number of subdivisions, movements, autonomous churches as well as numerous sects. The violent split of the original church still influences violence to this day. The Christian Goths destroyed the Christian Rome. The Christians crusaders of the 4th crusade destroyed the Christian city of Constantinople. The Christian Vandals destroyed North Africa with the bible in their hands. The bible has had more influence in the mind of humans and on history in general than any other book, unfortunately, not always positive influence. The immediate effects of the proclamation of Christianity as the only allowed religion, can be classified in two categories, the destruction of knowledge and the persecution of people.

Egypt
The Egyptian civilization, established by Enki and developed by his sons Thoth, and Marduk, as well as by his grandson Osiris, has suffered greatly. In fact, almost every aspect of this civilization has vanished. Arts, temples, codices and other forms of documented

achievements, knowledge about hidden things by Thoth, knowledge about metals, knowledge about other countries and people, have been declared as anti Christian. Books were burnt on fire. The Hellenistic world, centered in Alexandria, a great example of co-existence of different civilizations and cultures, could not survive because of the persecutions by the Romans, the Christians, and the Moslems. The same fate appeared to the great library of Alexandria, built by Ptolemaios Soter, (Ptolemy I 306–282 BCE), the man who also built the temple of the Muses from which the word 'museum' derives, and later developed by Ptolemaios Philadelphos (Ptolemy II 282–246 BCE).

The Library deserves some thoughts by any one who appreciates any kind of written records. The library was under the protection of all the Kings and Queens of the Ptolemaic dynasty and was continually expanding.

It was probably the world's oldest university. The library housed works by the greatest writers of the ancient world. There, Archimedes invented the screw-shaped water pump still used today. Eratosthenes measured the diameter of the Earth. Euklides discovered the rules of geometry. The library is believed to have stored 400,000 to 700,000 parchment scrolls. There is no real agreement about the time of the destruction of the library, although all references agree that it was burnt. According to Plutarchos, (47–127 CE), the library was destroyed in 47–48 BCE by Julius Caesar. If this is true, it might have been partly destroyed since there is evidence of the library's existence after that.

In 381 emperor Flavius Theodosius (378–395 CE) outlawed visits to the old temples. Public talks on religious matters were no longer allowed. He ordered the destruction of all pagan temples and the extermination of thousands of Gentiles in the whole Roman Empire. In Egypt the task was assigned to Theophilus, Patriarch of Alexandria (385–412 CE) and in Cyprus to bishop Epiphanius. Both executed the task with great passion and even greater fanaticism. They launched a program of heavy persecutions against the Gentiles. No place of worship remained, no stone upon another, no philosophers opposing the new religion. Laurence Gardner about Theophilus:

Led by the Roman-appointed Bishop Theophilus, they marched upon the Serapeum, where the collection was held in the great Library of Alexandria, and razed it to the ground in order to clear the field for the doctrines of new Church-approved literature. In this regard, Rome was said to have crucified the serpent of wisdom, just as Jesus (a purveyor of that wisdom) had been crucified by the same establishment.[2]

Theodosius has secured a place in the history books as one of the most iniquitous, equally most manipulated, Emperors. His allies like Theophilus and Epiphanius are not equally famous, as people have a propensity to forget after a few generations. Theodosius edict concerning Epiphanius says:

> . . . the one that won't obey pater Epiphanius have no right to keep living on the island.

We wonder what right, beside the imperial power, was keeping the non-Cypriot Epiphanius on the island!

The results of their sweep are the ruins still visible today. Sokrates Scholasticus (380–440) says about the destruction:

> Demolition of the Idolatrous Temples at Alexandria, and the consequent conflict between the Pagans and Christians.

One of the destroyed temples was the Serapeum, which was housed in the library building, and all the books therein.

Among the treasury books lost during the burning of the royal library, were most of the 42 books of Instructions, or the 42 Books of Thoth, as they are better known, some of them describing how to attain immortality, among other themes.

Clement of Alexandria, 2nd century CE mentioned 4 books on astrology, 2 on music, 10 about law, 10 about sacred sites, and some about medicine, cosmography, and mathematics. The survived books were buried in the desert. Through religious conflicts, we have succeeded in destroying the greatest gifts given to us by Thoth/Hermes. Most of the remains of those Hermetic books not consumed by fire have been corrupted, intentionally or not, through various translations and over writings.

Bishop Cyril of Alexandria (378–444 CE) led Christian mobs against both Jews and pagans. The Jewish synagogues were leveled to the ground and the Jews driven from the city. Another Christian mob, probably ordered by Cyril too, attacked and murdered the great philosopher and mathematician Hypatia of Alexandria (ca 370–414 CE).

We have the cruel details about her death passed down by Sokrates Scholasticus in The Ecclesiastical History from:

www.cosmopolis.com/alexandria/hypatia-bio-socrates.html

> . . . and dragging her from the carriage, they took her to the church called Caesareum, where they completely stripped her, and then murdered her with tiles. After tearing her body in pieces, they took her mangled limbs to a place called Cinaron, and there burnt them.

The year was 414 CE in the fourth year of Cyril's episcopate. Using a well-known building, the Caesareum, as church, witnesses of something we stated earlier here and there. That the Christians of those times were so unorganized they didn't even have churches of the kind we have today.

www.wisdomworld.org/setting/hypatia.html, says about Cyril:

> Cyril has come down in Christian history as one of the "Saints" of the Church, despite the well known fact that he was tried for stealing the gold and silver Church vessels and spending the money gained from their sale. But petty thievery has not earned for the name of Cyril of Alexandria its dark immortality in the annals of religious history. His real crime was much more serious-the crime of *murder*, deliberately perpetrated against one of the noblest characters in history: Hypatia, the last of the Neoplatonists.

That was also the end of the Neoplatonic school of Alexandria. Plato, who founded the academy in Athens, some thousand years earlier, would never dream that his philosophical ideas would threaten the most powerful man on Earth, the ruler Enlil/Yahweh. In fact, not only Plato and the Neoplatonists were threatening him, but also every freethinking person.

Paulus Orosius (385–420 CE), a historian and theologian stated in his 'History against the pagans' the following concerning the Serapeum:

Today there exist in temples books chest, which we ourselves have seen, and, when these temples were plundered, these, we are told, were emptied by our own men in our time, which, indeed, is a true statement.

The barbarians were proud by destroying the accumulated knowledge of the time in the name of the annihilator of humanity. According to other sources, the great library, or the remains of it, was destroyed in 640 CE by Amr, the leader of the Islamic forces that attacked and took Egypt, after the command of Caliph Omar.

On the question of Amr, on what to do with the books of the great library, Caliph Omar is supposed to have answered that the books should be destroyed because:

They will either contradict the Koran, in which case they are heresy, or they will agree with it, so they are superfluous.

Contradicting the Koran or contradicting the bible, the difference is only a matter of measuring the contradiction on different scales.

No matter how many lines all the writers of the world produced on the subject about the destruction of the greatest library of the time, it could never bring up the great lost of knowledge. The city of Alexandria was the capital of Egypt under the Ptolemaic era. It was the great trade center of the world. A roll the city inherited after the declination of Babylon. The library was the scientific center of the world. Even after the establishing of Christianity in Egypt, the library continued to house great writers and great inventions. But almost everything inside the building was declared as heretic by the agents of Enlil/Yahweh. Any civilization based on science was Enlil/Yahweh's enemy. The descendants of Serpanit, the Earthly wife of Marduk, as well as the descendants of the wise Isis, do not even know who is responsible for the destruction of their great Egyptian civilization. They can barely observe the remains of it. The whole civilization of their ancestors is gone together with their great gods, and most of their great achievements, as Enlil/Yahweh said: 'I will destroy the Egyptians and their gods and their pharaohs'.

Babylon

Babylonian astronomy, mathematics, and 'documents' about the early human history, even Sumerian, were condemned as heretical writings and had been destroyed or hidden. Except from the knowledge that Greeks and Arabs brought out from the city, the whole Babylonian civilization and the beautiful city is disappeared from off the face of the Earth. The rebellious city of Marduk, the symbol of resistance against Yahweh, could not be allowed to exist, as Enlil/Yahweh promised. Isaiah 13:19:

> And Babylon, the glory of kingdoms, the beauty of the Chaldees' excellency, shall be as when God overthrew Sodom and Gomorrah.

Hellas and Byzantium

Under the third and forth century CE, Greek art, even the statues of the gods themselves were destroyed as anti-Christian. The books of great writers, philosophers, historians, mathematicians, books about medical science, democracy, discoveries and much more were burnt on fire, or hidden away to avoid destruction. Books were even overwritten with religious texts, like the Archimedes Palimpsest.

> In the 12th century a monk in Constantinople scraped the parchment containing perhaps the only version of Archimedes' "Method of Mechanical Theorems," then overwrote it with healing prayers. The treatise described a calculus-like procedure that anticipated Newton's and, had it been published in the 16th century with the rest of Archimedes' then-known tracts, might have greatly accelerated the progress of mathematics. The parchment also held six other treatises, including the famous "On Floating Bodies," here alone in Archimedes' original Greek.[3]

By the year 2007 CE, sections of the book have successfully 'reappeared' through modern techniques. The book is now at the Walters Art Museum in Baltimore where restoration continues. This only book could have initiated a much earlier development had it not been hidden and overwritten. Ironically enough, it was thanks to the Greek language and the Hellenistic era that Christianity could be spread around. The Christian leaders and monks had little or none understanding about the damage their burnings had on human development. Those who knew were happy following the instructions of Yahweh, as stated in the 'holy scriptures'.

By the year 364 CE, the worship of Pagan gods was punished with the death penalty, by edict of Emperor Flavius Jovianus, who also ordered the burning of the library of Antioch.

In 370 CE thousands of books were burned in all cities of the Byzantine Empire after orders from emperor Valentinian I. From now on, only books about Judaism and Christianity were allowed.

Two years later, the same Emperor ordered the extermination of all Hellenes in Asia Minor and the destructions of all books associated with them.

The only and outstanding Global occasion of coming together, compete, and exchange ideas, of today is the Olympic Games. This activity was outlawed as anti-Christian in 393 CE by Emperor Theodosius. In the same way his God didn't want people to communicate with one another, Theodosius didn't want the spirit of athletics to unite young people. The Games were forgotten for 1500 years until they started again in 1870 CE in Athens after the initiative of Evangelos Zappas. Beside Zappas, Pierre de Coubertin is considering to be the father of the modern Olympic Games started again in Athens 1896 CE. Pierre de Coubertin wanted to bring the nations together and have young people to compete together in athletic activities instead of wars.

In 526 CE the Athenian Academy was closed and its property confiscated after orders from emperor Justinianus. The Academy, founded by the philosopher Plato in 387 BCE, had been a place of learning for some nine hundred years.

The systematic persecution of people under several hundred years by the Christian Church, powered with imperial decrees, witnesses of the great resistance against Christian beliefs. Not only philosophers responded negatively to the Bible, but also most ordinary people. Raised to act as freethinking individuals, they could never accept the intellectual bondage demanded by the new religion. Have the philosophers of today, the scientists, and the entire multitude of well educated people in general, no opinion about the doctrines of Yahweh? How can their silence be explained?

The inhabitants of Laconia in Hellas resisted all attempts by Byzantine Emperors, Patriarchs, and Christian mobs. Finally, they were forced to convert to Christianity as late as the 9th century, after a military attack. The number of Christians was once again increased by using imperial military power! Are the descendants of the people of Laconia aware of that?

The Greeks are also worshiping the man (Yahweh/God) who almost destroyed the great Hellenic civilization. Their ancestors were forced to replace Zeus, the chief deity of the Greek Pantheon, with Zeus, who now changed his name to Yahweh! They were forced to accept his demand that science should be subjected to his dogmas. They were forced to replace their songs with psalms, progress with declination, and free will with intellectual capitulation. The catastrophe brought by Christianity completed what wars left untouched. Nobody remembers the great ancestors who sacrificed their lives hoping to stop the darkness that would break down the great ancient civilization. The memory about what actually happened is gone, since time can pass anything into forgetfulness.

Rome
Roman literature, history, art, juridical achievements and much more were burnt on fire. People too. The once great city of Rome was reduced to a small city with no science, philosophers, culture or hygiene as Christianity took hold. The Church also demonstrated a passionate hatred for science. The Brotherhood of the papacy claimed to be the only true heir to human bodies and human souls after Yahweh.

Europe
Take a look about the greatest mathematicians and philosophers of this world from 624 BCE to 1079 CE.

Between 624 BCE–10 CE, under these 634 years, we count 51 famous mathematicians. Of them, 47 or 92% were Europeans (including the Hellenistic world of the eastern Mediterranean).

Under the next 550 years, from 10–560 CE, we count 30 famous mathematicians. Of them, 20 or 66% were Europeans (including the Hellenistic world of the eastern Mediterranean). The rest came from India, China and Arab countries.

Under the next 519 years, from 560 - 1079 CE, we count 43 famous mathematicians. Of them none was European. They all came from India, China, and Arab countries.

The number of great philosophers in Europe between the years
0–1100 CE is not a very exciding lecture either. There was only
one, Marcus Aurelius (121–180 CE).[4]

The Europeans, between 500 and 1000 CE, knew no books except for
the bible. Nobody wished to risk his life and the wealth of his family by announcing some discovery. Besides, almost all books were
burned on fire or hidden away. The slowing down of human developments was a fact. Darkness, the companion of Christianity, covered
the whole of Europe. The learned man of those times was something
similar to 'homo unius libri', 'a man of a single book', the bible. Compared to the learned man of ancient or modern times, the knowledge
of the learned man of the middle ages was miserable.

In some European countries, the priests were regularly visiting
people at their homes to control the status of their bible-knowledge.
The church fathers of all degrees were practicing a fanatic dictatorship. Punishment for insufficient bible-knowledge was usual!

Nearly every scientific achievement was abandoned as being
against, not only the bible, but also the teachings of the Church fathers. Music too. Every other form of entertainment that made life
worthy to live was against the dogmas of the church. People, who
could use some sort of entertainment, after a hard day's work, could
only read the bible, or sing psalms. Except for the drinking of wine,
of course, as Jesus himself drank wine, otherwise the art of making
wine would have vanished too. Things like, reading a hidden book
was a matter of life and death. Even after the dark ages, the reading
of books was still impossible because there were no books to read,
or the pressure of the society was so strong that it could completely
destroy people's social life.

Consider the case of Galileo, well known to almost everybody.
The Italian astronomer Galileo Galilei (1564–1642 CE) was one of
the first to use a telescope to study the stars. His theory was that Earth
was orbiting the Sun and not the other way around, as the church fathers believed. The church declared his theory as heresy and he was
imprisoned. At 1992, 350 years later, Galileo was formally exoner-
ated, in other words, he was forgiven for being a heretic. The case of
Galileo is just one of many witnessing that the church has been as
successful as Enlil/Yahweh was in manipulating people.

Was there somebody before Galileo with the same thoughts? Nobody knows, because nobody dared to utter anything contradicting

the church doctrines under the theocratic era, from year zero to the eighteen century.

What about before that? Indeed we have many theories, both right and wrong, as the authorities of those times didn't forbid people to think or express their thoughts. Expressions like 'against God' or 'contradicting the teachings of the Church' were unknown. The knowledge of ancient philosophers and writers was either lost or hidden until the time of the renaissance or even later.

Under the dark ages between the years 300–1300 CE, religion and 'holy' scriptures became the only way of communicating by written language. People knew nothing of the contents of the bible because most people couldn't read. Except for the narratives passed to them by the priests. It was a 'one-way-communication', and thorough-paced manipulation, similar to that practiced by Enlil/Yahweh. The people were not participating, only forced to listen and accept.

Most Christians have never heart the name 'Enlil'. Not 'Marduk' either. Yet, we refer to them several times per day in our churches. Moslems call their God 'Allah', probably from 'al' (the) and 'Ilah' (god), the God, or the deity. Others think that Allah is the same as Ilu, Elil, and Enlil. It is perhaps more accurate since the God of Islam is the same as the God of the OT, the God of Abraham.

He said to Abraham 'I am the god of your fathers' and to Moses 'YHWH'. He didn't wish to reveal any of his names, which created a serious problem for the Jews. Since God didn't want to reveal his name, a human must not pronounce that name either, although it is not a name at all. So they use 'Adonai' the Canaanite-Phoenician name that means 'My Lord', referring to the god Adon. This god, also called Adonis, is supposed to have been either the son of Inanna-Ishtar-Aphrodite or her lover. His origins are both in Cyprus, where his father was supposed to have been Pygmalion and in Phoenicia where his father was supposed to have been Phoenix, the father of the Phoenicians. Paradoxical enough, by calling the name of their 'only' god, they are adducing the name of another god.

The Egyptians used to pray to Amun with the words 'Amun Amun our father in the heavens'. They also used to complete their preys with 'Amun', meaning something like: 'Let it be as Amun will'. The Jews say 'Amin' and the Christians 'Amin' or 'Amen' with the same meaning, also derived from Amun. So when we say 'our father in the heavens . . . Amen' we refer both to Enlil, the god of the

Christians, and to Marduk, 'let it be according to Marduk's will', his adversary. Mysterious are the ways of human intelligence!

It's remarkable that all three religions introduced by Enlil/Yahweh have symbols associated with stars and Enlil's family. The symbol of Judaism is the Star of David. The six-edge Star of David is also the symbol of the planet associated with Enlil's son, Ninurta/Mars, the god of war.

The symbol of Islam is the crescent moon and a five-edged star. The crescent moon was the symbol of Nannar/Sin, the moon god, the son of Enlil who became Mikael in the bible. The star is also the symbol of Jupiter/Enlil.

The symbol of the Christians is the cross, associated with the Crucifixion, but it is also the symbol of the planet Nibiru, 'the planet of crossing', Enlil's home planet.

Emperor Constantine officially introduced the cross as the symbol of Christianity in Constantinople, after he decided to make it the Capital of the Roman Empire. Mehmed II introduced the crescent moon, as the symbol of Islam after he captured Constantinople. Both were military leaders, and both are supposed to have done so after they saw a vision in the sky!

Another confusing fact is the Egyptian ankh cross, a very old, and much revered symbol in ancient Egypt, symbolizing eternal life. In Mesoamerica one can observe a lot of cross-symbols curved in stones long before the time of Christianity. But when the Christian Spaniards saw those cross-symbols, they couldn't understand how the native people of those areas could have known about the Crucifixion of Jesus. The Christian cross is preventing us from searching about the meaning of the cross-symbol associated with the home planet of Yahweh.

The Western civilization

As long as the Western civilization was based on the Judeo Christian pillar alone, there was only darkness. The rulers were blind priests (from educational point of view). Fortunately, today this civilization, influenced by the knowledge of ancient civilizations, especially the Hellenic one, is on its way to free itself from the power of the dogmas. Science and discoveries are no longer subjected the authority of the Church. Development is escalating with, or, without the blessings of the Church fathers.

The more, the western civilization is relying on science, the more, it will distance itself from the doctrines of Yahweh. Unfortunately, it would also evoke the anger of Yahweh, the enemy of knowledge. We hope, however, that scientific and spiritual achievements will allow us to survive the approaching 'battle'. We hope that the battle about the Planet of Gold would be curried out in the science field between the forces of dogmas and the forces of science, or as Enlil/Yahweh said, between 'the forces of darkness and the forces of light'. William Bramley says:

> Yes, spiritual salvation and a thousand years of peace are goals well worth having, and are long overdue, but there is no need to pay the price of an Armageddon to achieve them.[5]

---

[1]Laurence Gardner, Genesis of the Grail Kings, p. 149
[2]Laurence Gardner, Lost Secrets of the Sacred Ark, p. 89
[3]William Cannon, Archimedes Unbound from: www.americanscientist.org/template/ Assetdetail/assetid/15726
[4]The origins of the statistics come from the School of Mathematics and Statistics, University of St Andrews, Scotland, www.history.mcs.st-andrews.ac.uk/ Indexes500_999.html
[5]William Bramley, The Gods of Eden, p. 143

Chapter 22

CORRUPTED TECHNOLOGY IN THE BIBLE

Helicopters, attack aircrafts and Holographic technology

The OT is full of divine vessels, hailstones from heaven killing people, illustrious angels who had the appearance of Man, 'God' himself entering through clouds and many other 'unexplainable' events. In the New Testament, we find visions of lights, visions of Jesus and incredulous descriptions of supernatural character.

The scribes of those times had no possibility to give us credible information since their knowledge did not include any technical expressions to describe what they saw. Another reason was that what they actually experienced was so powerful that they could only explain it as 'the work of God'. The prophets would 'speak the words of Yahweh' and were thus manipulated to ascribe such events to the alien god and his messengers. Two thousands years later we are able to understand the nature of most of those events due to our technical knowledge. Other descriptions, like 'visions appeared in dreams' or 'visions like in a dream' are still behind our comprehension.

This is natural as we always use to relate events to the knowledge of our times. So, after more than two thousand years we are at last able to understand parts of the OT. It might take another thousand years or so before we can explain the rest. If the protagonist of the OT, the alien Enlil/Yahweh, counted on that, then the plan was indeed ingenious. We wonder what would happen if we had been able to establish much earlier that those gods were just humans with

273

some advance knowledge. On the other hand, we know that some did just that in the first centuries of the current era. The results of their works, their warnings, and even their lives have been wasted. Enlil/Yahweh and his representatives on Earth didn't allow any opposition. The darkness created by his doctrines is still here.

The ruins of the destructed civilizations are still visible. But the destructors are still justifying the great lost of knowledge as the work of God. That is why we might need another thousand years to free us from the mental bondage created by his religions. But by then it would be too late because that would be all the time he would need (the orbit of Nibiru takes 3600 years). The difference between the level of the civilization we may have in a thousand years and the one we might have had could be enormous. As his worshipers we would certainly deliver the gold to 'the house of God'. As free humans we would not. If we do not understand his purposes ('the mysterious ways of God') then we might not be worthy to know either.

The information we are able to extract out of events described in the bible is covering almost any branch of our knowledge of today.

The name of God, like 'YHWH' and the name of his archangels, like 'Gabriel' or 'Michael', was given to the scribes by God himself or his messengers.

As we have seen, those aliens demanded to be called 'Gods' and 'Lords' by the humans. They also used titles describing their mission and duties at different times.

'Enlil' means 'Master of the Air' and 'Master of the Command'. 'En' means 'master' and not 'Lord' as it often suggests. 'Master of the Command' is describing his post as the High Commander of the Gold Mission on Earth. In the bible he is called 'Yahweh' meaning 'I am that I am'. Since Moses was a Jew and an Egyptian prince, it is logical to assume that he could speak Jewish and Egyptian. But Enlil/Yahweh could not. We do not believe he found any of our languages worthy to study. Asked by Moses about his name, he answered 'YHWH'. If it was the spur of the moment or something he wished to be called we never know. This 'I am that I am' has been abbreviated as 'I am', and then by using a lot of imagination into 'I am the one I am', 'I am whatever I need to become', 'He who causes to become' and the next thing we know 'He who causes to exist' which is the same as 'The Creator'. Beside the interpretation 'I am that I am', and 'cause to happen' there is no support for any other imaginary interpretation. 'Cause to happen' is equivalent to 'I command', which, in turn, is equivalent to the authority of the Commander of the Gold Mission. The most obvious evidence that Yahweh is not the creator god, is that the gods, including Enlil/Yahweh, believed in God, the creator of all.

In order to find some comprehensible information about the mystical 'name' Yahweh, we consult his own book, particularly Ephesians 2:2:

> Wherein in time past ye walked according to the course of this world, according to **the prince of the power of the air**.
> [emphasis added]

The 'prince of the power of the air' has been changed to 'the ruler of the kingdom of the air' in the mew International version of the Bible, while in the Greek original version is 'αρχοντας της εξουσιας του αερος' meaning just 'Commander of the Air'. Now 'Enlil' means, as we have seen 'Master of the Air' (master of the command) which is the same as 'The Commander'. By saying 'I am that I am' he was telling the truth, that he was the 'Commander', which is equivalent to 'Enlil'.

Beside the many connections between the character of Enlil and the character of Yahweh, this is one even connecting his names.

His human servants have always managed to ascribe some divine properties to his name, although any searching about such properties continues to be without result. Had they been paid to expand his reputation, hade they not been that successful! Christian theologians try to elevate the study of this 'name' alone to some kind of science, or philosophy. Are they driven by a genuine wish to solve a mystery, or are they receiving their 'divine' ideas as 'like in a dream'? Exodus 3:14 says:

> And God said unto Moses, I AM THAT I AM: and he said, Thus shalt thou say unto the children of Israel, I AM hath sent me unto you.

Consider the above statement according to the explanation of his 'name'. Note that he didn't say 'tell them that God has sent me to you'.

> And the Master said unto Moses, I am the commander: and he said, Thus you shall say unto the children of Israel, the Commander has sent me to you.

By following the OT it is easy to establish that, in the beginning, only some persons manipulated by him (like the prophets) believed in him as God. He had a hard time to convince the Israelites about that, and he succeeded only by using a lot of threats, violence, killings, and genocides. Most of the crimes begotten by him and his angels are documented in the OT. Christians, who have a documented abhorrence against Jews in general, should know that they are as much manipulated by Yahweh as the Jews.

'Gabriel' is a Hebrew name meaning 'Strength of El' or 'strong man of god' and he is supposed to be the highest chief over the angels. His real name was Ninurta, the son of Enlil and his half sister Ninmah. Not surprisingly, Nin-ur-ta also means 'hero of the Lord' in the tongue of the Anunnaki. Ninurta was the most trusted and perhaps the most beloved of his sons. They were always working together and the two that contributed the most in bringing the gold operations forward. They were, of course, the highest members of the Brotherhood of the Gold. It was also Gabriel who informed Mary that the time had come to conceive a son. He is 'Jabriel' in the Koran and the one who instructed Mohammed about the introduction of Islam.

'Michael' is Hebrew too, meaning 'he who is like El'. He is not mentioned in the bible by name but in many other Christian writings. His real name was 'Na-nnar' meaning 'bearer of heavenly power'. He is supposed to lead the souls to Hades and therefore seen only by the dead. In some icons he is depicted without face.

He is identical with Enlil's son, Nannar/Sin, the governor of Eden, the lands of the Enlilites. He was responsible for the administration, and for sending young men and women to work in the underground gold mines. He often represented his father when absent. His symbol was the crescent moon, and he is also mentioned in the Koran as 'Makail'. He probably was the architect behind the religions established by the Enlilites.

'Raphael' means 'Healer of El'. He was probably the man behind the visions, the plagues, and many other chemical and biological 'punishments'. His name was Ishkur/Adad, son of Enlil/Yahweh, and the storm god in many cultures. His temple was called 'the house of the seven storms'. Ish-Kur probably means 'Main physicist' which became 'healer'.

'Uriel' means 'Fire of El'. 'The fire of God' used to come down from the heavens. Uriel was the same as Utu, the grandson of

Enlil/Yahweh and the commander of the air forces of the Enlilites. Utu means 'The Shining'.

Jesus was the Son of God, according to the Bible. The name Ye-hoshua (Friend of Yahweh) was decided before his birth. In the OT he is referred to as the 'Messiah', meaning the 'anointed'.

In the Hebrew Bible, the term was also used to describe significant individuals, like king Cyrus, prophets and priests anointed with oil, who had been chosen for some divine task. The kings of Sumer were always chosen for some specific divine task. Messiah means thus no more than the 'Chosen'.

The name that became the most usual one is 'Christ' from the Greek 'Christos'. This is, however, not a name but an epithet, meaning 'useful'. Chosen by Yahweh to be useful to the brotherhood of the Gold, we presume.

Medical information is to be found in Genesis 2:21 where the Lord is supposed to perform a surgical operation on Adam. First we note that the surgeon has been using some anesthetics that caused 'a deep sleep' on the patient. We also note that it was not God who acted as a surgeon but the Lord. The most significant however, was that the operation was the only way, even for the Lord, to achieve the desired result. We wonder why the Creator of the Universe must have special surgical instruments, and a very suitable accommodation for the task, in order to give the first earthlings the ability to procreate. The truth is that is was Ningishzidda, the son of Enki, who performed the operation. Enlil/Yahweh had not been asked, but when the operation was already done, he expelled the young couple from the Edin (Sumer). By using the scribes of the OT he loaded a negative value on the event, as the 'original sin'. The very reason behind our existence was 'evil' according to the Christian Bible!

Missiles from airborne vessels are described as 'hailstones from heaven' in the bible. The missiles are not just falling down from heaven but are directed against the target with great precision. In Joshua 10:11 we read that the Lord cast down hailstones from heaven and killed men, women and children fleeing from the sword of Joshua.

Here we find information that they had aircrafts, imported from their home planet or manufactured on Earth, and that they were armed with missile-like weapons. It could be a kind of attack planes or helicopters operated by pilots with the necessary education. The pilots who killed many innocent people at different occasions are called 'the angels of the lord' in the Christian bible. No Christian can explain why the 'angels of god' made use of helicopters armed with missiles!

They also had very advanced chemical and biological weapons, which they often directed against innocent people, like the plagues in Egypt and elsewhere, not to mention the nuclear-like weapons that destroyed many cities. The genocides and killings through use of such weapons are called 'the punishment of god' in the Christian scriptures.

It is not easy to understand people propagating peace and fighting against the use of weapons, while they on Sundays pray to the most warlike man ever on Earth. They have managed to create a new word, 'hypofaith', by merging hypocrisy and faith!

Information technology was used to create holograms and voices, among other purposes.

The illustrious angels in the bible stress us to believe they are some kind of superior beings of divine nature, but it is not what it seems to be. The reason why those aliens appeared as illuminated every now and then was very simple. The effect was tremendous. No human could see such a being without feeling very small.

As we have seen, there are several examples of gods appearing as shining both in the bible and elsewhere. The consuming of certain amount of gold dust, which is a monatomic super contactor, brings so much energy that the light is flowing around the body. Those messengers and gods used to do that before marching in battles, and other very important occasions.

It is nothing supernatural about it, not even godly, but simply scientific. The using of such scientific discovery to impress on some humans can only be classified as forgery.

The lack of knowledge of the scribes of the OT along with the cemented doctrines that everything they saw was 'the glory of the Lord' has resulted in great corruptions. The flying vessels and helicopters became 'the chariots of God', the missiles became 'hailstones from heaven', the chemical and biological weapons became 'the punishment of God' and the alien pilots became 'the angels of God'. We would not be surprised if those alien pilots are laughing at us right now! Why shouldn't they? Their manipulations created a long thick darkness we just began to see through.

Angels and Holograms

Many unexplainable phenomena, like visions, are not limited to the bible pages. We have visions in the sky, voices that could be heard along great distances, lights stronger than the Sun, flying vehicles, hailstones from heaven and many other similar events all over the world. Not surprisingly, Jews and Christians, associate visions with Yahweh/God and angels.

Since the messengers of Enlil/Yahweh could fly using both helicopter-like vehicles and attack aircrafts, the angels are also supposed to have the ability to fly. The wings attached to their bodies, although an invention of a rather artistic nature, was welcome as it helped to erase the presence of technological equipment. We believe that the biblical visions were a result of technology, created by the administrators of the 'Messiah project', alias the members of the Brotherhood of the Gold and their leader Yahweh.

The visions in the sky, the enlisting of agents and the appearance of angels were performed in such a theatrical manner in order to maximize the effects. It was rather important to show that both visions and angels used to make their appearance from the heaven. It was a marketing trick in order to involve God in this kind of communication. Num 12:16 says:

> And he said, Hear now my words: If there be a prophet among you, I the LORD will make myself known unto him in a vision, and will speak unto him in a dream.

Enlil was always using technical equipment to communicate with his own planet by 'beaming words'. If he could 'speak unto him in a dream' could therefore be just another way to communicate that we do not (yet?) have the knowledge to explain.

Although nobody knows how the visions were created, it is probably possible for professionals to explain them as some type of holographic projection, often followed by a voice. We know that the Anunnaki had every kind of controlling and watching instruments, high-tech tools, and communicating equipment. To exclude such capabilities from people who had space ships that could land, load tons of gold and then lift again from earth, would be foolish. The humans could not ignore such phenomena, only subject to them.

We have 'signs in the sky' every now and then, often appearing at the time of some important person's birth, or, when they needed assistance. We have such signs when Abraham was born, Apollonius of Tyana, Osiris, Jesus, Buddha and others, suggesting that those who had access to the required technical equipment freely exercised this kind of communication. Not only visions and angels are coming down from heaven but also a whole city. Rev 21:2 says:

> And I John saw the holy city, New Jerusalem, coming down from God out of heaven, prepared as bride adorned for her husband.

The messengers/angels, most of them members of the Jehovah family, have different abilities well in accordance with their different education and skills. They can fly in 'whirlwinds', 'sky ships' or with the help of some equipment attached to their bodies. Athena had sandals allowing her to fly as well as Hermes and Horus. Inanna (Aphrodite) and Ninurta/Ares had their own 'sky bird' armed with missiles. The higher members of the 'Gold Mission Corporation' are called archangels in the Bible while ordinary members are called angels and sometimes even 'men'! Ezekiel 1:4–5 says:

> And I looked, and, behold, a whirlwind came out of the north, a great cloud, and a fire in folding itself, and a brightness was about it, and out of the midst thereof, as the colour of amber, out of the midst of the fire.

> Also out of the midst thereof came the likeness of four living creatures. And this was their appearance; they had the likeness of a **man**. [emphasis added]

The whirlwind described by Ezekiel is easy to identify as some kind of helicopter. As the angels of God do not need such equipment, the whirlwind is replaced by 'windstorm' in the new international bible. It seems that the truth is also blown with the wind! The corruption that started in Babylon, under the Babylonian captivity, is still going on.

The angels who visited Abraham before the destruction of the military base on mount Sinai, the cities Sodom, Gomorra and the other cities of the plain, were also men, (Genesis 18:2) and even hungry. Abraham offered them food, even if it took quite a time to prepare a meal for three persons. Genesis 18:8:

> And he took butter, and milk. And the calf which he had dressed, and set it before them; and he stood by them under the tree, and they did eat.

The angels do not always kill people or destroy cities. They often have some message to pass down to their agents, and they even use drugs to make them understand and remember the message, as in Ezekiel 3:2–3:

> So I opened my mouth, and he caused me to eat that roll. And he said unto me, Son of man, cause thy belly to eat, and fill thy bowels with this roll that I give thee. Then did I eat it; and it was in my mouth as honey for sweetness.

Also in Revelations 10:9:

> And I went unto the angel, and said unto him, Give me the little book. And he said unto me, Take it, and eat it up; and it shall make thy belly bitter, but it shall be in thy mouth sweet as honey.

We admit that we do not know if there is some benevolent being, we could call 'the Creator of All'. The Christian bible claims that he not only exists but his angels also make use of drugs. Even women, like Yahweh's wife or his grand daughter Inanna could show up flying, as in Zecharia 5:9

> And lifted I up my eyes, and looked, and, behold, there came out **two women**, [emphasis added] and the wind was in their wings; for they had wings like the wings of a stork: and they lifted up the ephah between the earth and the heaven.

The 'ephah' is translated as 'basket' in the NIV of the bible. The reiterated instructions to the agents, the many visions at different times, and the great efforts of Enlil/Yahweh and his warriors witness of a plan spanning much longer than our lives. The prophecies were an effective way to reach the minds of people many generations later. Enlil/Yahweh used to say 'I am the god of your fathers' because that was the only way to convince people long after the time of Abraham.

There are numerous Christian sites on the web, selling angels as art items. It's possible to find the most amazing information. You can buy small angels, be informed that there is an angel guarding you, that there are a lot of angels among us. Some wish that some angel would visit them, or claiming that they use to communicate with angels. They claim that the angels are the 'pure spirits of God' or just 'let an angel guide you to find Jesus and the kingdom of heaven'!

Never before have these winged angels been so admired and so popular. Their own book, however, the Christian Bible, is full of their criminal actions against humanity and against individuals. Have they been the agents of Jehovah or the 'spirits of God', their guilt can never be revoked.

Angel is loaded with values and meanings very different the word actually has. Despite that the word means 'messenger' in English, even the English bible uses the word angel. It is hard to think of any cult around the word 'messenger' similar to that created around the word 'angel'.

Prophets
The visions were often directed to carefully selected individuals, like sears (prophets in the bible) instructing them about specific actions. The purpose was always to enlist suitable 'agents'. Sometimes the visions appear as dreams and even 'as in a dream' but the scribes were not able to determine the nature of the vision. Christian theologians refer to these phenomena as evidence of the supernatural power of God and his angels.

Some usual messages are of the type 'go teach', 'they will believe when it happens' (because I will cause it to happen), 'see how powerful I am' or 'I have been choosing you to be my 'servant' (agent).

Probably there is not a single human who wouldn't surrender to such supernatural visions demonstrated in much a theatrical manner creating both fear and hope.

There are many definitions of the word 'prophet' but most dictionaries have a similar definition as the following. 'The prophet, almost always male, is supposed to communicate the will of God after some divine inspiration'. The 'divine inspiration' is also supposed to handle some help to make the message understandable. Is everybody predicting the future a prophet? Only if God appointed him, otherwise he is considered to be a 'sear' and even an impostor. The best definition is to be found in the OT, Deuteronomy 18:18, where Yahweh says that he would raise the prophets, and they would act according to his orders. The prophets were thus appointed by him to communicate his message to the people. Then they were by definition his agents, or, at least, the agents of the Brotherhood of the Gold. Now look at an usual definition of the word 'agent'.

Agent is a person acting on behalf of another person or organization.

The messages were of two kinds, order-messages, and future-messages. If a prediction showed up to be true then the prophecy was considered as fulfilled.

Could Enlil/Yahweh predict the future? Did he really know what was going to happen? If that is true then how come that most of the prophecies have never been fulfilled? Was somebody troubling his plans? In 'The Lost Book of Enki' by Z. Sitchin (p.315), Enlil/Yahweh admits that nobody can foresee the fates of Destiny.

Who in them the hands of Destiny could foresee, Who could between our chosen fates and our unbending destiny distinguish?

The use of prophecies was indeed a very powerful weapon to convince ordinary people. The absence of education used to make prophesies easily acceptable. First he declared prophecies through his agents, and then he made things happen, through his 'angels', to fulfill them. It was as simple as that, although they were not always successful because Yahweh's adversary, Marduk, and his supporters counteracted his plans whenever they could.

Some predictions about future events are fulfilled, like Jesus entering Jerusalem riding on a donkey. This was, like many other prophecies, easy to manipulate in order to get it classified as fulfilled. In the book of Daniel, Jesus is supposed to 'arrive on the clouds' which was not as easy to achieve! Some prophecies were written after the actual events already happened, and yet most of the prophecies have never been fulfilled. Many prophecies are considered as fulfilled according to Christian writings only because they can be interpreted in several ways. So, neither Enlil/Yahweh, nor the prophets could actually predict the future.

We have more prophets in the small country of Jesus than in the whole world. Was the prophesying that much trendy? Did Enlil/Yahweh appoint all the prophets? Probably not. He actually had some problems with agents hoping to make a career. The control of agents, double agents, or adversary agents must have been a problem. In order to discourage non-official agents he ordered his supporters to kill uncertified prophets, as in Jeremiah 28:15–16:

> Then said the prophet Jeremiah unto Hananiah the prophet, Hear now, Hananiah; The LORD not sent thee; but thou makest this people to trust in a lie. Therefore thus said the LORD; Behold, I will cast thee from off the face of the earth: this year you shall die, because thou hast taught rebellion against the LORD. So Hananiah the prophet died the same year in the seventh month.

Was Hananiah a fortune hunter or the agent of some other god? Sometimes Yahweh kills prophets speaking 'lies' and sometimes he kills prophets speaking lies provided by him! Although it sounds like 'the ways of God are mysterious', his logics could be on a mystery path too. Ezekiel 14:19 says:

> And if the prophet be deceived when he hath spoken a thing, I the LORD have deceived that prophet, and I will stretch out my hand upon him, and will destroy him from the midst of my people Israel.

Were all the prophets appointed by him really manipulated to speak his words or did they chose that occupation for some other reasons? What about money? Micah 3:11:

> The heads thereof judge for reward, and the priests thereof teach for hire, and the prophets thereof divine for money.

Paul, John, James, Peter and many other apostles and co-apostles have said that Jesus would come back very soon, often under their lifetime. Were they false prophets, had they been exercising disinformation, or had they been provided with information they could not interpret correctly? Since not a single one of the prophets of the Bible has been one hundred percent right, they have, at some occasion, been either wrong or lying. Peter the apostle also claims that anybody who does not listen to the prophet (probably Jesus) would be killed! Acts 3:23:

And it shall come to pass, that every soul, which will not hear
that prophet, shall be destroyed from among the people.

Saints

There are numerous saints in Christianity. In case the days of the
year are not enough to honor every one of them, a special day is
collectively dedicated to all of them. A usual definition of saint
is: A person who has died and been declared as saint by canonization. Some Saints are recognized by all the major Christian
branches, while others are only recognized by a specific branch.
The saints are not elected by the people but by ecclesiastical authorities.

One would think that pure life and good deeds are the criteria
used for canonization. That would, perhaps be the case if the saints
were elected by the people. The Church uses to judge the life and
deeds of saint-candidates by taking into account some other factors too. Like how valuable they have been in elevating the status of
Christianity, or how renowned they were. Because of that, we have
saints that have never died, like St Michael, and saints with blood
on their hands.

The saints are also specialized in every kind of medical treatment. The pilgrims are visiting different places of worship depending of the kind of help they need. If someone has some eye-
problem, ear-problem, and the like, then the visit is directed to
different saints. The saints are specialized in every kind of disease, physical or not.

At the specific day of celebration, the space outside the church,
transforms to a market place where one can bye everything from
curing items blessed by the particular saint, to food. The church
charges different fees to the traders according to the space they use,
anice combination of religiosity and business!

What kind of people were the saints? It is, of course, impossible
to know much concerning the life of most of them. Some stories
about the life of some particular saints are written long after their
death. There is neither any possibility of knowing how most of them
looked like. This is the reason why most icons, particularly in orthodox churches, are so similar to one another, often painted by monks
of the same school. It is difficult to believe everything ascribed to
them. Like the killing of dragons, or the curing of serious diseases.
Even saints can be classified in different categories.

Admirable Saints

The main characteristic of admirable saints is that they spent their life in helping people. They lived a pure but rather ordinary life without any attempt to gain riches or advantages for themselves. They never hurt anybody, and they really deserve our veneration. Their message was: 'Be good to your fellow humans'. Any imitation of them would make the world a better place to live. At the same time, we ignore equally admirable individuals because they happened to live before the time of Christianity. This is another example of how religions are creating virtual domains separating people.

Eremite saints

Those people lived their lives outside the society. Their religious fanaticism drove them to some extreme kind of life and even extreme actions. They abandoned everything valuated by ordinary people. We find them spending their whole life in some cave, in the desert, or some monastery, away from anything reminding civilized existence. They avoided other people and their choice was directed out of egoistic reasons. They chose a life full of preys and silence, just to prove the power of their faith.

We are not criticizing them for their choice. They had the right to do whatever they wished with their life. They chose a life suitable to their faith, for their own sake, not for anybody else. Although we have not any right to blame them, we have no reason to venerate them either. Their message was 'adjust life to faith, not faith to life'. We have, indeed, no reason to even remember them. Yet, we have built churches for them. The churches are, of course, not for them but for us. We feel some kind of obligation to venerate their memory, but why? They probably don't even feel comfortable. They wished to avoid people, not to be surrounded by strangers every now and then. It is not easy to understand how they were imitating their god either. He was a highly living individual with no restrictions in every-day-life-pleasures. The church may preserve their memory in the annals of canonization as quite egoistic saints. Neither the church nor the people need saints of this kind any more.

Violent Saints

Some fanatic 'bishops' and emperors ordered destruction of knowledge, art, temples, libraries, and even murdering, because they had the power to do that, and because they believed they were following

God's will. They used violence to create fear in the same way Yahweh did. Their message was: 'Faith in Yahweh excuses disrespect for life'. Some dishonorable actions of some early church fathers contributed to the establishment of the Christian Church. For that, some of them have been rewarded and declared as saints, like Constantine, Cyril of Alexandria, Epiphanius of Salamis, Michael the archangel (alien god), just to mention a few of them, although no other criterion is applicable in their case. Additionally, they have never been tried for their crimes. The church demanding the adoration of men begotten criminal actions is not honorable either. We are venerating saints with blood on their hands, most probably out of unawareness.

Chapter 23

ST MICHAEL, MARDUK AND THE DRAGON

The Christian Hell and the Assassination of Marduk

According to Sumerian records, Nergal was the administrator of the underground mines in Southern Africa. He is known as Hades in the Greek Mythology, the god of the underworld and the god of the dead.

Most of the gods of the 'House of Enlil', who grounded the Brotherhood of the Gold, were living in Sumer. Nergal was the only one of the 'House of Enki' (son of Enki) who became member of the brotherhood after marrying Enlil's granddaughter Ereskigal. Their temple-adobe, also housing the headquarters of the gold mining operations, was surrounded by seven walls, witnessing of the immense importance of the place.

Most humans in the lands controlled by the brotherhood of the gold were partially free. They had a labor duty whenever the gods called. Others were fulltime servants. The unluckiest people were the lifetime workers in the gold mines. The two gods with authority and responsibility to provide mine workers were Nergal and Nannar/Sin. They used to select (capture) young men and women and send them to dig the gold in the mines of Abzu. Once they came into the underground mines, they never came up again. They were considered as dead by their relatives. They also had been manipulated to believe they were dead, hence the expression 'living dead in the realms of Hades'.

Nannar/Sin, probably meaning 'Bearer of heavenly power', the son of Yahweh born on Earth, was involved in most of the affairs of the gods. He was often representing his father when absent. He is considered as the great architect behind many projects, including the 'Messiah project'. In Sumer he was the governor of Ur under a long time and even the governor of the whole land of Sumer. He was also a member of the 'Council of Seven', the highest official authority on Earth. He is known as the moon god, his symbol being the crescent moon.

His reputation as 'slave supplier' managed to survive and find its way into Christianity. He is supposed to be the archangel Michael who collects the souls of the dead and delivers them to other administrators for 'judgment'. We find both the name, Michael, meaning 'He who is like El', and his duties as executive chief messenger (archangel), in agreement with his alien name. He was one of the highest members of the brotherhood, the Grand Master being Enlil/Yahweh. By studying the life and activities of him in different Christian books and web sites, we find that he was involved in everything, everywhere, at least. The Christian Church managed to create a fantastic myth by assimilating the activities of many other mythological characters.

One description is, however, true. Although Christianity adopted several mythological and pagan traditions, the duties of Michael in the Christian culture originate from real events. The deliverer of mine workers (by boat as Charon or not) became the deliverer of souls. Expressions like 'we have to go when the archangel Michael calls', or 'when St Michael comes for the soul' are not unusual among Christians. Thousands of years after Nannar sent the first slaves to dig gold in the underworld, the Christians still believe that he is the one, under his new identity as Michael, who will come to lead their souls to wherever they belong. It is also believed that only the dead, and dying can see Michael's face, thus often depicted without face on icons in many Christian churches!

The 'Saint' without face selected uncounted young men and women and delivered them to a place of no return. The great supplier of slaves has been declared as 'Saint' by the Church fathers, something we believe he is not worthy. His new epithet and his new name cannot ease the burden of his evil actions against humanity. Besides, Saints use to be recognized as saints after their death, while Michael is probably still alive, constituting a paradox concerning the rules of holiness.

According to the Catholic Encyclopedia, St Michael is supposed to 'fight against Satan'. If we consider that the word 'Satan' is a corruption of the Arabic word 'Shejtan' meaning 'adversary', 'antagonist', then St Michael is fighting against his and Enlil/Yahweh's adversary, i.e. another god. He is also considered as 'archistrategos' in Greek liturgy, meaning 'Chief of the Army' (of God). The only epithet, the Church lack to ascribe to him is probably the most credible one, as the architect of religions! The Catholic Encyclopedia says:

> It would have been natural to St Michael, the champion of the Jewish people, to be the champion also of Christians, giving **victory in war** [emphasis added] to his clients.

The chief of the army of God! We wonder why God has an army, or a chief of the army. Does he also have a 'ministry of attack', rather than a ministry of defense? Also from the Catholic Encyclopedia, we read that Nannar/Michael had a meeting at Constantinople with Emperor Constantine, about military or religious matters, we presume.

> At Constantinople likewise, St. Michael was the great heavenly physician. His principal sanctuary, the Michaelion, was at Sosthenion, some fifty miles south of Constantinople; there the archangel is said to have appeared to the Emperor Constantine.

It would be most interesting to know what the conversation was about, Constantine being an enlisted (by Michael?) agent of Yahweh and Michael being the son of Yahweh and the architect behind Christianity!

The archangel Michael intervened in many battles, depicted always with a sword, although we believe he had much more advanced and destructive weapons. He stuck the minds of the Christians like a disease. Suddenly he became very popular everywhere, even in countries, like Egypt, the Enlilites continually tried to destroy. The Egyptian Christians adopted St Michael as the protector of the life-giving Nile! Michael is usually honored on mountaintops. This caused some scholars to identify him as Yahweh, the 'God of the great Mountain'. The great literature about Michael is a worthy competitor to any Mythology. Jehovah's witnesses consider Michael as Jesus! Both Michael and Jesus are supposed to be the leaders of armies in heaven!

St Michael is something unique in the history of Christianity. He is the only alien (all the angels were aliens, members of the Gold Mission of Enlil/Yahweh/God) who has been declared as saint by the Christian Church. The Christians have no problem in accepting an alien Saint, (with or, without face) even if they do not really believe in extraterrestrials.

No other god or human has been honored with so many epithets, as St Michael. He is also considered as the patron of the church, and he was, during the Middle Ages, even the patron of the orders of knights! He is also considered to have been Adam! In Germany, he replaced Wotan, the weather-god honored on mountains tops and hills. He is also supposed to be the patron angel of countries, warriors, police and much more, although there is no support in the scriptures that he ever acted benevolent. As we have seen, even the help he provided Joshua (as the chief of the army) was, in reality, an undercover operation in order to exterminate the Anakim. The fully armed warrior messenger is also the father of Inanna/Aphrodite, the goddess of war! The good actions ascribed to Michael can only exist in the skies!

The worshiping of Michael as some benevolent being and Saint is quite unexplainable. Shall we worship him because he sent thousands of people to work and die in the gold mines, or perhaps, because he killed people that could have directed humanity into a better future?

St Michael and the dragon
Most known is the depiction of Michael as the vanquisher of a dragon. We wonder, St Michael is supposed to have done what? Did he kill a real dragon or is the dragon symbolic? There is, of course, no description and no details about the fight. St George of Cappadocia, a Greek soldier in the service of Rome, killed a dragon too. As St Martha of Tarascon, St Philip the apostle, and many others, most of them declared saints after they killed some dragon!

We wonder why all those saints had to kill dragons? Are they supposed to be regarded as liberators from some dragon ruler ship? Why are we supposed to admire dragon killers? Michael has many similarities with Heracles of the Greek mythology. He too killed a lot of monsters, but he has never gained the status of 'archangel', although a son of Enlil/Zeus too. Michael killing the dragon is supposed to symbolize the battle fought in heaven against the Devil. Why the symbolism? Why in heaven? What do theologians know about battles in heaven? Is the symbolism representing a real battle in heaven? If the fight was between him and the Devil, as Christian scholars are claiming, we would like to know the source of this knowledge. Most artists have been painting religious motifs, under the times of darkness, as it was the only kind of painting they possibly could market. We have, for example, angels with wings, the last supper, the crucifixion on the cross, the dragon-killing Saints, and many other paintings that are nothing else, but artistic expressions. Many of those paintings are invaluable items of art. Unfortunately, people also consider them as representing real events. Is the fight between Michael and the dragon an artistic expression, or was there a rebellion in heaven indeed? If 'heaven' is figurative, then a fight between two powers represented by two gods-men, could indeed have taken place on Earth. Laurence Gardner says about dragons:

> From the very earliest of recorded times, dragons have featured at the forefront of culture lore, where they have been portrayed in various conflicting guises. The ancient Greeks believed that dragons were benevolent creatures with the ability to convey the wisdom and secrets of life, while in contrast the early Hebrews saw dragons as the meddlesome purveyors of sin. The mighty dragon was the emblem of the Chinese Empire, being a national symbol of good fortune and outside the Hebrew tradition dragons were generally seen as the guardians of universal knowledge and the benign protectors of humankind.[1]

Did St Michael kill a purveyor of sin, or a bearer of wisdom and protector of mankind? What kind of sins is a purveyor of sin guilty of? Enlil/Yahweh has uncounted crimes to answer for! If Michael killed a purveyor of sin, then he could be the hero of the Christians. If Michael killed a protector of humanity, then he did something very wrong. The Church has, of course, to find some way to justify yet another crime begotten by its founders. Nobody is expected to sympathize with a dragon!

The foremost protectors of humanity among the gods were, as we have seen, Enki, Marduk, and Thoth. The dragon has also been the symbol of Kingship. Hermes is depicted as triumphant in the battle against the dragon Typhon. Seth became king of Egypt after he murdered his brother Osiris. Seth is Typhon in the Greek mythology. Hermes-Thoth helped Horus to defeat Seth, the illegal king. Did Michael kill some illegal king too?

Outside the scriptures of Enlil/Yahweh, the dragon is venerated as a symbol of kingship, and the serpent as a symbol of wisdom. We know that the Jews were not allowed to think outside the pages of the scriptures. No matter what opinions they had, no expressions contradicting the doctrines of Yahweh were allowed. Enlil/Yahweh declared Marduk as 'the evil serpent' and Babylon as 'the evil city'. That became also the opinion of the Jews, that later, uncensored, passed down to the Christians.

All those fights against dragons by men and women, that later became saints, must have been copied and repeated from one original fight, a fight between two gods. Since we know the name of one of them, it is easy to guess the name of the other one. The other god ought to be Marduk, the dragon king. His emblem was a serpent with a dragonhead, symbolizing wisdom and kingship. He was also the great adversary of Enlil/Yahweh and the Brotherhood of the Gold. If some of the Enlilites had challenged Marduk in wrestling or some other combat, then that one would have been Ninurta/Gabriel. Both of them wished to succeed Enlil and both had that right at different occasions. But then we would have had a fight, probably a fair fight between the two.

In the case of Michael we have no duel between him and Marduk (the dragon), only a killing. A killing without fight, and without trial (accused for sins?), could not have been anything else than assassination. So Nannar, the architect of the Enlilites, the archangel of the bible, had probably assassinated Enlil's adversary Marduk. St Michael didn't kill a dragon but a dragon king.

Some actions of the Enlilites, after that, support this theory. As we have seen, from about 1950 BCE until the return of the Jews from the Babylonian captivity (539 BCE) under the time of Cyrus the great, 550–530 BCE, all the wars in the Meddle East were fought by powers controlled by either Enlil or Marduk. Cyrus said that it was Marduk who delivered the city of Babylon into his hand.

After that we have no sign of Marduk neither in Babylon nor in Egypt. Did he left for Nibiru? It is most unlikely as his family members (children and grand children) were not welcome there. Most probably he was still around determined to stay on Earth. Unless, of course, he had been assassinated. We repeat the words uttered by the Enlilites in a previous chapter.

> Of Marduk, an evil serpent, Earth must be rid! Enlil with them agreed.

One of the members of the council was Nannar/Michael. The Brotherhood of the Gold succeeded to execute the decision taken by the Council of Seven after thousands of years. The Enlilites had reason to celebrate the assassination of a great friend and protector of mankind. With Marduk away from the scene, a new reality was created; they actually became masters of the Planet of Gold. Enlil/Yahweh could now style as 'the living god'. His adversary was dead.

Their actions, from ca 500 BCE to ca 650 CE, remained without any reaction from Marduk. Some two hundred years later, they probably poisoned Alexander the great who also threatened their plans. Later on, Gabriel announced the coming of the Messiah (even his name, Jesus), also undisturbed. Some three hundred years later, they needed a new power that could force Christianity on every citizen of the Roman Empire. The powerful agent was Constantine, (probably enlisted by Michael) who transformed a very unpopular and sectarian Christianity into a world religion by using Imperial decrees. The last project of theirs, also without any opposition of Marduk, was the introduction of Islam, (also announced by Gabriel) designed to balance the power of Christianity so that the people of Earth would remain divided for times to come. Islam is actually helping the Christians to stay Christians!

The killing of the dragon-king by Nannar/Michael can be considered as, either mythology, or real crime. The assassination of Marduk, as well as the poisoning of Alexander the great was, without any doubt, connected to the gold powder. The assassination of Marduk shifted the path of human history into paths decided by the Brotherhood of the Gold. History records witness that Marduk, Nimrod, Alexander the great, and Emperor Julian (just to name a few personalities of the old times) could have directed humanity into a better future.

---

[1]Laurence Gardner, Genesis of the Grail Kings, p. 1–2

Chapter 24

RULER OF EARTH

Christianity, Islam and Secret societies.
The Ruling Sisters

Under the last two millennia, laws and political acts have been con-
formed to the will of God as a modern contribution to his Gold Mission!

What happened to Enlil/Yahweh? The last documented encoun-
ter we have between some Anunnaki and humans, was when the
chief messenger (archangel) Gabriel/Ninurta instructed Mohammed
about the introduction of Islam. They could appear 'illustrious', after consuming enough gold powder, for many reasons; one of them,
not less important, was to make some irrevocable impose.

The 'illustrious Messenger', who approached Mohammed, said
to him that the new religion should be called 'Islam', meaning 'surrender' (to God), and that it was the latest edition by the same God,
the God of Abraham. Everybody, even Christians and Jews ought to
surrender.

The religious and military program launched by Mohammed
to execute the order of Gabriel and conquer lands and people in
the name of Allah, became soon a great empire, where people
not willing to accept Islam were forced to surrender to the new
religion. Islam, and the new Islamic Empire, became soon a political, military, and religious threat to both Christians and non-
Christians.

Was Islam really projected to replace the other two religions introduced by God? Two options are available. Either the latest release was an updated better version, which means that it must have been something wrong with the previous two, or the only purpose was to create conflicts between them. The latter is obvious. While the Moslems had been told that the worshipers of the two earlier religions had to accept the latest one, the Christians had been told not to believe in any prophet after Jesus. The two of them were designed to balance the power of each other preventing each other from becoming the only world religion so that they could rule the world together. That would keep humanity busy in religious conflicts for times to come.

Religious fanatic beliefs do not die with the bearer, as they are loaded over with great power to every new generation. The more, the humans were busy with conflicts, created by him or not, the more, the secret about the Gold Mission would be safe.

After that, there is no sign of Enlil/Yahweh and his associates. He said, he would come back all right, the final day, to participate in the final battle, and judge the people of the Earth. He is supposed to judge what? By what right is he to judge the people of the Earth? According to which laws? According to his dogmas? The Kingdom of Heaven? Heaven only knows!

At the day of judgment, Jesus is supposed to judge the deceased, giving the righteous eternal life in Heaven, while the sinful will be cast into Hell, all according to the bible, Mathew 25:31,32:

When the Son of man shall come in his glory, and all the holy angels with him, then shall he sit upon the throne of his glory: And before him shall be gathered all nations: and he shall separate them one from another, as a shepherd divideth his sheep from the goats:

Is he going to cast people into the underground gold mines of Nergal/Hades? Shall we be commanded to dig gold again? The Christian Hell is just another name of the gold mines.

The 'trial' is supposed to appear 'at the end of time'. Christians of different branches use to predict 'the end of the world', from time to time, although they have no idea why, or how that is going to happen! Christians are, of course, the people who are certain they will be saved and move into the Kingdom of Heavens! Not surprisingly, there is 'a Day of Judgment', even in Judaism, and Islam. The Jews and the Moslems are also certain they will be saved. Are we supposed to feel pity for people born into other religions than the three mentioned above? Who is going to judge them? Would they be condemned as unbelievers? Is the Day of Judgment some kind of joke, or is it the day he would come back, and demand the delivery of the gold?

If it is Enlil/Yahweh, who is supposed to come back, does that mean that he left? Probably. Nobody knows. He has been ruling the Earth since he came here, hundreds of thousands of years ago. He didn't even really accept to be replaced as the Commander of the Gold Mission. Is it possible that such a person would give up and leave the scene? And if he really did, who is ruling after him? It is certainly not his adversary Marduk, because we have no sign of Marduk either from about 539 BCE. That means that either they left, or they are still here operating under secret identities, living in underground cities, or simply, living among us. We choose to believe that all of them (except Marduk) left with the last cargo of gold. Not because the Gold Mission had been completed, but because they could not operate publicly any more. If the Gold Mission had been completed, he would never promise to come back. But he left behind instruments directing us to collect gold for him. So, in a way, the Gold Mission is still going on!

It is not possible to realize any right for Yahweh to judge the people of Earth. On the contrary, we have the right to judge him! Laurence Gardner says:

> It was he [Jehovah] who had brought about the devastating Flood, and it was he who had leveled the cities of Sodom and Gomorrah-not because of their wickedness, as related in Genesis (18-19), but because of the wisdom and insight of their inhabitants, as depicted in the Coptic *Paraphrase of Shem.*[1] It was Jehovah who had removed the Israelites from their homeland, sending them into seventy years of captivity by King Nebuchadnezzar II and his five Babylonian successors down to King Belshazzer (545–539 BC).[1]

The Ruler

Are we ruling ourselves then? It seems like we are. But everything is not always what it seems to be. He is still ruling through the 'holy' books, and some secret brotherhoods. No one could deny the fact that the bible has been dictating, not only the direction of human history in the West and development in general, but also matters concerning everyday life.

How often don't we hear 'It is stated in the Bible', 'it is a sign from God', 'God said that', 'God's will cannot be questioned' and things like that? How can we evaluate the actions of the god of the OT when every question is considered as sinful?

The Church fathers neither need evidence of God's existence, nor do they supply any, since, they say, it is a matter of faith. But if it is a matter of faith, why then persecute people with different, or even, similar beliefs? Why kill the unbelievers, like, both God, and Popes did? How many people go to church, not because they believe in God, not because they feel comfortable in doing so, but because they feel the social press from the society lying heave on them.

Almost all of the world's leaders have officially declared that their work follows God's will. This is the same as following the instructions stated in the three 'holy books', representing three different wills! Suppose God is not God. Then we are all following the instructions of somebody else. Leaders, church fathers and ordinary people want everybody to believe that they act according to religious instructions, doctrines, and dogmas even if they do not. The hypocrisy established in the bible by Enlil/Yahweh himself, is still exercised both inside, and outside the Church. What is for sure, however, collecting gold and killing 'unbelievers' is indeed the will of the God!

Although Christianity is a monotheistic religion, Enlil/Yahweh himself has been telling us that he had an adversary who also was a god. It was the god of Egypt, the god of Babylon, his nephew Marduk, the one he called evil. Both are gods but Enlil/Yahweh consider himself as superior in some way. We, his worshipers have transformed him from being a 'god' to be 'God'. It is also interesting to understand how Christianity has transformed this epithet, the 'adversary', into Satan. We have God and Satan, (a morally 'fallen' god according to Yahweh), and the two of them together, or each one of his own, have been directing peoples' lives for thousands of years now. In that, Christianity is no different from pagan religions, worshiping both a wise god and an evil one.

The people of Babylon and the people of Egypt sided with Marduk, not with Enlil/Yahweh. In fact nobody sided with him except for some prophets/agents, whom he had to manipulate for the purpose under a long time. It seems that all 'the nations were flowing together unto Marduk'. While Enlil/Yahweh was speaking about Marduk as 'the god of Babylon' and 'the god of the Egyptians', the Christian church avoided consequently the use the name 'Marduk', his epithet 'god', or even 'adversary'. The god of the Jews and the Christians couldn't possibly have had another god as his adversary, since he had declared himself as the only god. Several hundred years later, the church chose to use a 'more negative' synonym to 'adversary', from another language. How convenient that there were other languages to use, created by no other than Enlil/Yahweh. They chose to use a word from Arabic, 'Shejtan' which means adversary. 'Shejtan' became 'Satan' and the like in every Christian language. By that, the church created a conception loaded with no other meaning or explanation than 'evil', while the original conflict between Enlil/Yahweh and Marduk, was political and in some sense military, the supremacy on Earth. It was never a religious conflict. Marduk threatened the Gold Mission of Yahweh, not the beliefs of the humans.

The Brotherhood of the Serpent
The 'Brotherhood of the Serpent' is the oldest known brotherhood founded in Egypt in very old times. Egypt was the domain of Ptah/ Enki/Ea from the beginning, and later the domain of his sons. Enki being associated with the 'Serpent' as the god of wisdom, and even his son, Thoth, the 'winged Serpent'. Isis was the goddess of wisdom and Osiris the demigod who perhaps released most knowledge to the humans than anyone else. It is very likely that it was some of them who founded the brotherhood, most likely Ningishzidda/ Hermes who was commissioned by Anu to be mankind's mentor. Since it was the creation of some protectors of humanity, it is only logical to assume that the brotherhood's purpose was to pass knowledge to the humans, and mark out some paths leading to certain developments and perhaps, spiritual salvation. William Bramley says about the brotherhood of the Snake:

> This suggests that Ea intended his creation, Homo sapiens, to be suited for Earth labor, but at some point he changed his mind about using spiritual enslavement as a means. If Ea was a true historical personality as the Sumerians claimed, then he was the probable leader of the brotherhood at its founding on Earth.[2]

As we have seen, some books about 'immortality' are ascribed to Thoth/Hermes, the Egyptian god of science. One of those paths might have been to preserve and promote 'sacred geometry of Thoth/ Hermes', and 'the art of building', which later has been adopted by Freemasonry. The brotherhood of the Serpent was in ancient times divided in two branches. The Brotherhood of the Yellow Dragon, operating in the East, and the Brotherhood of the Red Dragon, operating in the West. Both were supposed to provide the humans with guidance and knowledge from the gods. Since that was against the will of the ruling Enlilites, the brotherhood had to operate secretly. The knowledge the Enlilites didn't want to be handled down to humans was called 'the forbidden knowledge', according to the book of Yahweh. The monasteries of Tibet are supposed to derive from the Yellow Dragon. It is worthy to mention that Marduk's symbol was a serpent with a dragonhead, symbolizing the combination of wisdom and kingship.

The brotherhood of the Serpent was taken over, and corrupted by Enlil/Yahweh, (probably under Tuthmosis IV (1413–1405 BCE) to use the brotherhood against Marduk, by passing corrupted knowledge to the humans. One of the results of the corrupted brotherhood was the falsehood teaching about the symbol of the Serpent as being an evil symbol. The original knowledge promoted by the brotherhood, was classified as forbidden knowledge. William Bramley:

> The Custodial teams known as "Jehovah" helped the Brotherhood of the Snake to embark on a program of conquest to spread the new "one God" religion.[3]

Another result was the hiding of knowledge. In fact, Freemasonry has never promoted 'the art of building'. If they have some secrets about this art, then they have been hiding it from the public. So the Serpent, the symbol of wisdom, most venerated by the House of Ptah/Enki and by all the people around the world, became the object of biblical hatred, and the knowledge the House of Enki, meant to be handled to humanity, became hidden among the higher degrees of some secret societies.

Hiram Abif was the master from Tyre, who was invited by King Solomon to administrate the building of the temple in Jerusalem. He is considered to have been the first Grand Master of the freemasons. The all-seeing eye, the damaged eye of Horus, and the pyramid, (appears also on the American dollar bill), are Egyptian symbols adopted by freemasonry. In modern societies where discoveries are protected by law, through patents, it seems rather strained to protect 'the art of building' by secret brotherhoods.

There are hundreds of secret societies, secret fraternities, and other secret establishments. The main characteristic of such societies is always a common secret uniting the members of the brotherhood and serving their interests, much like the alien Brotherhood of the Gold.

Here are some of them: The Knights of the Temple, better known as Templars, The Knights of St John of Jerusalem, later known as the Knights of Cyprus, the Knights of Rhodes, the Knights of Malta, or SMOM, meaning 'Sovereign and Military Order of Malta'. The Illuminati, The Jesuit order, Opus Dei, Ordo Templi Orientis, Hermetic order of the golden Dawn, The Teutonic Knights, the Rosicrucians, the Freemasons, the Ismaelites, and many other. The greatest and most evil brotherhood ever on Earth, the Brotherhood of the Gold, is neither documented nor mentioned anywhere. Enlil/Yahweh, the first and only Grand Master of this Brotherhood, declared himself as God to discourage any research about his real identity. What an effective way in preserving secrets!

We believe that all secret brotherhoods on Earth have their origins, in one way or another, in the two alien brotherhoods, the Brotherhood of the Gold and the Brotherhood of the Serpent. But not even the most ingenious writers have been able to unearth the deep secrets of those organizations. The reason is that they are very effective in protecting their secrets.

They cooperate, counteract, and even absorb one another from time to time, or they close down and start again with new names. They have their own agents in other brotherhoods. Some of them are of a double nature, having secret societies operating within them. One part of such a society is open to the public where almost everybody can enter as a member, and a higher part, which is known only to those of the highest degrees, is 'top secret'.

The Templars

We are about to take a brief look at the Knight Templars, and the Knights of St John, because their initial founding and later activities have been closely connected to both Christianity and Islam.

The Templars, or 'The Knights of the Holy Temple', as their initial name was, was founded, as far as it is publicly known, at 1118 in Jerusalem, by Hugues de Payen, a French nobleman from Champagne and special emissary of the Pope Gelasius II (1118–1119 CE), Geoffrey de Saint-Omer, and seven other French noble men. The purpose was to protect the pilgrims visiting the Holy Land. Their residence was a part of Solomon's Temple from which their name derives. They are also known as 'The Knights of Christ'. Since they were poor, they were depended on alms.

The Templars spent nine years excavating tunnels under their residence. About what they were seeking and what they might have found, there are a lot of speculations. They may have found the Ark, and brought it to Europe, scrolls about sacred geometry, and specific knowledge, and much more about 'hidden wisdom' of Egyptian origins. They may also have found scrolls concerning Jesus that partially contradicted the doctrines of the Christian church, that they decided to hide the information. They must have had some guiding documents directing their searching; otherwise they wouldn't spend nine years digging under the place.

They returned to France in 1127, and the next year they gained official recognition, by the Catholic Church, at the Council des Troyes. They also gained legal autonomy and their activities were beyond the reach of the rulers of Europe. Their Grand Master was responsible to the Pope alone. By the year 1307 the Knight Templars were a powerful and very rich organization. They owned estates in almost every country in Europe, and were operating farms, vineyards, mines, and a well-organized fleet, which was the biggest of the time.

In the Catholic countries the Templars were autonomous, protected by the Catholic Church. In Eastern Europe, as Hellas, Cyprus, and parts of the Byzantine Empire, they had their own small states, occupied by force and hold by power.

By protecting the pilgrims on their route to the holy land, and other routes as well, they were de facto controlling the trade in the whole Mediterranean Sea.

After Saladdin defeated Guy de Lusignan in 1187 on the plains of Hittin, England, France, and Germany began to summon armies for a Third crusade. Richard Coeur de Lion of England (Lionheart), and Philip, the king of France, took the seaway to Acre from Sicily, in 1191 CE. The fleet of Richard was scattered by a storm, and took refuge in Crete and Rhodes. Three of his ships sank outside Limassol, Cyprus, and the soldiers (including the crews) were taken prisoners by the king, Isaac Komnenos (not to be confused with the Byzantine emperor with the same name). The king suspected that their purpose was to attack and take the island. As we shall see, neither Moslems nor Christians could feel safe for the professional crusaders on the way to Jerusalem! Another ship with Richard's sister, the queen of Sicily, and his affianced Berengaria of Navvare, reached the harbor of Limassol. The king of Cyprus tried to induce them to land, first by cajolery and later by threats, although unsuccessfully. Richard then arrived to Limassol and ordered his knights to conquer the island.

As the new Master of the island he was offered to taste the famous sweet liqueur wine of the area, called by then 'Mana', which he found superior. The wine was produced in the same way as it did for more than two thousand years, and was known in Hellas, Egypt and Phoenicia. He is supposed to have said that the wine was 'the Wine for Kings and the King of Wines'. After he married Berengaria in Limassol, he left the island in charge of Richard of Camville, and Robert of Tornham, along with garrisons in every town and every castle; he then sailed for Acre with even more troops, as many Cypriots chose to follow him.

After his depart, the Cypriots revolted as they realized that not only their freedom but also their Orthodox religion were in dang. The Catholic crusaders, who were supposed to fight the Moslems, also tried to convert the orthodox Cypriots to Catholicism. The Cypriots were, however, defeated by Robert of Tornham. Richard could not afford to send more of his troops to hold the island by force, so he sold it to the Knight Templars for 100,000 bezants. It was a great amount of money, of which 40,000 were paid at once, and the rest was to be paid later, which witnesses of the Templar's great financial power.

The same year, 1191, the Templars moved their headquarters to Cyprus. Their rule was practiced with great severity and they soon became hated by the people. The Knight Templars, as well as the troops of king Richard before them, chased the Christian Cypriots as well. Although the Templars crashed the revolt, and slaughtered a great number of men, women, and children, they decided to leave Cyprus as they recognized that they were unable to hold it by force in the long run.

The Templars sold the island back to Richard, who gave it, or sold it (it is uncertain), to Guy de Lusignan, who now lost the kingdom of the Holy Land to Richard's nephew, Henri, count of Champagne. After the fall of Acre, Sidon, and Beirut to the Turks in 1291, Cyprus became again the base of the order.

The Templars transformed Europe under their short existence of ca 200 years. First they were involved in the financing and construction of the Gothic cathedrals in France. The buildings were much higher than those of the Romanesque style, with more windows, and greater spaces and fewer pillars. The Cathedrals were the works of the craft masons under the name 'Children of Solomon', instructed in sacred geometry by Cistercian monks. The Notre Dame (our Lady) cathedrals were considered at the time as impossible structures, because of their 'abnormal' high, and their venture architecture. The manufacturing of the luminous colored glass used in the windows of the buildings, is still a secret. As monatomic gold dust has no metal properties, no modern analysis would show if some of the material used was gold dust. The Templars transformed Europe from being an assembly of small kingdoms, and feudal fiefdoms, to an area where traveling and trading (global in some sense) were safe, and expanding. They are also credited with the introduction of the 'note of hand' from the Moslems, the banker cheque that became the pre-cursor to our paper money.

It was a sophisticated and efficient banking system evolved from their activities in protecting travel and trade along the major routes of Europe. Had the dark ages of Europe come to an end? Was a status of none development under more than a thousand years now to be followed by an era of achievements? Was the new situation mainly directed by the Templars through trade and some kind of wealth, and not by the Church, alarming somebody? Was the Catholic Church interested in putting their hand on whatever the Templars found, or to put an end to a transformation of Europe? A transformation partially based on knowledge and, God forbidden, not approved by the Popes.

Many writers explain the Templars incredible achievements as a result of their findings from the excavations under the Temple. Although nobody knows, it is possible that the Gothic cathedrals, for example, are the result of sacred geometry-documents. If this is true, then we can assume that the writer, probably Thoth-Hermes, wished such documents to be handled down to all humans. In that case the owner is the whole humanity and not only the founders. Other findings may belong to Israel and Egypt. In any case, the Templars had no right to keep what they found for themselves.

Another highly important aspect of their possible discoveries is however these and other documents, from and about the Anunnaki gods, were meant as a gift to promote human advancements and prosperity, or they were meant to put humanity on tracks pre-selected by some gods serving their own interests. That would depend if the documents were originals or corrupted. The answer for that would also give us the answer if the Templars were working for the benefit of humanity or not.

The new Grand Master, Jacques de Molay moved from England to Cyprus, in 1295. He would remain there until 1307 when Philip IV and Pope Clement V summoned him to France. The era of the Templars came suddenly to an end on Friday the 13th of October 1307, by the hands of the French King Philip IV (1268–1314 CE), in cooperation with Pope Clement V (1305–1314 CE). Jacques de Molay and sixty other high executives of the Templar organization were arrested and tortured under seven years. In 1314 Jacques de Molay and Geoffroi de Charney were publicly burnt on fire on the Ile des Juifs. Jacques de Molay 'invited' the king and the Pope to soon follow him. Ironically, both died within a year. It has been speculated that both the king of France and the Pope wished to put an end to the Templars extraordinary power, not to mention their enormous fortune, and their famous treasure, whatever it was. Apparently, that the Templar treasure had vanished without trace. Or, so it is rumored. Most of the Templar treasure was in the form of real estates, farms, ships, and warehouses. None of that could the fleeing Templars take with them. Their fortune was divided between the French king and the Pope, who transferred the portion of the church to the Knights of Rhodes, (St John) as their name was at the time. Another remarkable fact, concerning the Templars, was that this powerful organization of warriors chose to flee without resistance. Was it because they owned something more valuable to protect than their property?

Many of the Templars fled to Scotland, England, Spain, Portugal, Germany, and Italy, where they started new brotherhoods. In Portugal they renamed the order to 'The Knights of Christ', after the demand of the Pope. Vasco de Gama the explorer was a member, and Prince Henry the Navigator was a Grand Master of the new order. Bartolomeu Perestrelo, whose daughter, Felipa Perestrelo Moniz, married Christopher Columbus, (1479 CE) was a member of the order too. Columbus crossed the Atlantic using a flag with a red cross, the cross of the Knight Templars. Several secret societies evolved from the Templars. They also became powerful and in position to rule several countries affecting human history. The charge against the Templars by the church was that of idolatry. They have been accused for worshiping an idol called Baphomet, the skull, and the black Madonna. These accusations are in the best Enlil/Yahweh style, if one considers how the wise Serpent became the evil Serpent. The Serpent was (and still is) venerated in the whole world as the symbol of wisdom. Except for the book of Yahweh, the Christian bible. The Templars have also been accused, like the Cathars, for not recognizing Jesus as God but as a man.

The trial of the Templars in Cyprus, in 1310, commanded by a Papal bull in the same manner as it did in many other countries, (Cyprus was governed by the Catholic Frankish) brought no evidence of the charges against them. But the outcome of the accused 76 Templars is not known.

The history of the Knight Templars in Cyprus ended in 1571–2, when the Turks took the island. Most of the records about them, as well as many other historical records, were destroyed by the Turks. In the same year, the Turks attacked the knights of Malta (St John) at Malta but were defeated by the Spanish fleet.

Concerning the Baphomet there are a lot of theories. The many interpretations of the word could only be possible thanks to the confusion of the tongues by Enlil/Yahweh. One of them, by Idries Shah in the book 'The Sufis', claims that the word is but a corruption of the Arabic 'abufihamet' which is pronounced 'bufhimat' and means 'Father of Wisdom'. The skull is to be the head of St. John the Baptist who the Templars venerated. In the black Madonna, the Templars were venerated Sophia, the Greek mother of wisdom, the Egyptian Isis and Horus, or was it Madonna and Jesus? Isis is often associated with the black Madonna of Europe. The fact that they were venerating Sophia, the mother of wisdom, didn't hinder them from destroying the cathedral of Hagia Sophia in Constantinople. Since they participated in the sack of Constantinople during the fourth Crusade in 1203–1204, Robert de Clari states that among the numerous relics at the sacred chapel of the Boucoleon Palace, supposedly was the head of John the Baptist. Graham Hancock states in 'The Sign and the Seal':

By this analysis therefore, when the Templars worshiped Baphomet what they were really doing was worshiping the principle of Wisdom.

We know by now that 'the Father of Wisdom' was Enki. Our theory is that the Templars were venerating Enki, the Wise Serpent and Jesus the man, instead of the God of the OT and Jesus the God. That means that they probably knew something about the schism between Enlil/Yahweh and Jesus, as presented in a previous chapter. Had the Templars some evidence that Jesus was a man, and not God? In that case, the Templars were in possession of a great secret. In order to preserve the secret, the Templars had to be exterminated like the Anakim before them.

The Catholic Church has never withdrawn the accusations against the Templars. However, Internet continues to influence our lives in every possible way. A historical document by the name 'The Parchment of Chinon—The Absolution of Pope Clement V of the Leading members of the Templar Order', made its sudden appearance on the internet, at the site http://asv.vatican.va/en/doc/1308.htm. Jacques de Molay and other named leaders of the Templars are freed from the charges brought against them by the Inquisition. This is probably a reaction from Vatican after Dr. Barbara Frale in 2002 discovered the document and brought it into public knowledge. The Chinon Parchment has been in the Vatican Secret Archives since August 17–20 1308. Although Pope Clement knew that Jacques de Moley and the other accused leaders were innocent, he did nothing to save them from seven years of torture and finally from being burned!

The Cathars
There is another parallel, the Cathars, whom the Templars had some contact with. The Christian Cathars too, (from the Greek katharos meaning pure) a tribe in Languedoc, in South France, were persecuted and exterminated by the Catholic Church. Pope Innocent III (1198–1216 CE) ordered a crusade specifically against the Cathars, the Albigensian Crusade, in 1200 CE, and destroyed one of the highest west European cultures of the time. Arnold Aimery, the Papal emissary at the siege of Beziers gave the follow order to his men:

> Show mercy neither to order, nor to age, nor to sex. . . Cathar or Catholic, kill them all. . . God will recognize his own. . .

The above command sounds like an echo from the exodus operation. 'Anakim or not, kill them all'. Preserve the secret! Pope Innocent III was acting as Yahweh's representative!

One of the Papal allies against the Cathars, was Dominic Guzman, a Spanish fanatic with a declared wish to exterminate heresy. Guzman also established the monastic order of the Dominicans, (in his name) which, in turn, spawned the 'Holy Inquisition' in 1233 CE. Another theory supports the idea that the Cathars were in possession of some portion of the treasure of the Temple taken and brought to Rome by Titus, after the Jewish revolt in 70 CE. Then the treasure, being some ancient knowledge or not, was brought to the Visigoth kingdom of Rhaedae, (today's Rennes-le-Chateau), by the Visigoths who took Rome in 410 CE. About the connection among the Templars, the Cathars, the Merovingians, the Visigoths, the Trojans, and even Maria Magdalene, there are many theories and speculations, but unfortunately few documented historical facts.

The Cathars vanished after the final siege at Monsequr in 1244 CE, although their faith and memory still fascinates, like the Templars. We are again tempted to recall a common biblical statement often used by Enlil/Yahweh, 'wiped out off the face of the earth'.

What were the crimes of the Cathars? According to the church, they were heretics. The preachers of Cathar congregations were both men and women, while the whole Christian church was dominated by patriarchal principles, not allowing women to be priests. The Papal church considered the Cathar beliefs as a dreaded adversary to the Roman Catholicism. While the burning of books, and even humans, was still in practice in most places in Europe, the Languedoc area where the Cathars lived, was a place where learning, philosophy, poetry, Greek, Arabic, and Jewish, were flourished. The Roman Church declared the Cathars as heretics in the same manner as Enlil/Yahweh declared the Igigi as 'fallen angels'. Neither he nor the church needed to argue about different opinions. They only had to announce their own opinion. The words of Enlil/Yahweh echoed in the form of the Papal bull. The Cathars were Christians but they did not accept Jesus as God, and neither the God of the OT whom, they considered as **'not a good one'.** According to them, such a violent being could not be God. They too, like the Templars, venerated Maria of Magdala (Magdalene). According to another theory, the Cathars were descendants of the Merovingians, who were supposed to be descendants of Jesus and Magdalene. This is quite interesting because, if someone could have a credible knowledge about Yahweh, that should be the Cathars through the Jesus-Merovingian bloodline.

Heresy means whatever we want it to mean. It has no objective meaning other than 'opposition'. Accordingly, Catholicism was also heresy to the beliefs of the Cathars. Had the beliefs of the Cathars been dominating instead of the 'orthodox beliefs' established by Irenaeus, Christianity would be more human and more liberal. We would believe in God and not the violent god of the OT. Compare the Cathar expression 'not a god one' with the more powerful words of the god of the OT, about himself in Isaiah 45:5.

> I form the light, and create darkness; I make peace, and create evil. I Yahweh do all these things.

The Cathars practiced a civilized religious tolerance, much like that of ancient times. Saint Bernard proclaimed concerning the Cathars:

> No sermons are more Christian than theirs, and their morals are pure.

Here too, we can see the long arm of Enlil/Yahweh striking at all those who wish to thing by themselves, not recognizing him as god. Here too we can see that he is still ruling the Earth through the bible. His agents act through the book, which states 'You shall not have other gods than me'. The man's logics are not completely clear. By saying that, it is only logical to assume that there are indeed other gods too; he is not the 'only one'. Laurence Gardner says about the Cathars:

> Although their convictions were unorthodox in comparison with the avaricious pursuits of Rome, the Pope's dread of the Cathars was actually caused by something far more threaten-ing. They were said to be the guardians of a great and sacred treasure associated with a fantastic and ancient knowledge.[4]

Were all the Cathars exterminated, or have some of them managed to survive? Nobody knows, but M. Baigent, R. Leigh and H. Lincoln say:

> Indeed, the whole history of the region is soaked in Cathar blood, and the residues of that blood, along with much bit-terness, persist to the present day. Many peasants in the area

now, with no inquisitors to fall upon them, openly proclaim
Cathar sympathies. There is even a Cathar church and a so-
called Cathar pope who, until his death in 1978, lived in the
village of Arques.[5]

The Cathar hidden knowledge and the secrets they probably shared
with the Templars are, on the other hand, lost, or hidden in the lodges
of some brotherhood.

The Knights of St John

The history of the Knights of St John is quite fascinating too. In
the year 1048 CE, merchants of Amalfi, Italy, established a hospital
in Jerusalem to provide help to pilgrims visiting the Holy Land.
By the year 1093 CE, the administrator of the Hospital was Peter
Gerard of Florence, who is regarded as the man who turned the
'medical organization' into a Brotherhood. In 1113 CE, after the
first crusade, Pope Paschal II recognized the brotherhood as an
Independent Order, the Knights of St John, with Raymond du Puy
as its first Grand Master. The brotherhood was turned into a military Order, and soon became engaged in battles with the Moslems.
They also became the most powerful military and economic power
beside the Templars.

The Knights of St John moved their headquarter to Kolossi, near
Limassol in Cyprus, after the fall of Acre (1295 CE). They renamed
the 'Mana' wine to 'Commandaria', after their headquarters, the
'Commanderie', and introduced it all over Europe, where it became
much appreciated by all the royal houses. Despite great incomes of
the wine and other trade, and despite that they mastered, at least 60
villages, the Knights of St John wished a country of their own.

Some years later, in 1306, they invaded the island of Rhodes, and
in 1310 they controlled the whole island. They could hold the island,
despite several great attacks by the Turks, until 1523, when they
moved to Malta, known by the name 'The Knights of Malta'.

As Knights of Rhodes, and later as Knights of Malta, they would
fight the Turks, and against pirates in the Mediterranean Sea. The
Knights Templars too fought the Turks under their short history.
Both the Arabs and the Turks were under several hundred years busy
fighting the Knight Templars and the Knights of St John. It is possible that these two orders hindered the Turks from taking some of
the countries of Europe.

The reason we mentioned the activities of those two orders in Cyprus, is to show that their activities were not always according to their constitution. Despite the fact that they used the Christian religion, and the Christian cross as their symbol, they could also turn against Christians. They absorbed persons who were more adventurers than Christians. Not only the Moslems were regarded as their enemies, but also Christians of the Orthodox church of the East. In fact, they fought everybody threatening their interests.

As we have seen, some brotherhoods were cooperating (and still are) with the Christian church, and yet some others were considered as enemies of the church.

By this classification one could say that some brotherhoods are good and some evils. Here we have the ever going on struggle between good and evil, although the definition of good and evil is a monopoly of the Christian Church. As in the case of Enlil/Yahweh and Enki, 'the gods of good and evil', can be interchanged, in order to be in accordance with the truth. The important thing is which one is working in the interests of humanity and which one is not.

Many of the world's most famous men were members of secret brotherhoods. Some of the most famous members of freemasonry were several American presidents, Napoleon, members of almost all the kingly families of Europe, and even writers, philosophers, and scientists. By being member of the same brotherhood, they could influence human affairs, war, and peace, and human development in general. It is difficult to believe that presidents, and all the other prominent members of the different secret societies, had become members while they knew the real purposes of these brotherhoods. We like to believe that they had no idea about the hidden secrets in the lodges of these societies, or if they had, they were directed by their fundamental Christian heritage. In either case they have been used in precisely the same way Enlil/Yahweh have been using the Israelites. We are not happy in establishing this theory because this is but another evidence of Enlil/Yahweh ruling the world through the bible, and some secret societies. We can certainly assume however, that not all of the secrets brotherhoods are working for the benefit of humanity, since they have hidden secrets, opposing to public observation and control by any authorities.

The constitution of the Knights Templars was derived from Freemasonry. After the Templars fled from France, they established new Freemasonry orders in Scotland, and other places. According to one theory, the Knights of Malta, and Freemasonry, contributed to the persecution of the Templars. If that was the case, then a subsequent question arises. Was the work of the Templars somehow threatening the Church? Did the Church influence its associates, the King of France and the Knights of Malta, to cooperate against the Templars? Or was the purpose to take over, and corrupt (or to hide) some work of the Templars? Why was it so important to always exterminate everybody regarded as heretic? Were the Templars heretics in their Christian beliefs, or just according to the Church? Had they some evidence that the god of the OT was not 'God'?

Free Masons–Freres Maçons
Many scholars believe that the Templars evolved from freemasonry. Yet, others like General Albert Pike, in his book Morals and Dogma, believes that the very name 'Free Masons' is just another name of the Templars.

> Therefore it was that the Sword and the Trowel were the insignia of the Templars, who subsequently, as will be seen, concealed themselves under the name of Brethren Masons. [This name, Freres Maçons in the French, adopted by way of secret reference to the Builders of the Second temple, was corrupted in English into Free-Masons].

Even their name is a subject of disagreement. Are they 'Free Masons' or 'Freres Maçons' (Brothers Masons)? Had the corruption occurred by mistake, or was it intentional, in order to conceal the real purpose of the new brotherhood? Not even ex members, like the prominent writer Laurence Gardner, are sure about Freemasonry's real purpose.

> . . . after some twenty years in Freemasonry, I resigned in 1984, mainly because I got thoroughly bored with it all. I had expected to learn such a lot, but actually learned nothing of much consequence except how to perform ceremonial ritual.
>
> * * *
>
> All I really discovered in terms of "secrets" was that their biggest secret is that they've forgotten what their secrets are! . . . What I never experienced was anything covert in the way that

one imagines a secret society. So, either it wasn't there, or it was very cleverly concealed from me for twenty years.[6]

Some of the ceremonial rituals practiced by the Freemasons are not unlike the ceremonial rituals of the Christian church. Some of them, like the 'eating' and 'drinking' of Jesus' body and blood in the Christian Churches, are not much understandable either. It is not easy to understand the implication of this symbolic action of 'eating and drinking' of someone's body. It would be much more 'Christian' to use the money for providing food to starving children. About Freemasonry hiding its real identity, Manley P. Hall writes:

> Freemasonry is a fraternity within a fraternity—an outer organization concealing an inner brotherhood of the elect . . .
> it is necessary to establish the existence of these two separate and yet interdependent orders, the one visible and the other invisible. The visible society is a splendid camaraderie of 'free and accepted' men enjoined to devote themselves to ethical, educational, fraternal, patriotic, and humanitarian concerns. The invisible society is a secret and most August [defined as 'of majestic dignity, grandeur'] fraternity whose members are dedicated to the service of a mysterious Arcanum [defined as 'a secret, a mystery'].[7]

How can the Templar worshipers of Baphomet be classified as heretics, while the worshipers of Arcanum are considered to be good Christians?

Independent if only the name of the Free Masons evolved from the Templars, or the whole brotherhood, or probably the other way around, there are many evidence connecting the two brotherhoods.

These and other brotherhoods, together with some movements evolved directly out of the bible, have had a lot to do with human affairs the last two millennia.

Some of these have been involved in such different events, like the conflicts between Christians and Moslems, the French and the American revolutions, the rise and fall of Communism, and the neutralization of the influence of science introduced by the Hellenic civilization.

John Calvin and the Puritans

John Calvin (1509–1564 CE), the man who experienced 'a sudden conversion', like Paulus, claimed that 'the world was created so that humanity might get to know him' and that 'the New Testament, baptism and the Eucharist had been created to provide Man with continuous divine guidance when seeking faith'. Is there any significant difference between 'divine guidance' and 'ruling the world'?

He also claimed that some of the people of the Earth (the Elect) were predestined for eternal salvation, while others (the Reprobates) would suffer everlasting damnation. Needless to say that Calvin himself believed he was an Elect. The Christian Europe had nothing to challenge the ancient European philosophers. Thinkers like Calvin, was just about what the Christian Europe could produce under those times. He was a fanatic who considered himself as a seeing man in an assembly of blinds. As an enlighten man he was preaching subjection to a society already covered by darkness.

He created regulations, punishments and doctrines concerning all aspects of life. Dancing was for example sinful, jewels and fancy clothes too. Engagements were limited to six weeks and the function of marriage was to produce children, but without enjoying the sexual act, as it was a sinful act. We believe that his own God, Enlil/Yahweh appreciated that 'sinful act'. He also persuaded the humans to produce children to use them as gold miners.

Calvinism had played a major roll in many events around the world. In Great Britain it became the Puritan religion. The Puritans received the name because of the program they launched to purify the National Church of England. By the way, the name 'Puritans' is equivalent to the 'Cathars', despite their completely different program and fate. While the Hellenic civilization of the old times elevated science and philosophy above the worship of any god, the Puritans believed that Science was to be used in the service of God, that is to say, in the service of Enlil/Yahweh, not in the service of humanity. William Bramley in 'The gods of Eden' says:

> In the Netherlands, Calvinists had played a very large roll in agitating and bringing about the Eighty Years War, which gave us The Bank of Amsterdam.[8]

Oliver Cromwell, the leader of the Puritans in England, believed that the English Puritans were God's 'second chosen people'. Here we go again! While the 'first chosen people' were forced to surrender to a powerful alien through advanced manipulations, the 'second chosen people' managed to manipulate itself through the bible. This is a first class example of how the bible inspires people to contribute in Yahweh's attempts to rule the world. According to W.J. Bethancourt some 3–4000 people were executed accused of witchcraft, under Cromwell's rule in England. The Puritans loved to create wars. William Bramley says:

> It caused Puritans to view peace as an affront to God because peace meant that the struggle against 'Satan' had ceased! . . . The highest calling of a Puritan man was to march off to war for the glory of God. When there were (heaven forbid) no wars in progress, men were encouraged to attend military drills for recreation.[9]

The puritans didn't pick up the idea of 'war for the glory of God' from nowhere. Mark 13:7 states:

> And when ye shall hear of wars and rumors of wars, be ye not troubled: for such things must needs be;

Don't worry about wars, just join them, and fight! Wars and the consequences of wars, like atrocities, genocides and simple killings are justified in the Book of Yahweh!

How are we supposed to create some peace on Earth when God says that wars are unavoidable? How did he know? Who sowed the seed of wars! Laurence Gardner about the Puritans:

> What these Puritans achieved, however, was to become intolerant bigots, devoid of any spiritual intellect. Indeed, they were so undemocratic in their beliefs that their parliamentary head was a brutal despot who put even Tomâs de Torquemada in the shade. It was during the years of Oliver Cromwell's savage Protectorate, from 1649, that astronomers and mathematicians were forced to go underground as the Invisible College.[10]

One could say Calvin, as well as the Puritans, got it all wrong, that they were laughingstocks. Nevertheless their influence on human affairs, have been both great and malicious. Their source was the bible, the great instructions manual about conflicts and wars. It is ironic really, to think of holy wars between the Christians and the Moslems, or the Moslems and the Jews, their god being one and the same. These thousands of years old instructions of his are still creating conflicts. At least, as long as there are some fanatics around, like Calvin, Luther, or the Puritans.

The Gold

Many of these brotherhoods created different kinds of political and economic organizations, supporting both sides in ongoing conflicts, or just creating them. According to the OT, (Joshua), Enlil/Yahweh himself supported both sides in the conflict between the Israelites and the Canaanite cities. He persuaded the Canaanite cities not to capitulate, by 'hardening their hearts', whatever that means, and then ordered Joshua to kill everyone unwilling to capitulate. The Glorious revolution of 1688 replaced the king of England James II with his son in law, William III of Orange. The initiators of this revolution were some Englishmen and Scots based in the Netherlands, which was under the monarchy of the House of Orange. William Bramley says:

> Sharing in Fredrick's monetary profits were other German principalities, including Hanover itself. They all made their money by renting German soldiers to England at exhorbitant prices. Hanover had already been engaged in this enterprise for decades.

> The rental of German mercenaries to England was perhaps one of the great "scams" of European history: a small clique of German families overthrew the English throne and placed one of their own upon it. They then used their influence to militarize England and to involve it in wars. By doing so, they could milk the British treasury by renting expensive soldiers to England to fight the wars they helped to create! Even if the Hanoverians were unseated in England, they would go home to German Hanover with a handsome profit made from the wars to unseat them. This may be one key to the puzzle of why some members of this German clique supported Scottish Templar Freemasonry and later took on leadership positions within it.

England rented German mercenaries through the signing of "subsidy treaties," which were really business contracts. England began entering into subsidy treaties almost immediately after the German takeover of their country by the House of Orange in 1688. As we recall, one of the first things that William and Mary did after taking the English throne was to launch England into war.[11]

The gold standard of our monetary system of today has been greatly discussed since its introduction. Some say that it is not a discovery of someone but the result of centuries of experience, and that the system is preventing wars. Others say that we are just using it since we have not succeeded to come up with something better. We leave the discussion of our monetary system to world's economists. Monetary systems and gold standard are closely associated with ethics and wars, or with moral and peace if you like. Paper money and credit cards as well as other exchangeable bills, are here to stay, and are widely used in the global economy by states, traders and individuals. What we argue here is not the principle of a monetary system, but the relationship between our monetary system and gold.

The monetary system used by the House of Orange, which later has been adopted by all money printing Banks in the world, made it possible to start a war even with bad financials. It was all according to advertising principles of the type 'buy now, pay later'. We do not have to pay in gold. Prior to that, a king could only go to war if he had enough weapons or enough iron to manufacture weapons, and the country's store houses full of appliances. The paper money, introduced by the Templars, the House of Orange, Freemasonry and English/Scottish secret brotherhoods, made it possible to steel from the people to cover governmental mistakes, although the term is not steeling but 'devaluation'. Paper money does not offer any security to the owners.

The Other World

How would our present have been shaped without Enlil/Yahweh? Nobody knows, of course. On the other hand, we certainly know what events we would have been spared from. The struggle between the wise house of Enki and the warrior house of Enlil ended, as we have seen, with the victory of Enlil/Yahweh. Now, if we speculate, that the winner had been the house of Enki, would that had made any difference? They were not faultless either. Let us take a look at only a few events we would have been spared from.

1. History. Our early history, like the creation of man and the deluge, would have been passed to us uncorrupted. Neither the creation, nor the deluge, would have been the work of God. The deluge would have been less destructive, if the aliens were allowed to inform people about the coming calamity.
2. Language. We would speak the same language. Although different people in different parts of the world would develop own words, expressions, and dialects, it is possible that we would indeed understand one another all over the Earth. If we summarize the work effort to translate scriptures into other languages, to learn some other language, and things like that, then we would arrive at an enormous quantity of work hours. That work effort could have been used for other, more productive, purposes.
3. Judaism. We would not have something like 'Judaism', or 'the chosen people'. No plagues against Egypt. No killing of every Egyptian firstborn. No persecutions of the Jews either.
4. Christianity. We would not have Christianity. Not the burning of people and books on fire. No killings of non-Christians, and no killings of Christians. No oppression of ideas contradicting the Christian doctrines. No dark ages completely dominated by the authority of the Church. No holy wars.
5. We would not have Islam. No 'surrender' by force. No Islamic Empire. No 'jihads'.
6. We would not have secret brotherhoods, or other kinds of religious movements, inspired by the 'holy' books.
7. Development. The development, started in Egypt, Babylon, and Hellas, would not have been vanished because of the religious doctrines of Enlil/Yahweh. The lost of achievements because of Yahweh can be counted in thousands of years.

Hermes Trismegistos states in 'The key of Wisdom', and in 'The History of Thoth The Atlantean':

All through the ages,
The light has been hidden.
Awake, O man, and be wise.[12]

Great were my people in the ancient days, great beyond the conception of the little people now around me; knowing the wisdom of old, seeking far within heart of infinity knowledge that belonged to Earth's youth.[13]

What kind of world would we be living then without Yahweh? We might as well present some speculations based on facts.

1. We could probably be able to live some longer than we do today. If the Egyptian Pharaohs, the Anakim, and the Babylonians were consuming gold powder, then it is likely that the knowledge would have survived through the ages. Hopefully, most of the people since then would have lived in health. We do not need to emphasize the enormous importance of this only fact, since health is highly valued by everyone, and the most usual reason for early death is bad health.
2. Democracy. We know that Nimrod was elected 'by his brothers', that is to say, by his fellow humans. Then democracy would have started thousands of years earlier than it did. The introduction of democracy in Hellas in ancient times was just another reason the Hellenistic civilization was as much hated by Enlil/Yahweh as Nimrod was. Being hated by God for being democratic is like being hated by criminals for being honest.
3. Advanced space facilities. We might have some colonies on the Moon and on Mars. We could solve the problem of our overpopulated planet. We could be in contact with other worlds too, expanding our horizon beyond what we are able to see.
4. Energy. We do not know if Marduk, or Enki, would have given us the secret behind their energy source. The Earthlings in possession of such an energy source, combined with advanced space technology, human curiosity, and an overpopulated planet, would perhaps threaten the planet of the gods. On the other hand, the 'fire stone', (of gold dust?) that probably was the main energy source they used, would allow us to keep the environment and Earth's climate situation in a better condition.

What about 'God' then? Would we be worshiping the old gods, Zeus and Jupiter? We don't think so, although this is precisely what we are doing. Intelligent beings realize, or choose to believe, that there might be some kind of benevolent force out there in the universe, a force-God worthy our veneration and worship. A Godless world is certainly better than a world dominated by an evil God. Besides, no benevolent force would have interests in manipulating us. No benevolent force would demand from us to kill unbelievers. A benevolent, almighty, all-powerful force would not be interested in gold!

---

[1]Laurence Gardner, Genesis of the Grail Kings, p.148–149
[2]William Bramley, The gods of Eden, p. 54
[3]Ibid., p. 78
[4]Laurence Gardner, Bloodline of the Holy Grail, p. 222
[5]Michael Baigent, Richard Leigh & Henry Lincoln, Holy Blood, Holy Grail, p. 48
[6]www book-of-thoth.com/article1251.html Interview by Atasha McMillan
[7]Manley P. Hall, Lectures of Ancient Philosophy, p. 433
[8]William Bramley, The gods of Eden, p. 223
[9]Ibid., p. 224
[10]Laurence Gardner, Bloodline of the Holy Grail, p. 265
[11]William Bramley, The gods of Eden, p. 251
[12]www.crystalinks.com/emerald3bw.html
[13]www.crystalinks.com/emerald1bw.html

Chapter 25

YAHWEH, GOLD POWDER AND THE CLIMATE CRISIS

The Truth about the Gold Powder

Advanced Alien Technology
The 'Anunnaki Theory' is kind of religious and intellectual adversity
to established religious, and even to archaeological and historical
dominance. It is continuously replacing our view of the past as long
as contradicting evidence is not presented. Sumerian, Babylonian,
Egyptian and other clay tablets and texts, many writers and even the
Christian bible itself, support this theory.

Most Christians do not believe that those alien gods ever existed.
Although they have never heard of the 'Anunnaki' they have indeed
heard of the 'Nephilim', which is just another epithet of them. Christians who have read about them use to reject them as 'mythological
beings', unknowing that the god of the OT, was one of them. Most
people are unaware of why gold was so important even in ancient
times, although the Sumerians told us that gold was the reason the
gods came here for. Laurence Gardner says:

We have always known that gold is especially important. The
vulcans of Mesopotamia knew it, the craftsmen of Karnak
knew it, the Lord of Mount Horeb knew it, as did Moses, King
Solomon, and many others of the distant past. The difference
was that they knew "why" gold was important, whereas for

centuries since (like so many wisdoms of olden times) the nature of this importance was lost and forgotten.[1]

Is Nibiru a planet in our solar system as the Sumerians claimed? Is it a spaceship, a virtual world, a spiritual world, or a world in some other dimension? Does it matter? The significant fact is that the Anunnaki were real people, they left but said they would come back. The picture we make out of them is that they had a very advanced technology allowing them to undertake space travel. They had high-tech weapons, many types of aircrafts, like 'sky birds', (airplanes), 'whirlwinds', (helicopters), rocket ships, celestial chariots, (cargo space ships) and various effective tools.

We are therefore surprised when these, otherwise very high-tech oriented individuals, had no democracy. The decisions on Earth were taken, by Enlil alone, the 'Chief in Command', or sometimes, in the council of seven, where members of his own family were in majority. They had a strange system of succession. Heirs between half brother and half sister had higher priority. Some of them, including Enlil/Yahweh, perhaps all of them, seem to believe in God, the 'Creator of all'. Yahweh is actually functioning as an intermediary god! By believing in Yahweh who, in turn, believed in God, we have managed to enter a blind alley with no other exit than go back.

They said that their planet could be saved from 'dying'. They only needed some gold dust to repair the atmosphere. A combination of scientific observations and accidental circumstances leaded them to Earth, where they found a lot of gold. At the same time, they classified another usage of the gold dust as top secret, not to be revealed to the humans. What usage was that?

The Lord Yahweh, together with Moses or by Moses' help, transformed the gold calf into gold dust, the biblical 'manna', and gave to the Israelites to eat and drink. Why?

Enki tells Endubsar, just before he is about to begin writing:

eat the bread and drink the water, and be sustained for forty days and forty nights.[2]

What is it, what kind of bread is it, which can sustain a man for so long time? Is it the same as the 'manna" which means 'what is it'? Marduk/Ra said to the Egypt Pharaohs:

Gold is the splendor of Life to them he said. The flesh of the gods it is! to the kings Ra said. To make expeditions to the Abzu and the Lower Domain, gold to obtain, the kings he instructed.[3]

It was the 'flesh of the gods' according to one of them, Marduk. Or 'ambrosia', the food of the gods, according to the Greek mythology. By urging the kings of Egypt to make expeditions of their own to obtain gold, Marduk sided against the Gold Mission. The Pharaohs had been encouraged to obtain and use the gold for themselves.

Only a few authors and their readers are familiar with the expression 'white powder of gold' today. The Israelites knew that as 'manna', but did they know anything about the origins of the word? John 6:31 says:

Our fathers did eat manna in the desert; as it is written. He gave them bread from heaven to eat.

We don't know the sources of the scribe but the 'know how', the transformation of gold into gold powder was certainly the work of gods who came from the heaven, but the gold used was our own. Because of that, the gods are able to maintain health and longevity. All the records we have about them are telling us about their actions, evil or good. We also have some details describing their feelings at special occasions. Like how they reacted to tragic events, like the news about the death of Dumuzi:

When of what had happened word to Enki was sent, Enki rent his clothes, on his forehead he put ashes. My son! My son! for Dumuzi he lamented. What have I sinned to be punished? out loud he asked.[4]

Such a deplorable event must be hurting a god as much as any human. We agree with Enki that he didn't deserve such a punishment. This is however one of the very few details we have about their mental health. We have no record at all about their physical health. And of course, no records at all that any of them had been ill or suffered from any kind of disease. So we assume that they lived their long lives in health, partially thanks to our gold!

At the same time, they denied us this knowledge that could save hundreds of thousands of children from starvation, and killing disease. We would rather choose to live a healthy life, than the Anunnaki would live for 'ever'. Although the gold of Earth is ours, Enlil and his followers, seems to consider the whole planet of Earth as their gold mines.

Another fact, supporting the connection between the gold powder and the longevity of the Anunnaki is Alalu's death. He had been exiled to Mars, to die there, as a punishment. While none of the others died a natural death on Earth, in fact they lived hundred of thousands of years after Alalu's exile, he died soon there after. He was supposed to die on Mars but why? How did they know he would die? They knew because he was provided with food, but not with gold powder. That was the punishment. He could not have been much older than Anu; otherwise it would have been impossible for him to participate in the wrestling. Anzu, who accompanied Alalu on Mars, was still alive when Ninmah made a stop there on her way to Earth. It seems that Anzu had been provided with gold powder, but not Alalu.

The Babylonian Epic of Creation states that Enki, together with his half sister Ninmah, created the first Earthlings, to be used as workers in the mines. The Chief Commander was happy about that, since the Gold Mission was a matter of high priority to him. But when Ningishzidda, a son of Enki, transplanted two "branches" from Enki into Adamu, and two from Ninmah into Ti-Amat, Enlil was not happy. In fact he was very angry. He wanted dumb workers, not intelligent beings with the ability to procreate.

When Marduk married an Earthly woman, he was also expelled from Ki-Engi by Enlil. When the Igigi married Earthly women, Enlil was angry again, because 'the gods defiled themselves'. Although he wished to expel them too, from the area of Baalbek in now-days Lebanon, he couldn't, because the Igigi had fortified the place. Does that mean that they contributed in making the human race 'better'? Are they of some superior race? Offspring between Anunnaki and humans lived much longer than ordinary humans, due to genetic inheritance. Adapa (Adam), the son of Enki and an earthly woman, lived for more than nine hundred years, according to the Christian bible, as did Titi (Eva), also the daughter of Enki and an Earthly woman. The life length is thereafter decreasing after each generation. What we make out of this is that their long lives depend on two separate factors. The genetic factor and the effects caused by the consumption of gold powder.

At sometime during the Gold Mission, Enlil decided to exclude the Enkites from the Mission. The Enlilites established some kind of brotherhood with the sole purpose to manage the affairs of the Mission. They controlled the mines, the landing places, and the military equipment. The humans, however, sided with Marduk. This is another evidence that Marduk wished to bring the Gold Mission to an end.

David Hudson's monatomic gold-powder, we mentioned in a previous chapter, has many similarities with ancient terms and events. Our ancestors knew that the physical body, as well as the 'spiritual' body, had to be fed. By feeding the spiritual body makes it possible to elevate into a higher level of consciousness, and at the same time keep the physical body in harmony and health. Otherwise the physical body is exposed to sickness. Otherwise the physical body is 'only flesh'. That knew Enlil/Yahweh too. He told us that he had decided for us to be in bondage of the physical body, as it is stated in the OT, Gen. 6:3

> And the Lord said, My spirit shall not always strive with man, for that he also is flesh; yet his days shall be a hundred and twenty years.

We are supposed to live one hundred and twenty years, according to Yahweh's estimation. Some of our ancestors lived much longer than that, something that could be quite reachable to us too.

A physical body is doomed to live a short life without the participation of an active spiritual body. It becomes the prison of the spiritual body. We do not know how to activate the spiritual body. It seems, however, logical to assume that gold powder is one of those factors.

The Shining ones

In the Egyptian 'Book of the Dead' (from about 3500 BC), ascribed to Hermes Trismegistos, Pepi II (2300–2210) says:

> I am purified of all imperfections. What is it? I ascend like the golden hawk of Horus. What is it? I passed by the immortals without dying. What is it?

'Manna' in the Hebrew language means just, 'What is it'. That was precisely what Moses offered the Israelites to eat, gold dust. If the secret they don't want us to know is 'the white powder of gold', the 'what is it' of the Egyptian Pharaohs, the 'ambrosia', the food of the gods of the Greek mythology, then David R. Hudson, may have revealed the secret to humanity, like Azazel did before him. However, the archaistic spelling of Manna was mana. The origin of both the word and the substance is in the heaven according to the Bible (John 6:31). In the tongue of the gods, ma-na could mean **bearer of health,** or **bearer of life**. Laurence Gardner says:

> ... By virtue of this, and given that the kings were fed with the highward fire-stone of the *shem-an-na*, it seems beyond doubt that the substance carried by the Genies was not pollen, but *mfkzt* powder of gold.

> ... There are, in fact, two contrasting forms of physical gold-the straightforward metal as we know it, and a much higher (or 'highward') state of gold. The latter is gold in a different dimension of perceived matter, the white powder of gold, the hidden manna, whose secret was known only to the Master Craftsmen.[5]

Enlil and his staff could become 'shining' at will, that is to say, after consuming a particular quantity of gold dust. They did so when needed, although there is no explanation why. We can however allow us a qualified guess, that they, in this way, became better fighters, easy to move, with a higher level of consciousness and more alert in general. Zecharia Sitchin says:

> Riding in front of him (Enlil) were gods clothed with radiance; he himself set off brilliance like lighting.[6]

Graham Hancock says:

> One legend described Viracocha as being accompanied by 'messengers' of two kinds, 'faithful soldiers' (huaminca) and 'shining ones' (hayhuaypanti). Their role was to carry their lord's message 'to every part of the word'

. . . and when they (his companions) had joint him (Viracocha) he put to sea in their company and they say that he and his people went by water as easily as they had traversed the land.[7]

Exodus 34:30 says:

And when Aaron and the children of Israel saw Moses, behold, the skin of his face shone; and they were afraid to come nigh him.

It is not far fetched to assume that the Egyptian pharaoh Moses was consuming more gold powder than he portioned out to the Israelites. Remember David Hudson's words?

. . . you can walk on the water, because it's flowing so much light within you that you literally don't attract gravity . . .

Jesus could walk on the waters like Viracocha. He also 'visited a bodily dwelling' by becoming a spiritual being, not because he was the Son of God, but probably because he was allowed to consume gold powder! David Hudson says:

Christ said to his disciples, "Don't touch me, I don't have on my earthly garments." They asked, "When will we see you again?" He replied, "When you have prepared the proper food and have on your proper garments." What is the proper food? It's the food of the angels, the food of the gods, the manna, the "What is it?" And your proper garments is your garment of Or, your Meissner field (what science call it). And literally, it's about a thousand times what you have now.[8]

The great painters of the renaissance applied this quality to Yahweh's relatives and servants. The aura around them is representing the shining quality that is the result of consuming gold powder.

Enki attempted to obtain gold from the sea waters, but the quantities were not sufficient.

We assume that it was gold dust, not gold he was looking for. In Genesis 2:11-12 we read:

> The name of the first is Pison: that is it which compasseth the whole land of Havilah, where there is gold; . . . And the gold of that land is good.

The scribe of Genesis had certainly not the required knowledge of evaluating the properties of the gold. Perhaps 'good' was good enough.

In Iliad we read that when Aphrodite returned to Olympus from the battlefield at Troy, she gave the horses ambrosia to eat:

> . . . after Iris stayed the horses and loosed them from the car, and cast before them ambrosia to eat.

We do not know why the atmosphere of their home planet was containing gold dust, or for how long, or if it was there from the beginning. They said that the gold dust was almost gone. But if there had been gold dust in their atmosphere, as they say, one could logically expect that some of it would fall down with rain. Then some herbs, and trees, would take up different quantity of the essence, which would then appear in eatable herbs and fruits. Reworked by the herbs or not. Was this discovery their scientists made that could explain their good health and long life? In that case the story of 're-pairing their atmosphere', is both true and not true at the same time. Without the gold dust, the planet was not doomed to die, but they were doomed to live an ordinary life like us, unless they could find gold somewhere else.

That was the Gold Mission of Enlil. Now they would need different equipment, and the most important, they would need a lot of mine workers. It was by then their problems began, when their own miners demanded less work, and perhaps higher salaries. That became the reason for creating the Lulus, (primitive workers), on Earth. There was a great demand of labor in the mines, the transport section and the metal works. Then it would, of course, be nice if the human slaves also could serve them in their homes/temples as servants and hierodules.

Azazel revealed the knowledge concerning the metals of the earth and how to work them. If we assume that the humans had a limited use of jewels, then 'how to work them', could only mean that Azazel taught them how to transform the gold into gold dust. Because of that knowledge, every single one of the Igigi descendants ought to be exterminated. It seems that these Igigi descendants, were not willing to share this secrets with other people, since the access to the gold was limited, we assume. Despite that, Enlil/Yahweh couldn't allow them to live. He had no intention of sharing the gold with us. He could not allow that humans would transform into spiritual beings served by two equal poles. Hermes Trismegistos says in 'The Key of Life and Death':

> Know ye, O man, that your form is dual,
> balanced in polarity while formed in its form.
> Know that when fast on thee Death approaches,
> It is only because thy balance is shaken.
> It is only because one pole has been lost.
> In Spirit shall ye reach that Halls of Amenti
> And bring back the wisdom that liveth in Light.[9]

Even if we do not really understand the secrets behind the words of Hermes, we have never tried to reach the goals either. Somebody keeps telling us that the goals are unreachable. We believe in him because he has been much too successful in manipulating us. Consequently, we follow the doctrines of Enlil/Yahweh rather than the words of Thoth, the god of science. Awake, O Man and make your choice. Shall we go on being the gold miners of Yahweh, living a short life dominated by diseases, or free ourselves from the intellectual bondage and live in health? Can we afford to allow Yahweh to make the choice for us? We could 'bring back the wisdom'. Perhaps, we would know if, and when the Anunnaki would come back, and why. We would know how to defend ourselves and how to keep the gold on Earth. The gods would then meet their equals. William Bramley says:

> Custodial rulers knew that they needed to keep spiritual beings permanently attached to human bodies in order to animate those bodies and make them intelligent enough to perform their labours.[10]

How very true. Additionally, they prevented us from using gold powder that could feed the spiritual body. No brain in the highward state, would accept slavery. Remember that the man himself said that it is possible! Genesis 3:2:

> And the LORD God said, Behold, the man is become as one of us, to know good and evil: and now, lest he put forth his hand, and take also of the tree of life, and eat, and live for ever.

Let us make some serious research about the gold powder. Neither the old scriptures about the 'what is it', the 'manna', the 'ambrosia', the 'light bread' nor David Hudson's 'ORME' (monatomic gold dust) are made up. The truth must be out there, not only 'preserved in heavens' but somewhere in the labs or the heads of our scientists. David R. Hudson says:

> Did you know that over five percent by dry matter weight of the brain tissue is rhodium and iridium in the high spin state? Did you know that the way cells communicate with each other is by super conductivity?

> * * *

> Do you know what speed the superconducting wave travels? The speed of sound. This, in fact, is what is in your body that we call the consciousness. It's what separates you from a computer.[11]

Is the spiritual body the same as the super conducting waves within our physical body? Could we be like gods if we could feed it with, what they called, 'the food of the gods'?

Although those of our ancestors, who knew, have been exterminated, we are certainly intelligent enough to rediscover that lost knowledge, even if the research is overdue by thousands of years. Let us put forth our hand and take of the results of our research, eat of the tree of life and live for 'ever', in health. Even if we cannot live as long as the God of the OT, because longevity is partially depended on our genes, every extension of our lives would be welcome. The connection Gold–Gold Powder—Energy source becomes more and more obvious. We have been captured by religious doctrines long enough. The doctrine that spiritual salvation is only possible after death has been provided as disinformation. The purpose was to discourage us from making any research about things the god of the

OT doesn't want us to know about. The most effective way to manipulate people proved to be religious doctrines followed by fear for punishment. Note that Yahweh's punishments have come to an end after he left. The Kingdom of the aliens on Nibiru, the so-called kingdom of heavens would welcome none of us. Only our gold is welcome there! Laurence Gardner again:

> When gold and platinum-group metals are transformed into the monatomic state, a fine white powder is produced. This substance was used by pharaohs and kings of the ancient world. It was also part of the secret knowledge of mediaeval alchemy and the Knights Templar. Research on this has been forging ahead, and some amazing properties of high-spin monatomic elements have now been scientifically confirmed.[12]

Spirit and Flesh

We have presented a lot of accusations against Yahweh, his messengers, and his agents, officially enlisted or self-made. We have also presented supporting evidence from old Sumerian-Babylonian 'documents' as well from the Bible itself. We agree with the Cathars that this god is not a good one. But what about human behavior? What kind of beings are we? What is the nature of the most intelligent creature on this planet?

Osiris taught the humans of his time not to kill one another! That must have been a rather usual activity among them. They could probably kill one another for almost any reason. That could partially explain the low status of the human race. Most of the gods had no high thoughts about us. Although we practice similar activities today, it is indeed far away from normal behavior. A violent action directed by emotions and instincts is almost always destined to be subject to reevaluation.

It seems that violent characters have not the time to think before acting. One reason is, undoubtedly, lack of education. It is often enough with basic education about respect for people and their properties. Another reason is probably the passivity of the spiritual body, the lacking of high spin of mind. This is why we, sometimes, have to take time to think before we act (count to ten!). Our consciousness needs sometime to catch up. The high spin of mind and the super conducting waves in our body are working too slowly. For some people, those waves are moving much too slowly.

We cannot increase the amount of rhodium/iridium in our brain, as the amount of those super-conducting elements found in herbs is exceedingly low.

Our conclusion is that by increasing such elements in our brain, through the consumption of gold powder (and other high speed essences of precious 'metals'), we would be better beings. Logics would precede action. Health and longevity would be just a bonus. Escalation of development would be yet another bonus. We have been manipulated to believe that 'shining' is fro the gods alone, not for us. We have been prevented from understanding what kind of good life our gold could bring to us. It is Yahweh and the brotherhood of the gold that put an end to such a good life. No matter how intensively we are seeking responsibility for our unspiritual life, the evidence is persistently pointing up against the Yahweh in heavens.

Is it possible to enjoy watching humans killing one another because of the slow activity of their brains? We believe Yahweh could put an end to it and yet, he didn't care a bit about 'chosen or not chosen' Earth-people!

We have nothing to lose by taking the ancient information seriously. David R. Hudson's research ought to be followed up. Any research on gold powder could show up to be better than storing the gold, or hanging it around our necks. Laurence Gardner says:

> We have craved gold, killed for it, dug for it, and died for it, but when all is said and done, we took thousands of tons of the world's most enchanting substance, molted it into bars and locked it out of sight in barricaded vaults as if it had never been brought out of the earth![13]

Gold Powder and the Climate Crisis
Most people agree today that we have a climate and environmental crisis on our planet. Fortunately, we have accepted that, and are on a path eventually leading to live in harmony with the environment. Ordinary people understand that most of the pollution affecting the climate mainly comes from the use of oil and coal products.

Most of our oil reserves are in the Middle East, known to the old gods as Ki-Engi, 'land of the masters of Earth'. There they built the first cities on Earth, the bas of the gold operations. They certainly knew about the 'black gold' under their adobes. They certainly had the technological know how to use it too. But they didn't. Why? Did they have something better? As we stated earlier, the energy source they used was probably made out of Gold Powder. As D. Hudson says: 'Monoatomic gold is much more powerful, as in a fuel cell . . .'

Now think of the world we could be living in by using this clean energy instead of oil. But Enlil/Yahweh forbade everyone to reveal the secrets connected with gold and gold powder. Well, do we have any right to demand that this technology would have been passed to us? It was, after all, the property of those aliens. No, we have not such a right. Ironically, some of them did reveal that secret to us. Marduk and his brother Thoth/Hermes did. The Igigi-Titans did. The descendants of the Titans knew. This technology, once part of our knowledge, could help us to avoid the climate crisis we are facing now.

But Enlil/Yahweh was not interested in our environment or our health. We have been allowed to live just to dig the gold and store it. Not to use it. As we have seen, Yahweh exterminated all those who had that knowledge. He and the Brotherhood of the Gold even used nuclear-like weapons and assassinations for the purpose. As if that was not enough, he even manipulated us, through religious doctrines, not to make any research about his actions. He manipulated us to justify his actions as being right. Our church fathers are still persuading us to do so. This is the reason why we are unable to see that his actions were only serving his own interests. Do we have the right to accuse him for our climate problems? We certainly have. He has not only deprived us of a long and healthy life, but also of the most effective and most clean energy power, fueled by our own natural sources.

[1] Laurence Gardner, Lost Secrets of the Sacred Ark, p. 81
[2] Zecharia Sitchin, The Lost Book of Enki, p. 13
[3] Ibid., p. 296
[4] Ibid., p. 254
[5] Laurence Gardner, Lost Secrets of the Sacred Ark, p. 118 and 177
[6] Zecharia Sitchin, The Wars of Gods and men, p. 323
[7] Graham Hancock, Fingerprints of the Gods, p. 49, 57
[8] http://www.halexandria.org/dward467.htm
[9] www.crystalinks.com/emerald13bw.html
[10] William Bramley, The Gods of Eden, p. 43
[11] Lectures by David R. Hudson in the 1990's from: www.asc-alchemy.com/hudson.html
[12] www book-of-thoth.com/article1251.html Interview by Atasha McMillan)
[13] Laurence Gardner, Lost Secrets of the Sacred Ark, p. 81

Chapter 26

GALILI AND LULU

Great gods and Slave Man

We believe in the historicity of the persons described in this book. Some of them can be found in different mythologies and even in the Bible, although under different names. Despite the fact the Anunnaki called themselves gods, our opinion is that none of them is God. This is why we 'judge' them after their actions and not after their titles.

Here is a short description of them, their names, and their personalities. Some of the 'names' (of gods and demigods) are not names at all, but titles. Titles were used, instead of names, describing specific undertaken tasks. For example, Ea became 'En-Ki', (Master of Earth), after he accepted the mission to obtain gold on Earth. Nin-Mah, was called, 'Nin-Khur-Saq', (Lady of the high mountain), after she became the administrator of the military base in the Sinai mountains. It could also mean 'Head Lady of the mountain', i.e. the head administrator of the mountain-base.

The sources of the following descriptions have been Sumerian, Babylonian, Egyptian, Greek mythology, and the authors 'research' about the language of the Anunnaki. Yet, some are from the best possible source, Enki himself, in the 'The Lost Book of Enki' by Z. Sitchin.

En means 'Master' like in Enki and Enlil; no other gods on Earth, beside those two, had that title.

334

Nin means both 'Lord' and 'Lady' and was used only by members of the royal families. Actually there is no support for the biblical 'Lord' for Enlil/Yahweh. The right title should have been 'Master', unless referring to some other god than Enlil, like Nin-urta.

Lu means 'Man'. **Lulu** means 'Man-worker, Slave man'. **Lu-Gal** means 'Great Man', a title used by the kings of Sumer. In Egypt the kings used the title **'Pha-Ra-oh'** that probably means 'appointed by Ra/Servant of Ra'.

Nibiru, or Nibru is the home planet of the extraterrestrials Anunnaki. It is probably a Nibiruan name rather than a Sumerian.

An means 'heaven'.

Anunnaki or Anunna means 'those who came from heaven to Earth', the Nibiruan gods who came to Earth to obtain gold.

Alalu means 'The Son of Alal'. He was the king of Nibiru who had been deposed by Anu after a jade in wrestling, because he failed to restore the atmosphere of the planet. Fearing for his life, he escaped to Earth. Earlier scientific observations claimed that Earth was the Planet of Gold they were looking for. He found gold and messaged the news to Nibiru. He is probably Oannes in Greek Mythology.

Anzu means 'He who knows the heavens', the pilot of the chariot of Ea's expedition to Earth.

Igigi means 'The Watchers', 'The observers'. A name of the Anunnaki who were stationed on Mars, serving the rocket ships, and the Celestial chariots. In the Greek Mythology, they are called the **'Titans'**, the gods who revolted against Zeus. In the Bible they are the Nephilim.

Ki means 'Earth', 'Solid Foundation'. From Ki derives the Hellenic words 'Gi' and 'Gaia' for Earth.

Ab-zu. Different theories exist. According to N. S. Kramer it means 'abyss'. Most likely 'abyss' derives from Abzu. Some say Abzu was a water god. We believe Abzu represents a place in Southern Africa where the gold mines were located. The word probably means 'He who knows shepherding', applying to the administrator of the slaves on the surface before they were sent down to the underground mines. Abzu was, beside the mines, also a 'farm' producing human mineworkers.

Nephilim is the name used in the bible for the Igigi/Titans who married earthly women. It means 'those who came down' (from Mars), or 'those who fell down' also called 'the fallen angels'. In reality, it is just another name of the Anunnaki with no religious connection.

Neteru means 'Guardian Watchers', another name of the Igigi/ Titans used by the Egyptians after the confusion of the tongues by Enlil.

Elohim means 'gods', the plural form of Eloh in Hebrew.

Anakim is either a corruption of the word Anunnaki or a word to describe Anunnaki descendants. 'Anak' means also 'Anunnaki made', while 'im' represents plural in Hebrew i.e. those of Anunnaki roots. It is the name used in the bible for the descendants of the Igigi/Titans and earthly women. They were also called 'the people of the Shem', meaning 'the people of the rocket (ships). Their fathers, the Titans, revealed the secret of the gold dust to them. As this was classified as top secret, Enlil decided to punish them. With the help of Joshua and the desert army, together with some missiles fired from airborne vessels operated by some Anunnaki, the Anakim were exterminated.

Anu means 'Son of An'. He became king of Nibiru after defeating Alalu in wrestling. In Hellas he was known as Cronus.

Ea means 'He whose house is water'. He was the firstborn son of Anu with a concubine by the name Ninlul. He was 'a master of the secrets of the waters', often depicted as associated with stream waters and fishes. **En-Ki** means 'Master of Earth'. It was a title of Ea after he undertook the task to obtain gold from the waters on Earth.

To the Sumerians he was the god of wisdom, the Wise Serpent, also known as **Nudimmud**, 'he who fashions things'. His city was **E-rid-u** (The faraway Home) in Southern Iraq, from which the old German word 'Erde' derives, as well as the English 'Earth'. His temple was the E-En-Gur-a meaning House of the master of deep waters. He was a scientist, as his half sister Nin-Mah, and his son Nin-gishzidda. The three of them created the Earthlings, by genetic engineering, combining genes from, probably, Homo erectus, and the Anunnaki. The earthlings were supposed to be used as miners and servants. Their symbol was the double-coiled Serpent, probably symbolizing the combination of two different DNA's in creating the Earthlings.

He was the firstborn of Anu and supposed to succeed him, but meanwhile they changed the rules of succession in favor of Enlil, a son of Anu with his half sister (more royal blood). That was the start of the enmity and struggle between the two. **Ptah** was his Egyptian name after the confusion of the tongues, meaning the 'developer'. Egypt, or 'Magan', or the 'land of the two narrows', as the land was called earlier, was under the dominion of the 'House of Enki', called 'Ha-ka-Ptah', from which the Hellenic 'Egyptos' derives. In Persia he was known as **Ahura Mazda**, the god of Truth and Light. In Babylon he was known as Ea. In Hellas he was **Poseidon**, the god of the seas, and in Rome, as **Neptunus**. His espouse was Damkina, even called Nin-ki.

Damkina or **Nin-ki**, (Lady of Earth), was a daughter of Alalu, and the wife of Enki. She born Ti-Amat, conceived by insemination, the first Homo sapiens female.

Marduk means 'born in a pure place'. He was a son of Enki and Ninki. He was the commander of the Igigi on Mars. By marrying the earthling Serpanit, he lost his princely title and was expelled from Ki-Engi, the domain of Enlil and his family. His domain was Egypt, after his father. There he was known as **Ra** (bright), the sun god, worshiped in the city of Memphis, (Heliopolis, the city of the Sun). He introduced the sun calendar in Egypt. His symbol was a serpent with a dragonhead. Later, he became **Amun**, (the unseen one), because he was often punished to exile, or wandering around the Earth of his own. He was a protector of humanity, and the only god who challenged Enlil, the High Commander, by building, first a Tower, a Landing place, and later the city of Babylon (Babili) in the domains of the Enlilites. He succeeded Enlil as the Commander on Earth, although not peacefully. He was also the Supreme god of Babylon, even before that. His temple in Babylon was the 'Esagil' (House of the highest god).

Serpanit was of earthly, well-educated, parents working at the space facilities on Mars where Marduk was the chief of the Igigi/Titans. She was the first to marry a god.

Nergal or **Erra** was a son of Enki, probably with some concubine. He was the administrator of the gold mines in Southern Africa. The subterranean mines were also known as 'the underworld'. His consort was Ereskigal, a granddaughter of Enlil and Enki. The gold miners spent their whole lives inside the mines. They never came up again which gave name to the 'underworld' in the Greek Mythology. In Hellas he was known as **Hades,** the administrator of the underworld. Nergal/Hades had the authority to take as many humans as he needed and use them as labor in the mines. Although a son of Enki, he often sided with the Enlilites, especially against his brother Marduk.

Ningishzidda probably means 'Lord of the legitimate land'. He was also a son of Enki. He was also known as **Tehuti**, 'the divine measurer' **Thoth**. He was the best educated of the gods, and one of the most peaceful. According to old traditions, he preserved all kind of knowledge for the accounts of humanity. Much of the Hermetic knowledge not allowed to be passed down to humans by Enlil, is called 'hidden knowledge'. He was known as **Hermes** in Hellas, and as Hermes Trismegistos, (the three-hold great). He was not the scribe of the gods, as he is often referred to, but the great scribe among the gods. He was the mentor of humanity, although counteracted by the Brotherhood of the Gold. In Rome he was known as **Mercury**, and in Mesoamerica as Quetzalcoatl, 'the winged Serpent'. He introduced the moon calendar in Egypt. He built the two great pyramids at Giza and several other megalithic structures all over the world.

Gibil was a son of Enki educated in metallurgy. Probably was the one called Hefaistos in Greek mythology, the smith of the gods. Hefaistos was renamed to Vulcanus in Rome, which is the meaning of his name in Greek. Hefaistos was however, not Gibil, but Dumuzi/Tammuz.

Ninagal means 'great Lord of the waters'. He was a son of Enki too and the one who navigated Ziusudra's boat under the great Flood.

Dumuzi was the youngest son of Enki, probably with a concubine. He was educated in farming and domestication of animals, some brought to Earth from Nibiru. He was in love with Inanna, but died just before the wedding. Some scholars state that he died after the wedding. His death became the reason of a war between the House of Enlil, and the House of Enki, although Nergal sided with the Enlilites. He became the god of fertility in some mythologies. He is often confused with his father Ptah. He was also worshiped in Phoenicia and Canaan as **Tammuz**. He is honored with the name of the fourth month in the Jewish calendar.

Nin-Mah means the 'Firstborn daughter/Lady' (of Anu). She was a half sister to both Enki, and Enlil. She was a scientist and the chief of the House of Healing in Shurupak, or Shurubak. She was also known as **Nin-Khur-Saq**, 'Lady of the high Mountain', and as **Nin-Ti**, 'Lady of Life'. In the Kharsaq epic, she was called 'the Serpent Lady'. She born Adamu, the first Homo sapiens male, conceived by insemination. She was considered as the mother of the gods as well as the mother of the humans. In Hellas she was known as **Demeter**, meaning 'double mother'. In Rome she was known as Ceres. She never married but had a son, Ninurta, with Enlil.

Enlil means 'Master of the Command' or 'Master of the Air' or simply 'the Commander'. He was a half brother of Enki, mothered by Anu's espouse Antu. He was appointed to lead the Gold Mission after Enki, as the Commander in Chief on Earth. He was completely dedicated to the Gold Mission, which was the most important task above all others. His domain was the whole land of Ki-En-gi meaning 'Land of the master of Earth' (Shumer or Sumer, Mesopotamia and the lands around), except for the city of Eridu, which was under Enki's control. His city was Nibru-Ki, (Nippur), the 'bond Nibru and Earth', (or Nibiruan Land on Earth). Nippur had all the required equipment for communication among the gods and even between Earth and Nibiru. He was presiding the Council of Seven where democratic-like decisions were taken, although most the members were of the House of Enlil. After raping a young nurse, Sud (who later became his wife Ninlil), he was exiled to Abzu for sometime. Abgal (Great Shepherd), the same pilot who hid the seven 'nuclear weapons' together with Enki, brought him there and revealed the secret location of the hidden weapons. Enlil's temple was the E-kur, (house like a mountain). He was also known as 'Ilu-Kur-Gal' 'The god of the great Mountain'. He became the God '**El-Shaddai**' of Abraham, which also means 'God of the great mountain'. In Sumer he was called **Ilu**, in Assyria **Elil**, in Canaan **El**, in Phoenicia **Adon**, in Hellas **Zeus**, the thunder god, and in Rome, **Jupiter**. Under the exodus of the Israelites out of Egypt, he became 'Yahweh' (I am that I am i.e. the Commander), as he refused to reveal his name. To the Jews, he was known as **El**, **Eloh**, **Yahweh**, or **Jehovah**. He is also the God **Allah** of the Moslems. He was not known in Egypt since Egypt was the domain of the House of Enki, except for the short special performance as Aten. Note that the epithet 'Lord' used in the Bible for both Enlil and Enki is misinterpreted. The Nibiruan epithet 'En' means 'Master'. The Greek 'Κυριος' is equivalent to 'Αρχοντας της εξουσιας' meaning 'the Ruler'. Additionally, the Greek 'Αρχοντας της εξουσιας του αερος' applying to Yahweh, means 'Master of the air', which is a direct interpretation of the name 'Enlil'. This is yet another evidence connecting Enlil with the god of the OT.

Ninlil means 'Lady of the Command', 'Lady of the Air'. She was called 'Sud' (Long?) before she married Enlil. To the Jews she was known as **Asherah**, the female companion of El. In Phoenicia she was known as Asherah too, but also as **Beruth**, from which the name of the city of Beirut derives. In Hellas she was known as **Hera** and in Rome as **Juno**. She was the mother of Nannar/Sin and Ishkur/Adad.

    Ninurta, probably meaning 'Lord of strength', was a son of Enlil and Ninmah. He was a great champion, a mighty warrior and very loyal to his father. His emblem was the plough, probably because he helped the survived humans after the Deluge to make a new start. He had great skills about metals, and even some military education. He was the administrator of the metallurgical facilities in Bad-Tibira, 'the Metal city'. His city was Lagash, and his temple the 'Eninnu', meaning 'House of fifty', and protected by 'the Supreme Hunter' and 'the Supreme Smiter', weapons given to him by Anu. The Supreme Smiter was probably a defense weapon similar to the weapons called cherubim in the bible. The 'Girsu' was a building (hangar) for his 'Black Sky bird'. The Supreme Hunter was probably an attack airplane. He was in some poems called 'Enlil's hero' and 'the foremost son of Enlil'. In Hellas he was **Ares**, the god of war and also the god of war in Rome by the name **Mars**. Another epithet of him was NinGirsu, 'Lord of the Girsu'. In South America, he was known as **Viracocha**. He is the archangel **Gabriel** in the bible, 'Hero/strong man of El'.

    Nannar, probably meaning 'Bearer of Power', was born on Earth to Enlil and Ninlil. His emblem was the crescent moon. His espouse was Nin-Gal, great Lady, who was a daughter of Enki. His city was Ur, and later Harran. He introduced the calendar to the Sumerians. His Babylonian name was **Sin**. His temple was the E-Kish-Nu-Gal, 'Great House of the Throne Seed'. He was probably the architect behind Judaism, Christianity, and Islam. He was entrusted as his father's representative. He was also called 'He who is like Enlil'. In the bible he is **Michael**, meaning 'He who is like El', one of the archangels. Among his duties was to deliver mineworkers to Nergal/Hades. As archangel Michael he is supposed to collect the souls of the dead, delivering them for judgment

    Ishkur, probably meaning 'Head Physiologist', was also born on Earth to Enlil and Ninlil. His espouse was Shala. Although he had much knowledge about weapons, and had some kind of military education, he had also great knowledge in meteorology and chemistry. In Assyria he was called **Adad**. He was the Storm god, called **Baal**

(his father was El) by the Canaanites, **Teshub** by the Hittites, and the Hurrians. His house was called 'the House of seven Storms'. He could handle chemical and biological weapons that could cause plagues. He is probably the archangel **Raphael** in the bible, meaning 'Healer'.

Ereskigal was a daughter of Nannar and Ningal and the consort of Nergal. She was the queen of the underworld. Her name means probably 'House of the great queen on Earth'.

Inanna was a daughter of Nannar and Ningal too. Her name means 'Bearer of heaven'. She was a grand daughter of both Enlil, and Enki. She was the goddess of war who later, by unknown reason, became the goddess of love. In Babylon she was known as **Ishtar**, in Hellas as Aphrodite and in Rome as **Venus**. She was very closed to become 'the queen of the gods' on Earth, which could have changed the paths of development.

Utu probably meaning 'the Shining', was a twin brother of Inanna. He was the commander of the landing place at Sippar, the chief commander of the Enlilite air forces. His spouse was Aya. In Babylon he was known as **Shamash** (the shining). His city was Sippar and his symbol a winged sun disc. His house was called Ebabbar, 'the shining house'. It is possible that he was 'Ashur', the main god of the Assyrians, beside his father 'Elil'. He was probably the god known as Helios in Hellas, although Helios could also have been Marduk, the sun god. He is **Uriel** in the bible, the 'Light/Fire of El'.

Shamgaz was the leader of two hundred Igigi who came to Earth and married Earthly women against the will of Enlil. He was the father of Asta/Isis and Nebat, the wives of Osiris and Satu. In the Greek mythology, the leader of the Titans who revolted against Zeus is called Atlas.

Adamu, (one whose color is like Earth's clay), was the first Earthling Homo Sapiens male, created from the DNA of Anunnaki and (probably) Homo erectus. He is partially the Adam of the bible.

Ti-amat, (The Mother of Life), was the first Earthling Homo sapiens female, created from the DNA of Anunnaki and (probably) Homo erectus. She is partially the Eve of the bible.

Adapa, (The Foundling), was the first Homo sapiens male, a demigod son of Enki and an Earthly woman. He fathered Abel, Cain, Seth and many other children. He is also the Adam of the bible!

Titi (Life), was the first Homo sapiens female, a demigoddess daughter of Enki and an Earthly woman. She mothered Abel, Cain, Seth and many other children. She is also the Eve of the bible!

Ziusudra means 'He of long bright life days'. He was a son of Enki and the Earthly Batanash, the wife of Lu-Mach (Lamech). He is also known as **Utnapishtim**, **Atrahasis** and **Noah** (in the bible). In Greek mythology he is known as Deucalion, the man who saved himself from the great Flood authorized by Zeus. He was the survivor of the Deluge with his wife, their sons (and probably daughters), their wives, and some friends who helped him to build the 'boat'. Note that the Bible, as well as other sources, is referring to Noah or Ziusudra, and his sons by names, while the names of his wife, and his son's wives, are omitted.

Gilgamesh was a demigod, king of Sumer. He believed, he had the right to the 'elixir of life' that would make him 'immortal', like the gods. His adventures searching for Ziusudra who had been 'blessed with the plant of life' are described in 'The Epos of Gilgamesh'.

Asar/Osiris was the firstborn son of Marduk with his wife Serpanit. He became the king of Egypt after his father. He married **Asta/Isis**, who was also a demigod, daughter of the Igigi Shamgaz and his earthly wife. She was one of the most well educated and wise queens in human history. Together they civilized the inhabitants of Egypt. Osiris traveled around the world in a mission to bring civilization to all humans. Osiris was killed by his brother Seth, probably after a conspiracy to prevent the Enkites to release more knowledge to the humans.

Satu/Seth was another son of Marduk. He married Nebat, the sister of Asta/Isis. He was badly hurt by Horus, the son of Osiris and Isis, in an aerial battle, and punished to live the rest of his life among the humans, as mortal without descendants.

Horon/Horus was the son of Osiris and Isis under some mystical circumstances. Isis made herself conceive by the seed of Osiris, after Osiris died. She raised him up in secret and helped him to avenge his father. His uncle Gibil was his mentor and helped him to make weapons of iron, probably the first such weapons used by humans on Earth. He became the king of Egypt after Seth. A missile directed against Marduk by Inanna, after Dumuzi's death, damaged Horus' right eye. The well-known eye with the golden tear was to symbolize that tragic event and can still be seen at many sites in Egypt and elsewhere.

Nabu means 'the bearer of prophecy'. He was also a son of Marduk and Serpanit, although much younger than Osiris and Set. His city was Borsippa and his temple the E-zidda, probably meaning 'Legitimate House'. He was the patron of scribes, and it was known to ordinary people, that Nabu had the power to increase the length of human life. He helped his father to build both the Tower, (the E-temen-an-ki), and the city of Babylon. Babili (the Gateway of the gods) was so named by him to honor his father. His was against the Enlilite administration as much as his father was.

EPILOG

Enlil/Yahweh left Earth, probably in the middle of the 7th century CE, after the introduction of Islam. We assume he left with the last cargo of gold.

Beside the gold, the personal baggage of Enlil/Yahweh must have been quite heavy too. He plundered Earth of its gold at the cost of millions of human lives. He left behind a mankind living in fear! His doctrines are still directing human affairs. We would not be surprised if 'the ruler and his angels' sang, "In Gold we trust" all the way back to the Kingdom of Heavens! Back on the Planet of Gold, the former slaves, now under the mantel of religious bondage, persuaded to sing "In God we trust."

Many generations of humans later, a Christian woman said to her husband:

"Dear husband, since we expect another child, we would need one more room. As a bricklayer you could easily build one."

"It is the will of God to enrich us, his poor servants, with yet another child. With God's help, I will be able to do that," the husband said.

When at church, the priest went up into the pulpit, to remind the audience that he was the representative of the God who left, with words like these:

"God is not here any more. Gold left for home, the kingdom of heaven. By following the Holy Scriptures, our Lord Jesus Christ, and St Michael the archangel will open the gates to the kingdom of heaven for you too. If you don't, Satan is waiting to open up the gates leading all the way down to Hell, wherefrom no return is possible."

344

BIBLIOGRAPHY

Baigent, Michael and Leigh, Richard and Lincoln, Henry
Holy Blood, Holy Grail, Bantam Dell, New York, 2004.

Baigent, Michael and Leigh Richard
The Temple and the Lodge, Arcade Publishing, New York 1989.

Blum, Howard
The Gold of Exodus, Hodder and Doughton, London, 1998.

Bramley, William
The Gods of Eden, Avon Books, New York, 1993.

Cotterell, Maurice
The Lost Tomb of Viracocha, Headline Book Publishing, 2002.

Däniken, Erich von
Odyssey of the Gods, Vega, London, 2002.

Eisenmann, Robert and Wise, Michael
The Dead Sea Scrolls Uncovered, Element Books Ltd, Longmead, 1992.

Flem-Ath, Rand and Wilson, Colin
The Atlantis Blueprint, Warner Books, UK, 200.

Flem-Ath Rand and Rose,
When the Sky Fell, Orion Books Ltd, London 1996

Gardner, Laurence
Bloodline of the Holy Grail, Element Books, London, 2002.
Genesis of the Grail Kings, Fair Winds Press, Gloucester, 2002.
Lost Secrets of the Sacred Ark, Element Books, London, 2003.

Gill Anton
City of the Dead, Bloomsbury Publishing Ltd,
London 1994

Goldman, Emma
The Failure of Christianity www.positiveatheism.org/hist/goldman413.htm

Hancock, Graham
Fingerprints of the Gods, Three Rivers press, New York, 1995.
Underworld, Three Rivers Press, New York, 2002.

Homer
Iliaden, Wahlstrom & Wikstrand, Stockholm, 1990
Odysseen, International Book Automation, Uddelvalla, 1973.

Jacobsen, Thorkild
The Eridu Genesis, Yale University Press 1987
The Treasures of Darkness, Yale University Press, 1976, New Haven and
London

Kramer, Samuel Noah
History begins at Sumer, Thames & Hudson, London, 1958.

Manfredi, Valerio Massimo
Alexander child of a dream, Macmillan, London, 2001.
Alexander: The sands of Ammon, Macmillan, London, 2001.
Alexander: The ends of the Earth, Macmillan, London, 2001.

Martin, Phillip
Hammurabi's Code of Laws,
www.phillipmartin.info/hammurabi/hammurabi/_epilogue.htm

McCullough Colleen
The Song of Troy, The Orion Publishing Group, Ltd, London 1998

Muck Otto H
Atlantis, Askild & Kaernekull Foerlag AB,
Stockholm 1983

Picknett Lynn and Prince Clive
The Templar Revelation, Touchstone, New York 1998

S Acharya
The Christ Conspiracy, Adventures Unlimited Press, Canada

Sitchin, Zecharia
Den tolfte planeten, Bergs pocket, Stockholm, 1989.
Genesis Revisited, Avon Books, New York, 1990.
When Time Began, Avon Books, New York, 1993.
The Lost Realms, Avon Books, New York, 1990.
The Stairway to Heaven, Avon Books, New York, 1993.
The Wars of Gods and Men, Avon Books New York, 1985.
The Lost Book of Enki, Bear & Company, Rochester, 2004.

Wallis, E.A
The Babylonian Story of the Deluge and the Epic of Gilgamish,
www.earth-history.com/Babylon/story-deluge.htm

Ward, Dan Sevell
Enki and Enlil,
www.halexandria.org/dward184.htm
Anunnaki, www.halexandria.org/dward185.htm
Ha Qabala, www.halexandria.org/dward465.htm

Wilcken, Ulrich
Alexander the great, W.W. Norton Company, New York, 1967
www.angelfire.com/nt/Gilgamesh/assyrian.html
The Assyrian Empire, Early history of Assyria
www.angelfire.com/nt/Gilgamesh/akkadian.html
The Akkadian Empire

www.asor.org/HITTITE/Kings.html
The Line of Hittite Kings

www.crystalinks.com/emerald1bw.html (also emerald2-15)
The History of Thoth, the Atlantean
The Halls of Amenti
The Key of Wisdom
The Space born
The Dweller of Unal
The key of Magic
The Seven Lords
The Key of Mystery
The Key to Freedom of Space
The Key of Time
The Key to Above and Below
The Law of Cause and Effect and the Key of Prophecy
The Key of Life and Death
Supplementary
Secrets of Secrets
www.crystalinks.com/quetzalcoatl.html

Quetzalcoatl
www.faculty.gvsu.edu/websterm/Atrahasi.htm
The Story of Atrahasis

www.gatewaystobabylon.com/gods/lords/lordnaby.html
Nabu
www.gatewaystobabylon.com/myths/texts/kings/shulgi.htm
Hymn of Praise to Shulgi

The Nag Hammadi Library www.gnosis.ord/naghamm
The Second Treatise of the Great Seth, (Roger A. Bullard and Joseph A. Gibbons)
The Hypostasis of the Archons (The Reality of the Rulers) (Bentley Leyton)
The Gospel of Thomas (Thomas O. Lambdin)
The Testimony of Truth (Søren Giversen and Birger A. Pearson
Trimorphic Protennoia (John D. Turner)

www.homepages.ihug.co.nz/~freethought/foote/crimes/c6.htm
The Rise of the Papacy (G W Foote & J M Wheeler)

www.homepages.ihug.co.nz/~freethought/foote/crimes/c7.htm
Crimes of the Popes

www.livius.org/es-ez/etemenanki/etemenanki.html
Etemenanki (The Tower of Babel)
www.livius.org/es-ez/esagila/esagila.html
Esagila
www.livius.org/ba-bd/Babylon/babylonia.html
Babylonia: country, language, religion, culture

www.members.aol.com/XianAnarch/nimrod_1.htm
Nimrod: the first politician
www.members.xoom.virgilio.it/Farf/commanding.htm
The Commandments of Ancient Egypt

www.mindspring.com/~mysticgryphon/descent.htm
The Descent of Ishtar to the Underworld

www.mystae.com/restricted/streams/scripts/thoth.html
Thoth, the Great God of Science and Writing.

www.theology.edu/ugarbib.htm
Ugarit and the Bible

www.wikipedia.org/wiki/Assyria
Assyria
www.wikipedia.org/wiki/Marduk
Marduk
www.wikipedia.org/wiki/Babylon
Babylon
www.wikipedia.org/wiki/Sumerian_king_list
Sumerian King list
www.wikipedia.org/wiki/Kings_of_Assyrialist
Kings of Assyria
www.wikipedia.org/wiki/Kings_of_Babylon
List of Kings of Babylon
www.wikipedia.org/wiki/Sargon_of_Akkad
Sargon of Akkad

CPSIA information can be obtained
at www.ICGtesting.com
Printed in the USA
BVHW081003120620
581230BV00001B/23